Law and Technology in the Pacific Community

Law and Technology in the Pacific Community

EDITED BY

Philip S.C. Lewis

Routledge
Taylor & Francis Group
LONDON AND NEW YORK

First published 1994 by Westview Press

Published 2018 by Routledge
52 Vanderbilt Avenue, New York, NY 10017
2 Park Square, Milton Park, Abingdon, Oxon OX14 4RN

Routledge is an imprint of the Taylor & Francis Group, an informa business

A CIP catalog record for this book is available from the Library of Congress.

ISBN 13: 978-0-367-00910-6 (hbk)
ISBN 13: 978-0-367-15897-2 (pbk)

Contents

PART FOUR
Property Rights in an Advanced Capitalist Economy

PART FIVE
Education for the New Lawyer

Preface

This volume is based on a conference held at Stanford Law School on October 5–8, 1991, on "The Role of Law in the Pacific Community." It is part of a major project on law within the Pacific Basin high technology community, funded by grant 890-287 from the Hitachi Foundation to the Stanford Law School.

The Foundation's challenge to the law school was to respond to the growing role of international and of high technology issues in the world and in the law. The overall program thus included both curricular components and research components, and built heavily on the school's previous studies of and work in both Pacific Basin and high-technology issues, including the school's long-term study of law practice in Silicon Valley. The project included significant study of the evolution of law practice in the increasingly interdependent Pacific technological community, a student research seminar, and substantial thinking toward curricular revision.

The conference which is the basis for this volume was a centerpiece of the grant. Our fundamental goal was to attempt to understand the way in which the legal systems of the different nations responded to the emergence of new technologically-centered international economic activity. This new activity, for example, has led to a stronger emphasis on intellectual property, an emphasis felt throughout the Basin. It has led to the emergence of a law practice in most of the Pacific capitals that provides assistance to foreign firms dealing with local bureaucracies, even in sectors in which local firms do not use lawyers. It has placed pressure on the differences among the legal systems. And it poses new demands for legal education; the last three chapters of the book were written or adapted by participants to describe the problems facing legal education in the three countries mainly represented at the conference: Korea, Japan and the United States.

Nine of the papers in this volume are revised versions of papers given at the conference. Unfortunately we could not publish the paper given by Mark Ramseyer, which is now part of his book with Frances Kornbluth, *Japan's Political Marketplace*, but we were able to include a paper by Setsuo Miyazawa on the same subject; this was previously published in the *Kobe University Law Review*, but has not been readily accessible to many readers outside Japan. We are grateful to the Kobe Law Faculty for allowing its reproduction here. We are also grateful to N. M. Tripathi Private Ltd. for permission to publish Chapter 12, an updated version of an essay first published by them in 1973.

We owe a special thank you to Delwin Roy for his role and the Hitachi Foundation's role in making this program possible. We also wish to thank our research assistants including Kwaku Andoh, Ryan Botev, Elizabeth Kopelman, and Paul Williams. Joy St. John dealt with all the complicated arrangements for a conference involving visitors from all over the world and many long papers, some received at the last minute. Mary Tye dealt with much of the preparation of the manuscript, acting as translator of the publishers' house style for the editor and contributors, retyping contributions from incompatible Korean word-processing programs (would that all cultural differences could be so easily dealt with), and making many helpful suggestions for improving the sense and consistency of the essays by removing infelicities and obscurities. Barbara Saavedra calmly assembled the final typescript under considerable time pressure. We are also grateful to Rush Services, of Boulder, Colorado, for their efficiency in preparing the camera-ready copy, to Jeanne Remington for a sensitive index, and to Spencer Carr and Marykay Scott, of Westview Press, for their wise advice and ready cooperation during the editorial and production process.

John Barton
Lawrence Friedman
Robert Gordon
Philip S.C. Lewis

Introduction

Philip S.C. Lewis

This collection of essays focuses on the high technology industries of the Pacific and the legal institutions and occupations with which they are involved. Most of the essays are aimed at understanding and explaining existing institutions and practices; some look forward to the training that lawyers will require to operate successfully in the new environment in the Pacific Community.

The classical literature on the relation of law to economic development has seen the topic in terms of the relations of national laws, legal systems and legal occupations to national economies and technological advances. Both Weber and the more recent work of North use this approach, although each also discusses periods of early modern history predating the nation-state. In this collection, the focus is rather on the relationship of internationalized legal occupations with an internationalized economy. Particularly in the area of high technology, companies from different countries do not only compete, but also combine to improve their products, though against a background of competitions between nations. Law firms have a formal national home but deal with foreign clients, foreign transactions, foreign lawyers and the laws of foreign countries, have offices outside their country of origin, and are part of international associations of law firms. In their offices, professionals qualified in the laws of different countries cooperate, and the firm, at least in some of its offices, may lose its national character altogether.

To a growing extent, contracts are negotiated internationally, there is more and more use of international decision-making procedures such as arbitration, and the intellectual property rights which are particularly relevant to high-technology companies are increasingly the subject of international negotiation and treaty, whether bilaterally, under traditional treaties such as the Berne Convention, or under the GATT. Thus we seem to be moving towards a world legal order which may parallel the world economic order. In the meantime, we have a series of national systems, modified in various ways by international contacts; the gaps between these systems are bridged by the institutional and contractual mechanisms created by the new kinds of legal occupation rather than the activities of legislatures or judiciaries. Many of these mechanisms are, of course, conceived in the interests of particular private clients.

These new kinds of legal occupation that operate in this changing context will require new forms of legal education, no longer so locally oriented as has been the case. And this new legal education will require to be based on research on these occupations and their activities if it is to meet the demands of training for them. These are the premises of this volume, to explore this new field and to illustrate some of the intellectual approaches to it which are possible.

The essays in this volume deal with various aspects of the legal institutions and occupations which operate in the Pacific area, particularly in relation to trade between the United States, Japan and Korea. The relationships of supply, cooperation and competition between these countries can serve as illustrative of those in the world economy as a whole, without the special factors introduced by the presence of a supranational organization in Europe, but with the possibility of examining the differences that can be introduced into the internationalizing process by the persistence of national legal cultures. Apart from the essays at the end, which are concerned with policy issues in legal education the essays in this book are descriptive or analytic in their approach. Some rely explicitly on a social science approach, for instance, Friedman, Blankenburg and Miyazawa, but all are concerned to elucidate what is happening in practice and so provide a foundation for a secure research and teaching agenda.

In the introductory essay Friedman gives a theoretical overview of the relation of law to the economy, and shows how much more far-reaching law can be than is usually realized. In another theoretical essay Blankenburg places international law practice in its local, economic and management theory contexts, and shows how there is a certain amount of self-fulfilling prophesy in its development; on the supply side of legal services, lawyers promote the expected need for such services to clients who come to accept their predictions, as do the lawyers themselves. Similarly from the outside, the essay by Krislov looks past the current rhetoric of unfair foreign competition to examine the political advantages for the US government of actions on several fronts in the 1980s to strengthen the protection of intellectual property in relation to high-technology industries.

Two essays discuss the internationalization of the legal profession. In a large-scale survey, Barton reviews the legal professions of the Pacific countries, and shows their responses to the new international legal occupations. A striking finding is that overseas offices tend to make work for the home office, rather than taking away local work from local lawyers. Ahn discusses the growth of the bar and changes in the lawyer's role in Korea, as it has developed against a traditional assumption that legal education was only for judges and public prosecutors, who might enter private practice after retirement. International practice is only one of several elements in a move away from the centrality of litigation and adjudication.

In the next section, two of the three essays deal specifically with the semiconductor and computer industries, and with the role of law and lawyers in their development. In one Miyazawa suggests that a corporatist theory, taken from political science, should be used to guide comparative analysis, and that it may be the degree and nature of government intervention in industry which determines the involvement of lawyers. In the other Lewis considers the role of litigation in corporate strategies, and the extent to which it can be seen as part of an attempt to reshape prevailing systems of private governance in the interests of particular economic actors. Supplementing Miyazawa, Yang argues that the true contribution of law-trained people to Korean economic development has been in government, not the judiciary or private practice.

Two essays are particularly important in the context of North's theories about the significance of property rights and institutions for economic development. In one Matsui examines the development of judicial protection for economic and property rights in Japan, and argues that if they are protected for some, it is only through interactions between bureaucrats, business corporations and politicians, not through constitutional provisions or adjudication. In the other Miyazawa shows how administrative control of the Japanese judiciary has been used to control the decisions in cases of concern to the government, including some which might have imposed liability on the government for economic losses caused by its negligence. These essays suggest that quite considerable economic progress can be made without the protection for rights and certainty in institutions which North argues are required.

The volume concludes with three essays on problems of education in the new context. Barton is a U.S. lawyer, secure in control of his syllabus, and yet he has to concern himself with practical problems. He would like students to be introduced to the international dimension as early in their courses as possible; this can most realistically be done in the context of particular transactions. In the real world, however, transactions do not confine themselves to the contract law which students traditionally learn in their first year. This is particularly true in high-technology transactions, where intellectual property and regulatory aspects are likely to be important. In addition his very wide conception of administrative law emphasizes the importance of students' knowledge of a wide range of governmental processes, too.

But Song and Taniguchi have other problems to deal with first. In both their countries legal education is an undergraduate subject, and faculty have to cope not only with the tensions between a liberal and professional education but also those between a course which would prepare the vast majority of students for employment in the public and private sectors, and a course geared for preparing for the fiercely competitive entry to the official professional training courses. Then, too, in Korea (perhaps to a lesser extent in Japan) professional training and legal practice remain fairly conservative, whereas members of the law faculty have studied, many of them, in the United States and are most sympathetic to the form of education for practice needed to support international high-technology trade. In addition, as Song and Ahn both remind us, Korea has only recently emerged from an extremely authoritarian regime; Ahn in particular sees an increase in the number of lawyers, strongly opposed by the legal establishment, as a way of facilitating firm practice, but also as a way of enlarging the reach of democracy in Korean institutions. These last essays caution us, then, also to remember the context in which the reforms in which we are interested have to take shape.

PART ONE

Approaches from Social Science

1

Law, Legal Institutions, and Economic Development

Lawrence M. Friedman

The relationship between law and the economy is a classic issue in the study of law and society.[1] It is, for example, a central concern of Max Weber's work on the sociology of law.[2] This essay will explore a few general ideas and theories about this relationship.

Words like "law" or "economy" are, of course, conceptually difficult. They are trouble even in the context of a single society; and they need careful refinement before they can be used across cultures. "Law" or "legal system" carry different nuances and references in different languages and cultures, and even within a national population.

To lawyers and jurists, law is what lawyers think about, study and write; and, to a lesser extent, what lawyers actually do for their clients. Of course, this way of looking at law tends to elide issues of culture and social context; and it puts law at the mercy of the habits and customs of legal education, or the particular scholarly tradition, say, in Germany or Japan. Such customs and traditions may or may not connect tightly with legal and business affairs in the real world. Very often they do not. So, for example, Western lawyers on the whole do not think of industrial policy as "law" or fiscal policy as "law;" economic regulation is "public administration" rather than "law."[3] But the modern state governs through law; it uses rules and norms expressed in the form of law or enforced (or not enforced) by agencies and institutions whose work-sphere and competence are legally defined.

Another point: it is notorious that lawyers (that is, members of the bar) do not count for much in certain societies—Japan or Korea, for example—compared to the United States. Some people jump to the conclusion that there is less "law" in Japan or Korea; or that America is more "legalized" or "litigious" than Japan; or terms to that effect.[4] But unless we define "law" very carefully, it is not clear what these statements mean, beyond the obvious fact that there are more lawyers in some countries than in others. What lawyers *do* is culturally quite variable. Little if anything is *inherently* a lawyer's job. People in England go to a solicitor when they want to buy a home; in other societies this might be a job for law-trained people who are not members of the bar; in still others, lay people carry it out.[5]

Thus there are problems in comparing "lawyers" across cultures. These problems are magnified a hundred-fold if we try to compare "law" or "legal systems." For now, we will avoid the problem of definition, and assume that, at least as far as the countries of the West are concerned, there is some minimum of commonality and consensus about such terms as "law" and "legal system." At the end of the essay we will return to this issue.

Law and the Economic Order

We are interested in the general relationship between the legal and economic systems. At the outset, we will identify *three* very broad, possible forms of relationship, and the theoretical issues underlying each of them.

The Null Hypothesis

Legal scholars and theorists divide up bodies of law, conventionally, into various "fields." This essay is about business law, broadly conceived: how law relates to parts of the economy. The focus is on developed, industrial nations. These countries are all, at core, capitalist, though "capitalism" is a complex concept (and a complex reality); all of these countries, moreover, have modified their capitalisms in various ways; they have "mixed" economies, and they redistribute income through taxing and spending. Must there be *any* relationship between law and the economy? The first theoretical position is a simple no. The two systems might be totally unrelated—ships that pass in the night. This would happen if the legal system was completely *autonomous*. A system is autonomous if it is closed on itself, self-contained, responsive only to its own logic, traditions, and imperatives. Language, for example, is a (relatively) autonomous system. Since 1955, Korea's economy has been utterly transformed; the changes have affected politics, the family, popular culture; outlook on life; but the Korean language has changed, I presume, very little—some new vocabulary, a few terms of phrase, but nothing that disturbed the basic structure of writing and speech. An "autonomous" legal system would be equally independent; it would think and behave on its own, divorced from the needs and wants of the economy; it would march to an entirely different drummer.

Is the legal system autonomous? The issue has been much discussed in legal scholarship.[6] Modern legal systems are on the whole highly technical; they seem to have a tough, outer skin, a thick hide that separates law from the rest of the social order. Lawyers and judges talk in a special, powerful language; they filter or translate raw material from the social world into "legal" terms. A client goes to a lawyer with a story from ordinary life—an auto accident, a dispute with a neighbor. The lawyer passes the story through the prism of his legal consciousness; it emerges as a mysterious jargon of torts, contracts, and liability. The concepts are foreign to the client, but they can determine the fate of her claim.[7]

An autonomous legal system would have no *organic* relationship to development, the economy, commerce, or the business world. The two social spheres would each go their own way, following internal rules or an internal program. Probably nobody believes this *absolutely*; but lawyers (and laymen?) assume it is more or less true. "The law" seems *relatively* autonomous; in the short run at least, it seems rigid, immovable, unresponsive, rather than supple, plastic, and yielding. As Lempert and Sanders put it, law "looks to itself rather than to the standards of some external social, political, or ethical system for guidance in making or applying law."[8]

At times, Max Weber himself expressed views that seem close to the null hypothesis. Weber was troubled by the problem of English law. The industrial revolution began in England; but the common law was, from Weber's standpoint, crude and unsystematic; less "rational" than European systems. Yet capitalism seemed to need a rational legal order. Was this need an illusion? At one point in his work, Weber flatly stated that "England achieved capitalistic supremacy among the nations not because but rather in spite of its judicial system."[9] This suggested to him that "modern capitalism prospers equally...under legal systems containing rules and institutions which considerably differ from each other at least from a juridical point of view."[10]

A Mirror of Society

A second alternative is to consider the legal system as a precise, exact reflection of the forces which flow into it from "outside"; law is, in other words, a kind of mirror of society. This is probably the dominant view among social scientists who study law. In this view, a tight fit between law and society is inevitable and unavoidable; there is no tough barrier, no outer skin, protecting the system from the play and flow of social, cultural, political forces. The legal system is directly dependent for its life and soul on its surrounding society.[11] In fact, the legal system *is* the arena of these forces; they are not "outside forces" at all.

Indeed, some scholars argue that there is no true distinction between "legal systems" and "social systems." Law and society are intermeshed and intertwined; they are part of each other; they "constitute" each other.[12] We cannot even talk about an "economy" without using words like property, contract, partnership, company. But these are *legal* terms; they structure any conversation about the economy, or business; they demonstrate the intimate union between law and society.

Thus the legal system inevitably changed and developed, as capitalism itself changed and developed. Or, to put it another way, the actors (whoever they are) who call the tune in society shape the reality of legal institutions.[13] This is as true of capitalism and its modifications as it is of any other system. When you describe a system as (say) a welfare state, you are not only describing its economy or polity; you are describing its *laws*. Thus, if you could, in theory, draw a map of the *precise* field of social forces in a given society—the interests and desires of merchants, bankers, farmers, and every other group, multiplied by some figure indicating how much *power* the members have, multiplied again by some measure of intensity of the concerns or interests of each group on each issue, then take into account how much *actual* force, lobbying, or activity gets exerted on the issue—if you could do all this, you would be able to deduce the *exact* contours of the working legal system. Obviously, this exercise is impossible to carry out; but arguably it is in principle correct.

The Catalyst

The "mirror" concept seems to treat law in a rather passive, reactive way. Law is simply a dependent variable. But the legal system may connect with the economy in a more dramatic, active way—as an agent of modernization, perhaps even a functional prerequisite. Perhaps a modern economy *requires* some specific kind of law; perhaps it cannot live without this legal pattern. A dynamic legal order might be one factor that divides "take-off" societies—societies that grow rapidly over long periods—from societies stuck in the mud of tradition.

Talcott Parsons thought that the "long-run adaptive capacity" of complex societies required a "universalistic legal system."[14] Rosenberg and Birdzell, writing on "how the West got rich," stress the role of commercial courts, especially in England; in these courts, merchants got fair, honest, intelligent treatment. As a result, transactions became "more secure, more calculable in their consequences, less subject to the vagaries of sovereigns and changes of heart by one party or the other."[15] A "rational" legal order, in this view, is part of the process of birth or growth of modern capitalism; it is unclear which is the chicken and which is the egg. (Conversely, a legal system without the necessary traits may stifle economic growth, or prevent a take-off—Japan before the Meiji was a possible example.)

Rationality, Autonomy, and Economic Development

Is there any way to choose between these three alternatives? Obviously, none of the three can be "proven" in some scientific sense. I think, however, that we can say something sensible about plausibility.

No one can really resolve, of course, the argument over autonomy. There is no way to measure autonomy, or to test a system to see if it is truly autonomous. Changes in law do correlate with changes in economic organization. But correlation, of course, is not cause. People in "modern" countries wear business suits and dresses; they eat hamburgers and drink Coca-Cola. But nobody thinks the way to wealth is through importing fried chicken or outlawing native costumes and customs.[16]

In the long run, it seems to me, legal systems obviously are not and cannot be autonomous; they inevitably take on the shape and coloration of their social system. Modern Italian law is strikingly different from ancient Roman law—or medieval Roman law, for that matter; and in ways that parallel changes in Italian society since Caesar. Law, after all, is not about abstract issues, but concrete social problems; when a problem becomes obsolete, its law dies with it. Similarly, a new problem or new situation (in vitro fertilization, computer hacking) generates new law. To be sure, if we want to explain specific events, decisions, legal acts, over some short time-frame—if we want to know (for example) why a particular judge decided a case in some specific way—"internalist" (autonomous) explanations sometimes *may* be more convincing. But for the big picture and the long haul, the notion of autonomy has to be tempered if not discarded.

Any particular type of society (feudal, tribal, social, capitalist) implies, generates, or perhaps requires certain norms, including legal norms, which fit that type of society. This is surely true of modern economies. In some ways, legal structure *defines* the type of society. It would be hard to describe a feudal or capitalist system, without using words like property and contract; these are legal terms, intertwined with legal norms. The relationships are both subtle and deep. They are also not monolithic. After all, what passes for a "capitalist" system in modern Sweden or Japan is quite different from what passed for capitalism in 19th century England; each country, in each period, has its own dialect of capitalism. Each country, too, has its own dialect of law.

If we reject the idea of autonomy, we are left with some version of the other two hypotheses. Is rationality or some variant a functional prerequisite for a modern economy? This is a question that cannot be answered. But there is some reason to be skeptical here too.

We have already mentioned Weber's views on the "England problem." Weber's ideas about law and economic development were unusually subtle and complex. Modern law (at least continental law) was, in Weber's terms, "formally rational"; and this is what set it off from other systems in world history. A "formally rational" system, for Weber, is one in which the "legally relevant characteristics of . . . facts are disclosed through the logical analysis of meaning," and which emphasizes "definitely fixed legal concepts in the form of highly abstract rules."[17] Weber was thinking here, above all, of juridical thought in his own society: Germany, in the late 19th and early 20th centuries and the civil law tradition in general.

Weber never made it entirely clear exactly how formal rationality was connected to economic growth or the rise of capitalism. At times, he seemed to suggest that a formally rational legal system was some sort of prerequisite to capitalist development; but his views on the "England problem" contradicted this. European lawyers, understandably, tend to feel their rather formal systems are important for economic success and modernization. They appreciate order, system, conceptual rationality; their tradition of legal scholarship stresses these virtues, and legal education passes the tradition along to future lawyers.

Rosenberg and Birdzell, however, are not talking about formal rationality. Honest, competent, and reasonably consistent judges and civil servants certainly help support economic life. It is helpful, too, if judges know something about business or the customs of merchants. But institutions do not need formal rationality in Weber's sense; they do not need the system and order of continental codes.

Common law systems, for example, are much less "rational" than continental systems. The United States inherited (and magnified) "the England problem." It has been an absolute jumble of laws, scattered higgledy-piggledy among dozens of statute books and hundreds of volumes of decisions. The fifty separate states have legal sovereignty in matters of commercial law; and a federal layer sits on top of and alongside the states.[18] Nonetheless, the United States has managed to produce an enormous economy. The common law—complex, irrational, archaic, as it seems—has not held back the gross national product, or stifled business innovation.[19]

An economic system implies and contains legal norms and forms; but not *only* legal norms. The modern industrial world is more than an economic system; culture and the moral order change along with ways of doing business. Capitalism (and modernization in general) calls for, evokes, or produces a distinctive way of looking at the world.[20] A market system requires modes of dealing which "command trust and loyalty on some basis other than kinship." It requires a system of norms and understandings to "supply the personal loyalties necessary to the development of firms outside the family."[21] The "invisible hand" of the market rests on this foundation. The foundation does not, of course, come out of nowhere; it starts with some particular cultural base, and so France or Japan or Finland or Australia describe somewhat different trajectories, speak somewhat different languages of capitalism, and produce somewhat different institutions—including legal ones.

To sum up: there is at least some reason to think that economic development requires *some* sort of basic legal (and political and cultural) framework, within a market system. But what sort of framework? Not "rationality," in the technical *legal* sense; not formal order, clarity, and system, the glory of continental jurists. There are a number of possible types of framework; and we will mention them briefly.

One important caveat: it is easy to slip into language which suggests that legal systems in the West grew and changed to meet the "needs" of the capitalist order. This teeters on the brink of determinism. There is no reason to assume some legal version of the survival of the fittest. If a legal doctrine or institution has survived this far, it is safe to say that it is not a lethal trait, as far as the economy is concerned. Overall, of course, the system must meet *minimum* needs. But any statement stronger than that skates on thin ice.

History is strewn with the corpses of failed economies. A corrupt, unmanageable legal system sometimes bears *part* of the blame. The legal system has no mind of its own. A "legal system" is after all an abstraction; the behavior of actual actors—lawyers, judges, business people, the public— are the concrete reality. The system consists of these elements interacting with each other. If legal actors and the social forces they represent misconceive what the economy "needs," then the "legal system" will be equally foolish or misguided.

A fairly recent body of work (mostly by economists) argues that judge-made rules, in common law systems, evolve toward economic efficiency.[22] The facts hardly support this idea. Modern American rules of tort law, many of them created by judges, would not strike many economists as "efficient." It is hard to connect the "rights revolution" or the "due process revolution" with anything an economist would call efficient.[23] Even in the 19th century, the legal choices made "were certainly not always optimal or uni-directional toward increased productivity" or economic welfare.[24] In any event lawmaking (in contemporary times) is concentrated not in court decisions but in statutes and rules and regulations. Most of these are the obvious result of struggles and battles among interest groups. It is hard to make the claim that all this wheeling and dealing drives inexorably toward efficiency; and the evolutionists in fact do not make such a claim.[25]

Law and Business: The Framework

There are at least *six* kinds of legal framework, which can or do affect an industry or sector of the economy.

1. There are, in the first place, *general* legal institutions, which pertain to and support industry, business, economic activity in general. Modern economies presuppose markets. They presuppose buying, selling, trading, dealing. "Marketing," as Willard Hurst put it, "cannot go on save in a context of reasonably assured expectations." Hence the legal order is "indispensable to the existence of a market."[26] The legal order in one sense *is* the market—a zone of protected, licit dealings. This means, above all, a regime of contract—support for the market through "assurance and the procedures and tools necessary for the immediate operation and steadily expanding energy of the institution."[27] North and Thomas, too, stress the importance of the legal framework in supporting the operations of the market. Their emphasis is on property rights;[28] and the definition of what is and what is not "property," and what can be done with it, is another aspect of the general framework established through law.

A legal system whose rules totally prevented people from buying and selling goods, or which outlawed private property, could hardly make it in the modern world. No such system, of course, exists. Socialist systems, like older feudal systems, severely restricted the sale of land; these systems also tended to define the domain of private ownership quite narrowly. The feudal systems are of course extinct.

The socialist systems have mostly gone out of business, or given up some of their prohibitions. In capitalist economies, basic rules define a large zone of "property:" values which can be held, sold, inherited, acquired and exploited. Definitions of property, like those of contract, are of course socially determined; capitalist definitions are wide and expansive, compared to other systems. Basic laws against theft or invasive harm also serve to protect the institution of private property.

All Western legal systems contain general rules about the enforcement of contracts; they also contain extensive labor codes, and they lay down ground rules for business and competitive behavior. The legal system also regulates banks and banking, guarantees or regulates credit, and declares what is or is not legal tender or money.[29] Laws and rules guide the formation of business associations—corporations, partnerships—and specify their powers and duties. The list of fundamental laws could go on. People take a good deal of this legal framework for granted; but it is an important support for economic life. There are interesting variations in this framework of laws, from country to country, and some of the variations are quite significant. But the basic elements are everywhere quite similar, and have if anything *converged* over the last century or so.

Traditional legal scholars work with a rather narrow conception of what law consists of. The *law* of contract, for example, as expounded by 19th century jurists, was by no means the same as the *regime* of contract, that is, a *system* of contract—an economic order that permits or fosters the buying and selling of goods and services. Some scholars, however, confuse the two; they blur together the 19th century law of contract, the dogma of "freedom of contract," and an economic order in which there is a great deal of buying, selling and trading. Hence, they assume that contractual freedom has gone into some sort of decline, in the age of extensive regulation of the business, and the age of the welfare state. Patrick Atiyah, for example, is one of those who detects such a decline; he sees a "weakening of belief in the values involved in individual freedom of choice."[30]

The modern law of contract is, to be sure, far more complicated than the 19th century law of contract. It contains far more restrictions and regulations. But these restrictions and regulations do not imply the "death" of contract,[31] or even much of an illness. The restrictions on pure freedom of contract, the regulation of insurance and labor contracts, securities markets, and business practice in general, all *presuppose* a vigorous market, a vigorous regime of contract. The regulations monitor and patrol this market; they do not contradict it.

Jurists rarely concern themselves with the working reality of the rules they expound. They tend to ignore living law. Some sort of legal infrastructure is certainly useful in a capitalist economy; and a network of contract and property norms is *more* than useful. But the rules of the formal legal system are not the only rules in economic life, or even necessarily the most important. Historically, private associations—guilds of merchants, for example—performed some of the guarantee functions; the state had basically a back-up role. Bills of exchange and other instruments of credit and finance come out of the "custom of merchants." In the 20th century, too, the working norms of contract and property, the living law, the actual legal behavior, cannot be deduced from the surfaces of formal law.[32]

Does capitalism work best under some *particular* kind of general framework—some set of uniquely efficient legal rules and institutions? Those who cling to classical economics as the one true church tend to believe in a golden age of efficiency. This was the period of high *laissez-faire*, dated to some point in the 19th century. Scholars on the left had quite a different view of capitalism and its law. Law was a scheme to make sure owners of land, factories, and wealth had firm control over society—a scheme to suppress quite ruthlessly the rights of the working class.

But there are all sorts of societies on which we can plausibly stick the label of "capitalist." The paths they have traveled are so different that it is hard to imagine any particular form of legal order as uniquely necessary. The golden age of *laissez-faire* was never as golden or as *laissez-faire* as some have imagined. On the other hand, capitalism arguably survived and flourished precisely because it was able to give workers and their unions enough of what they wanted to keep society from going down in Marxist flames. Open political systems prevented complete domination. The record suggests that capitalism can flourish under many kinds of legal framework—once one goes beyond the minimal legal conditions that define a social and economic order as capitalist in the first place.

2. There is also the framework of *fiscal* and *monetary* policy. We have mentioned banks and legal tender. Governments today also manipulate interest rates and the money supply; they run or avoid deficits; they inflate the currency or, at times, drive it down. All this, of course, has a direct impact on business (exactly how much is a question). "Industrial policy" is another aspect of the legal framework. The term refers to government efforts to work with business, to guide the economy by promoting specific, promising areas of trade or manufacture. Some scholars think "industrial policy" has been critically important in the economic success of Japan[33] and some European countries as well; other scholars disagree. Industrial policy obviously plays a lesser role in the United States.

3. The *formal* arrangement of the legal system is a third kind of framework. Most civil law systems have been codified since the early 19th century; these systems place a high value on their formal order and conceptual clarity.[34] System and codification spread from Europe to Latin America; Japan and other Asian countries also translated and adopted Western codes as the basis for their own legal systems.

We have already referred to the debate over rationality; and expressed doubts about the impact and importance of these traits. Common law systems rank lower than civil law systems on the scale of legal rationality. The United States has become the richest country on earth notwithstanding the common law. Nor has the common law system held back Singapore, which got rich quicker than any other Asian country except Japan.

All modern legal systems, including common law systems, *have* system and order, though not necessarily of the civil law type. The basic rules of law, are formal, written, and *accessible*; there are ways to find the law, there is some more or less orderly arrangement, some indexing scheme or plan. In recent years, too, computers have come to play a role in legal research—notably in retrieving legal data. Whatever was true in the past, the computer imposes a kind of electronic order on the chaos of modern law. This if anything reduces still further the value of "system" in the formal sense.

4. Quite another kind of rationality and order, however, may be in fact highly significant. The countries of the West, and those of the far East that have grown spectacularly, tend to have *relatively* honest and competent court systems, and relatively honest and competent civil service. Countries that are standing still, or moving backward, often suffer from mammoth corruption and incompetence. This may be the single most important factor in failure or success.

Every bureaucracy, of course, harbors corruption, red tape, and stupidity. These pathologies may even affect the courts. But in successful countries, these (arguably) remain within tolerable levels. The bureaucracy is notoriously inefficient in certain rich Western countries (Italy is often cited). The civil service of the United States in the 19th century, was small but fairly corrupt. But in many poor and struggling countries, bribery and civil dishonesty reach intolerable levels; corruption drains resources, blocks investment and stifles growth. The causes and cures of corruption are worth further exploration;[35] the impact on development seems undeniable.

5. *Legitimacy* is another threshold requirement.[36] Legitimacy is difficult to define; scholars (and people in general) use the word in a number of different senses. We use it here to mean a belief in the rightness of authority. In most societies, most people consider

authority legitimate, that is, legally and morally entitled to govern. This may be because the leaders followed some road to the top that people label fair, just, or right—an election, for example. People also tend to ascribe legitimacy to their legal institutions.[37]

Legitimacy is an important social attitude because it probably has an impact on the way people behave. If the population, or some sizeable part of it, has confidence in the legal order, and believes it is worth obeying, they probably *will* obey. Conversely, if a system does *not* command allegiance, its stability may begin to totter. And it is hard to imagine rapid growth in *very* unstable societies.

Put in this way, *legitimacy* is not a normative but an empirical fact, in any given society. It is a question of public opinion, or some part of public opinion; a question of how the popular state of mind, or the mind of elites, affects obedience, disobedience, revolt, quiescence, militancy, and so on. But in all or almost all societies, there is little information about attitudes of legitimacy; and next to nothing about how attitudes translate into behavior.[38]

The basic theory is plausible, however, because a society is stable if most people in it obey most important rules, most of the time. People obey rules either voluntarily or because they are forced to. Voluntary compliance is preferable; force is expensive and sometimes self-defeating. Legitimacy gives a government an enormous boost, at no special cost. At least this seems a reasonable guess. The empirical basis for this guess is exceedingly weak.

Legitimacy, of course, is a general requirement of a legal system; it relates to all parts of it, divorce law and criminal law as much as the law relating to the economic order. It is not necessarily an all-or-nothing idea. Criminal law could be legitimate (in the sense we have used the word), while business law is not; and vice versa. The idea here is that the legal system must provide *some* sort of legitimate forum for business disputes and for legal problems of commerce and trade. If the business community has no confidence in the honesty, skill, and virtue of legal institutions, it will suffer unless it can develop parallel or rival institutions of its own.

6. Five general frameworks have been mentioned. A sixth is specific. Every industry has its own character, its own special problems, wants and needs. In a complex legal system, dozens and dozens of special laws and regulations control or encourage specific industries: laws about retail stores, steel companies, taxicab companies, drug manufacturers. Some branches of law are specific to *modes* of doing business—anti-trust laws and laws about fair competition. There are also specific branches of law relevant to particular industries or types of business; copyright law, for example,

is of special significance to publishers and software companies; trade laws to exporting companies; health regulation to makers of drugs and foods, and so on. These are all not merely "frameworks," they are also arenas of struggle *between* industries. But the same is true of other "frameworks."

Law, Culture, and Economic Growth

Nothing much has been said so far about culture, in the sense of customs, traditions, habits and ways of life. How far culture effects the economy is a controversial question. Do developed societies, however they differ, share enough *general* features that we can ignore "culture" as a factor in explaining development?

Many scholars answer no. In Max Weber's work, as we have seen, there was the "England problem," in part a problem of culture. Moreover, Weber saw a link between Calvinism, an aspect of Western religion, and the rise of capitalism. Today, one might speak of the "Japan problem;" or the "Far East" problem. A great divide supposedly splits legal and social cultures, East and West. Government in the West is open and accountable. The push and pull of interest groups determines the political-legal process. Law comes out of overt assertions of interest. Western societies also place high value on "the rule of law;" on formal legality, on a rational, impersonal legal system. Their systems bristle with rights and entitlements; there is no stigma in defending or asserting rights. Western societies admire and respect people who "stick up for their rights." The United States is a land of "adversary legalism."[39]

Asian societies, on the other hand, are described in very different terms. "Law" and "litigation" have pejorative overtones. As a prominent Korean scholar put it, law "has traditionally been an instrument of ruling and controlling;" in the Korean tradition, law was not connected with the "benefit and protection of the public."[40] The Japanese, too, are said to avoid litigation and open conflict if at all possible. They favor mediation, indirection, consensus, informality, compromise.

Japan has notoriously few lawyers, and little litigation. Many people, on both sides of the Pacific, see this as a great social advantage; it is even cited as one reason why the Japanese economy has flourished. Japanese industrial policy rests, it is said, on "harmony and consensus. . . . [T]he process is legally informal and unaccountable."[41] The Ministry of International Trade and Industry "shapes policy by private consultations with representatives of the relevant industry associations and individual firms. Only after a compromise . . . that all major actors can live with does the process become formal and official."[42] Administrative agencies in Japan try to reach consensus; they use "guidance," informal means, flexibility, persuasion; they try to avoid coercion.[43]

Other scholars are more skeptical about cultural explanations of the Japanese miracle. They suspect that too much has been made of Japanese ideology and tradition. If American businessmen are "rational maximizers" (that too is subject to dispute), then so are the Japanese. Litigation rates in Japan are low because the government discourages litigation, and because there are structural obstacles in the way; the Japanese claimant is reluctant to sue because he has little chance to win, not because of his "culture."[44]

No one, of course, thinks culture is totally irrelevant, or that Japanese or Koreans think and behave exactly the same as Americans or Italians. And "the West" itself is not a cultural monolith. Students of comparative legal culture have found significant differences, for example, between American and French legal cultures, or between German and Dutch.[45] Very likely the Japanese are not as conciliatory and deferential as conventional wisdom would have it; on the other side, some American scholars question whether Americans are incurably litigious, and whether the "litigation explosion" is real.[46] Legal behavior is a complex phenomenon, in which culture, legal tradition, and structure certainly make a difference; no one has been able, so far, to assign weights to the various factors. In any event, critics of "culture" certainly have a point: "culture" cannot be disentangled from concrete factors of politics and structure; and vice versa.

No doubt, "tradition" does account for some differences between legal systems. I am not here referring to the *legal* tradition as such. "Legal tradition," as it appears in the literature of comparative law, tends to be a fairly arid and formalist affair, divorced from context and the living law. It explains little about how legal systems work in the modern world. Probably each society, however, has its own context of historical and structural facts—size, weather, natural resources, wars and domestic violence, forms of social stratification. These help shape the operating system. Once a certain structure is in place, it generates its own chemistry of costs and benefits. "Culture" is not a matter of (presumably enduring) personality traits. Culture and structure evolve over time, in complicated ways, in a natural dance of interaction. This development is unique to each society. It is the chemical reaction between the *general* (a market economy, for example), and the *particular* (the society's traditions and situation).

The United States, for example, has an enormous legal profession—

very large in comparison to, say, the British profession; positively immense in comparison to the professions in Korea or Japan. Elsewhere I have tried to explain the American profession in terms of certain brute facts of historical experience.[47] The United States was the first middle-class country; the first country in which masses (of men, at least) owned land. Millions of people had a stake in the economy; they needed basic legal services and skills. This produced a large, active legal profession; and it generated a *concept* of lawyers as factotums, do-it-alls, general advisers, people who knew their way around in business and government. The profession in, say, France or Korea, or even in England, evolved in profoundly different ways.

If we say that Americans are "litigious" and the Japanese are not, we are of course talking about legal behavior. "Culture," in other words, is an aggregate; the word refers to *patterns* of legal behavior. It is an empirical question, and a tough one, to decipher such patterns in any given society. The question is crucial, however, not because "culture" is the key variable; but because these patterns of legal behavior *are*.

This brings us back to the question we raised toward the beginning of this issue, and then postponed. Clearly, we can only sensibly discuss how law and the economy are intertwined if our concept of "law" is behavioral, not formal. It has to be about what people actually *do* and why they do it; official documents and forms tell us very little. This is why "culture" is important—because it elucidates patterns of behavior.

But if we use a behavioral concept of law, how can we compare two societies? It is one thing to check to see if their commercial codes have the same language; comparing living law is quite another. But it is important nonetheless to draw a line between the two. I would go further, and make a distinction between two kinds of legal phenomena, which I will call *legal acts* and *legal behavior*. A *legal act* is conduct that takes place inside the sphere of action socially defined as "law" or "the legal system." In most modern societies, judges, lawyers, legislators, and officials of all sorts and conditions are legal actors. In some societies, one might throw in notaries. The legal acts themselves include statutes, rules, decisions, regulations, ordinances, commands, or orders, done through or under the umbrella of law. Enacting a law is a legal act. It is also a legal act if a policeman shouts at a thief to stop and surrender; or pulls out his gun and shoots.

Legal behavior is behavior in response to a legal act. The response or reaction may be obedient or compliant; misuse, abuse and noncompliance are legal behavior just as much as obedience and compliance. Filling out a tax return or an apartment lease can be legal behavior; or asking a lawyer for advice about a contract or a will; so is breaking a lease, or tax fraud.[48]

The terms, as defined, are admittedly not easy to delineate. If an accountant or a neighbor or friend gives someone advice about the law, is this a legal act? Legal behavior too is very hard to pin down. The following might or might not be legal acts: stopping at a stop sign, driving down the left side of the road, paying for a TV set in cash (legal tender), paying for a TV set with a check, buying food, ordering food in a restaurant (these are "contracts"), shoplifting, refraining from shoplifting even if tempted, driving carefully so as not to hit anybody, not driving carefully, opening the door to your own house, or keeping someone else out (asserting or exercising a property right), going to a friend's house for dinner (entering premises under a license or invitation), owning a share of stock, going to work (performing one's obligations under an employment contract), and so on.

The problem is to disentangle "law" as a distinct category of social action. Legal theory in the West has often presumed that its codes of law or systems of doctrine are "gapless." In other words, whatever one does can be analyzed in *legal* terms, even walking down the street or falling asleep; most definitely, buying a newspaper or driving a car. This, of course, makes all behavior "legal." But the concept of legal behavior is *potentially* useful, insofar as it is linked psychologically and socially to specific legal *acts*. The root idea is that legal systems are systems—chains of actions and reactions; and that all "legal" behavior takes place within a domain that can be defined—either broadly or narrowly—in social and behavioral terms.

Legal acts and legal behavior cannot be measured in the aggregate. These concepts form a framework, a way to approach the orbit or sphere of "law." The orbit must be broad enough to deal with whatever larger issue is on the table—law and economic development, for example. Cultures differ, of course, in the ways they define legal acts and legal behavior—they differ in the manner in which they map out the domain of the legal system, and the interpretation they place upon specific forms of "legal" or "non-legal" behavior. But if we link the two concepts, if we tie specific legal behaviors to specific legal acts, it might be possible to compare legal systems, functionally and sociologically. There is, of course, a field called "comparative law"; but its categories tend to be very formalistic, and not suitable for functional comparison.[49] It would be useful to shift emphasis to legal actors, what they do, and the legal behavior that comes about in response to their actions, rather than to "laws," "norms," "codes" or "doctrines" as such.

Most (not all) of the "frameworks" discussed here can be analyzed in terms of legal *acts*, and indeed of a rather conventional type: laws, rules, formal institutions. The real issue, however, is legal behavior, that is, social responses to these acts and other cues and responses which flow out of the legal system. The secret connections between law and economic development are hidden in the way legal acts and legal behavior influence and reinforce each other in the modern world. But our studies and understandings of this issue are still in their infancy.

Notes

1. I wish to acknowledge the help of Daniel R. Krislov, John Barton and Robert W. Gordon. Mark Ramseyer and Kahei Rokumoto made valuable comments on an earlier draft.

2. Max Rheinstein, ed., *Max Weber on Law in Economy and Society* (Cambridge, Mass.: Harvard University Press, 1954).

3. Similarly, lawyers tend to exaggerate the role of concepts, doctrines, or rules which loom large in their training or are juridically famous; but which have little or no behavioral or social consequence.

4. There is a large literature on this point, especially in regard to Japan; see text to notes 41-44.

5. Philip S. C. Lewis, "Comparison and Change in the Study of Legal Professions," in Richard L. Abel and Philip S. C. Lewis, eds., *Lawyers in Society*, Vol. III, *Comparative Theories* (Berkeley, Cal.: University of California Press, 1989), p. 27. He points out that a couple who want to get married in Belgium will go to a notary for a marriage contract; a couple in England would certainly not go to a solicitor. See also, in the same volume, Lawrence M. Friedman, "Lawyers in Cross-Cultural Perspective," p. 1.

6. See, for example, Roger Cotterrell, *The Sociology of Law* (London: Butterworth's, 2nd ed., 1992), pp. 44-46, 65-70, 84-86; Richard Lempert and Joseph Sanders, *An Invitation to Law and Social Science* (New York: Longman's, 1986), pp. 401-427; Niklas Luhmann, "The Self-Reproduction of Law and Its Limits," in Gunther Teubner, ed., *Dilemmas of Law in the Welfare State* (Berlin: De Gruyter, 1985), p. 111.

7. In simple (mostly pre-literate) societies, there are no specialized legal terms, no specifically legal job-slots; the system thus does not even *appear* to be autonomous.

8. Lempert and Sanders, *Invitation to Law and Social Science, supra*, n. 6, at 408.

9. Rheinstein, *Max Weber on Law in Economy and Society, supra*, n. 2, at 231.

10. Ibid., at 315. The rub, of course, is in the phrase "from the juridical point of view."

11. Lawrence M. Friedman, *The Legal System: A Social Science Perspective* (New York: Russell Sage Foundation, 1975).

12. For this point, see Robert W. Gordon, "Critical Legal Histories," 36 Stanford L. Rev. 102 (1984).

13. This statement does not assume that the legal system actually meets the

"needs" of the economic system, a point that will be discussed more fully later in this essay. Nor does it assume that "the people" make the law, or that the law is "responsive" in some ethical sense to the wishes and requirements of the population as a whole. By the same token, it does not assume that the law, as in classical Marxist thought, exclusively reflects the "needs" and desires of some narrow class of capitalist overlords.

14. Talcott Parsons, "Evolutionary Universals in Society," *Am. Sociological Rev.* 29:339 (1964).

15. Nathan Rosenberg and L.E. Birdzell, Jr., *How the West Grew Rich: the Economic Transformation of the Industrial World* (New York: Basic Books, 1986), p. 116.

16. A society trying to modernize might want to imitate everything Western; nobody is sure what *causes* modernization, anyway. Atatürk banned the fez. The correlation between dress and modernization is not random, though of course not causal.

17. Rheinstein, *Max Weber on Law in Economy and Society, supra*, n. 2, at 63. A system, according to Weber, is "formally irrational" when it uses "means which cannot be controlled by the intellect, for instance...oracles." Ibid.

18. Common law lawyers try to put a good face on the jumble of jurisdictions; Justice Brandeis, in a famous phrase, referred to the states as "laboratories" for experimentation.

19. There are also, to be sure, structural features in American government that *promote* economic growth. The states can generate their own commercial rules; but they cannot interfere with *interstate* commerce beyond a point. The Constitution guarantees a large, internal common market.

20. See, for example, Alex Inkeles and David H. Smith, *Becoming Modern: Individual Change in Six Developing Countries* (Cambridge, Mass.: Harvard University Press, 1974); Alex Inkeles, *Exploring Individual Modernity* (New York: Columbia University Press, 1983).

21. Rosenberg and Birdzell, *How the West Grew Rich, supra*, n. 15, at 114. Religion was one source of such a system; Weber's famous discussion of the Protestant ethic and the rise of capitalism is relevant here.

22. George Priest, "The Common Law Process and the Selection of Efficient Rules," 6 *J. Legal Studies* 65 (1977).

23. On this development, see Lawrence M. Friedman, *Total Justice* (New York: Russell Sage Foundation, 1985).

24. Douglass C. North, *Institutions, Institutional Change and Economic Performance* (Cambridge: Cambridge University Press, 1990), p. 9.

25. What can be claimed (not without some controversy) is that the give and take of legislative bargaining produces the best or fairest result politically obtainable. This is, however, by no means the same as economic efficiency.

26. James Willard Hurst, *Law and Economic Growth: The Legal History of the Lumber Industry in Wisconsin, 1836-1915* (Cambridge, Mass.: Harvard University Press, 1964), p. 285.

27. Ibid.

28. See Douglass C. North and Robert Paul Thomas, *The Rise of the Western*

World: A New Economic History (Cambridge: Cambridge University Press, 1973), Chapter 2; also North, *Structure and Change in Economic History* (New York: W. W. Norton, 1981), where he again argues that the success of England was "directly traceable to the system of private property rights that had evolved," p. 154; see also p. 190, on American economic development.

29. Conventional legal scholarship tends to ignore these aspects of the legal system; but see James Willard Hurst, *A Legal History of Money in the United States, 1774-1970* (Lincoln, Neb.: University of Nebraska Press, 1973).

30. Patrick S. Atiyah, *The Rise and Fall of Freedom of Contract* (Oxford: Oxford University Press, 1979), pp. 726-727.

31. The reference is to Grant Gilmore, *The Death of Contract* (Columbus: Ohio State University Press, 1974), p. 20; Gilmore refers to a "decline and fall of the general theory of contract and, in most quarters, of laissez-faire economics." Ibid., pp. 95-96. For a critique, see Lawrence M. Friedman, *The Republic of Choice: Law, Authority and Culture* (Cambridge, Mass.: Harvard University Press, 1990), pp. 80-83; on the reality of 19th century contract law in the United States, Lawrence M. Friedman, *Contract Law in America: A Social and Economic Case Study* (Madison, Wis.: University of Wisconsin Press, 1965).

32. Stewart Macaulay, "Non-Contractual Relations in Business: A Preliminary Study," *Am. Sociological Rev.* 28:55 (1963).

33. See Chalmers Johnson, *MITI and the Japanese Miracle: the Growth of Industrial Policy, 1925-1975* (Stanford, Cal.: Stanford University Press, 1982).

34. See, on the ethos of these systems in general, John Henry Merryman, *The Civil Law Tradition* (Stanford, Cal.: Stanford University Press, 2nd ed., 1985), pp. 61-67.

35. *Why* nations differ along these dimensions is a complex issue, which we do not pursue in this essay. See Rogelio Perez-Perdomo and Ruth Capriles, eds., *Corrupcion y Control: Una Perspectiva Comparada* (Caracas: Ediciones IESA, 1991).

36. On the meaning of the concept see, for example, Friedman, *Legal System, supra*, n. 11, 112-120.

37. There is, of course, an enormous literature on legitimacy. Hyde argues that the term is fundamentally useless, see Alan Hyde, "The Concept of Legitimation in the Sociology of Law," 1983 Wisconsin L. Rev. 379; but there is a core meaning that makes sense and seems to refer to a real phenomenon. Fundamental to any discussion of legitimacy is Weber's famous distinction between three types of legitimate authority, see Rheinstein, *Max Weber on Law in Economy and Society, supra*, n. 2, 336-337. What we discuss in the text is basically "rational-legal" authority, which has a heavy procedural element, see Niklas Luhmann, *Legitimation durch Verfahren* (Darmstadt: Luchterhand, 1975).

38. See, however, Tom R. Tyler, *Why People Obey the Law* (New Haven: Yale University Press, 1990).

39. Robert Kagan, "Adversary Legalism and American Government," *Journal of Policy Analysis and Management*, 10:369 (1991).

40. Pyong-Choon Hahm, *The Korean Political Tradition and Law* (Seoul, Korea: Hollym Corp., 1967), p. 165.

41. Frank K. Upham, *Law and Social Change in Postwar Japan* (Cambridge, Mass.: Harvard University Press, 1987), p. 24. See Setsuo Miyazawa, "Taking Kawashima Seriously: A Review of Japanese Research on Japanese Legal Consciousness," 21 *Law & Society Review* 219 (1987).

42. Upham, loc. cit.

43. See Michael K. Young, "Judicial Review of Administrative Guidance: Governmentally Encouraged Consensual Dispute Resolution in Japan," 84 Columbia L. Rev. 923 (1984).

44. See J. Mark Ramseyer and Minoru Nakazato, "The Rational Litigant: Settlement Amounts and Verdict Rates in Japan," 18 *J. Legal Studies* 263 (1989); Takao Tanase, "The Management of Disputes: Automobile Accident Compensation in Japan," 24 *Law & Society Review* 651 (1990).

It is also by no means exclusively Eastern for a culture to disfavor litigation. See, on Spain, Jose-Juan Toharia, *Pleitos Tengas* (Madrid: Centro de Investigaciones Sociologicas, 1987).

45. See Laurent Cohen-Tanugi, *Le Droit sans l'État: Sur la Democratie en France et en Amerique* (Paris: Presses Universitaire de France, 1985) (contrast between the United States and France); Erhard Blankenburg and J. R. A. Verwoerd, "Prozesshaüfigkeiten in den Niederlanden und in Nordrhein-Westfalen 1970-1984," in Erhard Blankenburg, ed., *Prozessflut?* (Cologne: Bundesanzeiger, 1988), p. 257 (Germany and Holland).

46. Marc Galanter, "Reading the Landscape of Disputes: What We Know and Don't Know (and Think We Know) about Our Allegedly Contentious and Litigious Society," 31 UCLA L. Rev. 4 (1983); Lawrence M. Friedman, *Total Justice* (1985), ch. 2.

47. Lawrence M. Friedman, "Lawyers in Cross-Cultural Perspective," in Richard L. Abel and Philip S. C. Lewis, *Lawyers in Society: Volume 3, Comparative Theories* (1989), pp. 1, 7-9.

On the role of the profession in the rise of business, see Kenneth Lipartito, "What Have Lawyers Done for American Business? The Case of Baker and Botts of Houston," 64 *Business History Rev.* 489 (1990).

48. See Friedman, *The Legal System, supra*, n. 11, at 4-5.

The use of the word "behavior" is not intended to exclude as irrelevant ideas, attitudes, motives and values; quite the contrary. Ideas and attitudes ("legal culture") are the direct source of legal behavior. Moreover, behavior is *legal* when the actor takes into account some legal act. It is legal behavior to jaywalk deliberately; knowing disobedience to the norm makes behavior "legal" that would otherwise be profoundly ambiguous.

49. The way legal acts and legal behavior relate *to each other* also differs from society to society, in interesting and patterned ways. This is not an obstacle to comparison, but in fact a precondition.

2

The Thomas Theorem of Mega Lawyering

Erhard Blankenburg

In the 1980s a wave of lawyerism swept over the centers of international trade and finance. Brussels, Rotterdam and Frankfurt saw law firms growing within a few years, just as did Tokyo, Singapore and Hong Kong. In the Netherlands an estimated ten percent of the bar organized into seven big law firms—none of which was very sizable prior to 1985. Most of the senior partners in these "mega law firms" were recruited by merging traditional attorney's firms; many juniors started at salaried positions on lower levels of what was new for the profession: a hierarchy ladder.

Wide publicity has been given to the new law firms in the professional journals as well as the mass media. A certain amount of self-presentation was also added, since the Luxembourg court of the European Community opened the gates for advertisement in the legal profession. Most of the attention value, however, came from the imagery of big office buildings, logos on personnel advertisements and more-shiny-than-usual self-presentations as "company representatives" which formed a radical change from the crafty image of old-fashioned solo lawyers. Change swept over into neighboring professions, too. Accountants, tax advisors and notaries joined the partnerships, thus forming service firms for all legal needs of a business clientele.

The rhetoric of the merger movement emphasizes the need to respond to the internationalization of big corporations and the increasing influence of supranational regulatory agencies such as the European Community. These arguments are based on client demand. For many, however, the trend is stimulated more from the supply side; they argue that law firms essentially link international corporations to the diverse national legal systems and to local networks, too. In their view the merger trend among lawyers is based on mutual make-believe according to the famous theorem of the Chicago sociologist W. I. Thomas: trends become real, because people believe them to be real.[1]

The Supply Side: Change and Resistance Among National Bar Associations

Looking at the European experience, my thesis that the market for legal services seems to be pushed from the supply side more than being pulled by demand has been confirmed already by the sudden speed with which new firms and mergers have swept over the profession. Part of the new market for legal services stems from the opening of closed networks under the impact of international competition. Some American law firms thought in the middle of the 1980s that in anticipation of the magic date of the liberalization of Western European trade in 1992 they should look for partners or open subsidiaries in European countries; they postulated that law firms should merge internationally to follow their clients. The trend was taken up by European lawyers who became frightened by their American competitors. Thus, many a middle-sized European firm started looking for partners in major European cities, German, British or Spanish lawyers looking for cooperation with partners near Brussels, and lawyers in Brussels forming multinationals together with New York and Tokyo-based law firms.

A major element of the trend was its visibility. Watching competitors change name tags, letterheads and office buildings made many a middle-sized law office think about joining the bandwagon. The element of make-believe in the movement has been documented by market research among business clients of Dutch lawyers: for them the international ties of a law firm seem much less relevant than the law firms themselves expected. Some hesitation about the international market strategy has also been exhibited by the law firms themselves: while a few have entirely specialized on business clientele, the majority still retain a broad array of legal activities for private clients. Caution has also been demanded by professional standards: the Dutch Chamber of Advocates warned fully specialized law firms that they might not be entitled to recruit lawyer-trainees unless they provided experience in the full range of legal services.

The traditional regulations which kept up professional standards and at the same time prevented competition were different among Dutch, British, German and French lawyers. In all cases, the bar organizations sent out signals of resistance to changes which were perceived as turning the professional profile on its head.

The German profession seems to have resisted most successfully: statutory law grants German attorneys a monopoly not only on representation in court, but also on legal advice (as far as this can be separated from advice on economic, financial and tax matters. In the view of many such separation is not feasible, but nevertheless the local bar associations do reprimand infractions by non-lawyer competitors). The other side of the privilege consists of traditional restrictions: not to form multi-disciplinary partnerships, not to practice at a court other than the one where the lawyer is registered, not to open subsidiaries in other towns, not to announce specializations unless licensed by the bar for it, not to advertise, etc. Some of these professional standards have been loosened in the last decennium, many have been circumvented. But while partnerships with international lawyers appear in the big cities and subsidiary networks are being formed (especially most recently in the move towards gaining the newly opened East German market), there are only a few "mega law firms" in the shadow of the big banking centers of Düsseldorf or Frankfurt.[2]

In sharp contrast to professional conservatism in Germany, the Dutch have traditionally been quite innovation minded. Part of the explanation lies in their legal status remaining unprotected from para-professional competition. Their legal market is open for competition by insurance and association-membership legal services. Except in their monopoly of representation in higher courts (which includes divorce—a highly controversial privilege), attorneys have to compete with legal advisors among business consultants, legal cost insurers, trade unions and subsidized legal aid bureaus. This competition has led to distinct waves of innovation: while in the 1970s the "social advocacy" grew as part of the welfare state, the 1980s saw a spectacular increase in business law firms. Both comprise presently little less than ten percent of the profession—the one at the lower, the other at the upper margin of the income distribution. Differences within the profession are spreading by these waves of extension: the Dutch bar being absolutely (6000 attorneys) as well as relatively small (it grew from in 1980 thirty attorneys per 100,000 inhabitants to forty at the beginning of the 1990s). The new professionals simply add to the legal market without taking away a share of the traditional services.[3]

The French legal profession has also traditionally been rather small (approaching 20,000 *avocats*, a rate of thirty-eight per 100,000). One-third of them practice in Paris. Until 1971 the profession was split up into a number of rather closed "clubs" (various specializations separated legal consultants and lawyers who mainly rendered legal advice from the closed shops of court admitted *avocats*, *avoués* and *agréés*). Even though in the twenty years that there has been a unified job profile of *avocats* and even though their number has grown rather quickly, their offices remain oriented to all-round litigation, maintaining small offices either as solo-practitioners or with a few partners. The new "consultancy firms" which have appeared in the capital in recent years have been led by American accountancy firms and law firm subsidiaries; they did not usually include continental attorneys. More slowly lawyer partnerships including French, German, Dutch or Brussels attorneys have followed suit. Their activities form a world of "internationals" on its own; they hardly mix with French *avocats* nor do they use French courts very often.[4]

The British starting position was similar: as most barristers stuck to their court centered activities, solicitors had a wider range of business including conveyancing and thus open to new forms of activities. They still cannot, however, have non-legal partners. This has allowed a separate market of accountants' bureaus and consultancy firms to develop. American law firms forming partnerships with them have opened the battle of competition across professional lines, and after some years of discussion the Lord Chancellor suggested in his "green paper on the legal profession"[5] that multi-disciplinary law firms should be recognized by the Law Society. So far a majority of solicitors have rejected the proposal, but de facto non-compliance assures that the issue will reappear on the agenda. Solicitors' firms in the City have passed the threshold of small-sized legal partnerships and are engaged in building up networks of subsidiaries in European as well as overseas economic centers.[6]

"Mega law firms" in all four countries have a special kind of international business client in common. They are concentrated in financial centers, and do not necessarily merge or interfere with the national lawyer culture. The more open the competition among and access to performing legal services, however, the more have attorneys entered into alliances with neighboring professions. Competition with other Europeans has further increased expectations that after 1992 when foreign lawyers will be entitled to perform across the European community, many of the protective regulations of the legal profession will be lifted. The anticipation of a common market is the force which might bring it about.

The visibility of changes represented by some "mega-law firms" in financial centers is increased by their clientele and the nature of their activities. Like themselves their clientele act on the basis of belief in the coming competition on international markets. The anticipatory business strategies are manifold: some simply want geographic diversification, others look for vertical cooperation in chains of production, they increase their market share by buying distribution nets. In highly regulated markets (like agriculture) they might try to strip the production quotas; they might look for sites without wanting the workers, they might take over the manpower but move the sites. Depending on how many divergent interests are involved, the strategies tend to be partly covert. Bankruptcy might be intended, in order to take over assets; dismissals might be anticipated, without being announced. Competitors usually have to be taken by surprise, sometimes they may have to be fought directly (for example by claiming patent rights, intellectual property or brand names).

It is evident that such business strategies involve corporations in many legal risks (besides economic and social ones). A specialized bar for "acquisitions and mergers," a professionalized "bankruptcy bar" and an exclusive club of "patent lawyers" have developed expertise for their respective variants. Their cases and the tactics they use fill the pages of legal and economic journals and occasionally reach the mass media. In the mega-law firms, however, they count only as divisions among others: setting up contracts, (re-) negotiating long standing relations and occasionally litigating a case still fill most of the time of most lawyers even in the international law firms.

The Demand Side: Known Facts and Make-Believe of Business Internationalization

While international business lawyering forms a thin layer on top of largely conventional professions, the same might hold true for the managerial role which they play in European business firms. Traditionally, big European industries have kept many of their legal services in-house; legal departments of insurance companies and multinational industries gave advice to managers who were not necessarily law trained. The pattern varied from industry to industry, and by country in addition: in France the *hautes écoles* provided a class of managers who were proud of their craftsmanship; the German mining and steel industry used to recruit its managers from the nation's mining academy, the electronic industry from engineering schools; Dutch managers mostly have a background of economic schooling and acquire basic occupational skills in company traineeships. Besides industry specific training, these systems have the advantage of forming "clubs": many French industries or German cartels did not need formal regulations as long as the relevant counterparts belonged to the network; and merchants in Rotterdam or Hamburg did not need extensive written contracts as long as there was mutual understanding of the terms of trade.

The success of many a multinational empire shows that managing by a combination of hierarchy and network can keep an organization stable and alive over long times. As long as big corporations are internally flexible and "intrapreneurial," they can benefit from moving production, costs and profits across national (loan-and-tax) borders. They can also invest in technological innovation on a continuous basis, calculating costs and benefits, risks of failure and chances for success in a long-term perspective.

In many sectors economic as well as technological change (as well as stand-still) are dominated by the strategies of such big actors. Industrial oligopolies, banking empires and (inter-) governmental interventions determine the course of developments. Yet, there are other sectors where modern technologies are related to small-scale entrepreneurs, and there are branches of industry and trade where internationalization is related to the nervous patterns of financial manoeuvers, short-term contractual relationships, acquisitions and buy-outs, growth by merger and strategic bankruptcies.

The dramaturgical effect of these strategies and the high visibility of the "mega-law" world leads one easily to overlook the more stable powers of the economy and the everyday practice of the profession. The imagery catches the outside observer as well as the inside actors: by believing in legal manoeuvers they resort to lawyers; by resorting to lawyers they create the "mega-law" supply; by creating the supply they stimulate the demand.

The Legal Arms Race as a New Style of Management?

I have been cautioning sufficiently that the wave of "mega-law" activities might be a secondary phenomenon accompanying a primary, more persistent pattern of the internationalization of a world economy. On the basis of such caution I might dare some more speculative hypotheses about the institutional impact of lawyer strategies. According to Chandler[7] vertical integration of mass production and mass distribution at the turn of the twentieth century, which let huge corporations grow, first in North America, later in Europe and even later in Japan, also gave birth to a managerial class with professional ways of running such empires. American business schools led in the professionalization movement, they also developed tool kits of organizational analysis, audits and consultancies to be offered whenever corporations got immobile with internal inertia. The infrastructure of consultant services seems to have been much more of an open market *external* to American business firms, while European, and even more Japanese, corporations tended to *internalize* such services.[8]

Presumably this holds true of legal as well as other types of in-house professionals; and also presumably they tend more toward stabilizing current organizational features than pushing for aggressive changes. Vertical integration usually decreases lawyer use in conflict situations, horizontal integration increases it.[9] The recent wave of mergers and acquisitions mainly increased the horizontal integration of businesses; and reaching over borders of legislation and taxation it challenged especially the professional services of lawyers. Even in countries and among corporations which used to internalize the professional knowledge they needed, they were provided by external law firms.

My hypothesis follows, if these assumptions and observations hold true: the incorporation of mergers and acquisitions, strategic bankruptcies and litigation as a means of competitive fights might affect only the margins of multinational growth, but they are sizable enough to change the flexibility of managerial strategies. The use of external law firms is part of a change towards increased flexibility in management; it at the same time creates a new (upper) class of lawyers breaking through traditional professional patterns.

As the result of the mutual stimulation of supply and demand for legal services an international legal profession might finally emerge. Just as Galanter and Palay[10] argue for American law-firms, the growth might in the first place be triggered by the supply side of the legal profession; fear of competition may have led European attorneys to form international mergers and to test a market for legal services without knowing whether there would be any sizable demand. If the demand side answers by changing its management style and using more external legal service, it would be partly because of the stimulus of the service offered by the mega-lawyers on the supply side.

Evidently, if the supply side of legal services manages to create its demand, the result will be a general increase of "law" in the distribution of economic growth. It may be one of the instances where even empirical research can find evidence for "autopoiesis" in legal evolution.

Notes

1. E.H. Volkart (ed.), *Social Behavior and Personality: Contributions of W.I. Thomas to Theory and Social Research,* Social Science Research Council, New York (1951).

2. Rogowski found only one German law firm in Pritchard's handbook with more than 100 partners, eleven with more than 50 partners; in 1989 there were

none in either category: Ralf Rogowski, "The Growth of Corporate Law Firms in Germany," in Pezalay and D. Sugarman, eds., *Professional Competition and the Social Construction of Markets*, Routledge, London (forthcoming).

3. Erhard Blankenburg and Freek Bruinsma, *Dutch Legal Culture*, Kluwer; Deventer/Amsterdam 1991.

4. Yves Dezalay, *Marchands de droit*, Fayard, Paris (1992) 221.

5. Lord Chancellor's Department, *The Work and Organisation of the Legal Profession*, Cm 570, Her Majesty's Stationery Office, London (1989) ch. 12.

6. John Flood, "Megalaw in the UK: Professionalism or Corporatism? A Preliminary Report", 64 Indiana L.J. 569 (1989).

7. Alfred Chandler, *The Visible Hand of the Managerial Revolution*, Harvard University Press, Cambridge (1977).

8. Alfred Chandler and Herman Daems, *Managerial Hierarchies: Comparative Perspectives of Modern Industrial Enterprise*, Harvard University Press, Cambridge (1980).

9. B. P. Pashigian, "The Changing Role of the Corporate Attorney", in W.J. Carney ed., *The Changing Role of the Corporate Lawyer*, Lexington Books, Lexington, Mass. (1982).

10. Marc Galanter and Thomas Palay, *Tournament of Lawyers*, Chicago University Press, Chicago (1991).

3

Computers, Competition, and the Revitalization of the U.S. Patent System

Dan R. Krislov

In this chapter, I will briefly describe the growth of a technological and legal center in "Silicon Valley," and also certain aspects of the interrelationship among technological, economic, and legal developments.[1]

"Silicon Valley" is a nickname given to part of the Santa Clara Valley, in Northern California. The valley is located on the San Francisco Bay peninsula, to the south of the city of San Francisco. The nickname refers, of course, to the fantastic, mushroom growth of high technology industries[2] in the valley during the period after the Second World War. At one time, the valley was most famous for fruits and vegetables, especially prunes; today, the valley is associated in the public mind with computers, software, and gene splicing and the prunes have become an endangered species. Silicon, of course, is the primary component of computer chips.

The growth of the legal community in the valley has been almost as spectacular as the growth of industry, though less well known.[3] In Palo Alto, a city of less than 60,000 population, there were about fifty practicing lawyers in the 1950s; today, more than one thousand lawyers practice within the city limits—one of the densest concentrations of lawyers in the United States, and perhaps in the world. Of course, these lawyers perform various functions, including some very standard ones, unrelated to the high technology industries: they write wills, they help transfer real estate, they handle divorces, personal injury cases, and the like. But this ordinary kind of practice does not explain the explosion of lawyers in the valley. The Palo Alto bar grew fat and mighty on the growth of the high-technology industries.

Among the most significant technological groups were the semi-conductor companies. This technology dates back to 1947-8, when scientists working for American Telephone and Telegraph invented the transistor.[4] In 1958-59, there was a further breakthrough with the advent of the integrated circuit—a chip of silicon which contains many transistors. After this, a single chip could replace large numbers of transistors wired together on a board. In the same period, technology to permit the mass production of integrated circuits was developed.[5]

These inventions made possible another breakthrough that would revolutionize the computer industry: the invention of the microprocessor in 1971, at Intel. This is an integrated circuit that performs all the primary functions of a computer.[6] The microprocessor has been at the heart of the electronics revolution. It made the microcomputer possible; and it spawned pocket calculators, digital watches, video games, CD players, and dozens of other consumer products. It is also vital to many other industrial applications: for example, it is used in the safety and emission control systems of cars.

The development of new kinds of software proceeded along with these developments. Affordable software—the programming that configures computers to perform useful tasks—is essential to the mass marketing of microcomputers. Sophisticated software, among other things, allows unsophisticated people to use high technology. It is the programs which do the complicated jobs; the human user needs to do nothing more than press a button or a key.

But for these purposes, the computer industry had to develop better data storage devices—relatively inexpensive disk drives were a major advance. Cheaper memory devices also had to be developed. A computer must be able to store its programs in its active memory, and gain access to this memory whenever it becomes necessary. When the technology to do this was in place, the microcomputer became a practical device. The first company to achieve mass sales by combining these elements in microcomputers was Apple.[7] Its major competitor became IBM and the various companies that are compatible with IBM—the so-called "clones," who now account for most of the market.

The various high-technology companies come in all sizes. IBM, whose name is almost synonymous with computers, is one of the largest companies in the world. But IBM did not develop in Silicon Valley. The companies which were born in the valley are much younger than IBM, and much smaller. They have, in some cases, reached respectable size, and a few have become gigantic multinational corporations. All, however, had tiny, and for the most part, fairly recent beginnings.

A new industry, almost by definition, begins with small firms. The high-technology industries of the valley were no exception. The bases for these industries were laid by the formation of many small "start-up" companies in Silicon Valley. Scientists and engineers, who had little business experience, were the founders of many of these companies. In the first phase, these businesses needed access to elementary advice about incorporation, drafting agreements, tax and accounting matters.[8] In the valley, the lawyers functioned as all-purpose intermediaries; they linked the small start-up companies with sources of money ("venture capital"); and they represented the companies before government agencies at all levels of government.

The high-technology industries have been, on the whole, amazing success stories. As the companies expanded, they needed a new range of legal services. If they "went public," that is, sold stock to the investing public, they had to comply with complicated federal laws and rules about the issuance of securities. When a company reached this stage, too, it needed advice on many problems that small companies do not face: employee pension plans, labor relations, corporate taxation. They might need advice about acquiring or merging with other companies (or on how to resist getting gobbled up by another company). The company might expand in other parts of the country, or form or buy foreign subsidiaries; engage in joint ventures with American or foreign companies; or arrange to cross license its technology.

The incredible growth of the early years has not been, and could not be, sustained. The industry has been subject to many "shake outs"; firms have merged, collapsed, risen and fallen. Companies struggle to gain and hold market share; there is no longer a sense that a rising tide will raise all the boats, no longer a vision of indefinite, incredible growth, of fortunes to be made overnight.

In the more mature stage of the industry, lawyers have become even more essential than before. They deal with the complex issues that come with size, and the shake-out phase. The larger, more mature companies have also built up relatively large staffs of inside counsel, "house counsel," lawyers who are on the payroll, to supplement or oversee the work done by the outside lawyers. In this phase, too, a great deal more of the legal effort goes into bringing or defending against *litigation*, for example, a case for or about patent or copyright infringement, or private antitrust suits. The stakes in litigation can be, and often are, quite high.[9] As we shall see, although cross licensing and joint ventures remain common, a competitive mode, in which litigation is frequent, now shares the scene with the cooperative modes of doing business.

Silicon Valley is often pointed to as a model, though it is not always clear what it is a model of. It has been a place of innovation and entrepreneurship; and in the process of growth, the new industries have created thousands of jobs, and generated enormous new wealth. Moreover, the high-technology industries are highly appealing to development-minded cities, more so than heavy industry. They seem relatively "clean"; there is a good deal of research and development, along with some light manufacturing (much of this is now offshore); they do not blight the visual landscape the way a steel mill does; they require, at the top, a relatively intelligent and educated work force; there seems to be less pollution than that caused by, say, a chemical plant.[10] These are all traits that operate to make high-technology industry seem a particularly desirable way of increasing wealth and making jobs. Many cities and areas have tried to duplicate the conditions which made Silicon Valley grow. Some cities and regions have, in fact, been successful in this quest. (In fact the labor practices of Silicon Valley, below the level of executives and engineers, are darker and more dubious than generally assumed; so too of the environmental situation.)[11]

Stanford University is located in the heart of Silicon Valley and has been closely associated with the growth of high-technology industry. Many of the major founders and inventors studied there, and relationships between its technical branches and the industrial complex remain close. Some of these founders fit the popular image of an inventor: a brilliant, single-minded individual, working on his own. "Innovation" is strongly associated in people's minds with lonely inventors, individual geniuses; the paradigm case is Thomas Edison, about a century ago.

The role of the individual inventor, engineer, or entrepreneur was in fact strong in the early days of Silicon Valley. But even then, innovation was in many ways a group phenomenon, or at least a process that demanded cooperation, collaboration. Innovation is not a socially isolated or mutant event. It comes out of a context, a climate, in which innovation, so to speak, is in the air. Individuals may dominate it but they in fact stimulate each other. They are aware of the work of their colleagues; they both compete and cooperate with each other.[12]

It is a little like a race where competition is a kind of cooperation or stimulus: everybody runs faster under the influence of the runners who are leading the pack. The early phases of high-technology industry were characterized by a subtle mixture of cooperation and competition; to describe it as a period of intensive and unrelieved competition would be profoundly misleading.

Very little has been written about the role of law and lawyers during the "take-off" phase of any industry. On the surface, it seems as if "government" and "law" played a minor role in the early phases of industrial development. Or, to be more precise, law has been significant, even vital, but only in the sense of a basic framework, as Friedman describes elsewhere in this book.[13] Although defense contracts did provide much of the funding needed for basic research on computers and integrated circuits, on the whole the new companies did not have a *specific* framework of regulatory or promotional law, at least not in the United States.[14] Nor was the early or take-off phase particularly litigious.

Lawyers, thus, would seem to have been of only limited utility to high-technology companies in the start-up phase. In fact, however, lawyers played an important role, even during this period. For example, they were often instrumental in finding sources of money ("venture capital"), and giving practical advice about the financial side of the business. In most societies, this would have been considered a purely *business* function and would not have been performed by lawyers. In later stages, the complexity of the legal environment—including specific laws pertaining to the industry—made the use of lawyers even more important; in addition, the companies made heavier use of litigation and were exposed to issues of labor law and to the demands of an increasingly international market. We will take a closer look at the intersection between law, lawyers and the Silicon Valley business community in the context of one "field" of law: intellectual property.

Intellectual Property

"Intellectual property" is a general umbrella term, which covers patents, copyright, trademark and trade secret protection. In the United States, patent and copyright law are specifically mentioned in the Constitution, and given federal status: "Congress shall have Power . . . to promote the Progress of Science and useful Arts, by securing for limited Times to Authors and Inventors the exclusive Right to their respective Writings and Discoveries." (Art. I, sec. 8, clause 8). "Patents" are rights granted with respect to inventions; "copyrights" cover books, articles, photographs, and so on. "Trade secrets, " which are generally protected by state (rather than federal) law, are secret devices, processes, formulas, machines or information, used in business, and which give the user an advantage over competitors who do not have the knowledge or use.[15] In fact, the line between patent and copyright blur in the computer industry: computer software, very notably, falls somewhere in between the two poles and the law has vacillated considerably on whether software could be patented at all (the answer was ultimately yes).[16]

Companies in the Silicon Valley stand or fall on technological innovation, that is, on developing products or processes which are or can be considered "intellectual property." A new high-tech company succeeds not by virtue of its holdings of real estate, or its good will, or its inventory, or even its marketing practices (though these are certainly important), but rather on the ingenuity and novelty of its products. The company must find a market niche, and this niche will depend upon some innovative feature of the product. To stay ahead of the pack is the name of the game of survival; and this, too, depends on constant innovation or improvement of products.

Different industries have different uses for intellectual property protection. Probably no two firms have quite the same demand for forms of protection. A company that manufactures soup will probably have a particular interest in trademark law, since brand loyalty is at the core of business success. A soup company manufactures a well-known and stable product; chicken noodle soup has, after all, a certain timelessness. In the soup business, there is a low level of technological innovation; copyright and patent protection are of marginal value.

On the other hand, a company in the entertainment business (making movies, for example) desperately needs some way to protect its product through copyright. Brand names do not matter much (the customer is interested in the movie itself, and perhaps its stars, director, and/or author, not at all in what company produced it); and patent protection is also much less important than in the high-tech industry. The pace of technological change in this industry is relatively slow.[17] On the other hand, the pharmaceutical industry is a heavy consumer of both patent and trademark protection.

Thus each industry will have its own profile of needs. This does not mean, to be sure, that *legal* protection of innovation necessarily plays a critical role for any particular company, or for the industry, or that it plays the same role in different stages of industry development. There is a strong argument, as we shall see, that intellectual property protection (and litigation in this field) moved to the center stage only in the "mature" phase of high-tech industry growth. And intellectual property law plays a different role in different legal systems.

Changes in Patent Law

Patent law is, as we have discussed, vitally important to industries that are based upon technological innovation. The importance of patents has, however, varied throughout the existence of the

American patent system. We can distinguish three historical phases of American patent law. The power to grant inventors the exclusive right for a limited time to their inventions is given to the Congress by Section Eight of Article One of the U.S. Constitution, and this is the fundamental legal basis for the creation of the patent system.[18] The first phase can be said to have begun with the passage of the first patent act (1790), which gave patent power to the Secretary of State, the Attorney General, and the Secretary of War, "or any two of them." In 1836, a Patent Office was established, headed by a commissioner of patents. Patents were granted to inventors, who were, of course, individuals. By present-day standards, the rate of patent issuance was quite low.

The rise of big business ushered in what we can describe as a second phase. There were still "inventors" who worked out of their homes and without institutional support, but now patents often came out of the laboratories and workshops of large corporations. Sometimes corporations bought up and swallowed the products of small inventors. For this and other reasons, the patent was legally unpopular. Patents were supposed to encourage innovation but the patent grant itself bore the stamp or image of a monopoly. It enabled a company to keep competitors' products off the market when it wished. Arguably, then, some patents could be used to *stifle* innovation. There was thus a complex interrelationship between patent law and antitrust law; indeed, in the twentieth century the Antitrust Division of the Department of Justice had a section "devoted to antipatent advocacy and litigation."[19]

In this phase of patent law, which lasted by some accounts until 1980 or so, the courts were on the whole rather hostile to patents. For example, between 1948 and 1954, over sixty percent of the patents considered in the United States courts of appeals were held to be invalid; another twenty percent or so were held not to be infringed; in less than one case out of five did the courts hold that a patent was valid *and* infringed.[20]

In the 1980s, a new phase of patent law began: one scholar has referred to this phase as a "startling comeback" for patents.[21] The appellate court structure of patent cases was drastically changed by the Federal Courts Improvement Act of 1982 (FCIA).[22] This legislation took away the regional circuit's appellate jurisdiction over patent cases,[23] and assigned it to the newly-created Court of Appeals for the Federal Circuit (CAFC). This new court was formed by merging the personnel of the Court of Customs and Patent Appeals (CCPA), which had held jurisdiction over appeals of patent denials from the Patent and Trademark Office (PTO),[24] and the United States Court of Claims, which had held jurisdiction over numerous types of claims against the government. The new court kept the jurisdictions of its predecessor courts, as well as acquiring its new jurisdiction over patent cases heard in the district courts.[25]

The CAFC began hearing cases on October 1, 1982. Immediately thereafter, the chances that a patent would be held valid and infringed rose dramatically. Within a few years of its creation, it was reported that the court was holding more than half of the patents which came before it valid; and similarly, the court was finding infringement in about half of its cases.[26] In 1989, a study of the court summed this matter up: the court had "taken on a decidedly pro-patent bias."[27]

What brought this change about? The coincidence between the institutional and the doctrinal change is of course very striking; it is tempting to attribute the doctrinal change to the creation of a specialized court, with expert knowledge and "repeat player" experience.[28] There is little doubt that changing the institutional structure of the courts did have some effect on the patent law. It is fairly obvious that placing the jurisdiction over patent cases into the hands of one court has been the cause of greater coherence in patent law.[29] Prior to the creation of the CAFC, patent appeals could be heard by any of the regional circuit courts of appeals. Since the precedents of one regional circuit were not binding on any other circuit, the circuits could and did show enormous variety in their interpretations of the patent statute. This difference in the interpretation was reflected in great differences in the percentages of patents held valid among the various circuits.[30] For example, during the period 1974-78, the Third Circuit found for the patent holder in 11 percent of cases in which the obviousness of the patents was at issue, while the comparable figure for the Fourth Circuit was 33.3 percent.[31] Thus, it is not surprising that much effort in patent infringement cases was spent on jurisdiction-shopping.[32] Placing these appeals in the hands of a single court has eliminated this aspect of patent law. What was not as obvious was whether the institutional structure determined that this more coherent body of law would be as favorable to the patent holder as it has been.

One of the explanations offered for the direction that the law has taken is that the technically trained judges are more likely to have pro-patent attitudes than those judges without technical training.[33] There are theoretical and empirical reasons to believe that this may be the case. First, the judges with technical degrees practiced in, and were recommended to the bench by, the patent bar.[34] It is logical to assume that the attitudes of judges chosen this way would reflect the preferences of the patent bar.[35]

The patent bar can in turn be expected to favor strong patents for at least two reasons. First, it would seem likely that the self-selection involved in joining the patent bar would tend to eliminate those people who did not believe in the efficacy of the patent system. Second, since such a large proportion of the business of the patent bar is the filing and prosecution of patents before the PTO, and the number of filings is likely to increase if the value of patents increase, the strengthening of the patent system is in the patent bar's economic interest.[35] Lawrence Baum has also shown that in the CCPA, the court that had been responsible for appeals from the PTO, judges who had been patent attorneys were 9.1 percent more likely to write an opinion reversing the refusal of patent grants by the PTO than were non-patent attorney judges.[37] This would indicate that, at least on the CCPA, judges who had practiced patent law were likely to take a broader reading of the patent statute than were the judges who had practiced in other areas. Thus, this would tend to support the theory that placing the law of patents into the hands of judges with patent experience would result in greater protection of patent rights.

However, the large majority of judges who have served on the CAFC have not been technically trained. Only two of the original fourteen judges on the CAFC had patent practice experience. The fraction of patent experienced judges on the CAFC has never exceeded 25 percent.[38] Since most cases before the CAFC are heard by three judge panels, and there are special efforts made to ensure that all the judges hear a variety of all the types of cases heard by the CAFC, it is highly unusual to have a majority of patent experienced judges on a panel.[39] It is not at all unusual to have no patent experienced judges on a panel hearing a patent case.[40] Thus, if patent experienced judges are more likely to find for the patent holder than are non-patent experienced judges, the patent experienced judges will, in most of the cases on which they sit, have to swing the vote of at least one of the non-patent experienced judges. Obviously, the patent experienced judges may exert more influence on the other judges by virtue of their expertise, but as the Baum study of the CCPA demonstrates,[41] this influence is by no means automatic. In other words, in order to explain the shift towards a more pro-patentee legal regime, one must analyze the behavior of the non-patent experienced judges.[42]

Consistent with expectations, non-patent experienced judges on the CAFC do seem to be more likely to rule against patent holders than are patent-experienced judges. In cases decided with published opinions in the years 1983-84, panels without patent experienced judges ruled for the patent holder 47 percent of the time.[43] Those panels with patent experienced judges ruled for the patent holder 56 percent of the time.[44]

Likewise, while opinions of the court written during the same period by patent experienced judges found for the patent holder in 63 percent of the cases, non-patent judges did so in only 53 percent of their opinions.[45] Also, in published opinions deciding appeals from the PTO during the period of 1983-88, panels without patent experienced judges reversed or modified PTO refusals of patent applications 46.67 percent of the time, while panels containing patent experienced judges did so in 54.5 percent of the cases.[46] Opinions written by non-patent experienced judges during the same period reversed or modified the PTO 41 percent of the time, while those written by patent experienced judges did so in 52 percent of the cases.[47] While none of these differences are statistically significant, the fact that they are all in the same direction and consistent with the direction of the findings of Baum's study of the CCPA suggests that there may be a real difference in the way in which patent and non-patent experienced judges are likely to interpret the standards for patentability, and in determining the presence or absence of infringement of patents. However, the percentage of cases in which non-patent experienced panels of the CAFC ruled for the patent holder was higher than that of any of the regional circuits prior to the creation of the CAFC, and the non-patent experienced judges of the CAFC were more likely to reverse or modify the PTO than were the non-patent experienced judges of the CCPA. Thus, in order to understand the shift in judicial attitudes towards patents, it would seem necessary to explain why the non-patent experienced judges of the CAFC have been more pro-patent in their attitudes than were the non-patent judges of the regional circuits and the CCPA.

One of the conventional explanations given is that the non-patent experienced judges may be deferring to the expertise of their technically trained clerks. However, the judges of the CCPA also had technically trained clerks,[48] thus this cannot explain the increase in PTO reversals by the non-technically trained judges after the creation of the CAFC. Also, if one assumes that the technically trained clerks are likely to have policy attitudes similar to the technically trained judges,[49] the differences between the reversal rate of technically and non-technically trained judges on the CCPA suggests that the non-technically trained judges were not deferring to their clerks.[50] If they are doing so now, this is a change that must be explained.

Dreyfuss is probably on the mark in explaining the change in direction in patent law when she alludes to a factor of social context: "a major reorientation of national competitive policy and increased appreciation of the role of high technology in the nation's economy"; the court has simply "geared its interpretation" of the law "to the current climate."[51] Patent cases do not necessarily come out of high-technology firms; but this does not affect the validity of Dreyfuss' point. Essentially, it is a point about legal culture. The judges are responding to a changing image of the role of intellectual property law in the economic order. What is to be protected now is not the lonely inventor, or the integrity of a system of free competition (which patents presumably may even threaten), but the very competitiveness of the United States—its ability to stand up to other countries (very notably Japan).

The Globalization of Markets

The new phase in the patent system thus reflects the globalization of world markets. In order to understand the reasons for the change in patent law, it is therefore necessary to understand the changes undergone by the U.S. economy. After World War II, the United States held a position of dominance in the world economy that was unparalleled in this century.[52] Most of this dominance was based on the United States' industrial might. The other industrialized economies of the world were devastated by the war, and could not rebuild quickly because the necessary capital was tied up by the financing of the conflict. In addition, much of the productive capacity that had been built for wartime weapons production in the United States was converted to consumer and civilian industrial production after the war. By 1952, the United States still held a 35 percent share of the manufactures and exports among the ten largest industrial powers (the comparable 1938 figures had been 26 percent of the manufactures and twenty-one percent of trade).[53] The United States had trade surpluses in every major industrial group except metals in 1952.[54] Thus U.S. manufacturers were able to exercise near-monopoly power in a number of industries.

One example of this was the U.S. automobile industry. Following the war, the United States was virtually the only country with the capacity to meet the needs of its domestic market as well as export to other countries. The economies of scale of this industry led to the elimination of all but three major manufacturers and one minor manufacturer from the U.S. market.[55] This became an oligopoly which was stable until other countries' industries were able to recover enough to begin exporting cars.[56] Some of the monopoly profits that the U.S. auto manufacturers were able to extract in this situation were passed on to labor in order to buy stability in the labor supply. Thus, a system emerged that essentially fixed the cost of labor throughout the industry.[57] This arrangement remained fairly stable until other national economies, especially those of Japan and Germany, had recovered sufficiently to compete quite successfully in the automobile industry. The arrangement might have remained had the U.S. prevented the foreign manufacturers from gaining access to the enormous demand in the domestic U.S. market.[58]

However, the United States had been committed to a system of "free trade" even before World War II ended. This commitment can be traced to a belief that the severity of the Great Depression had been due to the passage of the Smoot-Hawley Tariff bill in 1930 which led to the enactment of retaliatory tariffs by other countries and a concomitant decline in world trade.[59] It was also widely believed that the economic disruption caused by these events was the indirect cause of the world war.[60] In any event, since the United States was, in the post-war period, by far the world's leading exporter, it was in the interest of the United States to have open trade. Also, given the United States' dominance in most of the major industries, there seemed little to fear from open trade. Other countries' dependence on United States exports, as well as their ambitions to penetrate what is still the world's wealthiest market, led them to go along with this arrangement. Thus, the General Agreement on Tariffs and Trade (GATT) was established in 1947. Many countries maintained some protectionist policies under this supposed free trade regime, some with significant market distortion effects, but the United States was largely indifferent to these since they did not seem to present much of a threat to the United States economy, and served to help the economies of the allies of the United States.[61]

During this period, the United States was not generally very interested in a strong intellectual property regime since the United States' primary advantage in world trade was its industrial base, and its lead in technology seemed so enormous that there was little fear that other countries posed a threat.[62] The United States was therefore not terribly enthusiastic about international cooperation on intellectual property. For example, the United States was not a member of the Berne Convention, which is a multinational agreement on copyright standards, until 1989.[63]

By the 1970s, it was clear that the United States' advantage in industrial capacity had eroded. The economies of western Europe and Japan supported an enormous new industrial capacity. The United States had gotten into the habit of paying high wages domestically during the decades of the 1950s and 1960s. Other countries had not acquired this habit, and were thus able to undercut United States production costs. United States firms responded by moving much of their productive capacity overseas, which has allowed them to cut wages without facing disruptions caused by strikes.[64] This strategy has been of questionable success as the U.S. firms have lost large amounts of market share in most industries, and have even exited some markets entirely. It has also led to enormous trade deficits that have persisted throughout the 1980s and seem likely to continue for at least the near future. These deficits continued despite the rapid devaluation of the dollar in the last half of the 1980s.

These trends have led to a drop in the standard of living in the United States. It is quite understandable that politicians would feel threatened by the potential political fallout of a rapidly declining standard of living. In order to cushion some of this decline, the United States has raised capital by borrowing enormous amounts of money from other countries, as well as selling off assets to foreigners. Much of this borrowed money has financed the large federal deficit, which ballooned during the 1980s. This deficit has, in turn, enabled the government to maintain entitlement, defense, and other spending programs without having to raise federal income taxes.[65]

These are clearly only palliative measures that cannot solve the long-run problem—i.e., how to maintain the standard of living currently enjoyed in the U.S., or at least to make the decline slow enough that it does not cause massive displacement of the political status quo.[66] The most obvious strategy that is viable in the long run would be to find areas in which the United States can extract high rates of profit.

Intellectual Property and International Competitiveness

In the 1970s, it was largely taken for granted that the United States lead in high technology was so great that it would continue to provide the United States with the ability to extract monopoly profits.[67] A company that innovates is able to extract monopoly profits until other firms are able to duplicate the innovation. In the case of an innovation that allows the production at a lower cost of a product that is already on the market, the innovator is able to realize a profit that is equal to the difference between the cost of production by the old method and the cost of production by the new method. Once competitors are able to duplicate the innovation, the price will decline towards the marginal cost of production. In the case of an innovation that creates a new product, the innovator's monopoly profits will be equal to the amount of costs saved by the consumer of the product as compared to the products previously available (minus the costs faced by the consumer in switching over to the new product).[68] Since the rate of innovations in the high technology area was so high, it was believed that the U.S.

technological lead would allow U.S. firms to continue extracting monopoly profits from new innovations. Thus, with the decline of the United States' industrial sector, the importance of the high-technology sector to the future of the economy has increased.

In the early 1970s, however, it was not clear that a strong intellectual property regime was in the interests of the high-technology industry. This has to do with the *phase* of development that the high-technology industry was going through at the time. Industries go through definite life-cycles, as I have noted. In the computer industry, in the early phase, technological development took place at breakneck speed; small "start-up" companies sprang up like mushrooms; new companies constantly were in process of formation. In this phase, again, the companies operated within a loose legal framework; few rules were specific to the industry. Rules dictating behavior became denser, more rigorous, as the industry matured, and the period of shake-out and consolidation emerged.[69]

Thus, the use of intellectual property law in the semiconductor, microchip, and software firms varied according to the phase of industrial development. Until the 1970s, participants in these companies were not heavy users of patent and copyright law. Protection of intellectual property was not a central issue. Company executives may even have felt that sharing information was part of a positive-sum game. The market was expanding with lightning speed. A good many of the companies became quite profitable.[70] A free flow of information was important. Chipmakers, for example, because of the swift pace of innovation and the "large overhead costs of developing new chip products," were aware of a "common interest in the sharing of research and development information."[71]

As late as the 1970s, as I pointed out, patent law was full of uncertainties that lessened its protective value. It was expensive, protracted, and often ineffective. However, semiconductor firms did not necessarily have an interest in "tightening" the law of intellectual property. It is true that inventors of breakthroughs would want security in their intellectual property rights so that they could realize full profits by monopolizing the technology. Yet the firms may have profited more from *diffusion* of technology than they did from monopolization. The pitfalls and uncertainties of patent law were arguably a blessing in disguise: They stimulated accommodation and sharing.[72] Firms faced with uncertainty are more likely to enter into licensing agreements, granting rights to use technology in exchange for money or for the right to make use of the technology of a competitor.

This indeed seems to have been the case. AT&T decided to license other firms' use of transistor technology in exchange for access to innovations making use of that technology; and since then, licensing arrangements have been commonplace in the semiconductor area.[73] Other patents were also extensively licensed, including the planar process (Fairchild) and Texas Instrument's integrated circuit.[74] If one company improves on a device which somebody else has patented, neither company benefits unless they cooperate. The first company does not have access to the improvement; the second cannot make use of the technology it has improved. If they cross-license, they can both profit from the increased demand that occurs when a product is improved.[75] This "leapfrog" effect is obviously most striking in the early stages of a developing industry. Arguably, however, when the uncertainties are too great, they reach a point where these benefits disappear. There is no incentive for firms to compensate each other if there is no effective protection for intellectual property—when an inventor retains no rights. Firms then can simply grab each other's inventions, without paying for them. In fact, the inventing firm is at a disadvantage: it has borne all the costs of research and development, and the "copycat" gets a windfall for little or nothing, especially if (as in the case of software) the *costs* of copying are minimal. The "copycat" company can charge less and still make a profit. This kind of market, at least in theory, will become technologically stagnant; there is little or no incentive to sink money into research and development.

But such a stage would come *after* the breakthrough stage. Microprocessors and RAM chips were genuine breakthroughs but later changes were more incremental—they were refinements on the existing technological base. The paradox is this: in the post-breakthrough stage, intellectual property protection becomes truly vital, yet, legally speaking, this protection becomes more precarious. Refinements and small improvements are often easy to copy; and they are more vulnerable to the argument that they are not patentable at all (because they are not truly novel). A further irony is that the refinements may actually cost much more than the original invention. The first Intel microprocessor was developed in nine man-months (or woman-months); today, new microprocessors require as much as 100 man-years (or woman-years). Yet the new microprocessor might not be legally patentable at all. Therefore, even without foreign competition, we might expect that the U.S. semiconductor firms' demands for intellectual property protection would have increased.

The industry, however, was also facing external competition. By the mid-1970s, while it was clear that the U.S. was still leading in the high technology sectors, Japan had emerged as its closest competitor in the semiconductor and computer sectors. By this time,

Japanese firms had enormous success in the consumer electronics sectors. Yet it was believed that they did not have the technological ability to compete head-to-head with the United States in the cutting edge of the semiconductor and computer companies. By the late 1970s, however, the Japanese successes in the production of dynamic random access memory (D-RAM) chips made it clear that the United States lead was not unassailable. Since virtually all the basic technology to produce these chips had been developed in the United States, there was much sentiment that the United States government must do more to protect United States developed technology.[76] These sentiments grew as the Japanese began to gain market share in the computer area. Because it is now believed that maintaining America's economic lead over other countries depends on its continued leadership in innovation in high-technology, ways have been sought to protect this leadership. Patent law has been one of the strategies adopted to advance this goal. Litigation on questions of intellectual property has become much more common in Silicon Valley. The period in which cooperation is usually the best economic strategy has ended for many firms. In certain crucial instances, firms have turned to litigation.

Litigation has come to be used, then, as a mode of competition. Where there is not enough market share to go around—no sense of a rising tide—companies tend to fight market battles in the courtroom.[77] A patent infringement suit, or a copyright action, can be viewed as simply another way of fighting the competition—more effective, and potentially more devastating, than many of the alternatives. The high-tech industries stand or fall on their technology; brand-name recognition, advertising, marketing techniques—these are classic tools of competition, but (as I noted) they are much less crucial in the high-tech industries than in such other industries as soup or soap.

Changes in the law or in the behavior of legal institutions may encourage the use of litigation. I have already mentioned the new Court of Appeals for the Federal Circuit, and the increasing success of plaintiffs in patent actions. There has also been a decline in antitrust cases, and antitrust counterclaims in patent cases.[78] Part of this may be due to doctrinal changes, but the net result is to make it more difficult to defend a patent infringement case. Litigation is, of course, in many ways a more radical form of carrying on competition. If the subject matter of the litigation is a vital innovation, then litigation can make or break a company, in ways that alternative forms of competition cannot. It is hard to imagine one soap company driving another into bankruptcy by changing its advertising slogan, but some high-technology companies have been driven out of business, or irreparably ruined, when they were on the losing end of a lawsuit over intellectual property. The stakes in the cases can be amazingly high.[79] Of course, litigation and threats of litigation can also lay the basis for compromises; it is not foreordained that every battle shall be to the death. The industry, in short, has forged new tools for coping with foreign (and domestic) competition; and law, lawyers, and litigation, in various modalities, are central to the "mature" strategies. Even though executives may voice skepticism about the role of lawyers, or wish that business could be conducted in a world without lawyers (or in which nobody *needed* lawyers), and even though they may envy the image of lawyer-less Japan or Korea, the computer industry has, like it or not, become increasingly "legalized" in the course of development. There is no reason to expect that this trend will reverse itself.

Intellectual property law has become, in other words, an instrument of industrial policy; its function, in theory, is to protect innovative companies so that they may remain competitive in both domestic and foreign markets. The changes wrought by the American judiciary in the area of patent law, as broad as they are, must be understood as only part of the changes that have occurred in intellectual property law generally. Some of these changes have been the result of judicial decision-making, but many others are the result of the activity of the executive branch and the Congress. There have been so many developments tending in the same direction (increased intellectual property protection) that it is fairly clear that all three branches of government are following the same general policies.

For example, the copyright statute was amended by Congress in 1980 to make it explicit that protection was extended to computer programs.[80] Generally speaking, computer software fits into the conventional categories of intellectual property very poorly. It is, in fact, an "interesting overlap" between the kinds of items usually subject to copyright and those which can be patented.[81] There has been a great deal of discussion—and some litigation—over how to deal with software in the law of intellectual property. For a variety of reasons, there have been complaints that copyright protection is not the answer. There have been proposals for special laws to cover the situation.[82] However, Congress' 1980 action settled the matter. So much has been invested by software companies in the copyright protection of their product that it is unrealistic to expect any major changes in the form of intellectual property protection.

The 1980 change in the copyright law led to a series of cases in which it has been held by various courts that this protection extends to object code (which is, for all practical purposes, unreadable by human beings[83]), operating systems,[84] the "structure, sequence, and organization" of a program[85] and to some aspects of the "look and feel" of the interface aspects of a computer program.[86] While it is fairly clear that software does need some kind of intellectual property protection,[87] the inclusion of "look and feel" aspects in copyright protection begins to look more like patent protection over certain types of programs.[89] Considering the low level of standards needed to acquire a copyright,[90] this may be a rather extreme protectionist regime for computer software.[91] If one accepts the argument that the institutional reforms of the FCIA were primarily responsible for the shift in the patent law in the 1980s, one must also explain why the non-specialist courts hearing the copyright cases are reading the copyright statute in such a broad way.[92] Such a development strikingly parallels the patent-strengthening actions of the CAFC.[93]

Other congressional actions have also indicated a high level of concern for increasing intellectual property protection, especially in high-technology areas. For example, in response to the demands of Intel and other semiconductor manufacturers, Congress created an entirely new form of intellectual property protection in the 1980s. Intel was the company which developed the first reliable dynamic random access memory chip (D-RAM) and initially it dominated this market. In the late 1970s, Intel's lead began to slip, and Japanese companies took a leading position in memory chips. The Japanese chips were at first virtually identical to Intel's designs.[94] Today, Intel no longer produces RAM chips, and the Japanese have a virtual monopoly over this market.

As this process went on, Intel aggressively sought out new forms of protection for its chip designs. In 1978, it attempted to obtain a copyright for a chip, claiming it as a creative writing. The copyright office refused to oblige. Intel brought suit against the copyright office, to force them to accept the chip; but the company later dropped the suit and entered into a "compromise" with the copyright office—a compromise which was of little use to Intel.[95] Under terms of this compromise, the copyright office allowed Intel to register written or encoded plans for the chip; but there would be no protection against others who might want to produce the chip on their own.

At this point, Intel and other chip makers decided to seek a legislative solution; Intel went to Congress and proposed a change in the copyright act, making it possible to copyright semiconductor chips. The proposal (1979) went nowhere. Indeed, some chip companies were opposed to this change in the law; they wanted to retain the practice of "reverse engineering," and they were afraid the copyright laws would make this illegal.[96] Finally, in 1984, Congress enacted a special law, the Semiconductor Chip Protection Act (SCPA),[97] outside the framework of the copyright act, and applying solely to semiconductor chip mask works. The act created a new form of intellectual property protection, which was not a patent or a copyright, but *sui generis.*[98]

SCPA protected designs once they were embodied in semiconductor chips. It set up a system which, in many ways, resembled copyright protection and it was to be administered by the copyright office.[99] But in other ways there were major departures from copyright law. Copyright protection extends for the life of an author plus fifty years, or seventy-five years for corporate copyright holders. Mask works under the act are protected for a term of ten years only.[100]

Also, and deliberately, the act did not outlaw "reverse engineering."[101] A competitor is entitled to study a chip, even though it is covered by SCPA protection, in order to create a copy of the original mask work. The competitor can then use the information gained to design a new chip, which performs the same task as the original; the analogous activity in traditional copyright law would probably be outright plagiarism.

The act thus distinguishes between reverse engineering, which is acceptable, and bald-faced "piracy," which is not. If a competitor took a chip apart, and copied it slavishly, that would be piracy, and the act would not protect it. There is a substantial difference between piracy and reverse engineering. It might take a few months to pirate a chip; reverse engineering is a longer, slower process, which might in some cases take years.[102]

Chip inventors recoup their development and marketing costs by charging high prices during the time when they and they alone can supply the new product. The pirate, of course, does not have the same kind of development costs; and he can undercut the inventor when the pirate chip reaches the market.[103] A reverse engineer has costs lower than the inventor but higher than the pirate and by the time reverse engineering has succeeded the inventor has probably been able to cover the costs of development. Thus, in the judgment of the industry, the reverse engineer does not have a competitive advantage over the inventor. SCPA embodies this judgment in normative form.

In theory, American chip firms could have accomplished the same results by entering into an arrangement among themselves. But a statute is in fact much preferable to a voluntary arrangement, for a number of reasons: first, a private arrangement might run afoul of the antitrust laws; second, any firm would have an enormous short-run incentive to cheat, and thus the arrangement would be unstable; third, the domestic companies could bind foreign competitors through legislation, but not through a private arrangement. Although the usefulness of the SCPA has been questioned,[104] its enactment was a direct response by the Congress to the demands of domestic semiconductor chip manufacturers.

Much of Congress' actions in the intellectual property area have been aimed at protection of domestic manufacturers both in the American market and abroad. For example, the SCPA provides for protection for the rights of foreign chip makers if their home country provides such protection for American companies. Other acts have been designed to strengthen the ability of the International Trade Commission (ITC) to take unilateral action against imports that infringe on American intellectual property rights. In 1988, Congress amended Section 337 of the Trade Act to do away with the requirement that the ITC must find that the infringing imports harmed an existing domestic industry before it could exclude the items.[105] This change in the law, along with the high likelihood that their findings of patent infringement will be upheld by the CAFC, gives the ITC a freer hand to act against infringing importers.

Congress has also been concerned with strengthening the hand of the U.S. Trade Representative (USTR) in conducting multilateral and bilateral negotiations over intellectual property issues. Section 301 of the Trade Act as amended in 1988 required that the USTR compile a list of countries that were the worst violators of intellectual property rights, and impose sanctions if those countries did not respond. This has given the USTR leverage which she used to negotiate bilateral agreements with Japan, as well as with other countries.[106] The USTR is also conducting the negotiations in the Uruguay Round of the negotiations to renew the General Agreement on Tariffs and Trade (GATT).[107] At the insistence of the United States, the current negotiations include a component dedicated to reaching an agreement on standardizing intellectual property protection and enforcement among signatory nations.[108] The Senate has shown its support of this by enacting a "fast-track" procedure for expedited consideration of any agreements emerging from the Uruguay Round.[109]

Why has intellectual property law become so central to industrial policy in the United States? There are three basic strategies used by governments to encourage the growth of technology in a society—direct subsidy, indirect subsidy through favorable tax treatment, and protection from imports.[110] Import protection is also basically a subsidy paid by the consumers in the form of higher prices for the protected products. Internationalized intellectual property protection can itself be a form of import protection. For example, United States semiconductor firms have used the "revived" patent system as a tool to cope with foreign competition. United States tariff law bans imports that infringe on American patents.[110] In 1987, Intel filed a complaint with the United States International Trade Commission, complaining that seven companies (including Hyundai) had violated the law. Intel charged that the companies were manufacturing EPROMs ("erasable programmable read-only memory" chips) that had been made according to a process for which Intel held a patent. ITC held the Intel patents valid, and issued an order banning importation of the EPROMs. This controversy is currently before the courts.[111]

Intellectual property protection is a form of subsidy paid to the innovator in the form of higher profits. It does, however, have political advantages over the other forms of subsidies. First, it does not, on the surface, appear to be a subsidy. Rather, it appears as merely the granting of a property right. However, it is actually the granting of monopoly rights as a reward for innovations that the government decides merit such rewards. Thus, although a strengthening of the patent system represents a stepping up of government subsidization, it does not appear to be such. Therefore, it does not appear to be inconsistent for an administration elected on a platform of smaller government, as the Reagan administration was, to support increased intellectual property protection.

Another reason that politicians may favor intellectual property protection is that, unlike two of the other forms of subsidy, it does not require much in the way of central planning. (The other form that does not require this type of planning, favorable tax treatment, is more obviously a subsidy to business firms, and as such, attracts populist opposition from Democratic politicians.) Establishment of an agency to oversee direct subsidies or strategic market protection would have been incompatible with the stated objectives of the Reagan administration to decrease the direct involvement of the government in the economy. An administration that had been elected while espousing *laissez-faire* policies would have found it quite difficult to support a centrally planned industrial policy.[112] The coordination necessary for rational central planning, assuming such a thing is possible, may also be seen as being especially difficult in an era of divided government, a condition that persisted in national U.S. government until 1993.[113]

Yet another political advantage for strengthening intellectual property protection is that it costs the government very little. Like other forms of protection, the costs of the subsidies are borne by consumers.[114] Also, the planning that is necessary for some of the other forms of industrial policy is costly. The decision-making in an intellectual property system is decentralized, thus causing the costs to be diffused. Patentees, for example, must bear the costs of drafting the application and prosecuting it through the PTO. The government's main costs are the provision of examiners, an appeals process, a registry, and the costs of those aspects of the court system that are needed to enforce the patentee's rights. While this may sound like quite a bit, they are very low compared to the costs of the information gathering that would be necessary for centrally planning an industrial policy, as well as the costs of direct subsidies or those of enforcing a protectionist trade policy. Favorable tax treatment would also lead to a loss of tax revenues that would have to be made up from other sources (although its relative ease of implementation may make it politically preferable to direct subsidies). In contrast, the costs of enforcing intellectual property protection fall mainly on the holder of the rights, or on the infringer (if the rights holder wins a suit and is awarded attorneys' fees). Thus, while direct subsidy, market protection, or favorable tax treatment would require an increased or shifted tax burden that is likely to be unpopular, intellectual property protection requires very little spending on the part of the government. Market protection also has the political disadvantage of imposing the brunt of its costs on the consumers of the protected product in the form of higher prices. If these costs are high enough to be felt by those consumers, this can be the source of political opposition.[115]

Intellectual property protection, because of its nature, may be less likely to create this sort of opposition. This is because the consumer of the protected product will not pay the monopoly profits unless they are better off than if they buy an unprotected substitute. Since the consumer is better off in this situation than if the protected product had never been created, the consumer may not feel the burden of paying the monopoly profits, especially if the consumer believes that the product would not have been created if the producer had not had the prospect of realizing those profits. In contrast, simply protecting the market from imports may, by causing the prices of already existing products to rise, make consumers worse off than they were before the policy was implemented. A policy that makes a group of people worse off is very likely to encounter political opposition from that group.

Strengthening intellectual property protection may have been appealing to politicians who were risk-averse. The shift in intellectual property law would seem unlikely to produce any dramatic improvement in the competitive position of U.S. firms.[116] However, the shift is also unlikely to greatly harm competitiveness. Other forms of industrial policy, while they may have the potential to greatly enhance the U.S. competitive position, have the potential to create such harm. No one really knows what the vital factors are in determining the success of an industrial policy.

Commentators frequently point to the success of the Japanese economy as being a result of a successful economic policy. Yet, the world is full of examples of failed economic policies.[117] Kenneth Flamm has made a convincing case that the success of the U.S. computer industry is a direct result of defense programs and spending during World War II and during the 1950s.[118] However, there did not seem to have been any coordinated plan to produce the civilian computer industry.[119] Other countries' more conscious efforts have varied in their degrees of success. Certainly the industrial policies designed to produce strong computer industries in the European countries can be characterized as failures.[120] Flamm attributes the failure of these policies to their adoption of a "national champion" strategy that subsidized a single company in the theory that their markets were too small to support multiple competitors.[121] The lack of competition in their home market, according to Flamm, created companies that were too inefficient to compete in international markets. Japan's industrial policy in this area during the 1960s and 1970s was a deliberate effort to create a competitive computer industry.[122] They, however, used a strategy of protecting the market while fostering several competing companies.[123] Flamm points to the success of the Japanese policy, as well as to the fact that U.S. money was distributed among several competitors, and concludes that the subsidization of several competitors is a necessary component of a successful industrial policy. Further, the proper role of government is to foster the companies while they develop basic technologies; the competitors will then independently develop commercial uses for the technology.[124]

While Flamm may be correct that the existence of multiple competitors is a necessary condition for a successful policy, events subsequent to the writing of his book have made it clear that, even in combination with the basic technology condition, it is not a sufficient condition. In 1981, Japan announced the Fifth Generation Computer Program.[125] This program, coordinated by the Ministry of International Trade and Industry (MITI), was to be a cooperative effort by the major Japanese computer companies to leapfrog existing computer technology and become the world leader in supercomputer technology. This program, although it fulfilled both of Flamm's conditions, is widely acknowledged to have been a failure.[126] Thus, programs that attempt to subsidize the development of technology may be costly failures.[127]

Protectionism in the high technology areas may be even more risky than direct subsidy. This is because the consumers of high technology are often other high technology companies. For example, semiconductor chips are bought in large quantities by computer manufacturers. Thus if, for example, the U.S. were to protect the semiconductor chip industry, it might drive up the costs of American-produced computers. In other words, efforts to protect one area of the industry may harm other areas.

Enhancing intellectual property protection is also attractive in the international political context. Because of its putative reciprocity—i.e., the same protection that is available to American inventors will also be available to foreign inventors[128]—the United States is able to pursue this policy without having to abandon its commitment to free trade policy. This is a low risk strategy since it does not invite the sort of retaliation that might be invited by more overt forms of industrial subsidization or market protection.

To sum up this section, the reason that the United States has adopted the policy of strengthening the intellectual property system both domestically and internationally is that it is a low risk strategy. It does not require difficult choices in policy that a divided government may find impossible to make.[129] It also does not seriously threaten the international economic order.

Conclusion

As we have seen, the patent system was strengthened in order to enhance United States competitiveness. This particular strategy was selected largely because it was the politically easy thing to do, and there was considerable pressure on the government to do something. The courts were simply another government agency responding to these pressures. It is not the purpose of this chapter to evaluate how effective the new intellectual property regime has been in encouraging American competitiveness in high-technology, but some comment must be made as to where we are now.

In the computer, software, and semiconductor industries there has, since about 1987, been an apparent increase in the amount of intellectual property litigation.[130] Texas Instruments has been credited (blamed?) for sparking this round of litigation by adopting what is widely perceived as a strategy of raising revenues through patent litigation.[131] Other companies, such as Apple Computer, are perceived as attempting to intimidate competition through the use of copyright litigation.[132]

Perhaps the development that has raised the most apprehension among the United States companies has been the dramatic increase in the filing of patents by Japanese companies; the top four holders of United States patents issued in the last few years are Japanese companies.[133] The larger number of patents filed by these companies should not be taken as a per se indicator of Japanese technical superiority over United States companies. The Japanese system encourages the filing of many more patents than does the United States. As a result, the Japanese companies employ a large number of patent engineers to prepare applications. Since patent applications in the United States are generally prepared by attorneys (who are paid more than patent engineers), United States companies would find this level of filing cost prohibitive.[134] There is, however, much speculation that this large number of patents is enabling the Japanese companies to build up strategic "arsenals" of patents in which to gain leverage over their competitors. United States companies are also building up similar, if smaller, arsenals.

It is unclear what the effect of all this will be on the competitiveness of United States companies. There has been some speculation that the efforts needed to engage in strategic behavior and litigation will detract from their ability to create the new products that will keep them competitive, and that the Japanese ability to file large numbers of patents may give them an advantage in this sort of competition.[135]

There is also speculation that large companies may use their patent portfolios to prevent competition from small start-up firms.[136] Since start-up companies have historically been a major source of innovation, there is reason to be concerned that a regime that over-protects intellectual property may choke off a fundamental ingredient of U.S. competitiveness. However, if large U.S. companies begin to perceive that it is in their long-term interests to allow this sort of innovation to occur,[137] they may use their patents as leverage to gain access to the innovative technology, rather than choking off the start-ups. However, the start-ups, by definition, will not have had time to have amassed a portfolio of patents with which to counter this leverage. Thus, strengthened patent protection may allow the larger companies to acquire the innovative technology developed by start-ups at a lower cost. In other words, the strengthening of the patent system may, depending on the status of the innovating firm, paradoxically reduce the value of some innovations.

It is probably too soon to evaluate the effects of the strengthening of the intellectual property system on the competitiveness of U.S. firms. In any event, very little is known about what those effects might be. Careful study must be directed at this issue in order to determine whether the United States is helping or hindering itself by its new-found enthusiasm for intellectual property protection.

In any event, this paper has been an attempt to relate changes of one form of law (intellectual property) to changes in the nature of the American economy, and in particular to the increased importance and changing demands of the high-technology sector. This account, like all historical accounts, is a mixture of the concrete and the general. Some aspects of the story are clearly peculiar to the precise setting, the precise type of technology, the precise configuration of legal institutions in Silicon Valley, or, more generally, in the United States. Other points are, I hope, not bound to this one time and place, and point in the direction of more general understanding of the central relationships. Exactly where the boundary lies between the idiosyncratic and the general—how much can be applied in other contexts, to other countries, to other cultures and legal traditions—is a question that remains wide open for further debate.

Notes

1. I gratefully acknowledge the generous contributions of Lawrence Friedman, without whom this paper could not have been written.

2. For the purposes of this paper, high technology will include the computer, semiconductor, biotechnology, and aerospace firms.

3. See, in general, Lawrence M. Friedman, Robert W. Gordon, Sophie Pirie and Edwin Whatley, "Law, Lawyers, and Legal Practice in Silicon Valley: A Preliminary Report," *Indiana Law Journal*, Vol. 64, 1989, p. 555.

4. R. C. Levin, "The Semiconductor Industry," in R. Nelson, ed., *Government and Technical Progress* (New York: Pergamon Press, 1982), p. 12. Silicon, the basic element used in transistor technology, does not conduct electricity; when minute amounts of conductive elements are mixed in, the new material is "semiconductive."

5. Id., at 13.

6. Kenneth Flamm, *Creating the Computer* (Washington, D.C.: Brookings Institution, 1988), p. 24. But see Joyce Gemperlein and Pete Carey, "Hello, Mr. Chips?" *S. J. Mercury News*, December 2, 1990, *West Magazine* Section, p. 18 (Patent Office awarded a patent on July 17, 1990, to Gilbert Hyatt for his claim of inventing the microprocessor. Hyatt, however, never produced a working version of his design, and it is at least questionable whether anyone could have based production on his specifications—a requirement if the patent is to be held valid).

7. Michael Moritz, *The Little Kingdom* (New York: Morrow, 1984) at 209-10.

8. This point was stressed in a talk given at Stanford Law School, September 25, 1990, by Larry Sonsini, a senior partner in the largest law firm in Palo Alto, and a major legal figure in Silicon Valley.

9. See, for example, *Apple Computer, Inc. v. Franklin Computer Corp.*, 714 F.2d 1240 (3d Cir. 1983). The court held that the operating system of the Apple II could be protected by a copyright; and a preliminary injunction was granted against the defendant. If the court had held that the operating system was *not* copyrightable, then anyone could simply copy it. Arguably, Apple's operating systems are its most valuable products.

10. The belief that the high-tech industry does not pollute may, in fact, be a myth. See Everett M. Rogers and Judith K. Larsen, *Silicon Valley Fever: Growth of High-Technology Culture* (New York: Basic Books, 1984), pp. 195-199.

See also "EPA Orders Clean Up in Mountain View," *S. J. Mercury News*, December 1, 1990, B:1 (eight square mile site contaminated by nine companies' dumping of trichloroethylene is on Federal Super Fund list).

11. See Lenny Siegel and John Markoff, *The High Cost of High Tech: The Dark Side of the Chip* (New York: Harper & Row, 1985); Dennis Hayes, *Behind the Silicon Curtain: The Seduction of Work in a Lonely Era* (Boston: South End Press, 1989).

12. See "If Hyatt Didn't Invent the Microprocessor, Who Did?" *S. J. Mercury News*, December 2, 1990, *West Magazine* Section, at 27. Silicon Valley Scientist Carver Mead describes the origin of the microprocessor: "It was a time of ferment. If you put yourself back into that time, you know that everybody was talking about putting a computer on a chip....It was a matter of when you could do it." Id.

13. L.M. Friedman, "Law, Legal Institutions, and Economic Development," chapter 1 of this book.

14. This has, however, often been the case in the past. The railroad industry is an excellent example: it was the beneficiary of direct and indirect subsidies. The role of subsidy in the automobile industry has been much more muted. The case of the computer industry is less clear-cut. The Defense Department played an important though sometimes indirect role in subsidizing development—of miniaturization and increased speed of computers, for example. The military role in financing research and development (through universities and procurement orders) was about one-quarter of the total in 1958 and in 1984 only about five percent. Defense procurement consumed over one-third of total U.S. semiconductor production in 1955-1963; by 1977 it was down to twelve percent. Daniel Okimoto, "Political Context," Ch. 4 in Daniel Okimoto, Takuo Sugano and Franklin Weinstein, eds., *Competitive Edge: The Semiconductor Industry in the United States and Japan* (Stanford: Stanford Univ. Press, 1984), pp. 78-85.

15. See for example, *CVD v. Raytheon Co.*, 769 Fed. 2d 842 (C.A. 7, 1985).

16. See Willis E. Higgins, "Technological Poetry: The Interface between Copyrights and Patents for Software," *Hastings Comm/Ent Law Journal*, Vol. 12, 1989, p. 67.

17. "Special effects" are a partial exception; and of course technological breakthrough was present at the birth of the industry.

The motion picture industry's reaction to the VCR does, however, present a good example of how technological advances may lead an industry to seek changes in law. In *Sony Corp. of America v. Universal Studios, Inc.*, 464 U.S. 417 (1984), producers of television shows unsuccessfully sought to have manufacturers of VCRs held liable for contributory infringement of their copyrights. In *Columbia Pictures Industries, Inc. v. Redd Horne, Inc.*, 749 F.2d 154 (3d Cir. 1984) "in-store rental" arrangements that allowed customers to rent a movie and view it in one of the store's eighty-five viewing rooms was a public exhibition and thus infringed copyright holder's rights under 17 U.S.C. § 106 (1982).

18. "The Congress shall have the Power...[t]o promote the Progress of Science and useful Arts, by securing for limited Times to Authors and Inventors the

exclusive Right to their respective Writings and Discoveries..." This clause is also the constitutional basis for Congress' enactment of the copyright statute.

19. Martin J. Adelman, "The New World of Patents Created by the Court of Appeals for the Federal Circuit," *J. Law Reform*, Vol. 20, 1987, pp. 979, 980.

20. "Adjudicated Patents, 1948-1954," *J. Patent Office Society*, Vol. 38, 1956, pp. 233, 236. Plaintiffs did somewhat better in the district courts, though even here only thirty percent of the patents were held valid and infringed; the district courts, however, do not publish all their opinions, and it is impossible to tell if this percentage reflects the characteristics of the whole group of decisions. *Ibid.*, p. 237.

21. Adelman, "New World of Patents," p. 979.

22. 28 U.S.C. § 1295.

23. Jurisdiction over most cases at the trial level remained with the federal district courts. Cases alleging infringement by the government were assigned to the newly-created U.S. Claims Court.

24. The CCPA also had jurisdiction over appeals from the International Trade Commission (ITC).

25. Judge S. Jay Plager of the CAFC has compiled the following partial list of subject matters over which the CAFC has exclusive jurisdiction:

> Indian claims; tax refund claims; military discharge claims; property taking claims; government contract claims; import law, such as import classifications, anti-dumping and countervailing duties, and import exclusion orders; patent cases; patent grant refusals and interferences; trademark registration refusals, oppositions, cancellations, interferences, and concurrent use proceedings; civilian personnel demotions and discharges; federal employee annuities, disability retirement and payments; veterans benefit claims; and vaccine compensation cases.

S. Jay Plager, "The United States Courts of Appeals, the Federal Circuit, and the Non-Regional Subject Matter Concept: Reflections on the Search for a Model," *American University Law Review*, Vol. 39, 1990, pp. 853, 854 n. 1.

26. Donald R. Dunner, "Introduction," *AIPLA Quarterly Journal*, Vol. 13, 1985, pp. 185, 186 (1985).

27. Rochelle C. Dreyfuss, "The Federal Circuit: A Case Study in Specialized Courts," *N.Y.U. Law Review*, Vol. 64, 1989, pp. 1, 25; Cooley, "What the Federal Circuit Has Done and How Often: Statistical Study of the CAFC Patent Decisions—1982 to 1988," *J. Pat. & Trademark Off. Soc'y*, Vol. 71, 1989, pp. 385, 391.

28. By "repeat player" is meant a litigant or litigant type (or, as here, a tribunal) which deals repeatedly with one particular type of case. For the term, see Marc Galanter, "Why the 'Haves' Come Out Ahead: Speculations on the Limits of Legal Change," *Law and Society Review*, Vol. 9, 1974, p. 95.

29. On the greater coherence of patent law brought about by the CAFC, see Dreyfuss, "The Federal Circuit."

30. It would be circular logic to also state that the differences in the rates of findings of patent validity among the circuits were caused by the differences in

the interpretation of a statute. Such a statement would be the logical equivalent of stating that the difference in the holdings of *Plessy v. Ferguson* 163 U.S. 537 (1896), and *Brown v. Board of Education* 347 U.S. 483 (1954), was caused by changes in the interpretation of the Fourteenth Amendment. Such statements ignore the fact that the judges (or justices) are aware that their reasoning has real-world consequences (although obviously no one could foresee all the consequences of integrating the schools or invalidating large numbers of patents), and that the judges are concerned with those consequences. Although I know of no study that attempts to explain the cause of the differences in patent holdings among the various circuits, it might be reasonable to hypothesize that the causes may be differences in the political make-up of the courts, or differences in the economic conditions of the various regions served by the different courts. Testing such a hypothesis would be a very large project that is beyond the scope of the present work.

31. Author's calculations based on figures contained in *Federal Courts Improvement Act of 1981: Hearings Before the Subcommittee on Courts of the Committee on the Judiciary, United States Senate*, 97th Congress, 1st session, at 158-89.

32. Since the alleged infringer could sue for a declaratory judgment that the patent was invalid, jurisdiction battles often turned on which party had won the race to file the case.

33. See, e.g. Michael S. Malone, "The Great Patent War," *Upside*, January 1991, p. 32 at 35-38 (quoting Roger Borovoy and Susan H. Nycum, both Silicon Valley patent attorneys, as attributing the shift to the attitudes of judges with patent expertise). Membership in the patent bar requires, among other things, the holding of one of a group of academic degrees in the sciences. Since all the judges that have sat on the CAFC who have had technical degrees have been members of the patent bar, for convenience the terms "patent experienced judges" and "technically trained judges" will be used interchangeably throughout this paper.

34. Lawrence Baum, "Judicial Specialization, Litigant Influence, and Substantive Policy: The Court of Customs and Patent Appeals," *Law & Society Rev.*, Vol. 11, 1977, pp. 823, 843-44.

35. Id.

36. Id. at 835.

37. Id. at 843. Patent attorney-judges wrote opinions that reversed or modified the PTO decisions 45.3 percent of the time while non-patent attorney-judges did so 36.2 percent during the years 1956-75.

38. Four of the current fifteen judges are technically trained.

39. For example, both patent experienced judges sat together on only one patent infringement case in 1983. *White Consolidated Industries v. Vega Servo-Control*, 713 F.2d 788. Interestingly, this three judge panel found the patent involved in the case invalid and not infringed, even though two of the judges were patent experienced. (Although it may seem logically redundant to find a patent both invalid and not infringed, this is a common holding since it allows the review of both issues simultaneously if there is an appeal to the Supreme Court.)

40. For example, a Lexis search conducted by the author found that 36 of the 84 patent infringement cases in which the court issued an opinion on the merits of the validity and/or infringement claims in 1983 and 1984 were decided by panels that included no patent experienced judges. This is fewer than would have occurred if the panels were chosen by chance, but it indicates that the CAFC was quite willing to allow such panels to hear patent cases.

41. Baum, "Judicial Specialization."

42. I am grateful to Paul Goldstein for pointing out (personal communication) the importance of the non-patent experienced judges.

43. Author's calculations.

44. Author's calculations.

45. Author's calculations.

46. Author's calculations.

47. Author's calculations.

48. Baum, "Judicial Specialization."

49. This may be something of an heroic assumption. However, as these clerks are intending to practice in patent law, it would seem probable that these are people with pro-patent attitudes.

50. Unfortunately, Baum did not perform a test for statistical significance for the difference between the patent experienced and non-patent experienced judges' opinions. However, the size of the sample (all the cases with opinions for nineteen years), and the size of the difference strongly suggests that the results would be statistically significant.

51. Dreyfuss, "The Federal Circuit," p. 27.

52. Indeed, one commentator has stated that the only comparable situation among industrialized nations was "Great Britain's position at the outset of the Industrial Revolution." Robert E. Baldwin, *Trade Policy in a Changing World Economy* (New York: Wheatsheaf, 1988), p. 22.

53. Id.

54. Id.

55. John B. Rae, *The American Automobile Industry* (Boston: Twayne Publishers, 1984), pp. 100-07. Economies of scale were also partially responsible for the inability of other countries to compete in the U.S. auto market. For all practical purposes, the U.S. was the only country in the immediate post-war period with a standard of living high enough to maintain a high level of consumer demand for the "family car." Firms in countries that did not have this level of domestic demand would have to export a much higher proportion of their production in order to match the U.S. firms' economies of scale. Thus, non-U.S. firms were not competitive with U.S. firms until their domestic economies had recovered enough to create consumer demand for cars. Robert Sobel, *Car Wars* (New York: Dutton, 1984), pp. 25-26.

56. The first foreign country to attain significant penetration of the U.S. automobile market was West Germany with its Volkswagen "Beetle." Id. at 25-50.

57. Rae, *American Automobile Industry*, p. 106.

58. Although the U.S. firms might have lost market share in foreign markets,

protecting the U.S. market would have allowed them to extract monopoly profits domestically, and thus preserve the stability of the arrangement with labor.

59. Robert E. Baldwin, *Trade Policy in a Changing World*, p. 138.

60. Id.

61. Id., pp. 209-10.

62. The one country that was seen to pose a technological threat was the U.S.S.R. However, that perceived threat was mainly military, rather than economic, in nature.

63. The United States was, however, a signatory to the Universal Copyright Convention (UCC) which was an agreement providing for copyright protection among its member nations. The requirements for protection under the UCC were less stringent than those under the Berne Convention, and were drawn up specifically to accommodate the less stringent copyright protection accorded by U.S. law. Helena Stalson, *Intellectual Property Rights and U.S. Competitiveness in Trade* (Washington, D.C.: National Planning Assoc., Committee on Changing International Realities, 1987), pp. 25-27.

64. It is not a very credible threat on the part of labor that they will disrupt the closing of a plant through the use of a strike.

65. This strategy, which is obviously not tenable in the long term, has had limited success in the short term. While personal federal income tax rates decreased during the 1980s, Social Security and state taxes increased during the same period.

66. I am not suggesting that it is necessary to preserve the status quo. I am merely making the not too startling suggestion that some of the seemingly illogical policies adopted by the government can be explained by politicians' wishing to remain in office.

67. Monopoly profits are defined as amounts the producer is able to charge that are over the marginal cost of production.

68. If the costs of the switch to the new product are greater than the amount saved by making the switch, then the consumers will not make the switch, and the value of the innovation will be zero. The most famous example of this is the standard QWERTY typewriter keyboard. The arrangement of the letters on this keyboard was not designed to facilitate or promote typing speed (indeed, legend has it that it was designed to slow up typists to prevent the jamming of the keys), and more efficient arrangements have been made available. However, since it would cost more to retrain typists to type with the new keyboard, there is no market for these keyboards. Paul A. David, "Clio and the Economics of QWERTY," *American Economic Review*, Vol. 75, 1985, p. 332.

69. On this point, see Michael Moran, "Investor protection and the culture of capitalism," in L. Hancher and M. Moran, eds., *Capitalism, Culture and Regulation* (New York: Oxford Univ. Press, 1989), p. 49.

70. But by no means all. See Albert V. Bruno and Arnold C. Cooper, "Patterns of Development and Acquisitions for Silicon Valley Startups," *Technovation*, Vol. 1, 1982, p. 275.

71. Leo J. Raskind, "Reverse Engineering, Unfair Competition, and Fair Use," *Minnesota Law Review*, Vol. 70, 1985, pp. 385, 386.

72. The English economic historian H. I. Dutton has argued that the ideal system for encouraging the diffusion of inventions may be a patent system with some degree of uncertainty built into it. This does not allow inventors to become overly-confident, and stimulates them to reach some sort of accommodation with competitors; but it also does not allow competitors to copy inventions without fear of consequences. H. I. Dutton, *The Patent System and Inventive Activity during the Industrial Revolution,* 1750-1852 (Manchester: Manchester Univ. Press, 1984), pp. 204-205.

73. R. C. Levin, "The Semiconductor Industry," pp. 80-1.

74. Interestingly, the Japanese patent office did not grant Texas Instruments a patent for the integrated circuit until 1989. TI may earn from $320-800 million a year in patent royalties from Japanese companies for this and other basic patents. *S. J. Mercury News,* December 12, 1990, G:1, col. 6.

75. Eric von Hippel, "Appropriability of Innovation Benefit as a Predictor of the Source of Innovation," *Research Policy,* Vol. 11, 1982, pp. 95, 102-3.

The Fairchild and TI patents in fact *required* each other; cross-licensing here was a virtual necessity. TI had no commercially practical method of mass-producing integrated circuits; and Fairchild's process technology was worthless without TI's patent as well.

76. On the competition between the United States and Japan in the semiconductor industry, see generally Daniel I. Okimoto, Takuo Sugano, and Franklin B. Weinstein, eds., *Competitive Edge: The Semiconductor Industry in the U.S. and Japan* (Stanford: Stanford Univ. Press, 1984).

77. Andrew Pollack, "The New High-Tech Battleground," *New York Times,* July 3, 1988, sec. 3 (Business), p. 1.

78. See Steven C. Salop and Lawrence J. White, "Economic Analysis of Private Antitrust Litigation," *Georgetown Law J.,* Vol. 74, 1986, p. 1001.

79. There have been allegations, too, that threats of patent infringement suits can be used, and are used, as a kind of "blackmail," to extort royalties from companies. See "A `White Knight' Draws Cries of `Patent Blackmail'," *New York Times,* January 14, 1990, F:5, col. 1.

80. 94 Stat. §§ 3015, 3028; 17 U.S.C. §§ 101, 117. The act defines a computer program as "a set of statements or instructions to be used directly or indirectly in a computer in order to bring about a certain result." Id., § 101.

81. The phrase is from Willis E. Higgins, "Technological Poetry."

82. Pamela Samuelson, "Creating a New Kind of Intellectual Property: Applying Lessons of the Chip Law to Computer Programs," *Minnesota Law Rev.,* Vol. 70, 1985, p. 471. But see Duncan M. Davidson, "Common Law, Uncommon Software," *University of Pittsburgh Law Review,* Vol. 47, 1986, p. 1037, arguing that the best way to develop appropriate protection for software is by grafting software protection onto the copyright statute, and allowing refinements to occur by common law adjudication.

83. *Apple Computer, Inc., v. Franklin Computer Corp,* 714 F.2d 1240 (3d Cir. 1983), cert. dismissed, 464 U.S. 1033 (1984). Programs are written in source code, which are the programming languages that are intelligible to humans (if they are "literate" in the particular programming language). In order for a program to run

on a computer, it must be "translated" into object code, which consists entirely of the binary signals that can be "understood" by a computer. This "translation" is performed by a computer program called a compiler. Although the binary signals can be symbolically represented by ones and zeroes, the information presented in this manner is so unwieldy that it is virtually unreadable by humans.

84. Id. Operating systems control the internal functions of a computer. Defendants had argued that copyright protection did not extend to aspects of the program with which human beings do not interact. The court held that human interaction was not a requirement for copyright in a computer program.

85. *Whelan Associates, Inc. v. Jaslow Dental Laboratory, Inc.*, 797 F.2d 1222 (3d Cir. 1986), cert. denied, 479 U.S. 1031 (1987). (Copyright on a computer program is violated by a program written in a different programming language that emulates the function of the copyrighted program.) Recent cases have indicated that the courts are retreating somewhat from the *Whelan* holding. See, e.g., *Computer Associates International v. Altai, Inc.*, 982 F.2d 693 (2d Cir. 1992).

86. By interface aspects, I mean those aspects that can be sensed by someone using a program (for example, screen displays) as well as those keystroke protocols which must be performed by a person using a program. One of the complicating factors in determining the scope of copyright protection for computer programs is that two pieces of software may contain very dissimilar programs but produce identical screen displays and/or be operated by precisely the same keystroke protocols. Likewise, very similar programs may have entirely different interface aspects. It has been held in one case, *Lotus Development Corp. v. Paperback Software International*, 740 F. Supp. 37 (D. Mass. 1990), that the copyright on the computer spreadsheet program "Lotus 1-2-3" protects the keystroke protocols that a user of that program must employ, as well as the layout of the screen display.

87. This paper is not the place to go into an extensive discussion of why software needs IP protection. However, a brief explanation might suffice. The development of software programs is often a very expensive proposition, yet software can generally be copied by anyone with an appropriate computer at virtually no cost to the copier. Thus, without some kind of IP protection, it would be likely that the economic incentives to produce new software would be low.

88. For example, if Apple had prevailed in its suit against Microsoft over the "windows" operating system, it would have given Apple exclusive rights over "window-type" screen displays involving overlapping icons. Since the screen display elements in the allegedly infringing program are produced by an entirely different program than Apple's, protecting these "look and feel" elements of programs is much like applying the doctrine of equivalents to software copyrights. The court, however, rejected that approach, arguing that a broad reading of "look and feel" doctrine would discourage efficient standardization and eliminate competition. *Apple Computer v. Microsoft Corp*, 799 F. Supp. 1006 (N.D. Cal. 1992). Other cases also seem to indicate that the courts have grown more sensitive to the potential problems of overbroad copyright protection. See, e.g., *Computer Associates International v. Altai, Inc. supra*, and *Sega Enterprises v. Accolade, Inc.*, 977 F.2d 1510 (9th Cir. 1992).

89. Eligibility for copyright protection is determined by § 102(a) of the Copyright Act, 17 U.S.C.A. §§ 101-810:

> Copyright protection subsists...in original works of authorship fixed in any tangible medium of expression, now known or later developed, from which they can be perceived, reproduced, or otherwise communicated, either directly or with the aid of a machine or device. Works of authorship include the following categories:
> (1) literary works . . .

Because computer programs are considered literary works for the purpose of the copyright statute, the only requirements for copyright protection of computer programs are that they be "original" and "fixed in any tangible medium of expression." The originality standard only requires that the work has not been copied from another's work. See e.g. *Sheldon v. Metro-Goldwyn Pictures Corp*, 81 F.2d 49 (2d Cir. 1936) cert. denied, 298 U.S. 669 (1936).

90. Pamela Samuelson characterizes the protection of all structure and "look and feel" aspects of a program as the "maximalist" strategy of copyright protection, as opposed to a "minimalist" strategy that would protect only against "outright piracy of the code." Surveying the literature on this subject, she finds that while "most commentators seem to think that" the proper level of protection "is in the middle ground between these extremes...no one has been able to articulate how" to determine the proper scope of that protection. She believes that this uncertainty is encouraging much of the current litigation. Pamela Samuelson, "Reflections on the State of American Software Copyright Law and the Perils of Teaching It," *Columbia-VLA Journal of the Law & The Arts*, Vol. 13, 1988, pp. 61, 62-64.

91. It should also be noted that the Congress has not moved to clarify whether the copyright statute extends protection to the "look and feel" aspects of computer programs. While Congress' inaction is, of course, an ambiguous piece of data (it might, for example, indicate lack of concern about the situation, satisfaction with the courts' actions, or uncertainty about the right course of action to take in this area), Congress has, in the past fifteen years or so, generally been rather active in the area of IP protection. Thus it seems unlikely that indifference is at the root of its inaction in this area.

92. It should also be noted that the Supreme Court seemingly reversed itself as to the availability of patent protection for computer programs in a case decided before the creation of the CAFC—*Diamond v. Diehr*, 450 U.S. 175 (1981) (patent protection was available for a process for curing rubber that involved the use of a computer to automatically monitor the temperatures within a mold, and to determine when the mold should be opened).

93. Intel's president, Andrew Grove, used the example of Japanese RAM-chip copying when arguing before Congress in 1979 for copyright protection for chips. See *Copyright Protection for Imprinted Design Patterns on Semiconductor Chips*, Hearings on H.R. 1007 Before the Subcommittee on Courts, Civil Liberties and the Administration of Justice, House Committee on the Judiciary, 96th Cong., 1st Sess. 32 (1979).

94. 1979 Hearings, pp. 17-18.

95. 1979 Hearing, pp. 50-79.

96. 17 U.S.C.A. §§ 901-14.

97. The act is 17 U.S.C. §§ 901-914 (1984). A mask work is defined in the act as "a series of related images...having or representing the predetermined, three dimensional pattern of metallic, insulating, or semiconductor material present or removed from the layers of a...chip...and...in which series the relation of the images to one another is that each image has the pattern of the surface of one form of the semiconductor chip product." 17 U.S.C. § 901.

98. Under the act, an applicant fills out a form, deposits the appropriate material, pays a fee, and protection is granted. 17 U.S.C. § 908. Patent protection, on the other hand, requires proof that the invention is novel; it takes an average of about two years before a patent is granted.

99. 17 U.S.C. § 904(b).

100. 17 U.S.C. § 906(a).

101. Hearings on H.R. 1028 before the Subcommittee on Courts, Civil Liberties, and the Administration of Justice of the Committee on the Judiciary, House of Representatives 98th Cong. 1st Sess. (1983), p. 32.

102. Statement of the Semiconductor Industry Association: The Economic Effects of Chip Piracy on the United States Semiconductor Industry, in the Semiconductor Chip Protection Act of 1983. Hearing on S. 1201, before the Subcommittee on Patents, Copyrights and Trademarks of the Senate Committee on the Judiciary, 98th Congress, 1st Sess. 122-36 (1983).

103. See, e.g., Robert Risberg, "Five Years Without Infringement Litigation Under the Semiconductor Chip Protection Act: Unmasking the Spectre of Chip Piracy in an Era of Diverse and Incompatible Process Technologies," *Wisconsin Law Review*, 1990, *p*. 241 (arguing that technological developments had made the direct copying of chip designs prohibitively expensive, and thus had rendered the SCPA obsolete by the time of its passage).

In interviews with the author, two in-house attorneys for a major high-technology firm referred to the SCPA as being a measure that "scratches a place that does not itch."

Only one case has been brought under the act: *Brooktree Corp. v. American Micro Devices, Inc.*, 977 F.2d 1555 (Fed. Cir. 1992). The CAFC heard the appeal because the case also involved a patent claim.

104. Other changes in § 337 were designed to bring ITC procedures more into line with GATT requirements.

105. Louis Uchitelle, "A Crowbar for Carla Hills," *N.Y. Times*, June 10, 1990, 6:20:1.

106. The GATT is the multilateral agreement that sets down the basic rules for international trade amongst its ninety-seven signatory nations. These include, among others, Japan, the United States, and the European Economic Community (EC) nations. GATT signatory nations account for two-thirds of all international trade. *Id.*

107. "Unreal Estate," *The Economist*, December 23, 1989, p. 100.

108. The current deadline at the time of this writing for fast-track consideration is Dec. 15, 1993. It has already been extended twice.

109. This sort of protection includes the imposition of tariffs on imports as well as the placing of quotas on or outright exclusion of imports.

110. 19 U.S.C. § 1337. Until 1988 there had to be a showing of a threat to destroy or damage a United States industry that was operating efficiently and economically; this was removed in the Omnibus Trade and Competitiveness Act of 1988, 102 Stat. § 1107 (Aug. 23, 1988).

111. *General Instrument Corp. v. United States International Trade Commission* No. 89-1534 (filed before the Federal Circuit June 19, 1989), and *Atmel Corp v. United States International Trade Commission*, No. 89-1476 (filed May 30, 1989). Another case, *Hyundai Electronics Industries Co. v. United States International Trade Commission*, 899 F.2d 1204 (Fed. Cir. 1990), upheld the exclusion of secondary products that include the infringing chips.

112. The one major exception to the *laissez-faire* rhetoric of the Reagan and Bush administrations was their support for a high level of defense spending. Thus, it is not surprising that what direct subsidization of high-technology that occurred under the Reagan and Bush administrations did so under the guise of defense expenditures.

113. David B. Yoffie, "American Trade Policy: An Obsolete Bargain?" in John E. Chubb and Paul E. Peterson, eds., *Can the Government Govern?* p. 100 (Washington, D.C.: Brookings Institution, 1989). Divided government refers to a situation in which the legislative and executive branches of the government are controlled by different political parties. The Republican party controlled the executive branch throughout the 1980s, as well as the Senate from 1981-1986. The Democrats have been the majority party in the House of Representatives throughout the 1980s, as in the Senate after 1986.

114. If the intellectual property protection is international, it offers the additional advantage of passing some of the costs of the subsidies on to foreign consumers of protected products that are exported.

115. The persistence of government farm price supports, which raise the price of food paid by consumers, demonstrates that these types of programs may not engender effective political opposition if the costs are sufficiently diffused.

116. This is not to deny that the shift will have some effect. I am only arguing that such effects will be marginal.

117. Examples of such failures include the Japanese aircraft industry, the U.S. steel industry, and the Soviet economic system. For a list of Japanese failures in economic policy, see Daniel I. Okimoto, *Between MITI and the Market: Japanese Industrial Policy for High Technology* (Stanford: Stanford Univ. Press, 1989), p. 3.

118. Kenneth Flamm, *Creating the Computer.*

119. Id.

120. Ibid., pp. 134-71.

121. Ibid., p. 170.

122. Ibid., pp. 172-202.

123. Ibid.

124. On these points, see generally Kenneth Flamm, *Targeting the Computer* (Washington, D.C.: Brookings Institution, 1987).

125. David E. Sanger, "Japan Sets Sights on Winning Lead in New Computers," *N. Y. Times*, April 30, 1990, A:1:6.

126. Id.

127. One explanation for why Japan's earlier industrial policies in the computer area succeeded, while the Fifth Generation project failed may be that the Japanese strategy worked well as a strategy for catching up to the U.S.' technological lead, but was not suited for developing new technology.

128. As Professor John Barton has pointed out (class lecture), countries whose comparative advantages are in lowering the costs of production rather than in the development of new technology (e.g. Thailand) will not see the distribution of the benefits and costs of strengthening international intellectual property protection as being reciprocal. This change in the law is clearly not in their interest.

129. I am not predicting that intellectual property protection will decrease during the Clinton administration as a result of the demise of divided government, only that we might see a greater variety of strategies pursued to enhance competitiveness in the high-tech sector.

130. M. S. Malone, "The Great Patent War," *Upside*, January 1991, p. 32. In-house patent counsel at a major electronics firm interviewed by the author also indicated that they thought that patent litigation had increased in the last few years.

131. Ibid., pp. 34-35.

132. Author's interview.

133. Malone, *Great Patent War*, p. 40.

134. Author's interviews.

135. Malone, *Great Patent War*.

136. The large companies, for example, may refuse to allow the start-up firms to use patented technology necessary to develop the innovations, or may hinder the financing of new firms by threatening to bring patent infringement suits.

137. For example, a large company may be better off if it can license the technology from the small innovative company than if that technology had not been developed.

PART TWO

The Internationalization of the Legal Profession

4

The International Legal Community in the Pacific Basin

John Barton and Susan Jordan

American law firms' global expansion reached Asia in the late 1980s.[1] Previously, some American firms had expanded to Europe, some following the creation of the European Economic Community in 1957 and some in a second wave in the 1970s and 1980s.[2] More recently, since 1987, when the European Community adopted the Single European Act, and separately Japan loosened its restrictions on foreign lawyers, American law firms rushed to both Europe[3] and Asia.[4]

The two hundred and fifty largest firms in the United States had one hundred and eighty or more foreign offices by late 1989, compared with one hundred and twenty four in 1985.[5] These offices included forty six in London, twenty one in Tokyo, nineteen in Paris, fifteen in Hong Kong, and thirteen in Brussels.[6]

In most foreign cities, American law firms predominate among other foreign firms.[7] But the American firms are not alone: British, Australian,[8] and Canadian[9] law firms are also venturing overseas. Canadian law firms of all sizes have opened offices in London, Paris, New York, Washington, Geneva, Brussels, Hong Kong, Shanghai, and Taipei—starting in the 1970s and accelerating in the late 1980s.[10] Many Australian firms have set up Asian offices staffed with Australian lawyers fluent in Asian languages, laws, economics, and customs.[11]

This paper explores the evolution of these international law firms in the Pacific Basin, with particular attention to their role in the high-technology sector. It attempts to tie the law firm patterns to the changing economic needs of the burgeoning Pacific Basin high-technology community and to changes in relevant regulation of international practice.

Introduction

The Pacific Basin is highly integrated economically, especially in the high-technology sector: "High technology firms sell components to one another in an international 'food chain.' Trade among Pacific Basin nations is growing nearly twice as fast as trade in Europe."[12] "Firms within the region are increasingly entering international cooperative arrangements—for off-shore production and for technology development and acquisition."[13] "Firms are even formally integrating across national borders as capital-rich nations, formerly the United States, now Japan and Taiwan, set up operations or acquire substantial interests in firms elsewhere in the region."[14]

Implications for the Pacific Basin High Technology Legal Sector

It is impossible to imagine these trends occurring without creating new needs for legal business, both domestically and internationally. Nevertheless, one cannot expect the new legal business to follow a pattern similar to that elsewhere in the world. Indeed, to the contrary, for, in contrast to Europe, the other region of great economic integration, business arrangements are leading government arrangements. There is no significant regional organization. Even more important, as is well known, many of the Pacific cultures have a very different perspective of law and prefer direct human relations to the formalities of law. (For a sense of the difference, see Table 4.1, appended at the end of the text.)

Several themes can be expected to dominate in the high technology sector:

The High Technology Community Within Any One Nation Will Require New Forms of Legal Service. The most obvious example is the patent area, in which expertise is needed to prepare patent applications (a task which is not, in every nation, assigned to the legal community) and to represent firms involved in patent disputes or litigation. (See Table 4.2, also appended at the end of the text.) A second, and evolving, domestic example is that of representing firms in negotiations with the national governments in ensuring compliance and obtaining formal or informal approvals in such areas as technology transfer regulation, foreign investment approval, and the like. Although these areas have traditionally been handled informally (as through administrative guidance) or, if handled formally, often conducted without lawyers, the tendency is toward greater formality and legalization. This is in large part a result of international pressure toward installing mechanisms to ensure fairness between foreign and domestic firms.[15] In some cases, legalization may arise as a result of choices to follow an existing international pattern, as in the case of new environmental regulation.

The Increasing Variety of International Transactions Among Private Firms Is a Second Type of Legal Need. These transactions—license agreements, strategic alliances, financings and purchases—are, as noted above, increasing rapidly. Their character will vary from nation to nation as will the—probably slow growing—extent to which lawyers are involved. The need includes initial negotiation and structuring; and dispute settlement, whether through negotiation, arbitration or litigation.[16]

There Is a Growing Need for Lawyers in the Public Sector. The public sector, including the lobbying sector, needs lawyers as technology policies increasingly become subjects of international discussion (as in the case of the U.S.-Japanese semiconductor negotiations).

Hypothesized Impacts on International Legal Practice

A large portion of these demands can be supplied by the local bar. In general, for example, a Korean firm dealing with the Korean government or patent system will use a Korean lawyer—if it uses a lawyer at all. And one can anticipate a growth in the domestic bars, corresponding not only to the growth in the national economies but also to the increasing legalization of the high technology sector. Moreover, this domestic bar will attempt to capture a portion of the business from the international community, typically by hiring a number of lawyers who combine local background with the additional language and legal skills available through study in Europe or the United States. In some cases, these are even foreign lawyers, working in the local firm. These patterns of internationalizing local offices of local law firms, typically with heavy reliance on U.S. LLM degrees, are frequent in Korea, Taiwan, and Malaysia. This is what is described in this paper as the domestic international bar.

But the internationalization of the sector may also imply that the law firms themselves should have international offices. Arguably, international transactions and businesses plotting a Pacific Basin strategy require law firms that reach beyond one nation.[17] American law firms, for example, are both seeking new business and following their domestic corporate clients abroad, especially to the major financial centers: London, Paris, and Tokyo.[18] These branches both serve existing clients and develop new business, especially in financial services.[19] These branches of foreign firms will often be referred to in this paper as the foreign bar.

A priori analysis suggests that law firms are likely to be successful in an international strategy in only two ways: (1) using foreign offices as a way to gain clients for a basic home office, and (2) offering a unique specialty. This economics may, of course, be distorted by formal restrictions on access to the legal market.

The first of these points is the most controversial. It states, in essence, that overseas offices are far more effective in attracting clients to the firm's basic home than in representing home clients in the foreign nation. With respect to regulatory issues, the point is almost certainly accurate, for the local law firm in the overseas office appears likely to have a better understanding of the local law, culture, and politics, than will the local office of an international firm. In short, a company wanting assistance in a foreign nation is more likely to turn to a local firm (especially one that has ensured that some of its local lawyers have international training and language skills) than to the branch office of a firm it works with at home. The great possible exception is Baker & McKenzie.[20] Baker & McKenzie's head office is in Chicago, and the firm has a total of 1519 lawyers in fifty offices in thirty countries.[21] The Baker & McKenzie approach is distinguished not only by its sweeping coverage but also by the financial and managerial independence of its branches, the employment of local lawyers, and the tendency to expand through acquisition of local law offices.[22] In essence, it has become a network of local firms.

In general, however, the overseas office is likely to serve overseas clients in their transactions with the law firm's home nation. Thus, for example, one would expect Tokyo offices of U.S. firms to concentrate heavily on representing Japanese firms investing in the United States. This was the case when the weak dollar fueled a surge in the business of assisting Japanese and European investors in the acquisition of U.S. assets and companies in establishing U.S. operations in the latter half of the 1980s.[23] Twenty-six American law firms have opened Tokyo offices since restrictions on foreign lawyers were loosened in 1987, primarily to capture more of this investment business.[24] Most of the Canadian firms are said to use the foreign branches to direct work to the home office.[25] As Japanese investors and companies are increasingly seeking to invest in Europe in the face of Europe's 1992 reforms,[26] major American law firms such as Skadden, Arps, Slate, Meagher & Flom, are opening offices and forging alliances in both Asia and Europe in order to tap the emerging Pacific-Atlantic link.[27] Similarly, Los Angeles-based O'Melveny & Meyers has formed a strategic alliance with Macfarlanes of London.[28] British and American firms have entered joint ventures with Hong Kong law firms.[29] Sidley & Austin has formed an alliance with London's

Ashurst, Morris & Crisp to open a Tokyo office.[30] Firms with offices in Tokyo or Hong Kong, such as Paul, Hastings, Janofsky & Walker and Thelen, Marrin, Johnson & Bridges, are looking for alliances in Europe.[31]

The other area in which internationalization can be expected is that of global specialization in specific transaction types. Only a very small number of firms may have expertise in particular forms of environmental law or in specific forms of strategic alliances. These firms can parlay that comparative advantage into successful operation in a number of nations. Thus, environmental law is seen as a potential growth area for Australian firms.[32] The transactions and negotiations expertise of American law firms, perceived as being globally unique, gives them a distinct advantage over Japanese and European law firms in attracting international business unrelated to the U.S.[33] American firms are consulted on mergers and acquisitions, such as the hostile takeover of a Belgian conglomerate by an Italian industrialist, and privatization of major industries, such as a communications equipment manufacturer in Turkey and an electric utility in Spain.[34] In addition, English is the language of international business transactions in Asia.[35]

In light of the economics of opening a foreign branch, firms can be expected—at least in the mid-term—to restrict their branches to those that make sense economically. Firms opening overseas offices can expect to lose money for at least five years, compared with two to three for new U.S. branches.[36] Law firms have been said not to attempt a sophisticated accounting of the indirect profits generated by their overseas offices to weigh against the millions of dollars expended annually to maintain a presence;[37] whether this attitude will continue in light of current economic pressures on law firms can be doubted.

Some firms have sought alternative ways to maintain global practice.[38] The Los Angeles firm of Christensen, White, Miller, Fink & Jacobs has a mergers and acquisitions "SWAT team" that can be assembled in hours to go anywhere.[39] And, in another response, an estimated dozen or more confederations of law firms practicing internationally exist world-wide.[40] There are at least two consortiums of law firms specifically operating in Asia. In 1988, firms from France, Germany, Holland, Italy, Sweden, Australia, Hong Kong, and the United States opened a joint representative office in Beijing under the name Interjura.[41] Approximately seventeen major law firms work through a referral network known as the Pacific Rim Advisory Council (PRAC).[42] The largest formal network in the world is Lex Mundi, formed in 1989, with one hundred and five firms from forty-three states and fifty countries.[43]

Japan

One would expect the greatest internationalization of law practice in Japan,[44] where the concentration of high technology industry is so strong. Here, among all Asian nations, is the greatest variety of transactions and the greatest source of capital for export. Hence, in spite of the traditional Japanese reluctance to use lawyers, one would expect a rapid increase in international legal practice.

The Local International Bar

A compilation of the data on Japanese international law firms contained in the 1989 Martindale-Hubbell directory revealed that among the five hundred and sixty-one bengoshi, one hundred and seventy-one had earned degrees from U.S. law schools, a significant number had studied law in the United States, and a number had studied law in other foreign countries.[45] More than two-thirds of the firms have one to ten lawyers, and only two firms have more than forty lawyers.[46]

The partners of these Japanese firms are in great demand, traveling frequently and devoting much less time to new clients than is expected in the U.S.[47] Hourly rates correspond roughly to those of the largest U.S. law firms.[48] To meet demand for foreign legal services following the 1955 repeal of the Practicing Attorney's Law, Japan continued to admit foreign lawyers as "trainees" who served as apprentices to bengoshi but could not practice law.[49] The trainees typically assisted bengoshi in preparing English-language documentation for international transactions, enduring low wages, long hours, and little respect.[50]

Legality of Practice by Foreign Lawyers[51]

Japan's system governing foreign lawyers is based on the Foreign Lawyers Law[52] enacted on May 23, 1986 and effective April 1, 1987, ordinances promulgated by the Ministry of Justice (MOJ),[53] regulations adopted by the Japan Federation of Bar Associations (JFBA) (a nongovernmental body) and local Japanese bar associations,[54] and written and oral understandings reached by the Japanese and U.S. governments during bilateral negotiations on the issue.[55]

Administrative responsibility over foreign lawyers is divided between the MOJ and the JFBA.[56] This sharing of authority represents a compromise which is reflected in the official title that foreign lawyers must use, "gaikokuho-jimu-bengoshi" or "foreign law solicitor."[57] The MOJ determines whether applicants are qualified,[58] while the JFBA controls registration[59] and discipline.[60]

The Foreign Lawyers Law allows the foreign law solicitor to perform legal business concerning the law of the "country" of primary qualification.[61] This provision has been interpreted to limit American lawyers to advising only on the law of the state in which the lawyer is licensed to practice.[62] However, foreign law solicitors can obtain a designation for a foreign "country" (or additional states) by demonstrating to the MOJ familiarity with the laws comparable to a qualified practitioner and at least five years experience with those laws.[63]

The Foreign Lawyers Law forbids a foreign lawyer to employ a bengoshi, tax specialist (zeirishi), patent specialist (benrishi), administrative scrivener (gyoseishoshi), or judicial scrivener (shihoshoshi), and prohibits revenue-sharing arrangements or partnerships between the foreign lawyers and the Japanese legal or quasi-legal professionals.[64] However, the Japanese government has agreed to define "partnership" narrowly to allow the sharing of such major expenses as office space and staff, but not profits.[65] In addition, bengoshi are permitted to employ foreign law solicitors, provided that the foreign attorney represents herself to the public using only the name of the bengoshi.[66] Foreign law offices may be staffed with essentially unlimited numbers of junior foreign attorneys not licensed as foreign law solicitors.[67] Foreign law offices may also employ Japanese who have studied law or who have law-related experience but who are not licensed to practice law in Japan.[68]

In addition to the Foreign Lawyers Law, foreign law solicitors are subject to regulations and edicts promulgated by the Ministry of Justice, the JFBA, and their local Japanese bar associations.[69] For example, the JFBA specifies how the foreign law solicitors' name and firm are to be displayed, requires the disclosure of the limited license to practice, forbids the foreign lawyers from referring to themselves as "experts," and prohibits the inclusion of client names in brochures and sharply limits their distribution.[70]

A series of talks between USTR and MOJ officials has been held, beginning in February 1990, to review the restrictions on foreign lawyers' practice and the range of legal services available to foreign firms operating in Japan.[71] One important issue is that the Japan Commercial Arbitration Association and the Japanese Bar have interpreted their Lawyers Law[72] and Code of Civil Procedure[73] to prohibit foreign lawyers from acting as arbitration counsel of record until very recently.[74] Although the Japanese Federation of Bar Associations voted in April 1990 to allow foreign legal consultants to represent parties in Japanese arbitrations where the lawyer is qualified to practice the governing or applicable substantive law, it expressed the desire that a bengoshi participate in the proceedings and affirmed that the foreign counsel could not file a motion in court or appear before a public agency.[75] Moreover, no Japanese court has endorsed arbitration representation by foreign legal consultants.[76] The central item on the agenda of the 1990 talks, however, was the restrictions on associations of foreign law solicitors and bengoshi.[77] American firms representing U.S. companies want to hire experienced bengoshi because their former classmates run the MOJ and MITI.[78]

The U.S. Trade Representative (USTR) has taken the position that the various restrictions prevent American lawyers from providing the trade and investment facilitation to American businesses in Japan that is readily available to Japanese corporations advancing into U.S. markets.[79] A USTR official asserts that American lawyers in Japan are the functional equivalent to Japanese trading companies in the United States and should therefore have the same ease of entry.[80] (Note that this argument is in direct contradiction to one of the basic hypotheses of this paper, that such Tokyo offices of U.S. firms are more important in attracting Japanese clients with U.S. legal needs than in serving U.S. clients with Japanese legal needs.)

Role of Foreign Lawyers

Practice under the law, however, confirms the hypothesis. Local practice is almost unappealing. The cost of establishing and maintaining even a small office in Japan is so high that even if each attorney bills 2,000 hours per year at New York billing rates, the Tokyo office will still lose money.[81] Indeed, a substantial part of the research on foreign (non-Japanese) law is done in the home offices.[82] The cost problem is exacerbated by the typical American preference for prime location, exemplified by Sullivan & Cromwell and Morrison & Foerster, by contrast to British solicitors, who are more willing to rent smaller quarters located off of the main streets.[83] However, Coudert Brothers, concerned that clients would be "turned off by excessive displays of money," has opted for a cramped office.[84]

Nevertheless, since the Foreign Lawyers Law took effect in 1987, fifty-seven or fifty-eight foreign law solicitors have been licensed; two-thirds of these lawyers are Americans.[85] A significant number are from the United Kingdom, and one is from France.[86] This relatively low number has surprised the bengoshi,[87] if not foreign bars, whose members may be staying away largely because of the ban on partnerships.[88] Yet combined with the unregistered foreign attorneys on the staffs of the foreign law solicitors (numbering fifty to sixty in late 1988), these attorneys represented a fifty percent increase in the number of transnational law specialists in Japan in an eighteen-month period.[89]

By mid 1990, approximately two hundred foreign attorneys were working in Japan in various capacities.[90] According to at least one American attorney in Japan, the Ministry of Justice has been quite willing to designate American attorneys as qualified to give advice on the laws of all fifty states, excluding Louisiana, upon demonstration of even minimal exposure to those laws.[91] As of late 1988, all of the twenty-two Americans who formally applied for designation with respect to at least one additional state were approved.[92]

In terms of firms, Martindale-Hubbell's 1991 directory of international law firms lists twenty-six American firms and nine British firms—compared with eighty Japanese international law firms—in Tokyo. Based on a review of the names in Martindale-Hubbell, only two of the American firms, Baker & McKenzie and Milbank, Tweed, Hadley & McCloy, and one of the British firms were present before 1987. In addition, six "post-occupation" firms founded by American attorneys qualified in Japan were listed in the 1990 directory. Baker & McKenzie, the American law firm with the largest presence abroad, is also the largest American firm in Tokyo, with twenty-seven lawyers.[93] Since its establishment in Tokyo in 1963, the firm has expanded its practice in part by incorporating local practitioners who could appear in Japanese courts.[94] Milbank, Tweed, Hadley & McCloy established an office in Tokyo in 1977 with special permission from the Japanese government.[95]

Fifteen of the American firms in Tokyo are New York based, three are Los Angeles based, two are San Francisco based, and the remaining firms have their principal offices in Chicago, Philadelphia, and Washington, D.C. Note that only Baker & McKenzie and the Los Angeles based firms are likely to be specialists in high-technology law.

Observers are speaking of a "second wave," which will be lighter than the first wave in 1987 but will again consist primarily of East Coast firms.[96] Simpson, Thacher, & Bartlett, and Winthrop, Stimson, Putnam & Roberts recently announced openings, while Arnold & Porter planned to open in early 1991.[97] Sidley & Austin of Chicago is awaiting approval to open a Tokyo office with London's Ashurst, Morris & Crisp.[98] Opening a Tokyo office is said to be high on the agenda in the merger of San Francisco's Pillsbury, Madison & Sutro and Los Angeles's Lillick & McHose.[99] By contrast, San Francisco's Thelen, Marrin, Johnson & Bridges, which has longstanding Japanese relationships and international clients including Bechtel and Kaiser, is not planning a Tokyo office.[100] Instead, the firm relies on real-time communications with clients there, close alliances with bengoshi, a regional presence in Hong Kong, and membership in Interjura, the consortium of about one dozen law firms which opened a Beijing office.[101]

"Ironically the only foreign law firms that will enter Japan under this bill will be those whose primary interest is in assisting Japanese businesses in solving their problems of market access and investment abroad."[102] This prediction, made upon the enactment of the Foreign Lawyers Law five years ago, has proved accurate with respect to at least the practice of most American law firms in Japan, if not to the express objectives of all of them.[103] Most of their work involves assisting Japanese entities with investments and financial transactions in the U.S.[104] In this capacity, their practice covers a wide array of matters: mergers and acquisitions, financing, leasing, real estate purchases, intellectual property, venture capital investments, licensing and distribution arrangements, trade disputes, immigration and labor issues, and arbitration and litigation.[105] This tendency to focus on Japanese clients is so strong that the chairman of the legal services committee of the U.S. Chamber of Commerce in Japan accuses the New York firms of prioritizing the representation of Japanese investors and companies in their overseas acquisition and ignoring U.S. companies' needs for representation in Japan.[106]

A Skadden, Arps senior partner says that the firm is in Tokyo to create a deal-oriented practice, not merely a marketing office, around reinvestment of Asian excess dollars into the U.S.[107] Yet the deal-oriented practice focussed on Asian clients with U.S. business. Specifically, Skadden announced prior to opening its Tokyo office that it hoped to provide collection and analysis of trade-related information on the U.S., consultancy and intermediation for investment in the U.S. by Japanese firms, and legal representation of Japanese firms in the U.S.[108] Similarly, Los Angeles based O'Melveny & Meyers works out Japanese connected mergers and acquisitions in the U.S., Europe, and Southeast Asia.[109] About eighty percent of San Francisco based Morrison & Foerster's Tokyo clients are Japanese companies with overseas operations or investments.[110] Squires, Sanders & Dempsey advised the Bridgestone Corporation in its takeover of the Firestone Tire and Rubber Company.[111] Coudert Brothers represented Sumitomo Life Insurance Company in a transaction involving a $300 million convertible mortgage with Olympia & York for a major Manhattan officebuilding.[112] Other major Coudert clients represented by the Japan partner include Japan Air Lines, Co. Ltd. and Fuji Photo Felin Co. Ltd.[113]

Among Japanese corporations, the greatest need for foreign law solicitors probably exists at medium-sized enterprises planning to venture abroad.[114] Large corporations fill most of their legal services needs with extensive in-house legal staff, including specialists in international transactions and persons trained in part at American law schools.[115] They use established contacts with foreign law firms for detailed, specialized advice, which the small representative offices generally cannot provide directly.[116] Still, many Japanese corporations have been quick to utilize the services of the foreign law solicitors: in a survey by the Association of Japanese Corporate Legal Departments of one hundred and thirty-eight of its member companies only a year after the Foreign Lawyers Law took effect, forty percent indicated that they had already had some contact with foreign law solicitors, either for periodic consultation (33.3%) or as primary legal advisors (5.9%).[117]

There are exceptions to the trend described here and a very limited amount of the work of American lawyers has involved representing American and other non-Japanese clients regarding business interests in Japan.[118] They have assisted in business and financing negotiations (loans, leases, and debt or equity offerings), provided informal advice on Japanese law with the assistance of Japanese counsel, and collected and analyzed information.[119] A major example is Philadelphia based Morgan, Lewis, & Bockius's Tokyo practice: forty percent has involved representing business inbound to Japan.[120] In addition, some American firms are in Tokyo mainly to represent financial institutions, and some product liability firms and patent firms also have offices.[121] For example, Coudert's resident partner represents Citicorp.[122] And the New York firm of Wilson, Elser, Moskowitz, Edelman, & Dicker, specializing in insurance and reinsurance, has established a Tokyo office to become more competitive by providing clients a service center.[123]

As a result of this balance, many U.S. and European business executives view the Foreign Lawyers' Law as a setback to their efforts to expand operations in Japan.[124] They claim that it denies foreign lawyers the opportunity to be trade facilitators and business advisors, expertise which Japanese lawyers are rarely trained to offer.[125] This view is echoed in a position paper of the American Chamber of Commerce in Japan, presented to Prime Minister Nakasone on May 12, 1986.[126] The U.S. Government's concern about barriers to American lawyers in Japan is linked to the argument that many Japanese trade concessions are meaningless if American businesses are not also permitted to employ the legal counsel to which they are accustomed.[127]

In light of the costs, one American attorney in Japan forecasts a shakeout of the American firms that have opened in Tokyo: three or four would maintain more than a nominal presence and grow to the size of the larger Japanese international law firms, that is, forty-fifty attorneys, including many bengoshi, and develop the name recognition enjoyed by the post-Occupation firms.[128] The current decrease in Japan's role as a capital exporter trends in the same way. Yet the partner heading O'Melveny & Myers Tokyo office observes that "Its psychologically easier to go to Tokyo than to leave Tokyo. Firms didn't want to be forced to close an office and suffer the negative publicity."[129] The chairman of the legal services committee of the American Chamber of Commerce predicts that firms will eventually be forced to become full service when there is full liberalization of the legal services market.[130]

Korea and Taiwan

In Korea and Taiwan, one would expect a legal situation similar to that in Japan, but perhaps lagging by a decade—this is certainly the case for the overall and international roles of lawyers noted in Table 4.1. Both nations have large scale, rapidly growing high technology communities. In both cases, these communities are evolving in close articulation with the Japanese and the United States industries. And both nations share with Japan an Asian tradition of avoidance of litigation.

Differences between the two can be expected, however, derived not only from the cultural differences between the two but also from their rather different economic strategies: Korea relying more heavily on the *chaebol*; Taiwan more on small-scale enterprise. And, as noted in Table 4.2, the patent world in Taiwan is completely different from that in Korea. These differences have led to a difference in transaction character; for example, domestic Taiwanese firms interviewed in the summer of 1990 were much more familiar with the concept of a high-technology strategic alliance than were their Korean analogues. Similarly, Taiwan's emerging role as a capital exporter is likely to differentiate it from Korea so that it would seem more likely to appeal to the international legal community as a situs for branch offices; this is not reflected in the statistics of Table 4.1.

Korea

Martindale-Hubbell lists fourteen international law firms in Seoul in 1991, compared with ten in 1985 and five in 1980.[131] None are foreign. Virtually all of the Korean international law firms, however, employ foreign legal consultants admitted to practice in the U.S.[132] The largest international law firm has sixty lawyers, including twelve foreign legal consultants.[133] Interestingly, all of the domestic international law firms are headed by Korean lawyers qualified in the United States.[134] According to discussions with lawyers at a number of these firms in the summer of 1990, the firms specialize in helping foreign clients deal with the Korean bureaucracy and even the language. On the whole, domestic clients do not use similar services and tend to deal with the bureaucracy directly without any form of legal intermediary.

Legality of Practice by Foreign Lawyers. This practice is well protected from foreign competition. Foreign citizens are generally prohibited from becoming lawyers, but they may be admitted to the Korean bar upon approval of the Ministry of Justice under an exception to the Lawyers Act.[135] Foreign lawyers are further prohibited from practicing law in Korea unless they receive additional special approval from the Minister of Justice.[136] Such approval is subject to withdrawal at any time.[137] In addition, the applicant's home state must have reciprocal provisions for Korean lawyers.[138]

The scope of practice is severely limited. Foreign lawyers "shall in no case handle matters other than those related to aliens or foreign laws."[139] Nor are they allowed to represent clients on legal matters or appear in court.[140]

Foreign legal consultants are not required to register with the Korean bar, which views them as outside the scope of the Lawyers Act provided that they work only as employees.[141] The Ministry of Justice regulates foreign legal consultants through immigration controls.[142] The employment contract must state that the foreign legal consultant will not engage in the practice of law in Korea, *whether foreign or Korean*.[143]

Any foreign law firm or lawyer that obtains approval to practice law from the Minister of Justice will undoubtedly be rejected by the Minister of Finance.[144] The Minister of Finance has jurisdiction over foreign legal service offices under the Foreign Capital Inducement Act.[145] The Ministry's guidelines severely restrict foreign investment in legal services.[146]

Role of Foreign Lawyers. Between 1949 and 1977, two hundred and eighty-five foreign lawyers were admitted to the Korean bar as honorary members for diplomatic reasons.[147] None have been able to obtain permission from the Minister of Justice to practice law.[148]

Approximately forty foreign lawyers work for Korean law firms and in law departments of major corporations.[149] The foreign legal consultants draft agreements for negotiation with foreign parties, translate documents, advise Korean lawyers informally on the laws of their home countries, and develop strategies for foreign clients seeking expansion in Korea.[150] In addition, they commonly give informal advice to foreign clients on the Korean laws with which they become familiar.[151]

Korean law firms, like their Taiwanese counterparts, do not want to establish an affiliation with a single foreign firm because the volume of referrals makes it more profitable to remain impartial.[152] However, Korean firms may be amenable to training foreign lawyers in exchange for training of their lawyers by foreign firms.[153]

Baker & McKenzie successfully circumvented restrictions on foreign law firms by hiring a Korean qualified lawyer, having him qualified and trained in the United States, and sending him back to set up a firm.[154] As a registered Korean firm, it can be staffed with American lawyers working as foreign legal consultants.[155]

In contrast to Taiwan and Japan, Korea has not yet been a major exporter of capital, capable of creating substantial legal business in foreign markets. Its debts have been too significant and its firms have not yet created legally-elaborate foreign affiliates. Real pressure to open the Korean legal services market may materialize, however, with the liberalization of the financial market, just as it did in Japan.[156] In late 1988, the Korean Ministry of Finance announced a plan to substantially liberalize the Korean financial market by 1992.[157]

Taiwan

The domestic international bar consists of several large law firms such as: Lee & Li, Tsar & Tsai, Baker & McKenzie, Formosa International Law Firm, and Ding & Ding. (Baker & McKenzie has hired local lawyers and can practice local law.) All the Taiwanese international law firms have foreign lawyers on staff. Counseling American companies primarily involves providing guidance on investment regulations and assistance in applying for patent and trademark licenses. (IBM, however, is said to have in-house counsel in Taiwan and to consult local firms infrequently.)

It is common for the partners in the major Taiwanese law firms to receive legal education in the United States. JSD and LLM degrees are preferred to JDs. In addition, many of the partners have practiced in American law firms, forming valuable relationships.

Taiwan has no laws specifically directed at foreign lawyers, but the government seems to want to mimic Japan's policy. Taiwan applies strict restrictions to its own bar and has, in some recent years, permitted fewer than ten persons to pass the bar examination. Foreigners are not allowed to take the bar exam. Lawyers must be licensed in Taiwan to practice *any* law, including foreign and international law. However, foreign lawyers may act as advisors and apparently foreign firms with branch offices can operate legally by having some locally qualified lawyers on staff.

The result is a larger role for the foreign bar than in Korea. Martindale-Hubbell lists twenty-three international law firms in Taipei in 1991, including three American firms, three Canadian firms, and one Australian firm. The American firms are Baker & McKenzie (twenty-five attorneys, including fifteen admitted), Jones, Day, Reavis & Pogue (eleven attorneys), and McCutchen, Doyle, Brown & Enerson (nine attorneys).[158] McCutchen is said to have opened this and several other Asian offices to avoid competing directly with American firms in Tokyo.[159] It advises American, European, and Japanese firms in shipping, trading, automobiles, computers, banking, chemicals, and real estate.[160] Although it is hard to be confident, the capabilities of the firms involved probably suggest a relatively strong high-technology orientation.

American and Taiwanese law firms regularly trade clients. Their ties are informal. For example, Sullivan & Cromwell has good relationships with several of the large Taiwanese firms. It may be a disadvantage to have a branch office in Taiwan because of fears of being seen by the Taiwanese firms as competitors to whom clients should not be referred. Overseas financial transactions originating from Taiwan are just beginning to happen; they may change the role of the foreign bar.

Hong Kong, Malaysia, and Singapore

These three nations are important centers of the Pacific Basin high-technology community. None, however, has the well-balanced large high-technology communities of Korea or Taiwan. Rather they concentrate in specific areas such as finance or offshore production; in the cases of Malaysia and Singapore, they have provided a home for multinationals rather than concentrating on encouraging indigenous firms. The high-technology legal needs will, therefore, be narrower than those of Korea or Taiwan. At the same time, for Hong Kong and Singapore, as indicated by the numbers on Table 1, international transactions form a large portion of the total legal business.

Legally, all three share a Commonwealth tradition, superimposed, of course, on an Asian tradition. Thus, the general openness and character of the legal systems can be expected to differ radically from those of Korea or Taiwan.

Hong Kong

Legality of Practice by Foreign Lawyers. Hong Kong[161] has permitted foreign law firms to open offices since 1972.[162] Under the Legal Practitioners Ordinance, admission to the legal profession is controlled by the Supreme Court of Hong Kong. However, entry and restrictions on practice of foreign lawyers are effectively controlled by The Law Society of Hong Kong, which is composed of all admitted solicitors in Hong Kong.[163] The Law Society has published detailed guidelines for applicants.[164] The guidelines limit any country to two firms, unless the applicant presents "evidence of a very substantial demand" for advice on its country's laws.[165]

Individual foreign lawyers, other than residents of the United Kingdom, have little chance of qualifying for admission to the Hong Kong bar, and if they do, they cannot practice Hong Kong law under the employment of a foreign firm.[166] A very limited number (twenty-two in 1986) of Queen's Counsel have a resident practice in Hong Kong, perhaps due to the reluctance of local counsel to take them and the readiness of Hong Kong judges to admit them on an ad hoc basis.[167] By contrast, over three hundred junior barristers are in Hong Kong.[168]

Restrictions on the practice of foreign lawyers are contained in the Law Society guidelines and the Form of Undertaking which it requires of each applicant firm.[169] Foreign lawyers may advise on the law of their country of origin and on international law or conflict of laws, but cannot advise on Hong Kong law.[170] Apparently, American lawyers are not restricted to consulting on the laws of the state in which they are a member of the bar, in contrast to the rules in Japan.

Recent amendments to the Hong Kong Arbitration Ordinance[171] enable foreign lawyers to directly participate in international arbitrations in Hong Kong without violating the prohibition on local practice.[172] However, a local solicitor and perhaps a barrister would have to be engaged for any ancillary court proceedings.[173]

While foreign law firms may not hire Hong Kong solicitors, local firms can hire foreign lawyers and thereby provide integrated legal advice.[174] An amendment to the Legal Practitioners Ordinance[175] proposed by the Hong Kong government, at the prompting of American law firms, would have allowed foreign law firms to hire Hong Kong solicitors and to practice Hong Kong law.[176] The Law Society agreed to terms providing for close association between foreign and local law firms on fee-sharing arrangements, but opposed the hiring of local lawyers by foreign firms.[177] The amendment reportedly also would have formalized the admission of foreign law firms and lawyers through the courts, and established explicit powers for the Law

Society to discipline foreign law firms.[178] The government expressed the belief that this amendment would help the development of a multi-jurisdictional legal community in anticipation of 1997 and would "enhance Hong Kong's reputation as a major international financial centre."[179] Then, in July 1990, the Hong Kong Attorney General informed foreign law firms and the Law Society that the rules would not be altered.[180] The foreign law firms have been asking the U.S. government to intercede.[181]

Role of Foreign Lawyers. Despite the Law Society guidelines limitation on the number of firms from any one country, nineteen American firms have offices in Hong Kong.[182] Half of the firms are New York based.[183] United Kingdom lawyers have a comparable presence with twenty-two offices—more than in any other foreign legal center.[184] Canadian law firms are entering the territory in response to major Hong Kong investment in western Canada.[185] Five Canadian law firms were listed in the 1991 Martindale-Hubbell directory. One Bermudan, one French, and one Philippine firm were also listed. A total of fifty-seven international law firms were listed in the 1991 Martindale-Hubbell directory.[186]

In both Hong Kong and Singapore, the international legal market is extremely competitive, and the earliest established foreign firms have had the advantage.[187] Coudert Brothers, the first foreign firm to open an office in Hong Kong in 1972, upon its arrival petitioned for and received permission to practice local law.[188] In the early 1980s, Coudert Brothers was capturing more bank business than any other American law firm.[189]

The banking sector has been more important to these firms than the high-technology sector. Some firms have branched out to Hong Kong or Singapore largely on the basis of a major banking client; relationships established by major American and British banks with law firms in New York and London tend to be carried over to Hong Kong and Singapore, with notable exceptions.[190] The regional syndicated loan business was thriving when many American law firms opened offices in Hong Kong in the early 1980s.[191] More recently, the syndicated loan business has fallen off, and foreign law firms as a group have lost bank clients to local lawyers as the banks have emphasized trading.[192] There are many joint ventures between British and Hong Kong law firms, with the Euromarket work tending to be channeled to the British partners.[193] Graham & James closed its Hong Kong office and moved three lawyers to Deacons, a ninety-lawyer Hong Kong law firm, as foreign legal consultants in August 1990.[194] The arrangement is apparently the first such affiliation between a Hong Kong and American law firm.[195]

The immediate past president of The Law Society contends that the American law firms are not doing very well in Hong Kong.[196] Six American law firms have closed, most in the past two years, due to insufficient business.[197] The firms are Winston & Strawn of Chicago, Dorsey & Whitney of Minneapolis, Heller, Ehrman, White & McAuliffe of San Francisco, and Shearman & Sterling, Simpson, Thacher & Bartlett, and Paul, Weiss, Rifkind, Wharton & Garrison of New York.[198] Simpson, Thacher insists that its September 1989 closing was in recognition of limited opportunities to advise on U.S. law in transactions rather than a response to political turmoil in China, and the firm will continue its Pacific Rim operations from Tokyo.[199] Shearman & Sterling had anticipated much work from Citibank when it opened its office in 1978, but the bank used local lawyers.[200] However, Thelen, Marrin, Johnson & Bridges and Gibson, Dunn & Crutcher opened Hong Kong offices in 1988, and Skadden, Arps, Slate, Meagher & Flom opened its Hong Kong office in 1989.[201] Thelen, Marrin uses its Hong Kong office as a regional staging area for the Orient.[202]

The American firms that remain in Hong Kong may differ from the firms that have left in terms of their client base.[203] At least some American law firms are involved in domestic-based Asian transactions;[204] it may be that getting significant business from Asian companies, especially given the slowdown in syndicated loans, has made retaining an office worthwhile. Morrison & Foerster is principal American counsel to six Hong Kong real estate development companies listed on the Hong Kong stock exchange, and has represented Esprit Far East.[205] Thelen, Marrin's clients are evenly divided between Hong Kong based companies including the Mandarin Oriental hotel group and Arral & Partners (a Hong Kong venture capital firm) and U.S. and European clients doing business in Asia.[206] Pettit & Martin opened a two lawyer branch, completely linked by computer to its San Francisco office, primarily to service a growing Asian client base, including Mitsui Bank and Hyundai.[207] Pettit arranges international financings and U.S. investments for its Asian clients.[208]

Because much of the international law practice in Hong Kong is at least indirectly related to China,[209] continued unrest there could set back American law firms in Hong Kong. However, many American law firms in Hong Kong—accustomed to the cyclical, transactional nature of China practice and responding to a significant decline in China work prior to the crackdown[210]—diversified their practices before the crackdown.[211] In the immediate aftermath of the Tiananmen Square incident, many were upbeat about their prospects, relying on the Chinese government's assurances that it will maintain an open door investment policy.[212] In fact, two areas of business should pick up as a result of the China turmoil: facilitating reinvestment following capital flight and advising Western investors and companies with projects in China.[213] The experience varies by firm: Gibson, Dunn has seen a slight decline in China related business but says overseas investment in China, especially from Taiwan, continues to grow, while Morrison & Foerster has seen China related business decline from fifteen to twenty percent of the Hong Kong office's revenues to virtually zero.[214] Skadden, Arps has a substantial base of clients in the PRC whom it assists in making acquisitions and strategic alliances in the U.S.[215]

The political changes in China have prompted foreign law firms to evaluate their presence in Hong Kong and at least contemplate whether they should wait to act.[216] Emigration not only threatens the overall economy by depleting the professional cadres, including lawyers, but also already is draining law offices of skilled secretarial and administrative staff.[217] According to a law professor at the University of Hong Kong, sixty percent of Hong Kong lawyers are planning to leave the country.[218]

Malaysia

Malaysia[219] has tended to be primarily an off-shore production center and legal needs have been slight. According to the former manager of one of the U.S. multinationals operating in the nation, there was no need for a resident counsel. Thus the nation is just beginning to evolve a substantial need for international legal services. There are three Malaysian international law firms listed in the 1991 Martindale-Hubbell directory. There were no listings for Malaysia in the International Law Firms section of the directory in 1980 and 1985.

Legality of Practice by Foreign Lawyers. Under Section 18 of the Legal Profession Act of 1976, the High Court of Malaysia may at its discretion admit for the purpose of specific causes (1) a Queen's Counsel qualified in the U.K., (2) a person with special qualifications or experience with regard to the matter, or (3) an advocate or solicitor who has been in active practice in Singapore for at least seven years.[220] Alternatively, under Section 38(1)(d) of the Act, foreign lawyers can work as in-house counsel so long as their work is limited solely to matters to which the company is a party.[221] These in-house counsel may not appear in court.[222] In addition, Section 28A of the Act gives the Attorney General broad discretion to admit foreign lawyers for a specified period through a Special Admission

Certificate.[223] Foreign lawyers may appear as advocates in arbitrations in Malaysia, site of a Regional Arbitration Center in Kuala Lumpur.[224]

Role of Foreign Lawyers. Malaysian advocates and solicitors employ foreign lawyers practicing on an ad hoc basis under Section 18 of the Legal Profession Act and frequently collaborate with foreign lawyers.[225] Only ten non-citizens are admitted as advocates and solicitors in Malaysia, all of whom are permanent residents and were practicing in the country before it gained its independence.[226] A few large companies have in-house foreign lawyers.[227] In addition, four foreign members of the Faculty of Law of the University of Malaysia in Kuala Lumpur are authorized to act in an advisory capacity under instructions from a practicing advocate and solicitor.[228]

Singapore

The high-technology sector in Singapore[229] consists in large part of large-scale subsidiaries of multinationals. In addition, there is a thriving financial sector. Thus, there are substantial needs for international legal practice. These have been met by both local and foreign firms; policy on admitting the latter has tended to be highly discretionary.

Legality of Practice by Foreign Lawyers. Several American law firms were allowed to open offices in Singapore on a trial basis in the early 1970s to help Singapore develop as a regional financial center, but in 1974 all except Coudert Brothers were asked to close.[230] A policy of granting entry to selected firms has been in effect since 1979,[231] and no written guidelines for entry had been issued, at least as of 1984.[232] The government's approach appears to have been that the foreign lawyers are welcome if they will add to Singapore's business potential.[233]

Foreign lawyers must apply to the Singapore Attorney General.[234] The Attorney General's authority is not specifically established by statute, but his practical discretion is complete: the immigration authorities will not issue the necessary work permits without his consent.[235] A foreign law firm's application to the Attorney General must describe its proposed areas of specialization in Singapore, the staff and their qualifications.[236] A 1984 government proposal would have given the Law Minister discretion to admit qualified attorneys from any jurisdiction, and would have exempted from the minister's approval lawyers from Australia, New Zealand, Canada, Malaysia, and Hong Kong.[237]

Foreign law firms are generally not allowed to practice or advise on

Singapore law.[238] Foreign and Singapore law firms are not allowed to share profits.[239] A recent High Court decision[240] barring foreign lawyers from appearing as advocates in arbitration proceedings surprised the legal and arbitration professions.[241] In *Turner (East Asia) Pte. Ltd. v. Builders Federal (Hong Kong) Ltd. & Anor.*, the Court held that the common law right of parties in arbitration proceedings to retain whomsoever they desired had been taken away by the Legal Profession Act,[242] and that only Singapore advocates and solicitors can appear in arbitrations where the dispute involves questions of law and legal rights and obligations.[243] Under the logic of this case, foreign lawyers *could* be precluded from *any* act in Singapore involving the practice of law.[244]

Role of Foreign Lawyers. The impetus for opening Singapore to foreign lawyers a decade ago was the desire to become competitive with Hong Kong as a financial center, particularly in Eurocurrency syndications.[245] The Monetary Authority of Singapore, cognizant of bankers' complaints that the necessary legal expertise was lacking, persuaded the Attorney General's office to admit Euromarket law firms to Singapore.[246] Within three years of the policy shift, at least eighteen foreign law firms (not all Euromarket specialists) had opened offices.[247] In 1991, seventeen foreign law firms—five American, five English, four Australian, one German, one Indonesian, and one Dutch—were listed in the Martindale-Hubbell directory. Ten Singaporean international law firms were also listed.[248] The American firms that joined Coudert Brothers and Graham & James in the early 1980s were Simpson, Thacher & Bartlett, Baker & McKenzie, Sidley & Austin, and White & Case.[249] New York-based Simpson, Thacher closed its offices in Singapore and Hong Kong due to insufficient business.[250] Despite the Singapore Law Society prohibition on profit sharing between local and foreign law firms, some work in "friendly association."[251] Local lawyers, especially in medium-sized firms, would enter into joint ventures with large foreign firms to acquire international banking expertise but for the official Law Society disapproval.[252] Bankers already consider several of the larger Singapore law firms as competent as the best foreign firms at handling large, complex financial transactions, particularly for Singapore dollar loans.[253]

This nation, then, shows the role of the international bar as being primarily one of providing a very specific form of expertise. And, like the other Commonwealth jurisdictions, the nation shows a special role for Commonwealth firms and lawyers, as distinguished from the dominance of U.S. firms in non-Commonwealth jurisdictions.

Peoples' Republic of China

China[254] is a quite different kind of special case. The role of law itself has, until recently, been minimal and there is still relatively little high-technology business. The potential, however, is enormous.

Legality of Practice by Foreign Lawyers

China prohibits foreigners from becoming Chinese lawyers.[255] Foreign lawyers in China are regulated by a very restrictive 1981 Ministry of Justice Circular. The 1981 Circular prohibits foreign lawyers from:

- setting up a practice in China
- establishing law offices
- setting up a practice in partnership with Chinese legal consultancies
- handling lawsuits or representing clients in Chinese courts
- proffering legal assistance to both parties involved in the same lawsuit
- being engaged by Chinese government organizations, social groups and enterprise units as legal consultants
- providing consultancy service and other legal assistance to both the Chinese and the foreign party involved in economic and technological cooperation or trade negotiations
- participating in activities which may be harmful to the sovereignty and interests of China.[256]

Revised regulations proposed to the State Council in the spring of 1988 by the representatives of the regional justice bureaus reportedly contain some of the same restrictions as the 1981 Circular.[257] The proposed revisions would clarify the limitations on foreign lawyers by specifying that they may advise foreign clients only on matters involving foreign law.[258] Apparently, foreign lawyers would be allowed to advise on Chinese law in association with Chinese lawyers.[259]

The proposed regulations do not address the issue of foreign law firms advising Chinese entities on foreign law in China.[260] Nor do they refine the distinction between permissible "consulting" services on trade and investment matters integrally related to Chinese law and the unauthorized practice of Chinese law.[261] The proposed regulations are not expected to be promulgated soon.[262]

Role of Foreign Lawyers. Despite these official restrictions, at least two international law firms have registered as "consultancy firms" in China and nearly a dozen foreign law firms and individual lawyers claimed some form of resident representative in 1989.[263] Six American law firms listed Chinese branches in the 1991 Martindale-Hubbell directory. All six have offices in Beijing, and Baker & McKenzie also has offices in Shanghai and Guangzhou, Guandong.[264]

In response to rapid expansion of United States trade with China in the few years preceding the issuance of the 1981 Circular, five American law firms—Coudert Brothers, Baker & McKenzie, Graham & James, Heller, Ehrman, White & McAuliffe, and Paul, Weiss, Rifkind, Wharton, & Garrison—established essentially permanent offices in Beijing.[265] The 1981 Circular was a setback to these firms,[266] as was China's repression of the June 1989 pro-democracy uprising in Tiananmen Square.[267] By mid-1991, all were back except Heller, Ehrman; moreover Skadden, Arps, Slate, Meagher & Flom finally opened a Beijing office that it had postponed earlier.[268]

In 1988, a group of firms from France, Germany, Holland, Italy, Sweden, Australia, Hong Kong, and the United States opened a joint representative office in Beijing, headed by a U.S.-trained Chinese lawyer.[269] Apparently, the consortium, known as Interjura, has had some success.[270]

Foreign legal consultants, including American lawyers, have been employed by state organizations and enterprises.[271] For example, the Salt Lake City law firm of Woodbury, Jensen, Kesler, & Swinton was engaged in 1990 to represent the Szechwan province in business matters and legal disputes between U.S. and Szechwan organizations.[272] Arnold & Porter successfully defended the Chinese sewn headwear industry against dumping charges before the U.S. International Trade Commission.[273] And Baker & McKenzie represents the U.S. subsidiaries of Chinese state enterprises in their investments in the United States. The New York law firm of Kaye, Scholer, Fierman, Hays & Handler created a wholly owned subsidiary, China Business Consulting Group Ltd., as an outgrowth of its legal work for Western companies doing business in China.[274] Work for China may dominate over work in China.

Foreign legal consultants have also been allowed to act on behalf of foreign clients in mediation and arbitration.[275] The China International Economic and Trade Arbitration Commission has amended its rules to allow non-Chinese nationals to serve as arbitrators.[276]

Conclusion

It is quite clear that the hypotheses presented at the beginning of this article are verified:

> A branch legal office is generally much more important for generating home office business than for generating local business, and such an office may alternatively gain a comparative advantage through its expertise in a specific form of legal transaction.

From this perspective, the laws and regulations designed to protect home legal markets against foreign lawyers are nearly irrelevant—they reach a form of practice that is only rarely the goal of the foreign firms. Moreover, it is abundantly clear that firms have generally found successful ways to evade some of these rules, either through dually-trained persons or through formal or informal alliances with other firms. Thus, neither the regulations, nor the ongoing efforts to break them down as through U.S. Section 301 actions or through GATT negotiations, are likely to be as important as often described.

Looking toward the future, one can anticipate that there will be strong pressures for more offshore offices as more nations, e.g., Taiwan, become important sources of capital. There will probably also be significant concentration in certain specific legal areas, e.g. computer software disputes or new kinds of venture financing transactions.

Several other points should be noted. The surprise is that the internationalization of the high-technology economic community has had relatively little to do with the growth of the global network of law firm branches. That network appears to have been driven much more by financial and real estate transactions. The bulk of the real high-technology work is still done in California or in a few internationally-oriented domestic firms in such nations as Korea and Taiwan.

For the United States, Japan, and China, there is no indication that the nationalism of the bars themselves is likely to break down in the near future in this region. The contrary is true in the smaller nations of East Asia, for which the internationally-oriented bar constitutes a large portion of the entire bar. It is impossible to imagine this not affecting the bar's outlook. (And the same may be true for the high-technology U.S. bar, as distinguished from the U.S. bar as a whole.)

TABLE 4.1 The International High Technology Bar in the Pacific Basin

Nation	*Population (M)*[1]	*Lawyers Total*	*Lawyers Intl*[2]	*Lawyers per M*	*% Int'l*
U.S.	248.8	460,200[3]		1,850	
Japan	123.1	13,902[4]	1120	113	8.1
Korea	42.4	2,568[5]	340	61	13.2
Taiwan	19.7[6]	1,950[7]	380	99	19.5
Hong Kong	5.7	1,332[8]	500	234	37.5
Malaysia	17.4	1,300	40	75	3.1
Singapore	2.7	990	220	81	22.1
China	1113.9	50,000	25	45	<0.1

[1]Data for mid-1989, from World Bank, *World Development Report 1991*, except as noted.

[2]Approximate count of number of lawyers listed in domestic and foreign firms in 1991 Martindale-Hubbell.

[3]Data for 1985, rounded, from U.S. Department of Commerce, *Statistical Abstract of the United States 1988.*

[4]Data from JETRO.

[5]Data for 1993 from K.W. Ahn, "The Growth of the Bar and the Changes in the Lawyer's Role," chapter 5 of this volume.

[6]Data for 1987 from Pacific Basin Economic Council, Japan Member Committee, *PEC Statistics 1990.*

[7]Statement from Taiwanese Embassy.

[8] Data for Hong Kong, Malaysia, and Singapore is for 1983 and is taken from Table 8.1 in S.P. Magee, W.A. Brock and L. Young, *Black hole tariffs and endogenous policy theory: Political economy in general equilibrium*, Cambridge, Cambridge U.P. (1989), 120-121.

TABLE 4.2 Relative Importance of Patents in the Pacific Basin High Technology Community

Nation	GNP[9] ($B)	Patents[10]	Patents per $B GNP	% Domestic
U.S.	5,156	77,924	15.1	52.0
Japan	2,819	55,300	19.6	86.6
Korea	212	2,174	10.3	26.4
Taiwan	83[11]	12,216[12]	147.2	54.8
Hong Kong	53	1,070	20.2	0.8
Malaysia	37			
Singapore	28			
China	418	1,025	2.5	60.2

[9]Data for 1989 from *World Development Report 1991*, except for Taiwan.

[10]Data for 1988 (grants to residents and non-residents, for U.S., Japan, Korea, Hong Kong, & China) from WIPO, IP/STAT/1988/A. The data for non-residents is used in the "percent domestic" index.

[11]Data for 1987 from *Pacific Economic Community Statistics 1990.*

[12]Data for 1988 grants for "Chinese" and "foreigner" taken from National Science Council, Taiwan, Republic of China, *Science and Technology Data Book 1987*.

Notes

1. *See generally* K. M. Dewey, "Business in Europe Remains Elusive for U.S. Law Firms," *California Law Business* (Los Angeles Daily Journal), Feb. 11, 1991 at 14; T. Carter, "The Great European Gold Rush," *California Lawyer*, July 1990, at 36; S. R. Sontag, "Opening Offices Overseas; Does the Payoff Warrant the Huge Expense?", *National Law Journal*, Feb. 12, 1990, at 1, col. 4; C. Roberts, "Globalization: Law Firms Gird for 90s, Beyond," *Los Angeles Daily Journal*, Dec. 29, 1989, at 1; T. Harper, "Going Global; Big Law Firms Expand Overseas," *ABA Journal*, Sep. 1989, at 68; S. Labaton, "U.S. Law Firms Expand to Reach Global Clientele," *New York Times*, May 12, 1988, at A-1, c. 4.

For historical trends in international law practice, *see* M. Brothwood, "International Law Offices," 1979 *J. Bus. L.* 8; S. M. Levy, "The American Lawyer in Paris," 52 *N.Y.St.B.J.* 647 (1980); Note, "Providing Legal Services in Foreign Countries: Making Room for the American Attorney," 83 *Colum. L. Rev.* 1767 (1983) (authored by Kelly Charles Crabb).

2. Dewey, *supra* note 1, at 14.

3. Dewey, *supra* note 1, at 14.

4. Two reference works on rules governing practice by foreign lawyers in various countries are S. M. Cone, *Regulation of Foreign Lawyers,* Chicago: American Bar Association (3d ed. 1984), and D. Campbell, ed., *Transnational Legal Practice,* Deventer: Kluwer (1982).

For analyses of barriers to trade in legal services, *see* Comment, "Toward Institutionalization of Reciprocity in Transnational Legal Services: A Proposal for a Multilateral Convention under the Auspices of GATT," 13 *B.C. Int'l & Comp. L. Rev.* 91 (1990) (authored by Annie Eun-ah Lee); R. J. Goebel, "Professional Qualification and Educational Requirements for Law Practice in a Foreign Country: Bridging the Cultural Gap," 63 *Tul. L. Rev.* 444 (1989); H. P. de Vries, "The International Legal Profession—The Fundamental Right of Association," 21 *Int'l. Law* 845 (1987); M. C. Shiono, "Foreign Attorneys in Japan: the International Practice of Law as a Question of Unfair Trade Practices," 2 *Am. U.J. Int'l. L. & Pol'y.* 615 (1987); J. H. Barton, "Negotiation Patterns for Liberalizing International Trade in Professional Services," 1986 *U. Chi. Legal Forum* 97; Crabb, *supra* note 1.

5. Sontag, *supra* note 1, at 1 (data from The National Law Journal's 1989 survey of the 250 largest law firms in the United States, Sep. 18, 1989).

6. Sontag, *supra* note 1, at 28.

7. According to the American Bar Association, there are 90 foreign firms in London, including 55 American firms. C. Roberts, "Around the World: A Panoply of Legal Opportunities," *Los Angeles Daily Journal*, Dec. 29, 1989, at 6. In Tokyo, there are approximately 21 American firms, compared with about eight British firms.

8. *See* K. Wilson, "Law Firms Move into Asia," *Law Institute Journal*, June 1990, at 513.

9. *See* M. Kideckel, "Going Global," *Canadian Lawyer*, June 1989, at 14 (describing and critiqueing Canadian law firms' expansions into foreign markets).

10. Kideckel, *supra* note 9, at 14, 17 (list of firms).

11. Wilson, *supra* note 8, at 513.

12. According to GATT numbers, Asia-Asia and Asia-North America trade total about 21% of world trade compared with intra-European trade that totals about 31.1% of world trade. Trade in the Pacific region, however, is growing at approximately 10% per year compared to a 6% rate in Europe, GATT, II *International Trade 89-90* 10 (1990). The rates are based on 1980-1989 averages.

13. The number of strategic alliances between U.S. and Japanese firms in the semiconductor industry has, for example, increased, according to one source, from three in 1980 to 180 in 1991. Statement by Richard Johnson before the Subcommittee on Intellectual Property and Judicial Administration of the Committee on the Judiciary, May 16, 1991, p. 8.

14. In 1988, the United States invested almost $127 billion in the area; Japan invested $32 billion, up from $9 billion in 1985, Pacific Basin Economic Council, *PEC Statistics, 1990*, pp. 198-201 (1990). For the first five months of 1990, Taiwan's outbound investment was $456 million, of which about half was to the Pacific region, Investment Commission, Ministry of Economic Affairs, Republic of China, *Statistics on Overseas-Chinese & Foreign Investment, Technical Cooperation, Outward Investment, Outward Technical Cooperation* (May 1990).

15. Thus, the proposed GATT Service Code is expected to include provisions requiring "transparency" of regulations affecting international service transaction. The mid-term services agreement of the Uruguay Round stated: "Provisions should ensure information with respect to all laws, regulations and

administrative guidelines as well as international agreements relating to services trade to which the signatories are parties through adequate provisions regarding their availability." General Agreement on Tariffs and Trade, Decisions Adopted at the Mid-term Review of the Uruguay Round, Part II, Negotiations on Trade in Services (April 8, 1989), reprinted in 28 I.L.M. 1023, 1037.

Similarly, in the Structural Impediments Initiative, Japan has promised: "In order to ensure transparency and fairness of administrative guidance, the Government of Japan will see to it that administrative guidance is not intended to restrict market access nor to undermine fair competition. The Government of Japan will implement its administrative guidance in writing as far as possible, and unless there are good reasons not to do so, it will make the administrative guidance public when it is implemented." *Interim Report by the Japanese Delegation*, April 5, 1990; available in 7 *B.N.A.I.T.R.* 531 (April 11, 1990).

16. International arbitration revenues at the largest law firms may now account for 5-10% of overall billings. Labaton, *supra* note 1 at D20.

17. In the analysis in text, we are assuming that the competitive forces involved in creation of branch offices are those associated with relative ability to provide legal services themselves. We do not emphasize another possible role of a legal network, that of providing a client of one office with a way to be confident of the quality of services to be performed in another city or country. Although this information service may have played a role in the creation of legal networks in the past, its importance is declining as corporations have better and better internal mechanisms of evaluating the quality of legal services offered in different markets. See generally R. Gilson, "The Devolution of the Legal Profession: A Demand Side Perspective," 49 *Md. L. Rev.* 870 , especially 899-903. The factors described by Professor Gilson will be very strong in a community as integrated and as replete with international repeat players as the Pacific Basin high-technology community.

18. Harper, *supra* note 1 at 68; Labaton, *supra* note 1.

19. Wilson, *supra* note 8, at 513. Australian law firms also practice maritime law in Asia, and export legal education and judicial assistance to island nations. *Id.* at 515.

20. Harper, *supra* note 1, at 69. *See also*, "Baker & McKenzie—*The* International Law Firm," *New Law Journal*, Jan. 2, 1987, at 12.

21. *See* "The National Law Journal's Annual Survey of the Nation's Largest Law Firms," *National Law Journal*, Sep. 24, 1990, at S1, S4.

22. *See* Harper, *supra* note 1, at 70.

23. Labaton, *supra* note 1.

24. *See* text to notes 44 ff.

25. Kideckel, *supra* note 9, at 14, 15.

26. L. Forte, "Despite Barriers, Firms Head to Japan," *California Law Business* (Los Angeles Daily Journal), Sep. 10, 1990, 3, 10; Dewey, *supra* note 1, at 16.

27. Forte, *supra* note 26, at 10.

28. Roberts, "Around the World," *supra* note 7, at 6. O'Melveny is also opening an office in Brussels with a British and a French firm. *Id.*

29. *See* text accompanying footnotes 161 to 253.

30. Forte, *supra* note 26, at 10.
31. Forte, *supra* note 26, at 10.
32. Wilson, *supra* note 8, at 515. The Australian firms of Clayton Utz (through PRAC) and Freehill Hollingdale & Page already practice environmental law in Asia. *Id.*
33. Forte, *supra* note 26, at 3; S. W. Stein, "Go East, Young Lawyer," ABA Journal, Sep. 1989, at 74; Roberts, *supra* note 7, at 1.
34. Labaton, *supra* note 1, at D20.
35. Stein, *supra* note 33, at 76.
36. Sontag, *supra* note 1, at 1.
37. Sontag, *supra* note 1, at 28.
38. R. Smith, "Attorneys Still in Demand for Foreign Investors," *California Law Business* (Los Angeles Daily Journal), Feb. 11, 1991, at 19.
39. Smith, *supra* note 38, at 19.
40. W. E. Green, "Law Firms Link to Serve Clients Around the Globe," *Chicago Daily Law Bulletin*, July 10, 1990, at 1. Insofar as the driving force behind these networks is probably the ability to assure clients of the quality of the other firms in the network, this approach will probably lose competitiveness as clients build their own capabilities of evaluating foreign legal services.
41. "Law Firms Join Together for PRC Rep Office," *International Lawyers' Newsletter*, Vol. X, No. 1, 1988, p. 3. The American firms are Thelen Marrin of San Francisco, Bracewell & Patterson of Houston, and Wilmer, Cutler & Pickering of Washington, D.C. *Id.*
42. Wilson, *supra* note 8, at 513.
43. Green, *supra* note 40, at 1. The major American firms based in New York, California, Washington and Illinois have declined to join Lex Mundi, presumably because they do not need assistance in making contacts. *Id.* at 16.
44. For the history and structure of the Japanese legal profession, *see* M. K. Young, *American Lawyers in Japan: Opportunities and Obstacles for Clients and Practitioners*, 5-10 (November 3, 1988) (report of conference sponsored by Japan Society, Center for Japanese Legal Studies at Columbia University, and the Section of International Law and Practice, American Bar Association), and for a thorough discussion, M. K. Young and V. L. Hamilton, "Introduction to Japanese Law," in M. Matsushita, ed., *Japan Business Law Guide*, Para. 7-010 to 7-900 ("The Legal Profession of Japan") (Sydney: CCH Australia 1988).
45. *See* E. W. Libby, "Retaining Legal Counsel in Japan: Guidelines for New-To-Market Firms," *East Asian Executive Reports*, July 15, 1990, at 17, 18.
46. Id.
47. Libby, *supra* note 45, at 19.
48. Libby, *supra* note 45, at 19.
49. Richard H. Wohl, Esq., "Operating Under Japan's Foreign Lawyers Law; Japan's System for Governing Foreign Lawyers," *East Asian Executive Reports*, Aug. 15, 1990, at 18 n 6 [hereinafter Wohl, Part I].
50. Id.; M. N. Tuchow, "Living on Tokyo Time," *California Lawyer*, July 1990, at 35. Apparently, the Foreign Lawyers Law, discussed below, does not preclude bengoshi from hiring trainees. Young, *supra* note 44, at 13.

51. This subject is treated thoroughly in R. H. Wohl, S. M. Chemtob, and E. S. Fukushima, *Practice by Foreign Lawyers in Japan* (American Bar Association, 1989) [hereinafter *Japan Practice*] (including forty-four related documents). Wohl, an attorney with Morrison & Foerster in Los Angeles, was Attorney-Advisor for East Asian and Pacific Affairs in the Office of the Legal Advisor of the U.S. Department of State from 1985-1987, when he was one of the principal U.S. negotiators in the U.S.-Japan talks on the foreign lawyers issue.

52. Special Measures Law Concerning the Handling of Legal Business by Foreign Lawyers, Law No. 66 of 1986, reprinted at 26 I.L.M. 881 (1987) [Translation based on version in Appendix 4 of Young, *supra*.] [hereinafter Foreign Lawyers Law].

53. The Foreign Lawyers Law contains a broad provision for procedures and enforcement as stipulated by the Ministry of Justice Ordinance. *See* Foreign Lawyers Law, *supra* note 52, Art. 62.

54. *See* Foreign Lawyers Law, *supra* note 52, Art. 21-23 (broadly providing, *inter alia*, for the regulations of the JFBA and Bengoshi Associations to include "other necessary provisions concerning a gaikokuho-jimu-bengoshi [foreign law solicitor].")

55. Wohl, Part I, *supra* note 49. Japan enacted a new Bengoshi Law in 1949, during the allied occupation, allowing foreign attorneys to practice in Japan without passing the national bar examination if they possessed "an adequate knowledge of the laws of Japan." When this provision was repealed in 1955, a handful of American attorneys who had obtained licenses were grandfathered. Similarly, foreign attorneys admitted to practice in Okinawa before 1972 were grandfathered when the territory reverted to Japanese control. *Japan Practice*, *supra* note 51, at 10-11.

The award of a special entry visa in 1977 to Isaac Shapiro (now with Skadden, Arps) to establish Milbank, Tweed, Hadley, & McCloy's Tokyo presence triggered JFBA opposition to licensing of foreign lawyers and halted the granting of work visas to foreign lawyers other than trainees. V. Slind-Flor, "U.S. Lawyers Say Japan Opens Door Only to Shut it," *Los Angeles Daily Journal*, June 2, 1986, at 1.

The ABA engaged the JFBA in discussions on opening the Japanese legal services market from 1974 to 1982. The failure of these attempts prompted the ABA to seek assistance from the U.S. government. In March 1982, the U.S. Government formally designated the issue for government-to-government consultations at a meeting of the U.S. Japan Trade Committee chaired by the Deputy U.S. Trade Representative. Intermittent U.S.-Japan discussions occurred from 1982 to 1985. In 1985, pressure from Congress and the private sector to open the Japanese market in general, dissatisfaction among American lawyers working as trainees, and the admission to the New York, California, and Washington, D.C. bars of a number of bengoshi, together with the JFBA's expression of a tentative willingness to admit foreign lawyers followed by the Japanese government's announcement that it would amend the Bengoshi Law prompted acceleration of the talks. Intensive bilateral consultations took place from September 1985 to February 1987. *Japan Practice*, *supra* note 51, at 11-12.

In April 1986, a group of American attorneys filed a petition with the Office of the United States Trade Representative under §301 of the Trade Act of 1974, alleging that the Japanese regulations preventing foreign attorneys from practicing law constituted illegal nontariff trade barriers to legal services and violated treaty agreements between Japan and the United States. Shiono, *supra* note 4, at 615. The USTR dismissed the petition without prejudice and decided not to initiate an investigation based on progress in the bilateral negotiations and the enactment of the Foreign Lawyers Law. *Id.* at 618. A second petition was filed in response to the proposed regulations to implement the law in January 1987, followed by the announcement of a U.S.-Japan negotiated agreement in February 1987. *Id.* at 651.

For further background on the dispute and the bilateral negotiations that led to the enactment of the Foreign Lawyers Law, *see Japan Practice, supra* note 51; Wohl, Part I; Young, *supra* note 44; M. R. MacMullin, "Foreign Attorneys in Japan: Past Policies, the New 'Special Measures Law' and Future Expectations," 4 *Florida International Law Journal* 51 (1988). *See also* H. W. Tan and A. J. Alexander, *Entry Restrictions and Japanese Lawyers' Incomes in International Legal Practice* (Santa Monica: Rand Corp., May 1987).

56. Part I, *supra* note 51, at 13.

57. Young *supra* note 44, at 12; Wohl, Part I, *supra* note 49.

58. Foreign Lawyers Law, *supra* note 52, Art. 7-15. The qualifications to become a foreign law solicitor include two particularly controversial requirements. Probably the most contentious is the necessity of "having engaged in practice as a foreign lawyer in the foreign country where he acquired such qualification for five years or more after acquiring it." Foreign Lawyers Law, *supra* note 52, Art. 10.1. The period is effectively six years in most cases because it commences on the day of admittance to the bar. Young, *supra* note 44, at 19-20. As a result, qualification is met at a time when, for purposes of promotion to partnership, it is difficult for American attorneys to go abroad for an extended period. *Id.* Following complaints by American lawyers who had spent time practicing in Japan as employee "trainees" of bengoshi, a supplementary provision was enacted to allow those so employed at the time of execution of the Foreign Lawyers Law to count up to two years of that experience toward fulfillment of the five-year requirement. Wohl, Part I *supra* note 49, at 14; Young, *supra* note 44, at 12. For translated text of the supplementary provision, *see* Young at 56.

Reciprocal treatment of bengoshi under the law of the applicant's home jurisdiction is the other controversial requirement for approval. Young, *supra* note 44, at 12. An application will not be approved "unless substantially equivalent treatment as accorded by this Law is given in the foreign country." Foreign Lawyers Law, *supra* note 52, Art. 10.2. This means that the applicant must be licensed in a jurisdiction that has rules permitting bengoshi to practice as foreign legal consultants, regardless of whether any bengoshi actually want to work there. Wohl, Part I, *supra* note 49, at 14. Because Japan's reciprocity rule applies on a state-by-state basis with respect to American lawyer applicants and the key U.S. jurisdictions now permit foreign legal consultants, this should not be a problem for the large American law firms. Wohl, Part I, *supra* note 49, at 14; Young, *supra* note 44, at 13.

Other requirements are designed to protect the Japanese Bar and the clients of the foreign law solicitors. They include references, absence of criminal convictions or disciplinary actions, ability to compensate clients in case of malpractice, and a business plan and the financial backing to implement it. *See supra* note 52, at 14-15; Young, *supra* note 44, at 13. The business plan and financial test, which are not required by the U.S. states with foreign legal consultant rules, are intended as consumer protection measures. Wohl, Part I, *supra* note 49, at 14.

Interestingly, being a foreign national is not one of the tests for qualification, and Japanese should be treated identically to foreigners under the Law. Young, *supra* note 44, at 18. This "back door" to a practice comparable to that of the 1.5% of bengoshi elite who cultivate an international clientele, was purportedly a prime concern of the JFBA, but the five-year requirement makes this route less attractive. M. McAbee, "Foreign Lawyers Law Faces Review," *East Asian Executive Reports*, February 15, 1990, 6. Two of the "U.S." foreign law solicitors are Japanese nationals who qualified as New York lawyers. Wohl, Part II, *supra* note 49, at 15.

59. Foreign Lawyers Law, *supra* note 52, Art. 24-36.

60. Foreign Lawyers Law, *supra* note 52, Art. 51-54. However, a refusal to register or an imposition of disciplinary sanctions by the JFBA must be reviewed by a committee composed of representatives of the Japanese government, the judiciary, the JFBA, and other groups, with a final right of appeal to the Tokyo High Court. Foreign Lawyers Law, *supra* note 52, Art. 37-39 (Registration Screening Board), Art. 55-58 (Discipline Actions Committee and Discipline Maintenance Committee), Art. 60 (Right of Appeal).

61. Foreign Lawyers Law, *supra* note 52, Art. 3. Six areas of practice are prohibited:

(1) representation in regard to procedures before a court, public prosecutor's office, or other public agency, or the preparation of documents for such proceedings;
(2) acting as counsel in criminal juvenile protection, or extradition cases;
(3) expressing an expert opinion or other legal opinion regarding laws other than the laws of the country of primary qualification;
(4) service of documents in regard to the procedures taken for a foreign court or administrative agency;
(5) representation in regard to the entrustment of preparation of notarial deed under Item (5) of Article 22 of the Civil Execution Law (Law No. 4 of 1979);
(6) representation or the preparation of documents (excluding written expert opinions) in regard to a legal case, the primary objective of which is the acquisition, loss, or change of rights concerning real property in Japan, or of industrial property rights, mining rights, or related rights. Foreign Lawyers Law, *supra* note 52, Art. 3.1, 4.

Where rights concerning real property in Japan or industrial property are at issue but are not the primary objective of a case, the foreign law solicitor must obtain written advice from or work jointly with a bengoshi. Foreign Lawyers Law, *supra* note 52, Art. 3.2. Foreign law solicitors must also act in consultation with bengoshi on family relations and estate cases involving a Japanese national. Id.

62. Young, *supra* note 44, at 12.

63. Foreign Lawyers Law, *supra* note 52, Art. 16.2.

64. Foreign Lawyers Law, *supra* note 52, Art. 49; Wohl, Part I, *supra* note ___, at 15 (noting the extension of the provision applying to bengoshi to quasi-legal professionals).

65. Wohl, Part I, *supra* note 49, at 15.

66. Young, *supra* note 44, at 13.

67. Wohl, Part I, *supra* note 49, at 15-16. A U.S.-Japan understanding limits the entry controls to the normal immigration criteria of (1) the need for the employee's services and (2) the unavailability of a qualified Japanese worker. Wohl, Part I, *supra* note 49, at 17.

68. Wohl, Part I, *supra* note 49, at 17. Many of the Japanese who study law in college do not pass the rigorous national bar examination. *Id.*

69. Young, *supra* note 44, at 14.

70. Id.; Wohl, Part I, *supra* note 49, at 17.

71. M. McAbee, "Japan's Foreign Lawyers Law: U.S.-Japan Talks Near Impasse," *East Asian Executive Reports*, Mar. 15, 1991, at 10; M. McAbee, "U.S. Continues Pressure," *East Asian Executive Reports*, June 15, 1990, 14. The chief U.S. negotiator is Deputy USTR Linn Williams. McAbee, "Foreign Lawyers Law Faces Review," *East Asian Executive Reports*, Feb. 15, 1990, at 6.

U.S. Trade Representative Carla Hill's formal request in late 1989 to begin the review cited five obstructions, which were raised by the American Chamber of Commerce in Japan: (1) the rule that foreign lawyers must use their personal names and jurisdiction of primary qualification, with firm names appended, is unwieldy and hinders development of goodwill; (2) the qualification requirement of five years practice in a particular jurisdiction and the exclusion of time spent working in Japan together discourage younger attorneys, interfere with continuity of personnel (which is vital to client relations), and complicate replacement of the qualifying partner who heads the office; (3) the prohibitions on foreign lawyers employing or (4) entering into partnerships with bengoshi create inefficiencies for Japanese and foreign clients seeking advice on matters involving both foreign and Japanese law and reduces competition between foreign lawyers and bengoshi; and (5) the interpretation of the prohibition on appearing before a public agency to restrict the right of foreign lawyers to represent foreign parties in commercial arbitrations. Wohl, Part II, *supra* note 49 at 16; McAbee, "Impasse," *ante* at 10. A sixth firm restriction not then formally recognized by the USTR prevents law firms from having branch offices. L. Forte, "U.S. Lawyers Must Deal with Japanese Restrictions," *California Law Business* (Los Angeles Daily Journal), Sep. 10, 1990, at 10. The rule applies to both foreign and domestic firms. Id.

72. Article 72.

73. Article 801.

74. C. Ragan, "Preparing for the Pitfalls of Arbitration in Japan," *East Asian Executive Reports*, Jan. 15, 1991, at 9 (Charles R. Ragan, Esq. is a partner with Pillsbury, Madison & Sutro in San Francisco).

75. Ragan, *supra* note 74, at 13 (citing summary translation published by the Committee on Gaikokuho-Jimu-Bengoshi of the Nichibenren in A Guide to Rules for Foreign Special Members (1990)); McAbee, "U.S. Continues Pressure," *supra* note 71, at 14.

76. Ragan, *supra* note 74, at 13 (citing summary translation published by the Committee on Gaikokuho-Jimu-Bengoshi of the Nichibenren in A Guide to Rules for Foreign Special Members (1990)).

77. Wohl, Part I, *supra* note 49, at 15. This is a key demand of the business community, as distinguished from the major American firms in Tokyo focusing on Japanese investment work, and the USTR's prioritization of the issue was in direct response to a request by the American Chamber of Commerce. *See* J. Fuhrman, "Lions at the Gate," *California Lawyer*, July 1990, at 30, 31.

78. Id., at 32 (quoting David A. Livdahl, partner in Tokyo office of Graham & James). It is said, however, that major firms relying on overseas transactions practice are generally not interested in hiring bengoshi. Id., at 34. Rather, they have referral arrangements with Japanese law firms which would be threatened by bringing bengoshi functions in-house. Id., at, at 34.

79. McAbee, "Impasse," *supra* note 71, at 10; McAbee, "U.S. Continues Pressure," *supra* note 71. Bengoshi cannot fill this gap because they traditionally specialize in litigation and rarely act as continuing consultants to corporations in business planning or transactions structuring. McAbee, "U.S. Continues Pressure," *supra* note 71, at 15.

80. Forte, *supra* note 71, at 12 (Lewis I. Cohen, USTR director of Japanese Affairs [mistakenly referred to as "Mr. Lewis" by Forte]).

81. Young, *supra* note 44, at 21. Because these additional costs are primarily attributable to office rents and cost of living allowances, there would not seem to be real economies of scale.

See generally Sontag, *supra* note 1.

82. Young, *supra* note 44, at 19.

83. Young, *supra* note 44, at 21; V. Slind-Flor, "Scenes from the Japan Practice," *American Lawyer*, March 1988, 22.

84. Id. at 22 (quoting Charles Stevens). For anecdote about American lawyers attempting to fit in to local culture, *see* id.

85. Forte, "Barriers" *supra*, note 26, at 3; Fuhrman, *supra* note 77, at 30, 32, 33.

86. Wohl, Part II, *supra* note 49, at 9.

87. Young, *supra* note 44, at 18.

88. Miller, "Few Foreign Lawyers Apply to Practice in Japan," *Japan Times Weekly*, May 23, 1987, at 5, col. 1.

89. Young, *supra* note 44, at 18.

90. Fuhrman, *supra* note 77, at 33.

91. Young, *supra* note 44, at 19 (citing Charles Stevens, Senior Partner, Coudert Brothers). For example, Stevens believed that the fifty-state surveys of Blue Sky laws frequently executed by young attorneys in New York would constitute sufficient exposure. Id.

92. Young, *supra* note 44, at 19. Foreign law solicitors have also accompanied bengoshi to court. Young, *supra* note 44, at 19 (citing Stevens). At least one American firm that opened an office next door to a Japanese firm with which it had a longstanding relationship was required to submit to the JFBA a floorplan confirming the existence of a wall between the firms. Young, *supra* note 44, at 21.

93. *See* Labaton, *supra* note 1 at D20; National Law Journal 1991 survey, *supra* note 21.

94. Labaton, *supra* note 1, at D20.

95. Slind-Flor, "Japan Opens Door," *supra* note 55, at 1.

96. Forte, "barriers," *supra* note 26, at 3.

97. *Id.*

98. *Id.* at 3, 10.

99. Id. at 9. A partner in the firm, Yugi Iwanaga, is a Japanese bengoshi licensed as an American lawyer. Id.

100. Id. at 9.

101. Id. at 9.

102. Michael McAbee, "Foreign Businessmen Critical of New Lawyers' Rights Law," *East Asian Executive Reports*, June 15, 1986, at 18.

103. *See* Slind-Flor, "Scenes," supra note 83, at 22 (noting the range of professed objectives of American firms in Tokyo).

104. Wohl, Part II, *supra* note 49, at 16. In serving Japanese corporate clients, the foreign attorney usually meets with a "kacho," a manager with a rank equivalent to assistant vice-president or section chief. Slind-Flor, "Scenes," *supra* note 83, at 23 (quoting Elliot Gewirtz, partner, Milbank, Tweed, formerly in Tokyo office).

105. Wohl, Part II, *supra* note 49, at 16; Young, *supra* note 44, at 19.

106. Fuhrman, *supra* note77, at 31 (citing Ned Perry).

107. Slind-Flor, "Scenes," *supra* note 83, at 23 (quoting Joseph Flom, senior partner).

108. Michael McAbee, "Foreign Businessmen Critical of New Lawyers' Rights Law," *East Asian Executive Reports*, June 15, 1986, at 18.

109. Forte, "Barriers," *supra* note 26, at 9.

110. Fuhrman, *supra* note 77, at 34.

111. Labaton, *supra* note 1, at D20.

112. Id., at D20.

113. Slind-Flor, "Scenes," *supra* note 83, at 22.

114. *See* Young, *supra* note 44, at 23.

115. Id., at 23.

116. Id., at 23.

117. Id., at 23, 74. The bulk of the client companies were capitalized at or above ten billion yen, which the surveyor designated as "big" companies. Id. at 74.

118. Wohl, Part II, *supra* note 49, at 16.

119. Id., at 16.
120. "Barriers," *supra* note 26, at 10.
121. Id., at 9 (quoting Grayson Bryan, Tokyo Partner, O'Melveny & Meyers).
122. Slind-Flor, "scenes," *supra* note 83, at 22.
123. Id., at 23 (quoting Thomas Tobin, Tokyo partner).
124. Mcabee, "Foreign Businessmen," *supra* note 108, at 18.
125. Mcabee, "Foreign Businessmen," *supra* note 108.
126. Id.
127. Young, *supra* note 44, at 1; *supra*, text accompanying notes 79 to 80.
128. Young, *supra* note 26, at 21 (citing Charles Stevens).
129. Forte, "barriers," *supra* note 77, at 9 (quoting Grayson Bryan). Note that half a dozen firms have closed their Hong Kong offices.
130. Fuhrman, *supra* note 77, at 34 (quoting Ned Perry).
131. For an overview of the Korean legal profession and qualifications for domestic lawyers, *see* E. Oh, "The Practice of Law in Korea: A Canadian Lawyer's Perspective," 48 *The Advocate* 741, 741-43 (Sep. 1990); S. H. Song, *Introduction to the Law and Legal System of Korea* (1983); C. J. Kim, "The Role of Lawyers in Trans-Pacific Cooperation," in C. J. Kim, ed., *Business Laws in Korea* (2d ed. 1988), p. 3. See also chapters 5, 11, of this book.
132. See listings under Korea in Martindale-Hubbell International Law Directory, 1991.
133. Oh, *supra* note 131, at 744.
134. Oh, *supra* note 131, at 744.
135. Article 6, Lawyers Act, Law No. 63, promulgated November 7, 1949, amended by Law No. 3594, December 31, 1982. And see, "Enforcement Decree of the Lawyers Act,: Decree No. 11061 (February 23, 1983). [Cited in R. C. Brown, "Foreign Lawyers on Foreign Soil: Changing Regulations and Opportunities in International Practice in Asia and Hawaii as Foreign Legal Consultants," Vol. 20 *Hawaii Law Journal* 75, 79.

Foreign lawyers are exempted from taking the National Judicial Examination and completing the two-year educational program at the Judicial Training and Research Institute required of Korean applicants to the bar. Oh, *supra* note 131, at 742-743.

136. Oh, *supra* note 131, at 743.
137. Lawyer's Act, *supra* note 135, Art. 6(3).
138. Lawyers Act, *supra* note 135, Art. 6(2).
139. Lawyers Act, *supra* note 135, Art. 6(2).
140. Oh, *supra* note 131, at 744 (citing Lawyers Act) [which article?].
141. Oh, *supra* note 131, at 746.
142. Oh, *supra* note 131, at 746 (citing Article 9(11) Immigration Act Enforcement Decree, Presidential Decree No. 11456, 1984).
143. Oh, *supra* note 131, at 746.
144. Oh, *supra* note 131, at 746.
145. Foreign Capital Inducement Act, Law No. 1082, promulgated on August 3, 1966; amended on March 12, 1973, Law No. 2598; amended on December 31, 1983, Law No. 3691; amended on June 16, 1989, Law No. 4128.

146. Oh, *supra* note 131, at 746 (citing "Guidelines for Foreign Investment," Ministry of Finance Notification (No. EC-89-24), issued January 1990, p. 33).

147. Oh, *supra* note 131, at 744.

148. *Id.*

149. Oh, *supra* note 131, at 744.

150. Oh, *supra* note 131, at 744.

151. Oh, *supra* note 131, at 746.

152. *Id.*

153. Oh, *supra* note 131, at 748.

154. Oh, *supra* note 131, at 747.

155. *Id.*

156. Oh, *supra* note 131, at 747.

157. Oh, *supra* note 131, at 747 (citing Ministry of Finance, "Jabon Shigang Kukjyehwa e Kwedanjok Hwakdae Chujin Kewhoek: 88-92" (Plan for the Gradual Expansion of the Internalization of the Capital Market: 88-92), December 12, 1988).

158. *See* Martindale-Hubbell International Law Director, 1991. *See also* Smith, *supra* note 38, at 15. In 1980, only six international law firms had been listed, including Baker & McKenzie and Kirkwood, Kaplan from the U.S. and none from Canada.

159. Smith, *supra* note 38, at 17.

160. Smith, *supra* note 38, at 17.

161. Solicitors and barristers in Hong Kong generally perform the same functions as in England. For an overview of the legal profession in Hong Kong, *see* M. Sandor, "The Legal Profession," in Raymond Wacks ed. *The Future of the Law in Hong Kong*, Hong Kong; Oxford University Press (1989) p. 219.

162. A. E. W. Conner, "Debate Heats up on Proposal to Allow Foreign Law Firms to Hire Hong Kong Lawyers," East Asian Executive Reports, Nov. 1988, at 14.

163. *See* Cone, *supra* note 4 at 75. Foreign lawyers must obtain visas from the Director of Immigration, Note, "Are Large Law Firms Legal?" 17 *Hong Kong Law Journal* 188, 191 (1987) (authored by Michael A. Olesnicky), who requires that their law firms obtain permission from the Law Society before he will grant visas to the individual lawyers. Cone, *supra* note 4 at 75. The Law Society accepts applications from firms, not individual lawyers. Id.

164. Cone cites The Law Society of Hong Kong, "Foreign Law Firms Establishing Themselves in Hong Kong: Guidelines to Applicants."

165. The Law Society of Hong Kong, *supra* note 164 at para. 2, as quoted in Cone.

166. Conner, *supra* note 162, at 15. A foreign lawyer can either qualify as a solicitor in the United Kingdom and apply for what has been effectively automatic admission in Hong Kong, or complete a limited enrollment, one-year certificate program followed by a two-year articled clerkship. Id. Note that the provision in Section 27(1)(e) of the Legal Practitioners Ordinance that an applicant seeking to practice as a barrister must have been "ordinarily resident in Hong Kong for a period of at least eight consecutive months immediately prior

to the date of his application for admission" or satisfy the court "that he intends to be ordinarily resident in the colony" has been interpreted narrowly to deny admission to a British barrister in at least one case. *Re John Caldwell Beveridge QC*, HCt, MP No 603 of 1981. Barristers admitted in the United Kingdom with at least five years experience can practice as solicitors in Hong Kong after passing one examination. Cone, *supra* note 4, at 73. However, non-Commonwealth citizens ordinarily cannot qualify until they have been resident in Hong Kong for seven years. Id. The Law Society may be concerned about lawyers from throughout the European Community seeking admission as British solicitors after the European Community Directive on Mutual Recognition of Professional Qualifications enters into force in 1990 or 1991. Sandor, "The Legal Profession," *supra* note 161, at 224 n. 18 (citing "Law Society Strategy 1988/89" (1988) 85 *Law Society Gazette*).

167. Case Note, *Re Nicolas Dusan Bratza*, HCt, MP No 2526 of 1985, 16 Hong Kong Law Journal 420, 423 (1986) (Malcolm Merry).

168. *Id.* A 1986 decision of the high court refusing admission of junior counsel from England with special expertise for a particular case involving a building dispute signalled a stricter approach to the ad hoc admission of junior counsel, by contrast to admission of Queen's Counsel. Note, *Bratza, supra* note 167, at 422. The determination of the public interest with respect to the admission of Queen's Counsel involves the weighing of several factors, including the encouragement of a strong local Bar, the desirability of importing specialized skills, the financial and legal interests of the client and the views of solicitors. *Id.*, citing *Re the applications of Simon Goldblatt QC and John Uff QC* (1985) HCt, MP Nos 1196 and 1213 of 1985. The court held that the public interest requires a strong and independent local bar, which requires that local counsel should be briefed in preference to London counsel even if the local skill and experience available is not of the standard which would be available in England. Note *Bratza, supra* note 167, at 420. A commentator remarked that this "sounds uncomfortably like an import ban on overseas counsel because they are, or may be, better." Note, *Bratza, supra* note 167, at 424.

169. Cone, *supra* note 4 at 76. A critic of the location of this power in the Law Society comments that the "restrictions [on the practice of foreign law firms], enforced through the granting of work permits to employees of such firms, are imposed in the public interest, but there is no public knowledge or approval of them....In effect this scheme grants legislative authority to the Law Society...." Editorial, "Law-making by Strings and Mirrors," 12 *Hong Kong Law Journal* 257, 259 (1982).

Foreign law firms operating in Hong Kong apparently are in technical violation of legislation intended to safeguard the territory from triads, political organizations, and other groups which threaten the "peace, welfare or good order." Olesnicky, *supra* note 163, at 188. The Hong Kong practice of a foreign partnership would be illegal under the Societies Ordinance, Cap. 151, LHK (1982) unless conducted through a separate partnership of no more than twenty partners. Olesnicky, *supra* note 163, at 191.

170. Cone, *supra* note 4 at 76-77. Cone cites The Law Society guidelines and

Form of Undertaking Addressed to The Law Society of Hong Kong. Note that this restriction is imposed by The Law Society, as advising on either Hong Kong or foreign law does not constitute unauthorized practice under the Legal Practitioners Ordinance. Cone at 74.

171. Arbitration (Amendment) (No. 2) Ordinance 1989, Part IA, Sections 2F and 2G.

172. Donald T. MacNaughton, "Arbitrating International Disputes in Hong Kong," *East Asian Executive Reports*, Oct. 15, 1990, at 9.

173. Id.

174. Conner, *supra* note 162 at 15.

175. Laws of Hong Kong, cap 159.

176. S. Jones, "Hong Kong Proposes Guidelines to Allow Law Firms from Abroad to Hire Locally," *Wall Street Journal*, May 5, 1989, at B-5A; Conner, *supra* note 162 at 14-15. In a 1988 petition to the Governor, seven American firms asked for a simplified admissions procedure (on a motion to the high court) for American lawyers and the right to hire or take as partners locally qualified solicitors. *Id.*; M. Thompson, "Hong Kong Bar Fights Proposal by U.S. Firms," *Daily Journal*, p. 1, June 15, 1989; C. Morton, "Hong Kong Lawyers Face the Future," *International Financial Law Review*, Nov. 1989, at 11, 12-13. The first demand was rejected by the Chief Justice's Committee in January 1988, but the government agreed to push a new law in response to the second demand. M. Sandor, "The Legal Profession," *supra* note 161 at 224, n. 20; M. Thompson, "Hong Kong Bar Fights Proposal by U.S. Firms," *Los Angeles Daily Journal*, June 15, 1989, at 1. The seven law firms are Coudert Brothers, Dorsey & Whitney; Gibson, Dunn & Crutcher; Jones, Day, Reavis & Pogue; Kaye, Scholer, Fierman, Hays & Handler; Paul, Weiss, Rifkind, Wharton & Garrison; and White & Case. The Law Society, at least initially, vehemently opposed the proposal, citing threats to the independence and ethical standards of the profession, but apparently motivated by economic reasons. Conner, *supra* note 162, at 15-17. Both sides have used the tactic of evoking fears about China, especially in the wake of the 1989 crackdown on political dissent. Thompson, "Hong Kong Bar," at 1. Unfortunately, the timing of the government's announcement seemed to indicate that it had capitulated to the American law firms' threat to seek action on any further rejection as a restraint of trade contrary to GATT. Sandor, "The Legal Profession," at 224; Thompson, "Hong Kong Bar," at 11. Interestingly, Morrison & Foerster declined to join the law firms who petitioned the governor, in part because its resident partner did not perceive the situation in Hong Kong as a free trade problem, in contrast to Japan. Thompson, "Hong Kong Bar," at 11.

177. "Law; American Firms in Hong Kong," *Wall Street Journal*, Aug. 2, 1990, at B2, col. 6.

178. Conner, *supra* note 162 at 15. The Law Society does not object to these proposals. Morton, "Hong Kong Lawyers," *supra* note 176, at 11, 12.

179. *Id.* at 12-13 (quoting Hong Kong Attorney General Jeremy Matthews).

180. "Law; American Firms in Hong Kong," *supra* note 177 at B-2.

181. "Law; American Firms in Hong Kong," *supra* note 177, at B2.

182. *See* Martindale-Hubbell International Law Directory, 1991.

183. *See* Martindale-Hubbell International Law Directory, 1991. *Compare* Morton, *supra* note 176 at 12, (observing that most of the American firms are West Coast based because of the enormous Hong Kong investment in that region).

184. The number is taken by count from Martindale-Hubbell, 1991. Morton, *supra* note 176 at 12, gives a number of nineteen.

185. Morton, *supra* note 176, at 12. In 1989, an estimated C$280m per month flowed into Vancouver. Id.

186. In 1985, Martindale-Hubbell listed thirteen American firms, ten English firms, three Canadian, and one Philippine. In 1980, five American firms, five English firms, and one Canadian were listed.

187. Thomas, "The Leading Euromarket Law Firms in Hong Kong and Singapore," *International Financial Law Rev.* June 1983, at 4.

188. Thompson, "Hong Kong Bar," *Supra* note 176 at 1.

189. Thomas, *supra* note 187 at 5.

190. Thomas, *supra* note 187 at 5–6. For example, the New York firm of Milbank, Tweed, Hadley, & McCloy followed Chase Manhattan to Hong Kong in the late 1970s. Chase used Coudert Brothers in Singapore, where Milbank, Tweed was not established [as of 1983]. Chemical Bank used Cravath Swaine & Moore, Cleary, Gottlieb, Steen & Hamilton, and Coudert Brothers in New York, but chose Milbank, Tweed as its principal law firm in Hong Kong after shopping around. Id.

191. J. Altschul, "U.S. Firms Pulling Out of Hong Kong," *Legal Times,* Nov. 19, 1990, at 12, col. 1.

192. Altschul, *supra* note 191 at 12.

193. Thomas, *supra* note 187 at 7. The two oldest associations include the largest Hong Kong firms: Linklaters & Paines with Deacons, and Norton, Rose, Botterell & Roche with Johnson, Stokes & Master. Id.

194. Altschul, *supra* note 191 at 12; G. Stricharchuk and A. D. Marcus, "Law: Hong Kong Practices of some U.S. Law Firms Prove Disappointing," *Wall Street Journal,* June 19, 1990, at B8. The two firms merged their Beijing offices and affiliated with an Indonesian firm, Hanfiah Soeharto Ponggawa. Altschul at 12.

195. *Id.*

196. Thompson, "Hong Kong Bar," *supra* note 188 at 11 (quoting Simon Ip). *See also* Stricharchuk and Marcus, *supra* note 194 at B8.

197. Altschul, *supra* note 191 at 12.

198. Altschul, *supra* note 191 at 12.

199. Morton, *supra* note 176 at 11; *see also* Altschul, *supra* note 191 at 12. Simpson, Thacher also closed its Singapore office. Labaton, *supra* note 1.

200. Altschul, *supra* note 191, at 12.

201. Morton, *supra* note 176 at 14; M. Thompson, "U.S. Lawyers in Hong Kong Sad, Hopeful," *Daily Journal,* p. 1, June 8, 1989; Altschul, *supra* note 19 at 12. The London firm of Allen & Overy also opened an office in 1989. Morton at 14.

202. Forte, "Barriers," *supra* note 26 at 9.

203. *See, e.g.,* Altschul, *supra* note 191 at 12.

204. Altschul, *supra* note 191 at 12.

205. Altschul, *supra* note 191 at 12.

206. Altschul, *supra* note 191 at 12.

207. Smith, *supra* note 38 at 17.

208. *Id.*

209. Thompson, "U.S. Lawyers in Hong Kong," *supra* note 201 at 1.

210. The Chinese government had restrained foreign investment to control inflation and developing imbalances in the economy accompanying rapid growth in some regions, such as the southern provinces adjacent to Hong Kong. Thompson, "U.S. Lawyers in Hong Kong," *supra* note 201 at 24.

211. Thompson, "U.S. Lawyers in Hong Kong" at 24.

212. *See* Morton, *supra* note 176 at 12; Thompson, "U.S. Lawyers in Hong Kong," *supra* note 201 at 24.

213. Thompson, "U.S. Lawyers in Hong Kong," *supra* note 201 at 24.

214. Altschul, *supra* note 191 at 12.

215. Altschul, *supra* note 191 at 12.

216. Morton, *supra* note 176 at 11.

217. Morton, *supra* note 176 at 13 (observing that the biggest problem to date has been a "brain drain" rather than a capital drain). *See also* Smith, *supra* note 38 at S. 17.

218. P. Wesley-Smith, "The Future Development of Hong Kong Law," *Law Institute Journal*, June 1990, at 521.

219. For an overview of the Malaysian legal system and profession, *see* A. Ibrahim and A. Joned *The Malaysian Legal System* Kuala Lumpur, Dewan Bahasa den Pustaka (1987).

220. J. S. H. Skrine, "Malaysia," in *Transnational Legal Practice, supra* note 4 at 245, 251-252. *See id.* for text of selected provisions of the Legal Profession Act and discussion of qualifications for admission to the Malaysian Bar.

221. Skrine, *supra* note 220, at 255-256.

222. Id.

223. Skrine, *supra* note 220, at 249-250. This Section was added to the Act in 1977 for the purpose of assuring that an accused could find counsel willing to represent him, and apparently no person has been admitted through this mechanism. Id.

224. P. Mooney, "Representation in Arbitrations in Malaysia and Singapore," [1989] *Malayan L. J.* cvii, cviii (Dec. 15, 1989). Concerned by the Singapore High Court's interpretation of an essentially identical Legal Profession Act to bar foreign lawyers from arbitration proceedings, the Bar Council of the State of Malaya sought a ruling by the High Court in Kuala Lumpur in the case of an American attorney seeking to assist in cross examination in an arbitration between a Malaysian company and a German company. Mooney, at cviii; *Zublin Muhibbah Joint Venture v. Government of Malaysia*, [1990] 3 *Malayan Law Journal* 125, 126 (1990). The Court held that the American attorney need not apply for ad hoc admission in order to appear as an advocate because there was no necessity for him to be an admitted advocate and solicitor in order to make such an appearance. Mooney, at cviii. The Singapore case is discussed below.

225. Skrine, *supra* note 220, at 257.

226. Skrine, *supra* note 220, at 256.

227. Skrine, *supra* note 220, at 256.

228. *Skrine,* supra note 220, at 255, 256. *See* Section 38(1)(g) of the Legal Profession Act.

229. For an overview of the legal profession in Singapore, see Boo King Ong, "The Structure of the Legal Profession," in Walter Woon ed.,*The Singapore Legal System*, 277-289 (Singapore: Longman 1989).

230. Cone, *supra* note 4, at 102-103; Thomas, *supra* note 187, at 7.

231. Cone, *supra* note 4, at 102-103.

232. Cone, *supra* note 4, at 102-103.

233. Thomas, *supra* note 187, at 7. Two of Hong Kong's largest law firms were refused entry. Id.

234. Cone, *supra* note 4, at 102.

235. Cone, *supra* note 4, at 102.

236. Cone, *supra* note 4, at 103.

237. "Singapore: Easing Restrictions on Foreign Lawyers," *East Asian Executive Reports*, Sep. 15, 1984, at 6. Attorneys from Hong Kong could not practice independently unless they had either resided in Singapore for one year and practiced with a local attorney for two years, or had been specifically exempted from these conditions by government authorities. Id.

238. The Attorney General did permit the London firm of Freshfields to maintain a local practice by exempting two of its solicitors from the statutory pupillage and examination processes requisite to admission to the Singapore bar. Thomas, *supra* note 187, at 7. Because of subsequent protests by local firms, however, Freshfields will likely be the only foreign firm licensed to practice local law. Thomas, *supra* note 187, at 7.

239. Thomas, *supra* note 187, at 7.

240. *Turner (East Asia) Pte. Ltd. v. Builders Federal (Hong Kong) Ltd. & Anor.*, [1988] 2 *Malayan Law Journal* 280.

241. Mooney, *supra* note 224.

242. Cap. 161 (1985).

243. *Turner*, *supra* note 240.

244. D. Rivkin, "Keeping Lawyers Out of International Arbitrations," *International Financial Law Review*, Feb. 1990, at 11, 12.

245. Thomas, *supra* note 187, at 4; "Foreign Lawyers Admitted to Aid Financial Community," *East Asian Executive Reports*, July 15, 1980, at 9.

246. Thomas, *supra* note 187, at 4.

247. Thomas, *supra* note 187, at 4.

248. There was no listing for Singapore in 1985, and the only foreign law firms listed in 1980 were Coudert Brothers and Graham James.

249. Thomas, *supra* note 187, at 4.

250. Labaton, *supra* note 1, at D20.

251. Thomas, *supra* note 187, at 7. For example, Lee & Lee have a close association with Norton, Rose, Botterell, & Roche. Id.

252. Thomas, *supra* note 187, at 7.

253. Thomas, *supra* note 187, at 7. These firms are Lee & Lee, Drew & Napier, Allen & Gledhill, and Shook Lin & Bok.

254. For a description of the practice of law and the regulation of lawyers in China, *see* H. Zheng, "The Evolving Role of Lawyers and Legal Practice in China," 36 *Amer. J. Comp. Law* 473 (1988).

255. Civil Procedure Law of the People's Republic of China (for trial use) promulgated on 8 March 1982 by the 22d Session of the Standing Committee of the Fifth National People's Congress, CCH Australia, *China Laws for Foreign Business* para. 19-200, art. 191 [As cited by Zheng. p. 473]

256. C. Oechsli, "Regulating Foreign Lawyers in China," Vol. I, ALP 2, March 6, 1989, at 35. (Oechsli is with McCutchen, Doyle, Brown & Enersen in Shanghai). This Circular is probably the same as a law promulgated in March 1982.

257. Oechsli, *supra* note 256, at 36.

258. Oechsli, *supra* note 256, at 36.

259. Oechsli, *supra* note 256, at 36. Oechsli could not confirm whether the proposed rules would allow joint ventures or other permanent office arrangements between Chinese and foreign lawyers. Id.

260. Oechsli, *supra* note 256, at 36.

261. Oechsli, *supra* note 256, at 36.

262. Oechsli, *supra* note 256, at 36.

263. Oechsli, *supra* note 256, at 35-36.

264. One German firm was listed in the 1991 Martindale-Hubbell directory.

265. F. Butterfield, "Law Firms Capitalize on China Trade Boom," *New York Times*, Oct. 25, 1981, at 30.

266. F. Ching, "Peking Restricts Foreign Legal Firms, Dealing Setback to Some U.S. Lawyers," *Wall Street Journal*, Jan. 8, 1982, at 26.

267. One report was that these firms were still fully staffed. E. Adams, "U.S. Lawyers in China: Slower Business Makes Some Put Off Expansion," *National Law Journal*, Oct. 23, 1989, at 24. *Compare*, however, J. Boatman, "International Reactions: Diplomatic and Commercial," *East Asian Executive Reports*, June 15, 1989, at 6 (reporting in early June, 1989, that "foreign law firms have gone for now," noting that Paul, Weiss and Baker & McKenzie moved their China based attorneys to Hong Kong, and that in many cases Chinese staff were keeping the offices nominally open).

Paul, Weiss and Heller, Ehrman did not list China offices in the 1991 Martindale-Hubbell directory. Two recent additions in that directory are Buxbaum & Choy (apparently a partnership of David C. Buxbaum of New York) and Rice, Fowler, Kingsmill, Bance, Flint & Booth.

268. E. Adams, "Two Years Later, Firms Are Back in China," *National Law Journal*, June 17, 1991, at 27.

269. "Law Firms Join Together for PRC Rep Office," *International Lawyers' Newsletter*, Vol. X, No. 1, 1988, p. 3.

270. Young, *supra* note 44, at 21 (quoting Isaac Shapiro, Partner, Skadden, Arps, Slate, Meagher, & Flom).

271. Cone, *supra* note 4, at 61.

272. E. Felsenthal and W. Lambert, "Chinese Province Appoints U.S. Lawyer as Legal Representative," *Wall Street Journal*, May 31, 1990, at B-11, col. 3.

273. Jill Abramson, "Firm Puts on its Thinking Cap to Win Trade Battle for Chinese," *Wall Street Journal*, May 15, 1989, at 5.

274. T. Lewin, "Outside Ventures Transform Law Firms," *New York Times*, Feb. 11, 1987, at D-1.

275. Cone, *supra* note 4, at 61.

276. "Arbitration Rules Amended," *Int'l Fin'l Law Rev.*, June 1989, at 46. China has proposed drafting a separate arbitration law in the near future. *Id.*

5

The Growth of the Bar and the Changes in the Lawyer's Role: Korea's Dilemma

Kyong Whan Ahn

Introduction

The Korean legal community is struggling over a critical question: to increase or not to increase the number of lawyers. For the last several years no single issue has more haunted the entire Korean legal world than the optimal size of the bar. In the last fifteen years, the number of lawyers in active practice has tripled, from 811 in 1977 to 2,568 in 1993.[1] Every year approximately 150 new lawyers are expected to join the bar. Such a sharp increase in lawyers has been accompanied by many problems, some expected, others totally unexpected. This paper is an overview of the new phenomena that have accompanied the numerical growth of the Korean bar over the last fifteen years.

The next section discusses the pros and cons of the growth of the bar which have been vehemently asserted by two sharply divided proponents: the legal establishment and the academics. A further section introduces the changes in the role of lawyers in recent years. The author argues that such changes were primarily caused by the numerical expansion of the bar. Throughout the entire paper the author maintains the position that Korea critically needs a larger bar.

Too Many Lawyers?

The only practical path to becoming a licensed attorney in Korea is to pass the National Judiciary Examination[2] run by the government.[3] Successful candidates must complete a two years' training course at the Judicial Research and Training Institute (hereinafter referred to as the

"Institute") before qualifying as a lawyer (*Byun Ho Sa*).[4] This examination has been almost a myth to Koreans. It has been a symbol of opportunity, fairness and intellectual achievement. The myth was further solidified by its almost prohibitive pass rate —less than a few percent.[5]

A Copernican revolution took place in 1981. The Korean government broadened this narrow footpath to a public boulevard. Without any public hearing or equivalent open discussion, the government announced its decision to set the new yearly quota for the entering class of the Institute at 300.[6] This figure was astronomical to Korean legal society which had been so accustomed to a family-sized, exclusive monopoly on the practice of law. On the other hand, this drastic decision, although tainted by the arguable legitimacy of the deciding body,[7] was generally accepted by the public as a "democratic" measure, as it paved a way for easier access to a legal career. Ever since its inception, this democratic measure has been constantly criticized by the legal establishment, and as the fear of losing a restricted market becomes a reality, a systematic movement has been launched to reduce the quota to a "practical" number. Typical are the recommendations and declarations issued by legal institutions such as the Korean Bar Association, the Office of Judicial Administration and the Ministry of Justice.[8]

The rationales given by these institutions may be summarized as follows. First, this number simply exceeds the demand for legal services. They point to the fact that the yearly demand for judges, public prosecutors and military attorneys, for which the graduates of the Institute are qualified, is no more than 100.[9] This argument, however, does not merit serious discussion. It is based on the assumption that the Institute is a preparatory school for judges and public prosecutors. The assumption may have been justified up to 1980, for then private law practice came at the conclusion of one's legal career. The unrebutted convention and practice were that one engaged in private practice only after considerable service as a judge or public prosecutor. Under such circumstances one can agree that the judiciary examination was equivalent to an employment examination for a judge or public prosecutor, at least in the short term. However, Queen Anne is dead! For present purposes, the Institute is a training school for attorneys as well as for judges and public prosecutors. Annually at least 150 new graduates of the Institute choose (or are forced to choose) private practice as their initial legal career. Therefore, this cannot be a persuasive reason for limiting the numbers passing the bar.[10]

Their second argument concerns quality of legal service. They claim that, as a consequence of "mass production," the quality of the bar has been so impaired that there is serious potential for malpractice.[11] To support this argument they draw attention to two recent incidents in which three young attorneys were arrested for "ambulance-chasing" in violation of the relevant statutes.[12] However, this argument is defective in two respects. First, the intellectual quality of those taking the examination recently (mostly college graduates with a law degree) is becoming ever higher. All the statistics show that at every university, with rare exceptions, the law department is the most popular and hardest to enter. Every year only the best qualified 6,000 students out of approximately 200,000 are admitted to the law departments of 65 universities.[13] The quality of law school education has been substantially improved during the last decade. For example, the total number of law faculty doubled to 677 by December, 1992.[14] Every consideration negates the claim that the best 300 law students are sub-standard. A more basic problem is the adequacy of the bar examination in assessing the quality of the prospective jurist. As one foreign observer has sarcastically but correctly pointed out, the Korean bar examination may be characterized as a system of "meritocracy of memory."[15] In Korea, an extreme emphasis on rote memorization discourages those taking the examination from building up any integrated vision of law.[16] Aside from this rather fundamental suspicion, the statistics of the bar examinations indicate that there is very little, if any, discernible difference in numerical scores among the successful 300.[17] Secondly, in Korea malpractice is more a matter of legal ethics than professional intellect. Therefore, post facto disciplinary measures, not prior numerical restraint, should be the prime remedy against malpractice.

The third argument of those in favor of reducing the quota is relevant to understanding the basic goal of legal education in universities. They define the fundamental character of Korean law schools as institutions for general education, not professional legal education,[18] and argue that for the sake of an adequate distribution of human resources, law school graduates should be encouraged to take jobs of a non-legal nature. They claim that widening the door to the bar in fact narrows students' career choices. It entices many "hopeless" examinees, who could succeed in other fields, to hold on a futile dream, thereby causing a disastrous waste of human resources.[19] This argument is equally defective. First, it is true that the Korean law school is not a professional school in the American sense. Still, it has some of the significant characteristics of a professional school. A student is required to take three years' education in law in addition to one year of education in general subjects.[20] Any law school graduate, therefore, is most naturally expected and entitled to capitalize on their legal education in legal practice. Although diversity in employment for law graduates is to be encouraged, this does not serve as a valid reason to discourage taking the orthodox route. The argument of "false expectation" is too trivial for serious consideration. From the beginning, there have been numerous "hopeless" repeaters. The Bar examination in Korea is, as I have mentioned, almost a myth. It is the best known way of realizing the "Korean Dream." No formal schooling is required before taking the examination. In theory, any Korean may legitimately take up the challenge, and on the rare occasions when "no schoolers" do succeed, intensive media coverage dramatizes their sagas. Under such circumstances, mass production of hopeless repeaters is inevitable. If prevention of the waste of human resources is a real issue, some other direct means should be employed. The most effective would be to implement a "strikeout system", by limiting the number of times one can take the examination.

Their fourth argument has some substance. This is that the legal market is already over-supplied. As a partial justification, they emphasize the unique nature of legal practice in Korea. Traditionally much of the non-litigious legal work has been handled not by lawyers, but by so-called "quasi-lawyers."[2] The patent agent (*Byun Ri Sa*), tax agent (*Se Mu Sa*), judiciary agent (*Bop Mu Sa*, formerly called *Sa Bop Soe Sa*, literally "legal scrivener"), administrative scriveners (*Haeng Jong So Sa*), and labor agent (*No Mu Sa*) are prime examples of these. There are over 6,000 of these quasi-lawyers.[22] Further, in many companies legal matters are dealt with entirely by their in-house legal departments composed of non-lawyers. They also claim that many recent Institute graduates are unemployed or underpaid, and there is an imminent threat of serious unemployment among lawyers.[23]

While the first part of this argument has some validity, it is partly the bar's own fault. They confine themselves to the traditional types of criminal and civil cases, and neither possess the professional knowledge required in these fields nor desire to explore unaccustomed fields. In terms of both practical knowledge and accessibility, these quasi-lawyers can offer a far better service to the public.[24] In one sense, this means that lawyers feel no necessity to explore the non-traditional fields of legal practice. Most lawyers are well off with their income from civil and criminal litigation. Fees for litigations are incomparably high, and there is no reason for extra effort in return for much lower fees.

The second part of this argument depends on the level of income to which society agrees that lawyers are entitled. There is no single reported incident of a "jobless" lawyer. Some may have trouble in being hired by a law firm, or in running their own office in Seoul. However, no lawyer is indigent. Disappointment comes mainly from the unreasonably high expectation of financial remuneration. Starting salaries at the first class law firms are disproportionately high compared with other occupations. Smaller sized firms also pay substantial salaries to their rookie associates. It is undisputed that even a novice lawyer is paid more than a director(*I Sa*) of a top-ranked company with a twenty year career.

In any case, there have always been alternative ways of working as a lawyer. Many companies would be glad to have in-house counsel, as long as their demands are not unreasonably high. For those having trouble in working in Seoul, local practice is an alternative guaranteeing high income and reputation. From the perspective of the general public, lawyers are definitely overpaid.[25]

Besides these arguments, the Ministry of Justice has raised a peculiar argument, which I take the liberty of calling the "Karl Marx argument." It claims that many "dissident lawyers" are the by-products of the desperate competition among Institute graduates, and it is therefore desirable to take preventative measures to avoid the production of these "undesirable" dissident lawyers.[26] Their reasoning is that these young civil rights lawyers are unsuccessful applicants for jobs as judges or public prosecutors. It seems to be based on the assumption that unemployment among intellectuals is the prime cause of social disturbances.[27] Whatever the justification for such an idiosyncratic attitude may be, it cannot be a persuasive reason for curtailing the legitimate exercise of the constitutional right of Institute graduates to freely choose a lawful occupation and to challenge governmental action in a lawful manner.

The proponents of the continuing growth of the bar are mostly academics. In 1984, the Korean Law College Association gave its official view in the form of a recommendation to the government.[28] In opposing the reduction of the annual quota, it went one step further. It claimed that the door to the Institute should be widened so as to allow at least 600 people to pass yearly.[29] Arguments in support of a larger bar have been presented by many academics in their individual capacities as well.[30] Their reasoning has been discussed in in the context of the opposing views above. To repeat, however, the gist can be summarized under two classifications—philosophical and practical. Their philosophical ground is democratization of the society cannot be achieved without the systematic guarantee of fair competition in legal services. Practically, they emphasize that from the consumer's point of view, all the statistics favor a larger bar.[31]

New Patterns of Practice

My argument in this section is that the increase in the size of the bar has already led to changes in the patterns of legal practice which benefit consumers and increase social justice. The changes are in the growth of law firms to serve commercial needs, the spread of local practice outside metropolitan areas and the development of non-traditional areas of practice.

Law Firms

One distinctive pattern of legal practice that has flourished since 1980 is the law firm. Until 1980, only a few "firms" existed in Korea. It was not until 1982 that the law officially recognized the "law firm" (*Bommu BopIn*) as an independent legal entity.[32] As of March, 1993, there are 37 law firms with 206 lawyers in Korea; 26 firms with 151 lawyers are concentrated in Seoul.[33] A decided majority of these firms specialize in international transactions, as did the pioneer ones in the 1970s. In most cases, the clients of these "international law firms" are limited to big companies, including foreign ones. These firms typically consist of a few partners, junior partners, and associates. The senior partners are the founders of the firm, who in most cases have licenses from both the Korean Bar and at least one jurisdiction of the United States. These founding partners have some experience in the Korean judiciary either as judges or public prosecutors. Junior partners may be regarded as the product of the expanded bar, and the associates undisputedly are. The junior partners are either promoted from among the associates after considerable years of work, or invited from outside for their potential contribution to the firm.

In the first case, they would have been given the opportunity for a foreign education and training as a part of their work. Not all the firms have junior partners. In smaller sized firms, one founding partner directly controls the associates. Associates are recruited from among the recent graduates of the Institute. Disproportionately high salaries with various fringe benefits work as an incentive for the young Institute graduates who are interested in international practice. These firms also hire a substantial number of foreign lawyers, sometimes purely for their linguistic capacity.

Until recently, students and laborers sharply criticized these international law firms for their "anti-patriotic" and "anti-populistic" activities. In a sense, such criticism may be unfair. As long as their foreign corporate clients rely on the procedures of favorable Korean laws, including labor laws, they had no alternative. The same may have been true in the case of domestic corporate clients. Anyway, from the standpoints of the corporate clients, these law firms are valuable partners.

Only a few firms deal with purely domestic, non-commercial cases. Civil rights cases, labor cases, and small claims cases are the usual kinds of cases they handle. Commonly these are run by young lawyers sympathetic with the causes of the social underdogs. The pioneer of such firms was founded by a well known former student activist and has survived his premature death.[34]

Legal practice in the form of a firm could not have been expected to flourish without the consistent supply of young lawyers. Law firm practice is largely a product of the recent numerical growth of the Korean bar.

Local Practice

As of March 1993, 88 percent of lawyers are in active practice in the Seoul Special City and five Direct Control Cities (Pusan, Taegu, Kwangju, Taejon, Inchon).[35] The proportion of metropolitan practice becomes 94 percent if the provincial capitals are included.[36] These rates, seemingly disproportionately high enough, have remained unchanged for the last ten years. Until recently, there were many cities with courts that had no lawyers. Even today, there are a few. Although the rates of local practice have remained extremely low, there is one positive sign. The number of lawyers in local practice is increasing. Considering the fact that local population has actually been decreasing, the increase in the number of attorneys in local practice has helped considerably to remedy the decided imbalance of legal service between the metropolitan areas and the local cities. This is further supported by the sharp increase in the total number of attorneys in recent years. Having maintained the same rate of local practice, however low, does indicate that a significant change has happened in the pattern of legal practice.

Local practice guarantees financial success, even for a novice lawyer. And, it can serve as a valuable stepping stone towards national politics, the fundamental goal of many young lawyers. It may be a legitimate dream for a young attorney from that locality to become a politician. A resident lawyer is a great source of pride for many small cities, and the pride may easily turn into affection when the lawyer has local origins. There are instances where relatively young lawyers have been elected to the National Assembly after a brief period of local practice.

Recently quite a few young lawyers have set up their offices in the local cities. Without exception, they have made an economic success within the shortest period of time. This supports the claim that there is a market in the locality, where a Korean lawyer can be assured of deeper pocket. Local practice is a definitely new phenomenon for young lawyers. In the past, it was something that they never dreamt of at the beginning of their legal career. In a sense, it was a forced choice. The choice was motivated by survival instincts and market analysis of comparative advantage. The choice, however, turned out to be right, for themselves as well as for their communities.

New Areas of Practice

The basic character of the traditional legal work of a Korean lawyer may be defined as remedial. Litigation comprises almost all the work. Preventive legal practice (roughly classified as "general practice of law" under the Attorneys' Act[37]) has been almost abandoned. Litigation for the recovery of money or involving real property are the two major types of civil litigation handled by Korean lawyers.

On the criminal side, petitions for *habeas corpus*, suspended sentence or probation are the most popular patterns of legal practice, because they guarantee the attorneys maximum income with minimum effort. This is mainly attributable to the almost hysterical fear of physical incarceration prevalent among Koreans.[38] From the sad experience when the authoritarian regimes abused their powers with every kind of violence, Koreans now accept a cardinal commandment—"Use every means to get yourself out. Forget about Money."

In recent years there have been considerable changes in the nature of the legal work handled by Korean attorneys. On the government side, the long-pursued idea of legal aid has become a reality. In 1987 the Korean Legal Aid Corporation was founded under the Legal Aid Act of 1986.[39] The Corporation, established with government funds, hires young lawyers, although only a limited number, as its full-time staff. This is something unprecedented in the history of Korea. The Corporation was the first governmental institution which ever hired lawyers for their professional capacity. Thus, although still at a primitive stage, the Corporation has paved one alternative form of legal practice for the brand-new lawyers. Until recently, it was impractical, if not impossible, for a public institution to hire a staff attorney. Salaries for civil servants were simply too low to entice someone from this privileged occupation. However its noble ideas might have appealed to young lawyers, the Corporation could not have recruited its legal staff had "young lawyers" not been available at all, as was the Korean situation before the 1980s.

During the 1980s many non-traditional areas of legal practice have been explored by young lawyers. Labor cases, consumer law cases, civil rights cases are some of the prime examples. The exploration was accelerated partly through the political democratization of Korea since 1987. Traditionally labor law had been largely a matter of academic principles. Labor laws were heavily criticized for their unrealistically high goals and standards. As economic progress made the provisions workable principles, workers' claims surged. Although occasionally their claims were expressed by more violent means, workers did not totally disregard the authority of legal institutions. Lawyers played decisive roles in keeping labor claims within the ball park of the law. The law of industrial accidents and workmen's compensation is the area where attorneys' services have conspicuously improved. This was possible owing to the dedicated efforts of a few young attorneys.

Consumer law cases had been largely neglected by the lawyers. Consumer law itself was not mature enough for the public to rely on. The economic stakes were too trivial to attract lawyers. In the recent years, some lawyers have been heavily involved in this area of law, with the support of many citizens' movement groups.

The term, "civil rights lawyer" in Korea generally indicates those lawyers who actively defend political dissidents. The name originated in the 1970s when the authoritarian government suppressed the legitimate claims of the people. Claimants for rights often ended up as political prisoners. Even the judiciary did not enjoy full independence. There were only a few lawyers who argued, instead of merely pleading for mercy, for these political defendants. There was an instance when the defending counsel of the dissident students was imprisoned for his oral defense contemptuous of the military tribunal set up under martial law. From this background, the term "civil rights lawyer" carries to Korean minds an overtone of "righteous fighter".

In May, 1988, 51 lawyers organized a group under the banner of "Lawyers' Group for the Achievement of Democratic Society" (commonly called "*Min-Byun*").[40] Led by the pioneer civil rights lawyers of the 1970s, the Group launched its systematic activities for the full "democratization" of Korea. However, their activities were not confined to litigation for specific clients. They included preventive measures aimed at educating the general public. The Group held a series of public debates, issued statements and declarations on important legal and political issues, and published much informative material.[41] This group has emerged as one of the biggest pressure groups in the modern history of Korea. As of March, 1993, it possessed

225 lawyer members.[42] Three quarters of them are recent graduates of the Institute, who chose (or were forced to choose) initial legal careers as attorneys.These young lawyers are playing an active role in raising many issues which had been resignedly regarded as belonging to the "realm of politics." At its 1992 Annual Convention, the Seoul District Bar Association elected a core member of *Min-Byun* as its new President for a two year term. This is something phenomenal in Korean history. It may be regarded as a public recognition of their past contribution to the political democratization of the nation.

This group could not have functioned as effectively as it did, had there not been an adequate supply of young lawyers.

Conclusion

Many writers have argued that traditionally Korea has been a non-litigious society. Conciliation and mediation were far more the preferred and prevalent form of settling disputes in Korea, they argue.[43] It is not the intention of the author to raise a counter argument in this paper. Suffice it to say, for present purposes, that it is no longer true. Floods of legal disputes are attacking the Korean courts and other quasi-judicial institutions.[44] Judges are constantly complaining of overwork. A great majority of the disputes are disposed of without representation by a lawyer. On the civil side, the rate of *pro se* litigation exceeds 59 percent,[45] and the records on the criminal side is even worse.[46] In cases where public defense is available, the quality of defense is notoriously poor.[47]

Even so-called "Alternative Dispute Resolution" comes within the legal monopoly of the lawyers. Korean law prohibits non-lawyers from assisting others in their legal disputes in return for monetary remuneration.[48]

Regardless of what the prime method of disputes resolution may be, litigation or other alternative means, Korea needs more lawyers. The number of disputes is skyrocketing. This trend is irreversible. No other occupation can legitimately and effectively resolve legal disputes. Only lawyers can. Korea desperately needs a bigger bar.

Notes

1. The total number of licensed lawyers in Korea has increased as follows:

	Number of Licensed Lawyers		
Year	*Active Status*	*Inactive Status*	*Total*
1993(Mar.)	2,568	705	3,268
1991(June)	2,212	735	2,947
1990(Dec.)	1,984	757	2,741
1988(Dec.)	1,667	779	2,445
1987(Dec.)	1,521	791	2,312
1986	1,414		
1985	1,320		
1984	1,116		
1983	1,098		
1982	1,058		
1981	1,013		
1980	940		
1979	890		
1978	832		
1977	811		

Sources: The Korean Bar Association, 1981–1993; The Judiciary Almanac (*Sa Bop Yon Gam*), 1978–1986.

It is unclear whether the statistics for 1978-86 indicate the total number of licensed lawyers or only those in active status. In this paper an assumption has been made that they indicate the latter.

There were 1,068 judges as of October 1, 1991 and 868 public prosecutors as of August 1, 1992. They are potential lawyers. Including these figures, the total number of licensed lawyers amounts to approximately 5,200: Membership Booklet, The Seoul Bar Association (1993) p. 3; Also see Choi, K.R., "Proposal For Cooperation Between the Academy and the Bar," *The Justice*, Vol. XXIII, No.2 (1990), The Korean Legal Center, pp.53-67.

For an introductory overview of the Korean judiciary and the role of the lawyers, see Song, Sang Hyun ed., *Introduction To The Law And Legal System of Korea*, Kyung Mun Sa Pub. Co., (1983); Yoon, Dae Kyu, *Law and Political Authority In South Korea*, West View Press & Kyung Nam University Press, Seoul(1990) pp.109-149.

2. The other route is serving ten years as a military advocate after passing the Military Advocates' Examination (irregularly conducted: Law Concerning the Recruitment of Military Advocates (Law No. 243, Apr. 24, 1952, as amended on December 31, 1975). The requirements for this examination are substantially the same as those of the Judiciary Examination (*Id.* Article 5). The total number of lawyers produced in this way is not big enough for separate discussion.

3. Doubts have been raised intermittently regarding the adequacy of leaving the administration of the examination under government control. The Supreme Court of Korea has recently claimed jurisdiction in bar examination administration. *Judiciary Policy* (*Sabop Joengchaek Jaryo Jip*), Vol.8, March, 1993, p.7. A similar claim has been made by the Korean Bar Association. *The Law Times(Bop Ryul Shinmun)*, February 20, 1993.

4. This examination is also a prerequisite for a judgeship or a job as public prosecutor.

5. The pass rates for the last 29 years are as follows:

Year	*Number of Applicants*	*Numbers Passing*	*Pass Rates(percent)*
1993	19,441	289	1.5
1992	17,131	288	1.7
1991	16,310	287	1.8
1990	15,041	298	1.9
1989	14,202	300	2.0
1988	14,245	300	2.0
1987	14,963	300	2.0
1986	14,303	300	2.0
1985	11,743	298	2.5
1984	11,600	303	2.6
1983	10,530	300	2.8
1982	9,273	300	3.2
1981	7,983	289	3.6
1980	6,658	141	2.1
1979	5,788	120	2.1
1978	5,387	100	1.9
1977	4,767	80	1.7
1976	4,498	60	1.3
1975	4,119	59	1.4
1974	4,010	60	1.4
1973	4,575	60	1.3
1972	3,507	80	2.2
1971	2,776	81	2.9
1970(Aug.)	2,786	49	1.7
1970(Feb.)	2,561	33	1.2
1969	2,486	34	1.3
1968	2,203	37	1.6
1967(Aug.)	2,005	83	4.1
1967(Feb.)	2,390	5	0.2
1966	1,947	19	0.9
1965	2,263	16	0.7
1964(Aug.)	3,493	22	0.6
1964(Feb.)	3,904	10	0.2
1963(Aug.)	2,411	45	1.8
1963(Feb.)	3,532	41	1.1

From Kosige, November editions (1970-1993). By permission.

6. The relevant provision does not set any fixed number. Instead it leaves it to the decision of the Minister of Government Administration with the advice of the Minister of Justice and the Chief of the Office of Judiciary Administration for each annual examination: Article 3, Order on the Judiciary Examination, Presidential Order 4979, May 5, 1970 as amended by Orders of December 18,1980 and March 14, 1983. Since 1990, a "tacit understanding" has been observed that the number should be between 250 and 300.

7. The decision was made by the Kugga Bowi Ipbop Hoei (Legislative

Committee For the National Protection) which, on its own initiative, assumed the legislative function during the interim period following the assassination of President Park Chung Hee in October,1979. This Committee enacted 188 laws in total, whose validity was later ratified by the Constitution of 1980. Included therein was one giving birth to the Committee itself (Law No. 3260, October 28, 1980).

The most controversial law enacted this way was the National Security Act (Law No.3318, December 31, 1980) which was used primarily to suppress political criticism. For comprehensive analyses of the history of political misuse of this Act, see Park, Won Soon, *Kookga Bo An Bop* (National Security Act), Vols.I-III, YoekSa Bi-Pyong Sa (1992)

8. For examples,"Declaration on the Matter of Numerical Quota of the Judiciary Examination" by the Korean Bar Association, December 30, 1985 as reproduced in *Dae Han Byun Ho Sa Hoe Ji* (Korean Bar Periodical), January 1986, p.95: "irresponsible and arbitrary decision totally disregarding the opinions of the Minister of Justice and the Chief of the Office of Judiciary Administration "; "Opinion on the Quota of the Judiciary Examination," submitted to the Ministry of Government Administration on November 15, 1988 as reproduced in Choi, C.K.,"Proposal for the Improvement of the Judiciary Examination", *Seoul Law Journal*, Vol.XXX, Nos.1-2 (May,1989), pp. 5-34, at 14-15.; "Recommendation On the Judiciary Examination" by the Office of Judiciary Administration, November, 1987, as cited in Ahn, K.W., "Reducing the Numerical Quota of the Judiciary Examination Is An Undemocratic Measure," *Bop Ryul Shinmun* (The Law Times), December 7, 1987; "Opinion On the Judiciary Examination Quota," Recommendation to the Minister of Government Administration, by The Office of Attorney General, as cited in "Modern Society and Lawyers—A Symposium," *Inkwon Gwa Jeong-Eui* (Human Rights and Justice), Vol.XXVII (Feb. 1990), pp. 18-30 at 20. Similar statements have been repeated recently by the Office of Judiciary Administration and Ministry of Justice, respectively, *The Dong-a Ilbo*, February 23 and 26, 1993.

9. Choi, note 8 *supra*, at 16-17.

10. Ahn, note 8 *supra*.

11. The KBA Declaration, note 8, *supra*.

12. *The Dong-a Ilbo*, April 8 and 22, 1993. The Attorneys' Act, Art. 27, makes it a crime for an attorney to hire a non-lawyer for the referral of a client (Law No.3594, December 31, 1982).

13. *TongGye Yeonbo* (Annual Statistics), Ministry of Education, 1987, as cited in Choi, note 8 *supra*, at 15.

14. From Membership Booklet, The Korean Law Teachers' Association, 1993.

15. James M. West, *Education of the Legal Profession in Korea*, International Legal Studies, Korea University Press, Seoul, 1991, pp.18-31.

16. *Id*. at 21.

17. Almost half the successful 300 are concentrated within the range of one point near the "cut line" on a one hundred point scale. *Ko Si Gye*, November editions, 1984-1993.

18. The KBA Declaration, note 8 *supra*.

19. *Id.*

20. Typically, for a LL.B. degree, the student must have taken at least 100 semester units from law subjects, in addition to 40-50 units on general subjects.

21. For a general overview of the status of quasi-lawyers, see Shin,D.W. *et al.*, "Roles of Para-legals in the Changing Society," *Seoul Law Journal*, Vol.XXVIII, No. 3 & 4 (1987), pp.1-105; Jay Murphy *et al.*, *Legal Profession in Korea: The Judicial Scrivener and Others*, Korea Law Research Institute, Seoul National University (1960).

22. *Id.*

23. The KBA Declaration, note 8, *supra.*

24. Yang, S.K., "Optimal Size of the Bar," *Seoul Law Journal*, Vol. XXIX, No.1 (1988), pp. 68-79.

25. In a recent statement, the National Revenue Office enunciated a policy of ensuring that professionals such as medical doctors and lawyers pay taxes appropriate for their income. This statement was made in response to long-standing public criticism that these occupations earn more, yet pay less, than they deserve: *The Dong-a Ilbo*, April 20, 1993.

26. Recommendation by the Office of the Attorney General, note 8 *supra.*

27. McLellan,D., *Karl Marx: The Legacy*, British Broadcasting Corporation, 1983, p.18: "There are few things more dangerous than an unemployed intellectual. If the young Marx had got he really wanted [*sic*], things might have gone very differently for the world."

28. Choi, note 8 *supra*,.

29. *Id.*

30. For example, Yang, S.K., "Reformation of the Bar," *Seoul Law Journal*, Vol.XXIX, No.2 (1988), pp.1-19; Ahn, K.W.,"A Note On the Judiciary Examination," *SaBop YonSuWon HoeJi* (The Judiciary Training Institute), November 1988, pp.1-5.

31. "Proposal on the Judiciary Examination Quota," *Bophak Gyosuhoei Hoebo* (Law Professors' Association News Letter), August, 1991, pp.5-8.

32. Ch.5, The Attorneys' Act, note 12 *supra.*

33. "Current Status of the Members," Leaflet, The Seoul District Bar Association, March 1, 1993.

34. For his detailed career and activities, see "Creative Activities as A Human Rights Lawyer: A Special Symposium in Commemoration of Cho Young-Rae," *Bop Gwa Sa-Hoe* (Law and Society), Vol. 4, Spring, 1991, pp.82-104. The two most well-known cases he successfully litigated are the so-called "Sexual Torture Case" of 1986 and the Flood Cases of 1987. In the Sexual Torture Case, a female student sued the police officer who interrogated her for her alleged illegal anti-government activities as a "camouflaged factory laborer." She claimed that the officer sexually abused her as a means of obtaining a confession. The case lasted for almost two years, resulting in the prosecution of the officer concerned and many other high ranking police officials who authorized or condoned this method of interrogation. This case was a fatal blow to the Government of President Chun, whose moral integrity was under heavy attack. Throughout the entire proceedings, in multiple litigation, both criminal and civil, Cho played

decisive roles in overcoming the many systematic barriers set up by the government, till final victory. For details, see Human Rights Report of 1986, The Korean Bar Association, December 1986, pp. 147-178. The Flood Cases are a series of lawsuits filed by the residents of a downstream area of the Han River, Seoul, for the compensation for losses allegedly caused by the negligence of the government in controlling the water level during stormy rain. In 1990, the cases finally ended up in victory for the plaintiffs. The Flood Cases are phenomenal in two respects. First, these are the first cases where negligence of the government has been proved in such circumstances. Secondly, the cases were the first "class action" suits. Almost thirty thousand plaintiffs were involved in their individual capacities, owing to the limited availability of class actions under the Korean law (Article 49, Code of Civil Procedure). These cases caused serious discussion in the Korean legal community on the pros and cons of implementing the American-type class action. For detailed chronologies of the Flood Cases, see *Bop Gwa SaHoe* (Law and Society), Vol. 4 (1991), pp.107-109.

35. Leaflet, note 29 *supra*. Out of a total of 2,568 active members, 1,628 practice in Seoul, and 645 practice in five Direct Control Cities (Pusan,206; Taegu,170; Kwangju,109; Taejon,93; Inchon,67).

36. *Id.*

37. Article 3 (Duty of Lawyer): A lawyer shall handle matters relating to litigation, agency activities in applying for administrative decisions or other general legal affairs. . . .

38. Many literary works have accused the criminal justice system of illegal practices. One classical work is *Yuk-Jo-Ji* (literally meaning Six Devilling Tortures) by a novelist, Chung Eul Byoung (1965).

39. Law No. 3862, December 23, 1986.

40. Leaflet, *Min Byun*, January 1, 1993.

41. For example, *Inkwon-Bogosoe* (Human Rights Reports of 1989-1990), *Min Byun; Byunron-Jip (1)* (Collected Documents of Defences (1), May 25, 1991, *Min Byun*.

42. Leaflet, note 40 *supra*.

43. For a leading example, see Hahm, Pyong Choon, *Korean Jurisprudence, Politics and Culture*, Yonsei University Press (1986), pp. 241-245.

44. Between 1982 and 1991, there was an increase of 47 percent in the total number of legal disputes recorded (from 7,253,418 in 1982, to 10,621,950 in 1991). Regular lawsuits have also increased by 48 percent for the same period (from 385,311 to 569,086 in 1991). See *SaBop YonGam* (The Judiciary Almanac), 1992, p. 499. This means at least one of every four Koreans was involved in a legal conflict. The statistics cover all kinds of legal disputes handled by the judiciary branch, including regular lawsuits, some civil and domestic affairs cases subject to mandatory conciliation etc., and non-contentious cases, such as disposition of uncontested wills.

45. In 1991, in civil litigation at first instance, 65 percent of the plaintiffs and 53 percent of the defendants argued on their own behalf (*id.* at 670). For the second instance, *pro se* rates were around 7 percent for both sides.

46. In 1991, 64 percent (51,318 out of 147,691) of criminal cases at the first

instance, defendants were not assisted by a lawyer (*id.* pp.551, 900) No official records are available for appellate cases.

47. In 1991, in approximately 12 percent of criminal cases, an attorney was appointed by the government (*id.* at p. 904) as required by the law (Art.282, Code of Criminal Procedure, provides that a counsel should be appointed for indigent defendants charged with a crime which can be punished with more than three years' imprisonment).

48. Korean law prohibits a non-lawyer from involvement in the legal disputes of others in return for remuneration. Violators are subject to criminal sanctions (Sec.2, Art.78, of the Attorneys' Act, note 12 *supra*).

PART THREE

Law and Institutions on the Pacific Rim

6

The Role of Government and Lawyers in the Development of the Semiconductor/Computer Industry in Japan

Setsuo Miyazawa

Introduction

This paper is a study of the role government and lawyers have played in the development of Japan's semiconductor/computer (SC) industry in Japan.[1] I have interviewed the managers of the legal and/or intellectual property departments[2] of three major SC manufacturers in Japan. I also carried out archival research.[3] Theoretically, this is a comparative study of the relative contributions of government and lawyers in industrial development in two countries with different political structures, namely, Japan and the U.S. As I will explain in the next section, I borrow from political science the concepts of *pluralism* and *corporatism* in order to characterize the basic political structures of the U.S. and Japan and to construct hypotheses about the role of government and lawyers in the development of SC industries in both countries.

U.S.A.

Silicon Valley Semiconductor Industry, Lawyers, and the U.S. Government

From what Krislov describes in his paper, I have reconstructed the following three phases in the development of the Silicon Valley semiconductor industry and the role of lawyers and the U.S. government in that development.

First Phase (50s and 60s). A new industry began with small firms. These businesses needed access to elementary advice about incorporation, drafting agreements, tax and accounting matters. Regular corporate legal matters were major concerns during this phase, and intellectual property did not appear as a major concern, although those small companies were engaging in various technological innovations. Outside lawyers protected their corporate interests. During this take-off phase of the industry, law was significant only in the sense of a basic framework. New industries do not have a specific framework of regulatory or promotional law, nor is this phase particularly litigious.

Second Phase (70s). In the more mature stage of the industry, lawyers became even more essential than before. The major issues were intellectual property (patents and copyright), antitrust, and litigation in these fields vis-à-vis domestic American competitors. While protection of technological innovations became a major issue, there was still a strong antitrust opposition to the stifling effect of patents. In-house counsel appeared to supplement and monitor outside lawyers. The U.S. government did not appear to be a major factor at this phase.

Third Phase (late 70s–80s). The globalization of world markets marked this latest phase, and what was to be protected was the very competitiveness of the United States against other countries (particularly Japan). There was a major reorientation of national competitive policy and increased appreciation of the role of high technology in the nation's economy. With this general background, Congress, in 1982, created a new court, the Federal Circuit, and gave it jurisdiction over virtually all appealed patent cases, and the protection of patents became a major concern. To counter Japanese competition, Intel in 1978 tried to obtain a copyright for a chip and failed. Intel and other chip makers turned to Congress for help, and the Semiconductor Chip Protection Act of 1984 was enacted, establishing a *sui generis* intellectual property right that is neither patent nor copyright. Thus, the U.S. Congress became a major factor at this phase. Moreover, governmental agencies also became major factors at this phase, as litigation before these agencies became a mode of competition. For instance, in 1987, Intel filed a complaint with the U.S. International Trade Commission (I.T.C.) charging seven companies with infringement of its patent. While Congress and administrative agencies like the I.T.C. have come to play a significant role at this phase, their functions appear to be limited to establishing new, more stringent, and universally applicable conditions for competition. Krislov does not mention any industry- or company-specific promotional or protective policies established and enforced by the U.S. government.

To summarize, the dominant form of the relationship among industry, lawyers, and government has evolved from the combination of individual companies, their individual lawyers, and corporate legal matters common to many industries, to the combination of industrial organizations, governmental agencies, and uniformly applied conditions of competition. In other words, the policy-making process in the semiconductor industry appears to have moved from an extremely atomized mode to a more centralized one. As we are going to compare this development with those in Japan, where the central government appears to have consistently played an active role in many policy areas, the mode of governmental involvement should be a focus for comparison.

From **Pluralism** *to* **Corporatism?**

The development in the U.S. summarized in the previous section reminds me of a perspective on political structures used by Halliday in his comparative analysis of the relationship between lawyers and government.[4] This is called *corporatism*, and it emphasizes the active role of the state in the determination of the number of social sectors which may have access to the policy-making process, the number of organizations that may represent interests of a given sector in the policy-making process, and the admission of individual members to a given organization. A major proponent of this approach has set out a classification scheme for state structures,[5] which Halliday has applied to characterize the relationship between the legal profession and government in each country he described.[6]

Using the same scheme, the American semiconductor industry's relationship with law clearly started with an extreme form of *pluralism*. The central government does not assume much of an active role. Various arenas are available for an unlimited number of social actors to present their claims and, if anything, vaguely identifiable trends might appear as the result of individual negotiations in these diffuse processes. The state, and particularly the central government, does not intentionally try to lead or create such trends. Negotiations between individual companies in various markets and courts might be seen as one such process.

This situation appears to have changed since the late 1970s. Clearly identifiable parts of the government, such as Congress, the Federal Circuit, and the I.T.C., have become the most salient arenas of policy-making, and a group of companies in the same industry have acted in concert to mobilize these governmental agencies to their advantage. In other words, at least in relation to the semiconductor industry, the state structure of the U.S.A. appears to have moved from extreme *pluralism* to one containing more elements of *liberal corporatism*. These state agencies have recognized that the semiconductor industry is particularly entitled to have access to their policy-making processes. However, the state agencies have not created the specific groups that have emerged to represent this industry; they have been formed by companies such as Intel in a de facto manner and on an ad hoc basis.

Thus, one might entertain a hypothesis about the relationship between the structure of the policy-making process in a given country and its standing in global competition: the more the country enjoys overwhelming competitiveness in the global market, the more *pluralistic* the policy-making structure vis-à-vis the relevant social sector can be; the more the country loses its competitiveness in the global market, the more *corporatist* the policy-making structure will become.

However, even in the last phase in the U.S., Congress, the Federal Circuit, and I.T.C. were essentially formulating legalistic responses in order to establish universally applicable legal conditions for competition. They were not presenting any proactive policies to improve productivity and product quality or to assist technological innovation of a particular industry or a company. Particularly noteworthy, as far as I can tell from Krislov's paper, is a lack of involvement of agencies within the executive branch of the U.S. government.

The U.S. government in fact has had several national projects to promote the SC industry since the late 1970s. They include the VHSIC (Very High-Speed Integrated Circuit) project started by the Defense Department in 1979, the MIMIC project also started by the Defense Department in 1986, MCC (Microelectronics and Computer Technology Corporation) established in 1982, and SEMATECH established in 1987.

There has also been a series of important statutes. For instance, the new taxation system introduced in 1986 allowed a wider deduction of R & D expenditure, while the National Cooperative Research Act of 1984 reduced the antitrust risk of joint R & D activities and authorized MCC in 1985. The Semiconductor Chip Protection Act of 1984 might also be added to this list.

I wish to see analyses by American scholars of the policy-making as well as implementation processes of these projects and legislation. It would be particularly interesting to see if there is any possibility of the emergence of industrial policy in the U.S. as well as an increasing *corporatism* of the American policy-making process under the declining international competitiveness of high-tech industries.

For instance, a Japanese newspaper has recently reported an apparently interesting development.[7] Both the Senate and the House of Representatives of the U.S. Congress passed the so-called "High Performance Computing" bills. The main purpose of these bills was the investment of two billion dollars in the next five years in the development of a computer that is able to operate one hundred times faster than present super computers. Thus, the bills were introduced to promote a specific industry. Moreover, the House bill included Buy-American provisions that require the government to provide special justifications when it purchases equipment from foreign countries. This is clearly a protectionist measure. While the Bush administration reportedly opposed these bills and these promotional and protectionist measures might be insignificant if compared with the Japanese policies I will describe in later sections, these bills might nonetheless indicate an increasingly more *corporatist* political structure.

Another newspaper also reported a case of more tacit pressure to exclude Japanese SC companies from the U.S. market, this time allegedly involving both the Congress and the administration.[8] In June 1991, a Colorado-based environmental organization called MECCA asked Fujitsu to donate a super computer to analyze global weather changes. Fujitsu decided to donate a computer that was worth two billion yen (approximately 15.3 million U.S. dollars). However, in September 1991, some members of Congress protested the donation, citing national security concerns, and there were objections from within the administration as well. Fujitsu thus withdrew its offer. National security is, of course, an all-purpose justification of protectionist measures.

Nevertheless, the situation may be quite different in Japan, where the executive branch of the government has constantly introduced measures to promote the SC industry. With data from Japan, we might be able to expand the scope of our analysis and more fully examine the usefulness of the analytical scheme presented by Halliday in the analysis of the role of lawyers under different political structures.[9]

Japan

Japanese Industrial Policy Towards the Semiconductor/Computer Industry

The next section will present a historical sketch of the development of the Japanese SC industry, emphasizing specific laws and policies adopted by the Japanese government for protection or promotion of the industry and legal disputes with American companies. Before presenting this historical sketch, however, it is necessary to summarize the major elements of general Japanese industrial policy as they were mobilized to promote the SC industry. More specific legislation and promotion policies directly aimed at the SC industry were introduced and operated on the basis of the general legal and policy structure which I now describe.

Restrictions on Import and Direct Investment. First, the Foreign Capital Law (Gaishi ni kansuru Ho) of 1950 prohibited foreign computer manufacturers from owning more than 49% of the shares of a Japanese computer company. The only exception was IBM Japan that had been established in 1937. This restriction continued until 1975.

Second, the Foreign Currency Exchange Law (Gaikoku Kawase Kanri Ho) of 1949 authorized MITI to control importation of foreign computers and domestic manufacturing by foreign computer manufacturers. When a user wanted to import a foreign computer, he was required to go through a hearing before MITI on the necessity of a foreign computer. When a foreign computer manufacturer wanted to manufacture computers in Japan, the firm had to submit a request for permission to MITI about the type, the quantity, and the degree of expansion of production facilities proposed. IBM Japan was the only foreign computer manufacturer operating in Japan until 1975 and was subjected to this restriction. The *de facto* compulsory patent licensing might also be mentioned in this context. In the late 1950s, as a necessary condition of MITI's permission for IBM Japan's technology assistance contract with IBM USA and its dividend payment to IBM USA, IBM Japan was required to give a license for its patents to Japanese computer manufacturers.

Third, higher customs rates were applied to imported computers and parts. For instance, in 1978, the rate for an imported CPU in Japan was 13.5%, compared to 5.5% in the U.S.

These measures prevented the influx of both foreign computer manufacturers and their products into Japan.

Exemption from Antitrust Risk. As I will describe in the next section, MITI has introduced a series of R & D projects involving potential competitors in the Japanese SC market. The antitrust implications were obvious. However, when Japanese competitors joined in working on the production of a certain product, the projects were often based on specific legislation which authorized the government to adopt the relevant policies. Such legislation has generally been used to justify exemption from antitrust risk. The situation has been same in the case of the SC industry. Legislation that authorized MITI to organize R & D projects also exempted participating companies from antitrust risk.

Thus, the restrictions on import and direct investment protected Japanese manufacturers from foreign competition, and the exemption from the antitrust law reduced their legal risk. Major beneficiaries of these measures have been the six computer manufacturers (Fujitsu, Hitachi, Mitsubishi, NEC, Oki, and Toshiba). Except Oki, they were also major manufacturers of semiconductors in Japan. On top of these general laws and policies, more specific laws and policies were introduced to promote the SC industry in Japan.

Specific Legislation and Policies in the Process of Development of the Japanese Semiconductor/Computer Industry

Legislation and policies specifically aimed at developing the SC industry closely followed technological development in other countries, particularly in the United States. I can show this most easily by listing relevant legislation, policies, and technological developments in chronological order.

The semiconductor industry in Japan was founded in 1952 when Kobe Industries (Kobe Kogyo, later acquired by Fujitsu) was licensed to use transistor technologies by RCA. Tokyo Communications Industries (Tokyo Tsushin Kogyo, now SONY) also acquired transistor technologies in 1953 from Western Electric. Both companies started production of transistors in 1954. Transistors were soon used in radios and then in televisions.

In 1957, MITI enacted the Electronic Industry Promotion Law (Denshi Kogyo Shinko Rinji Sochiho or *Denshinho*). The purpose of this law was to foster the infant industry so that it could catch up with U.S. and European technologies, and to give MITI the power to create R & D programs, to provide financial assistance to manufacturers, and to realign and reorganize the industry. This law was in effect until 1971.

In 1958, Kilby of Texas Instruments (TI) invented the integrated circuit (IC). TI disclosed the prototype of its IC in 1959 and started mass production of ICs for military use in 1961. In 1964, TI applied for permission to establish a wholly-owned subsidiary in Japan, but its request was rejected by MITI.

Already in the early 60s, the Japanese government moved to provide financial assistance to the SC industry which was barely born at that time. In 1961, JECC (Japanese Electronic Computer Company or Nihon Denshi Keisanki Kabushikigaisha) was established with Fujitsu, Hitachi, Mitsubishi, Nippon Electric Company (NEC), Oki,

Toshiba, and Nichiden-Toshiba Information Systems (a joint venture of NEC and Toshiba) as shareholders in order to assist the shareholding companies to lease their computers to end users. The arrangement was as follows: when a computer manufacturer signed a lease contract with a user, JECC purchased the computer from the manufacturer, leased it to the user, and provided maintenance; when the term of contract expired, the manufacturer bought back the computer at a depreciated price. Through this arrangement, while the contract was a lease, the computer manufacturer could receive the full payment at once. JECC received loans for a large amount from Japanese banks at low interest rates and had spent a total of 3.6 trillion yen on the purchase computers by 1990.

In order to facilitate this arrangement, a tax deduction was introduced in 1968. One problem occurred when the manufacturer bought back a returned computer. Since the machine could be more obsolete than expected at the time of initial leasing and since the depreciated value that the repurchasing manufacturer had to pay might be higher than the real value, this arrangement could result in a loss to the manufacturer. Therefore, the Finance Ministry allowed computer manufacturers to establish reserves to cover such losses. The 1968 tax law amendment made such reserves tax deductible.

In the meantime, NEC acquired IC planar technologies from Fairchild in 1962 and started IC production in 1964. In 1964, Hayakawa Electric (Hayakawa Denki, now Sharp) started to use ICs in portable calculators and thus triggered the competition for lower prices and new products and contributed to the expansion of the IC market in Japan. In the late 1960's, 60% of ICs in Japan were used in portable calculators.

At a cabinet meeting in 1963, the "Buy Japanese" policy regarding computers was adopted. National and local governmental agencies were required to purchase Japanese computers, while the private sector was also requested to cooperate with this policy. This policy was lifted in 1972 for other products, but it is uncertain if the policy was also lifted for computers. The public sector was considered to account for 10% of the computer market and this policy reserved that share for domestic manufacturers.

In 1965, Nippon Business Computer (Nippon Bijikon, later bankrupted) approached Intel for microprocessors to be used in its portable calculators. Microprocessors quickly occupied the central position in technological innovation.

In 1966, MITI started the High Performance Computer Development Project (Kosoku Konpyuta Kaihatsu Keikaku) in order to develop large-scale business computers which would outperform the IBM S/360 series. The six Japanese computer manufacturers (Fujitsu, Hitachi, Mitsubishi, NEC, Oki, and Toshiba) participated and MITI subsidized the project with 10 billion yen until 1971. This project eventually produced computers such as the HITAC 8700 and 8800, and was also a prototype for later promotional projects. In such projects, participating companies were exempted from antitrust risk and were allowed to freely use the project results.

In 1968, following NEC and Hayakawa, Hitachi and other electronic manufacturers acquired IC technologies. However, Japanese manufacturers had to pay 10% of sales as royalty for basic patents and their products were not price competitive. Moreover, American semiconductor manufacturers were already changing from IC to LSI.

In 1971, MITI enacted the Specific Electronic and Machinery Industries Promotion Law (Tokutei Denshi Kogyo oyobi Tokutei Kikai Kogyo Shinko Rinji Sochiho or *Kidenho*). This law combined *Denshinho* with a similar law regarding the machinery industry in order to promote electronics, machinery, and related industries. The law also gave MITI the power to direct computer manufacturers to engage in joint research and development projects and the power to provide financial support. This law was in effect until 1978.

Also in 1971, MITI started the Pattern Information Processing System Project (Patan Joho Shori Shisutemu Kenkyu Purojekuto). The purpose of this project was the development of pattern recognition systems for characters, pictures, three-dimensional objects, and voice. Fujitsu, Hitachi, Mitsubishi, NEC, Toshiba, Sanyo, Matsushita as well as such optical manufacturers as Konishiroku (Konica) and Hoya Glass participated. By 1980 MITI had spent a total of 22 billion yen, and the project produced OCR for handwritten *katakana* (one of the two phonetic forms of written Japanese) and voice input devices.

In 1972, IBM adopted the so-called unbundling system in which software was marketed and priced separately from hardware. The property value of computer software thus became a legal issue.

In the same year, MITI started the New Series Computer Development Project (Shinkishu Konpyuta Kaihatsu Purojekuto). Anticipating eventual liberalization of the Japanese computer market, MITI encouraged Japanese computer manufacturers to develop a new series of computers in order to compete with the IBM S/370 series. The six computer manufacturers were regrouped into three groups (Fujitsu-Hitachi, NEC-Toshiba, and Mitsubishi-Oki) and MITI spent a total of 69 billion yen through 1976. The main results of this project were the IBM-compatible M- and ACOS-series computers. These computers are still the dominant domestic main frame computers.

In 1973, Japanese IC manufacturers started to export their products.

That year's exports totalled 2.6 billion yen, while imports were 33.2 billion yen.

In 1975, imports and capital investments regarding IC were finally liberalized. However, Japanese manufacturers were already catching up with U.S. manufacturers in LSI technology and, in the late 1970's, the technology gap disappeared.

In 1976, MITI started the VLSI Development Project (Cho LSI Kaihatu Purojekuto). IBM was expected to produce the so-called Future System computers at that time. The purpose of this project was to develop the VLSI products needed to produce computers that could compete with Future System computers. The VLSI Technology Research Association (Cho LSI Gijutsu Kenkyuu Kumiai) was formed with the five domestic computer manufacturers (excluding Oki[10]) and MITI spent a total of 29 billion yen through 1984. This project resulted in 64K bit DRAM and other products.

In 1978, MITI enacted the Specific Machinery and Information Industries Promotion Law (Tokutei Kikai Joho Sangyō Shinko Rinji Sochiho or *Kijoho*). Its purpose was the same as that of *Kidenho*, but it also placed computer software under MITI's jurisdiction. This law was in effect until 1985. There has been no promotional law enacted after that.

In 1979, MITI started the Next Generation Computer Development Project (Jisedai Denshi Keisanki Kaihatsu Purojekuto). The purpose was to develop computers that could compete with IBM 308X computers, and the project emphasized the development of basic software technology. In addition to the six computer manufacturers, Matsushita and Sharp participated, and MITI spent a total of 22 billion yen through 1983.

Also in 1979, IC exports exceeded IC imports for the first time. In 1980, IC exports to the U.S. exceeded IC imports from the U.S. In 1981, annual sales of the Japanese semiconductor manufacturers reached one trillion yen. The semiconductor industry continued to grow. In 1983, IC exports were 423.8 billion yen, while imports were only 152.6 billion yen. In 1984, annual sales of the semiconductor industry reached 2 trillion yen. In the late 1980's, while U.S. manufacturers still maintained a lead in technologies of microprocessor and circuit designing, Japanese manufacturers started to lead in VLSI-related technologies. Eventually, in 1990, there remained only two American IC manufacturers (TI and Micron Technology). While they still had a lead in micro processors, Japanese manufacturers controlled 90% of the mega-bit chip market.

In the meantime, MITI continued to introduce several more promotional projects. In 1981, MITI started the High-Speed Scientific

Computer Development Project (Kagakugijutsu Keisanyo Kosoku Keisan Shisutemu Kaihatsu Purojekuto). The purpose was the development of so-called super computers. The six computer manufacturers participated and MITI spent a total of 23 billion yen through 1989.

Also in 1981, MITI started the New Function Element Development Project (Jisedai Sangyo Kiban Gijutsu Kenkyuu Kaihatsu Purojekuto). The purpose was to promote the development of superlattice elements, three-dimensional circuit elements, and so on. The six computer manufacturers, Matsushita, Sanyo, Sharp, Sumitomo Electric, and SONY participated. The project was to continue until 1990, and MITI was to spend a total of 25 billion yen.

In 1982, MITI started the Fifth Generation Computer Development Project (Dai Go Sedai Konpyuta Kaihatsu Purojekuto). The purpose was to develop computers that could handle "knowledge base" with inference processing and intelligent interface technology. The six computer manufacturers, Sharp, and Matsushita formed the Institute for New Generation Computer Technology (Shin Sedai Konpyuta Gijutsu Kaihatsu Kumiai) and MITI spent 83 billion yen for the two fiscal years of 1983 and 1984. This project continued until 1990. It is now judged a failure. This result suggests a hypothesis that promotional policies such as those introduced by the Japanese government are effective only in so far as their purpose is catching up to leading countries, but not for making innovations.

While the projects described above were concerned with hardware technology, MITI also introduced software-focused projects around the same time. In 1985, for instance, MITI started the Interoperable Data Base System Project (Sogo Unyo Detabesu Shisutemu Purojekuto). The purpose was to develop a data base system that could operate with different information systems. The six computer manufacturers, Matsushita, Sumitomo Electric, and Sharp formed the Interoperability Technology Association for Information Processing). The project was to continue until the end of 1991 and MITI was to spend a total of 15 billion yen.

Also in 1985, MITI started the SIGMA (Software Industrialized Generator and Maintenance Aids) Project (Shiguma Purojekuto). The purpose of this project was the automation and mechanization of software development, and UNIX was selected as the base to develop a standard OS. The participants were the Information-Technology Promotion Agency (Joho Shori Shinko Jigyo Kyokai, established in 1970 for the development of software technology under the jurisdiction of MITI) and AT & T. MITI was to spend a total of 25 billion yen through 1989.

While MITI and Japanese SC manufacturers were carrying out these projects, the legal environment surrounding the SC industry started to change. In 1984, for instance, the Semiconductor Chip Protection Act was enacted in the U.S in order to protect masking technologies as a new type of intellectual property. It required the same protection in foreign countries in order for their products to receive protection in the U.S. Thus, the Semiconductor Integrated Circuit Masking Law (Handotai Shusekikairo no Kairo Haichi ni kansuru Horitsu or *Kairoho*) was enacted in Japan in 1985.

About the same time, legal protection of computer software became a major issue. Japanese computer manufacturers and MITI wanted to create *sui generis* "program right" (*puroguramu-ken*) under the jurisdiction of MITI, while IBM Japan and the Agency of Cultural Affairs (*Bunkacho*, an agency of the Ministry of Education, Science, and Culture) proposed an amendment of the Copyright Law (Chosakukenho). Practical issues were the length of protection (fifty years under the Copyright law and shorter protection proposed under the Program Right Law) and the respective expertise of MITI and *Bunkacho* to handle industrial products. MITI generally has enjoyed a stronger position in the Japanese policy-making structure than most other governmental agencies in Japan. However, the U.S. position that handles computer software under copyright law had a decisive impact, and the Copyright Law was amended in 1985 and went into effect in 1986.

Legal disputes and trade conflicts regarding the SC industry also started to appear in the early 1980s. In 1982, "spying" to obtain technological information from IBM was detected, involving Hitachi and Mitsubishi. In the same year, a copyright dispute also started between IBM and Fujitsu. In 1983, Fujitsu and Hitachi settled with IBM, while Mitsubishi pleaded *nolo contendere* in the "spying" case.

In 1984, IBM claimed infringement of the 1983 settlement contract by Fujitsu. In 1985, both parties sought arbitration from the American Arbitration Association (AAA). In 1987, the AAA issued an order and gave its opinions. Fujitsu was granted a limited extent of access to interface information in secured facilities, in return for payment of royalty and fees for access. In 1988, the AAA issued the final decision, specifying the amount of royalty and fees.

In 1990, TI sued Japanese manufacturers for patent infringement regarding DRAM. In 1991, TI asked Japanese and Korean IC manufacturers to include a payment for royalties for using the Kilby patent that had been registered in Japan in 1988 in their cross-licensing contracts with TI. While Toshiba, Matsushita (Panasonic), and NEC agreed to pay, Fujitsu refused and sued TI, arguing that Fujitsu was now able to produce ICs without using the patented technology. TI immediately countersued.

An Example of **State Corporatism?**

What we have seen in the previous two sections appears to be a good example of *state corporatism*. The Japanese government recognized the SC industry as a legitimate social sector which should have access to its policy-making process. The government designated the six SC manufacturers as the main members to represent the SC industry. Other companies have been allowed to participate in those projects on an ad hoc basis, but they have not established as stable a relationship with the government as have the six designated companies.

Moreover, the government appears to have *proactively* enacted legislation and organized projects. Either through archival research or in interviews, I have not encountered any data that suggest that the SC companies took initiatives to which the government *reactively* responded. No doubt, MITI consulted the companies before finalizing its bills and plans. But the government does not appear, at least, to have been a minor partner in its ongoing relationship with the SC companies. The managers interviewed occasionally mentioned the role of the Japanese Association of Electronic Industry (*Denshi Kogyokai*) as the peak organization of their industry in presenting coordinated responses to MITI and other governmental agencies. However, they did not mean that *Denshi Kogyokai* campaigned to demand certain policies from the government. It might not be too far from reality to say that MITI appointed itself as the champion of the Japanese SC industry, and so constantly surveyed the needs of the industry and took actions it deemed appropriate which were more or less acceptable to the designated major members of the industry.

This pattern has been broken recently, particularly under pressure from the U.S. government. The failure of "program right" is a good example. MITI was unable to protect the position of the SC industry in that case. However, MITI's compromise might still be seen as a paternalistic response to the changing environment. Considering two options, one being the loss of the U.S. market, the other being the longer protection of rapidly changing software, the compromise was better. After all, Japanese SC manufacturers are outcompeting American manufacturers in many areas regarding both quality and price. This compromise might not reduce much of their competitiveness.

At the same time, Japanese SC manufacturers have also been

forming joint ventures with their American competitors. Their ultimate purpose might be to reduce the risk of conflicts with them.

For computers, for instance, Matsushita purchased a super computer from Cray Research for one of its research centers and negotiated an agreement to sell its own computers through Cray's marketing network.[11] Nippon Electric signed a marketing agreement with Japan I.B.M. to sell Nippon's super computers. The first sales contract under this agreement was signed with Komatsu, a major manufacturer of machineries. Under this contract, Japan I.B.M. designs the entire system and Nippon's super computer will be used as part of it.[12]

For semiconductors, Toshiba and Japan Motorola agreed to jointly market their semiconductors. They agreed that if their respective customers need a second provider, they will introduce each other as a legitimate second source.[13] Toshiba was also to sign an agreement with U.S. I.B.M. before the end of August 1992 about a new generation of semiconductors Toshiba has developed. Toshiba would provide I.B.M. basic technologies and I.B.M. would start production in 1993, use them in its computers, and market them to other computer manufacturers.[14] Similar agreements with American competitors can also be seen for Hitachi, Nippon Electric, Mitsubishi Electric, Sharp, and other companies. Moreover, there are also industry-wide joint projects. For instance, ten semiconductor and electronics manufacturers in Japan and the U.S., including Matsushita and Nippon Electric in Japan and LSI Logic and VLSI Technologies in the U.S., announced an agreement to jointly develop LSIs in order to reduce the price of high precision televisions.[15]

However, similar agreements for earlier generations of semiconductors did not pose a significant barrier to market domination by Japanese manufacturers and, hence, failed to prevent legal actions taken by American manufacturers. The effectiveness of recent agreements remains to be seen.[16]

While Japanese SC manufacturers have been trying to form stable relationships with their American competitors, the Japanese government has also been working to ease tensions by giving American SC manufacturers an access to the Japanese market and research consortiums. For instance, MITI announced a bill that gives tax benefits to research consortiums including foreign companies,[17] while FACOM-HITAC, a joint venture established in 1974 by Fujitsu and Hitachi under MITI's leadership as part of MITI's policies for promoting domestic computer manufacturers, was dissolved.[18]

Following this new policy, MITI formed a consortium to develop technologies of quantum functional devices. Its members included Motorola, as well as SONY, Nippon Electric, Hitachi, Fujitsu, and

Matsushita.[19] A research institute of the Science and Technology Agency signed a lease contract for a super computer with Cray.[20] MITI and the Electronic Industries Association of Japan (EIAJ), an industrial organization of Japanese SC manufacturers, jointly announced a policy to help American SC manufacturers to expand their share in the Japanese market. One measure is to establish an organization in California that works as an intermediary for medium and small SC manufacturers there to sell their products to Japan. Another measure is for MITI to request Japanese companies to purchase American products.[21]

Nevertheless, elements of *state corporatism* are still apparent in these measures.

It is debatable, however, whether the protective and promotional legislation and projects are the main causes of the tremendous growth of the Japanese SC industry.

First, while SC manufacturers have been working together in government-sponsored R & D projects, they have competed very hard in both domestic and foreign markets. Since quality has often been comparable, price cutting has been prevalent. Fujitsu surprised everyone a few years ago, for instance, when it bid on the computer system of a local government for only *one yen*! This, of course, is an extreme case, but it nonetheless symbolizes the fierce competition among Japanese manufacturers.

Second, while the amount of subsidies by MITI may appear very large, they might still be relatively small compared to the R & D budgets of the manufacturers themselves. Here are some rough comparisons:

1. In 1966, MITI started the High Performance Computer Development Project, which it subsidized by a total of 10 billion yen (approximately 27.9 million U.S. dollars at the exchange rate of 1970) through 1971. In the single year of 1970, however, the six SC manufacturers spent a total of 33.5 billion yen for R & D.[22]
2. In 1971, MITI started the Pattern Information Processing System Project. It spent 22 billion yen (approximately 74.1 million U.S. dollars at the exchange rate of 1975) through 1980. In the single year of 1975, the six manufacturers spent in total 84 billion yen for R & D.
3. In 1976, MITI started the VLSI Development Project with only five manufacturers, excluding Oki. MITI spent 29 billion yen (approximately 121.5 million U.S. dollars by the exchange rate of 1980) through 1984. In the single year of 1980, the five

manufacturers included in this project spent a total of 183.8 billion yen.

4. In 1982, MITI started the Fifth Generation Computer Development Project. It spent 83 billion yen (approximately 357.7 million U.S. dollars) for the two years of 1983 and 1984. In the single year of 1985, the six manufacturers spent a total of 595.5 billion yen. In 1990, the R & D budget of the six manufacturers reached 1,173.2 billion yen (approximately 8,103 million U.S. dollars).

It might be the case that MITI and other governmental agencies had other projects that subsidized the manufacturers, while the R & D budgets of the manufacturers were not necessarily spent for semiconductors and computers. Therefore, these comparisons might have inflated the relative size of the R & D budget. In spite of this possibility, however, it still appears that the manufacturers invested heavily in R & D, much more than the subsidies they received from the government. MITI's R & D projects might have been helpful to the manufacturers in indicating the most promising areas for exploration, but the overall technological improvement might be largely the result of the manufacturers' own investment and effort.

Notwithstanding these reservations, however, it remains true that the role of law in the development of the Japanese SC industry until 1980's can best be understood in the framework of *state corporatism*.

Where Have All the Lawyers Gone?

Compared to the analysis presented by Krislov of the Silicon Valley semiconductor industry, curiously missing in my data is reference to practicing lawyers. In fact, the managers interviewed could not tell me much about their role. First, even when they dealt with domestic legal matters such as the *Kairo Ho*, the amendment of the Copyright Law, or suing American companies in Japanese courts, their main advisers were American lawyers from major law firms in New York, Washington, D.C., etc. Since their companies' survival depends on their access to the American market, particularly when legislation is concerned, they have to take into account consistency with the American legal system and possible reactions of the American government.

Second, even when they were involved in litigation in Japan and had to rely on Japanese lawyers, their lawyers' expertise was often not much better than their own, particularly in areas such as intellectual property. Hence, in most cases, in-house staff and outside lawyers sit together and hear advice from American lawyers.

Third, as part of the general international trend, major SC manufacturers have rapidly expanded their in-house staff in both general legal matters and intellectual property. A survey of 200 major companies in 1990 revealed that the average number of employees in the general legal department was 14.5, while that figure for the intellectual property department was 35.1.[23] The surveyed companies also expected that they would reach, respectively, 17.5 and 41.3 in three years. Considering that these results were obtained for the entire sample, the majority of which was no doubt outside the SC industry, we might expect that the figures for major SC companies were much higher. Moreover, increasingly large numbers of people from legal and intellectual property departments are sent to American law schools and take bar examinations in the U.S. While they are not admitted to the bar in Japan, their expertise in the areas most needed for their companies might often exceed the level of domestic Japanese lawyers.

Since domestic litigation is always rare, this combination of a large number of sophisticated internal staff and direct consultation with American big law firms will continue in major companies. The main market for both Japanese corporate and international lawyers and foreign law solicitors (*gaikokuho jimubengoshi*) will continue to be small- to medium-size companies. Japanese lawyers will remain largely outside the development of laws and policies as far as high-technology industries such as SC are concerned.

This picture might be unfair to Japanese lawyers. On the one hand, in the legislative process under the parliamentary cabinet system of Japan, major bills are always brought in by governmental agencies.[24] While the Japanese Federation of Bar Associations (JFBA) might have some influence over the policies of the Justice Ministry, it cannot do much vis-à-vis MITI and the other business-related ministries. On the other hand, in the judicial process, Japanese judges are extremely positivistic and, hence, reluctant to develop any new laws through their decisions. Powerful bureaucratic control of lower court judges by the Supreme Court General Secretariat insures this aversion to judicial activism.[25] The JFBA has been active in promoting civil rights and has taken some commendable initiatives in pro bono activities, including, most recently, the introduction of a Japanese version of the duty solicitor scheme that originated in the United Kingdom.[26]

It is undeniable, however, that lawyers have largely been excluded from important policy decisions in Japan. They have not been recognized by the government as a group to be included in the *state-corporatist* political structure, except on those issues which directly affect the judiciary and legal profession. Moreover, lawyers themselves have been reluctant to expand their sphere of influence. They have refused to increase the size of the bar and, as a result, have unintentionally contributed to the development of their own non-lawyer competitors, contrary to both their own interest and the interests of their potential customers.[27] In any event, their impact in the high technology area is difficult to discern.

Conclusion

An analysis of the relative contributions of government and lawyers to the development of high-technology industries and to related laws requires a theoretical framework about the different political structures in which government, business, and lawyers interact. The concepts of *pluralism* and *corporatism* seem to provide such a scheme. The situation in Japan until the 1980s can be characterized as *state corporatism,* in which the government provides paternalistic policies for the industries it selects. Under this situation, lawyers had virtually no chance to take initiatives in the development of laws in relation to new technologies.

In closing, two questions may be raised. First, how can and will Japanese lawyers expand the sphere of their influence, particularly in the development of new laws? And second, is the American political structure moving from *pluralism* to *corporatism,* and are lawyers losing their functions to the government? These are important questions whose answers must be sought in different papers.

Notes

1. In this paper I do not distinguish the semiconductor industry from the computer industry. There are five mainframe computer manufacturers in Japan. In order of overall annual sales in 1987, they are Hitachi, Toshiba, NEC (Nippon Electric Company), Mitsubishi Electric, and Fujitsu (Yasunori Omichi, *Handotai Gyokai* (Semiconductor Industry), Tokyo: Kyoikusha, 1990, p.101). They are all major manufacturers of semiconductors. As I will describe later, along with Oki Electric, now a major manufacturer of peripheral products, these firms have formed the core of the Japanese SC industry which MITI has been promoting. While incorporated in Japan, Japan I.B.M. has stood outside this group. The term "SC industry" will used in this paper to refer to this semiconductor/computer industry as a whole, except where it is necessary to specifically refer to semiconductors or computers.

This research was inspired by an earlier draft of the paper by Krislov, now chapter three of this volume, presented at the conference on the Role of Law in the Pacific Community, held on October 6-7, 1991, at Stanford Law School.

Earlier versions of this paper were presented at that conference, and at the 1992 annual meeting of the Research Committee on Sociology of Law of the International Sociological Association, June 29-July 3, 1992, Mexico City, Mexico. The Science Council of Japan provided a travel grant to attend the latter meeting. An earlier version was also published in *Kobe Hogaku Zasshi* (Kobe Law Journal), Vol.42, No.4, 1993, pp.659-689. Permission of the Kobe Law Faculty for publication here is gratefully acknowledged.

Ken'ichi Yoneda and Hiroto Hata, J.S.D. candidates at Kobe University Graduate School of Law provided research assistance. Andrew L. Beaton, also a J.S.D. candidate at Kobe, and David T. Johnson, a J.S.P. student at the University of California at Berkeley and Fulbright researcher at Kobe University edited earlier versions of this paper.

2. SC manufacturers usually have separate departments in charge of general legal matters (legal department) and of intellectual property matters (intellectual property department). The intellectual property department deals with applications to the patent and other governmental agencies and examines potential infringements, while the legal department reviews licensing contracts and handles legal actions once a dispute arises. While there is such a division of labor, they often work together in close coordination. Of the three companies I interviewed, I interviewed managers from both departments at one company and managers of only the legal department at two of the companies. Even when I interviewed only legal department managers, however, they appeared to be quite knowledgeable about intellectual property as well. As I promised when I requested interviews, I will protect their anonymity.

3. Main sources are: Yoshikazu Kano and Yoshikazu Takaishi (eds.), *Sentan Sangyo no Chiteki Shoyuken* (Intellectual Property Rights of High-Tech Industries), Tokyo: Toyo Keizai Shinposha, 1990; Shohei Kurita, *Konpyuta: Kaiteiban* (Computers, revised ed.), Tokyo: Nihon Keizaishinbunsha, 1989; Nihon Denshi Keisanki Kabushikigaisha (ed.), *JECC Konpyuta Noto 1991* (JECC Computer Note 1991), Tokyo: Nihon Denshi Keisanki Kabushikigaisha, 1991; Nihon Keizaishinbunsha (ed.), *Dokyumento Nichibei Homu Senso* (U.S.-Japan War of Corporate Legal Departments: A Documentary), Tokyo: Nihon Keizaishinbunsha, 1991; Yasunori Omichi, *Handotai Gyokai* (Semiconductor Industry), Tokyo: Kyoikusha, 1990; Yoshikazu Takaishi, "Wagakuni ni okeru Konpyuta Sangyo no Hatten to Sangyo Seisaku" (Development of the Computer Industry in Japan and Industrial Policy), 3 *Sangyo Gakkai Kenkyu Nenpo*, 1987, pp.24-38; Yoshikazu Takaishi, "Legal Dimension of High Technology Trade and Competition," Valerie Kusuda-Smick (ed.), *United States/Japan Commercial Law and Trade*, Ardsley-on-Hudson, N.Y.: Transnational Juris Publications, Inc., 1990, pp. 169–175.

4. Terence C. Halliday, "Legal Professions and the State: Neocorporatist Variations on the Pluralist Theme of Liberal Democracies," Richard L. Abel and Philip S. C. Lewis, *Lawyers in Society, Vol.3, Comparative Theories*, Berkeley: University of California Press, 1989, pp.375-426.

5. Philippe C. Schmitter, "Still the Century of Corporatism," and "Modes of Interest Intermediation and Models of Societal Change in Western Europe," in

Philippe C. Schmitter and Gerhard Lehmbruch (eds.), *Trends Toward Corporatist Intermediation*, Beverly Hills: Sage Publications, pp.7-52, and pp.63-94.

6. Halliday, *supra* note 6, pp.417-419. While Kahei Rokumoto contributed a paper to an earlier volume of the same publication ("The Present State of Japanese Practicing Attorneys: On the Way to Full Professionalization?", Richard Abel and Philip S. C. Lewis, *Lawyers in Society*, Vol.2, Berkeley: University of California Press, 1988, pp.160-199), it was not his concern to discuss the political structure in which Japanese attorneys operate and organize themselves. Halliday apparently relied on this paper for Japanese data and thus missed an important case of extreme *state corporatism*, where the national organization of lawyers (Nihon Bengoshi Rengokai or Japanese Federation of Bar Associations (JFBA)) was created by a state law, participation of private lawyers in the JFBA was made compulsory by a state law, competition among lawyers has been kept at a very low level through the state-administered bar examination, while, in spite of these close relationships with the government, the JFBA has had minimal power to *initiate* any policies that affect the government and has failed to prevent the competition posed by the so-called quasi lawyers, such as judicial scriveners and administrative scriveners.

7. *Nihon Keizai Shinbun*, October 27, 1992, morning.

8. *Asahi Shinbun*, November 1, 1991, evening.

9. T. J. Pempel and Keiichi Tsunekawa, "Corporatism without Labour?: The Japanese Anomaly," P. C. Schmitter and G. Lehmbruch (eds.), *Trends towards Corporatist Intermediation*, Beverly Hills: Sage Publications, 1979, pp.231-270, characterize Japan as a form of *state corporatism* with labor being excluded from policy-making process. Consumers might be another major social group that has been largely excluded. On the other hand, business interests have always enjoyed access to policy-making elites, and industrial policy has occupied a central position in Japanese politics. For a review of monographs on Japanese industrial policy, see Masaki Abe, "Japanese Industrial Policy in Perspective," 24 *Law & Society Review*, pp.1071-1088 (1990).

10. In fact, Oki expressed an interest in participating in the project, but MITI rejected it (Hiroshi Kitamura, "Japanese FTC should be involved in Export-related Problems" (in Japanese), *Nihon Keizai Shinbun*, March 5, 1992, morning). While Oki continued to participate in many later projects for computers, it was thus forced to survive not as a major force in the mainframe computer industry, but as a major manufacturer of peripheral products. This is an example of a well-known pattern in MITI policy of deliberately promoting larger companies.

11. *Nihon Keizai Shinbun*, November 2, 1991, morning.

12. *Nihon Keizai Shinbun*, August 29, 1991, morning.

13. *Nihon Keizai Shinbun*, September 26, 1991, morning.

14. *Nihon Keizai Shinbun*, June 20, 1992, morning.

15. *Nihon Keizai Shinbun*, November 15, 1991, morning.

16. *Nihon Keizai Shinbun*, June 21, 1992, morning.

17. *Nihon Keizai Shinbun*, August 28, 1991, morning.

18. *Asahi Shinbun*, October 31, 1991, morning.

19. *Nihon Keizai Shinbun*, January 30, 1992, morning.

20. *Nihon Keizai Shinbun*, August 29, 1991, morning.

21. *Nihon Keizai Shinbun*, March 19, 1992, morning.

22. Ken'ichi Yoneda calculated the R & D budget from the annual reports of the six SC manufacturers for 1960 (only Hitachi and Fujitsu), 1965, 1970, 1975, 1980, 1985, and 1990. He also found the yen-dollar exchange rates for these years. I am grateful for his research assistance.

23. Nihon Keizaishinbunsha (ed.), *Dokyumento: Nichibei Homu Senso* (U.S.-Japan War of Corporate Legal Departments: A Documentary), Tokyo: Nihon Keizaishinbunsha, 1991, p.123.

24. See Frank K. Upham, *Law and Social Change in Postwar Japan*, Cambridge: Harvard University Press, 1987, p.14.

25. See Setsuo Miyazawa, "Administrative Control of Japanese Judges," *Kobe University Law Review*, No.25, 1991, pp.45-61, reprinted as Chapter 10 of this volume.

26. See Setsuo Miyazawa, *Policing in Japan: A Study on Making Crime*, Albany: State University of New York Press, 1992, pp.239-240.

27. See J. Mark Ramseyer, "Lawyers, Foreign Lawyers, and Lawyer-Substitutes: The Market for Regulation in Japan," *Harvard International Law Journal*, Vol.27, 1986, pp.499-539. The situation changed slightly in 1990. The number of applicants who pass the annual bar examination had remained the same for several years at the level of approximately 500 in spite of more than 20,000 applicants. In 1990, the Japanese Federation of Bar Associations, the Justice Ministry, and the Supreme Court agreed to increase this number to approximately 700 by 1993. Nevertheless, the Justice Ministry, *not* the bar, made the initial proposal.

7

The Role of Lawyers in the Economic Development of Korea

Seung Doo Yang

This paper attempts to describe briefly what role the law, the legislation and lawyers play in the process of economic development in Korea. In terms of economic development, Korea is sometimes praised as one of the four "dragons" in the Asian region, which have achieved, to some extent, the goal of modernizing and industrializing their economies and their societies. They are admired for the economic progress achieved in such a short time. A simple figure shows how fast the Korean economy has grown: in the early part of the 1960s when General Park Chung Hee took over political power and initiated the First Five Year Economic Development Plan in 1962,[1] the Korean per capita income was less than U.S. $100 whereas it is now nearly U.S. $6,000.[2]

Numerous economists and economic policy makers in and out of the country have theorized as to the particular force absent in other developing countries but found in those four dragons which have made such drastic economic progress. Some have suggested that Confucian teachings might have been the effective force and others have enumerated other factors. But this writer believes that the law has contributed greatly to economic progress in Korea, and the purpose of this paper is to describe the contributory role of lawyers and legislation.

The Role of Lawyers in Economic Progress

Lawyers in Korea

In order to see the role of lawyers in economic progress in Korea, it is necessary to define the term "lawyer," as I use it in this paper, and to explain some of the features of the legal system pertinent to the training of lawyers in Korea.

The training of lawyers in Korea begins generally at the college level. The vast majority of high school graduates come to colleges of law hoping to follow a career as a judge, prosecuting attorney or practicing lawyer. But in reality, those who pass the judicial examination[3] during or after their college level education (the first step required by law in order to follow a legal career such as a judge, a prosecuting attorney or a practicing lawyer) number three hundred or less each year.[4] After passing the judicial examination, they are admitted to the Judicial Research and Training Institute for two years of legal training. The Institute is under the control of the Supreme Court of Korea, and the teachers there are mostly judges, prosecuting attorneys, practicing lawyers and occasionally law professors. Some of the graduates of that institute (roughly eighty each year) will be appointed as judges, some others (about seventy to eighty) prosecuting attorneys, and the rest (the majority) will go into the practice of law or find other jobs.

Each year Korean universities and colleges produce approximately seven thousand graduates, and as pointed out earlier, only three hundred pass the judicial examination each year.[5] Consequently, the remaining six thousand seven hundred have to follow careers other than the legal profession as they may choose or as circumstances allow. The vast majority of them are employed by private business corporations, though some of them go into public service on either the national or local level. The term "lawyer" then, applies only to those who have passed the judicial examination and trained at the Judicial Research and Training Institute.

Up to 1980, the number of those who passed the judicial examination was less than twenty. One particular year only five passed the examination. In those days all the graduates of the Judicial Research and Training Institute were appointed as judges or prosecuting attorneys. It was a general practice for retired judges and prosecuting attorneys to open individual law offices and the so-called law firms were very few—if not non-existent. The primary role of practicing lawyers was limited to the role of representing their clients in court.

Now, the Bar Association has altogether roughly 2,500 members while Korea has a population of about forty-two million people. So 2,500 or so lawyers seems too small a number to perform many of the significant roles expected in most developed countries. Hence, some roles which are performed by lawyers in other countries are in Korea performed by quasi-lawyers, such as patent attorneys, tax specialists, customs specialists, judicial scriveners, and the like. In theory, these quasi-lawyers have to pass national examinations, but the reality is that, by various laws and regulations, those who have retired after serving a specific period of time at the respective government offices are exempted from all or part of the examinations, making it easy for them to qualify. Presently the substantial majority of practitioners have followed these short-cuts.

As said before, a significant number of graduates of law colleges go into public service and eventually they occupy top seats in and out of government. They exercise great influence on legislation and policy formation, including economic policies.[6] Their voice seems to be louder in reality than that of the Korean Federation of Bar Associations.

It appears that there are very few qualified lawyers (those who passed the national judicial examination and completed two years of training at the Judicial Research and Training Institute) in the government. Even in the Office of Legislation, one can find normally only one lawyer—the Minister himself—while the rest are not. However, they are graduates of colleges of law, deal professionally with legal problems and issues related to legislation, and thus, in this sense, they deserve to be called lawyers. The identical phenomenon can be found in the Patent Office. A qualified lawyer is normally appointed as the Minister of the Patent Office, but virtually all the rest of the civil servants working with the Patent Office are not lawyers. It is quite rare for patent examiners to be lawyers. However, all of them successfully deal with cases related to the registration of patent rights, patent trials and the like.

In sum, it may be said that lawyers in Korea are chosen very selectively,[7] and their role has been narrowly limited to that of representing clients in court. They perform advisory functions for their clients on an ad hoc basis but their constructive role in and out of government is limited. However, fairly large numbers of graduates of law colleges, in spite of their "non-qualification" as lawyers, have been performing the role lawyers are expected to play in most foreign countries. In this sense they may be called lawyers. For the remainder of this paper, when I use the word "lawyer" I mean that person whose discipline was law and who performs the role of a lawyer in or out of government.[8] The role they play in economic policy formation and in the legislative process related to the economic progress deserves to be admired, as will be discussed below.

The Five-Year Economic Development Plans

The Park Chung Hee government, after the so-called May 16th Revolution led by General Park Chung Hee and his subsequent seizure of political power, published its intention of establishing the first five-year economic development plan in January, 1962,[9] in order to "eliminate social and economic vice and to formulate a solid basis for an independent economic development." This economic development plan was for the period from 1961 to 1965, and the primary goal they wished to achieve during the period was industrialization, by way of strengthening the export drive. Supporting these industries was a large quantity of relatively cheap labor, simply because the Korean economy lacked natural resources, capital and technological skills for industrialization.

During the period of the First Economic Development, the Law on the Inducement of Foreign Capital was amended to facilitate foreign investment; and, subsequently, the Law on Guaranteeing Payment for Foreign Loans and the Special Measure Law on Capital Inducement by Means of Long-term Payment were enacted and made effective (July 31, 1962) solely for the purpose of introducing much needed foreign capital into the Korean economy. At the same time, the Korean government established formal diplomatic relations with Japan which resulted in six hundred million dollars (U.S.) worth of Japanese capital being brought into the Korean economy. In 1965, the Korean government decided to send its fighting forces to Vietnam, and this decision to participate in the Vietnam War resulted in the influx of hard currency necessary for economic development.

The Second Five-Year Economic Development Plan was for the period from 1966 to 1971. During this period the primary goal was to solidify the infrastructure of viable economic development: the construction of a steel mill (Posco), highways (from Seoul to Pusan and from Taijon to Mokpo), and petro-chemical and heavy machinery factories which were started and completed during the period.

The Third Five-Year Economic Development Plan was for the period of 1972-1976, and its main goal was, firstly, to correct a social structural malaise—mitigating the huge discrepancy between "haves" and "have-nots," and between "urban areas" and "rural areas"—which resulted from rapid industrialization; and, secondly, to develop the economy in rural areas and fishing villages in a "revolutionary" way.[10] Thirdly, their goal was to drastically increase exports and to construct both heavy and petro-chemical industries.

The Fourth Five-Year Economic Development Plan was for the period 1977-1981. The main targets for achievement during this period can be described in three words: economic growth, efficiency and equity. Technical development in industries like electronics, shipbuilding and heavy machinery was emphasized and large scale investment in petro-chemical and heavy machinery was structured in order to maximize efficiency. In 1979, President Chung Hee Park was assassinated and the ensuing political and economic disorder resulted in a negative growth for 1980. The oil shock of 1979 also affected economic development adversely.

After the assassination of President Park, General Jon Doo Whan took power. His economic advisors saw that "economic development" should be replaced by "economic and social development." Therefore, the Fifth Economic Development Plan (1982-1986) set a goal of "stability, efficiency and balance" in economic progress. They did not produce a year-by-year economic plan. Instead, they tried to formulate plans only for those pertinent economic issues that came to the forefront. With dubious political legitimacy, President Jon's government saw economic progress as the most important task for the government. The government liberalized the import of foreign goods and sought to implement a policy aimed at suppressing inflation. The government further worked to lessen government interference in economic activity so as to ensure and strengthen initiatives from private business.

The Sixth Economic Development Plan (1987-1991) has now ended. Due to the so-called "three lows"—low oil price, low international interest rates and low purchasing power of the U.S. dollar—the Korean economy boomed. The international balance of payment turned to "black" from "red" for the first time in Korean history during the first part of this period. So the economic development policies during this time have been changed to stress efficiency and balance and leave aside the goal of development.

It may be said that the cornerstone of economic development was laid during the first and second five-year plans (the period of solidifying the basis), the trend toward massive economic progress was molded during the third and fourth five-year plans (the period of development), and economic stability was achieved during the sixth five-year plan (the period of economic stability).

The Role of Lawyers in Economic Progress

Numerous new laws and regulations were enacted to facilitate economic progress in Korea.[11] During the first of its three stages of Korean economic progress, namely the stage of solidifying the basis of economic progress, legislation like the Foreign Capital Inducement Act, the Korea Development Bank Act, and the Export and Import Bank of Korea Act contributed significantly to economic development. During the second stage of Korean economic development, numerous laws and regulations on tax exemption for export-oriented industries, labor regulation, and the promotion of small and medium-size industries facilitated and stimulated the development of the Korean economy. During the stage of stability, laws like the Consumer Protection Law, the Fair Competition Law, and numerous other laws on environmental protection and labor were enacted or amended to ensure so-called "social justice." Laws and regulations on intellectual property were also enacted or amended in accordance with current international practices.

All through the legislative process, lawyers (in the wide sense) in and out of government have contributed actively. They have participated in preparing bills in cooperation with economists. They have been the lobbyists and they have also been charged with implementing all laws and regulations. In this connection, an example of formulating a regulation related to intellectual property can be mentioned. An advisory committee composed of a judge, a prosecuting attorney, several law professors (who are not licensed lawyers), several patent attorneys, a few government officials from the Patent Office and other Ministries (they are not licensed lawyers either) and a few representatives from the Korean Association of Patent Lawyers were organized to advise the Minister of the Patent Office. On one occasion a member of the said committee deplored mere legislation and amendment of laws and regulations on intellectual property as being inadequate for the protection of intellectual property rights. The committee concluded by suggesting to the Minister of the Patent Office that an *ad hoc* committee be organized to restructure the curricula of primary and secondary education[12] so that the protection of intellectual property could be taught at primary, middle and high schools. The Minister of the Patent Office appropriated a research fund and asked the Korean Educational Development Institute[13] to study the feasibility of amending the curricula. An *ad hoc* committee of the KEDI, composed of experts on education and those non-licensed lawyers, is now studying and working to persuade the Ministry of Education to amend the curricula. It is likely that the curricula will be amended to include the protection of intellectual property rights and, thanks to the teaching in primary and secondary schools, intellectual property rights, which at present are somewhat unfamiliar to the common Korean people, will eventually be protected throughout Korea.

Conclusion

Lawyers in Korea, as said before, are recruited very selectively and the corps of lawyers is very small.[14] They have contributed to the country's economic progress in a limited way. But the role of those who have received a legal education at the university level and are working in and out of government toward economic betterment cannot be underestimated. They initiate or formulate economic policies and prepare government bills which are submitted to the National Assembly. They are the very people who execute the laws and regulations. Their role in Korea's economic progress deserves to be commended.

Notes

1. The first plan was for the period from 1961 to 1965, and the sixth five-year plan was for the period running from 1987 through 1991. The seventh is now in operation.

2. And there seems to be a harsh critical voice that they are spending too much if they are earning annually more than U.S. $20,000.

3. The judicial examination is provided for by a Presidential Decree and is under the control of the Ministry of General Affairs. Each year a committee for the examination is organized; most of its members are law professors, judges, prosecuting attorneys and practicing lawyers. Otherwise, it is quite similar to the bar examination in the United States.

4. The number of applicants for the national examination for the past five years has been: 1987, 14,963; 1988, 14,245; 1989, 14,202; 1990, 15,041; and 1991, 16,296.

5. The number is fixed by government regulation at between two hundred and fifty and three hundred.

6. Once it was half jokingly said that there was a political party named *Yookboeb Tang*, members of which were graduates of the Military Academy and the College of Law of Seoul National University. The joke went on to say that the party is mightier than any other political party in its influence on the domestic political scene.

7. The Ministry of Government Administration, the government office which is in charge of managing the national judicial examination, which for some years selected 300 each year, has selected less than 290 for the three years 1991-3.

8. In Japan where there is an identical system for recruiting lawyers, some Japanese scholars call these people "legal staff."

10. For detailed information on this section, see Economic Planning Board, *Economic Policies During the Years of Development, Twenty Year History of the Economic Planning Board*, 1982 (in Korean).

11. The term was the government's. Massive support was given for agricultural subsidies and for "New Village Movements" to enhance rural living conditions.

12. For the role of law in Korean economic progress, see Jang Hie Lee, "The Role of Law in the Process of Korean Modernization" (in Korean) in Sung Chick Hong, *et al.*, *Research on Social Development in Korea* XXI) Asian Research Institute, Korea University, pp. 141 *et seq.*

13. The curricula of primary and secondary education are regulated by the Ministry of Education.

14. A government supported research institute.

15. For comparative figures for countries in the Pacific Basin, see J. Barton and S. Jordan "The International Legal Community in the Pacific Basin," chapter 4 of this volume, Table 4.1.

8

Litigation in Silicon Valley Industries

Philip S.C. Lewis

Complaints of a "litigation explosion" have led to a recent acceleration of interest in the study of litigation.[1] Recent work has most significantly concentrated on documenting changes in the quantity of litigation cases and the categories in which they fall. In the most significant paper Galanter and Rogers[2] show that much of the increase is in cases between businesses, and tentatively associate it with changes in business relationships, in particular the means available for businesses to achieve "orderly commercial dealings" (p. 35). On this basis the study of litigation is not just a response to concerns about waste or lawyer misbehavior, or a specialist field of study of the braking effects of lawsuits on national productivity; Galanter and Rogers show that the study of litigation can be a signpost to the nature of changing business relationships. But it may be more: we may be going through a period where the establishment of rights and litigation to enforce them is increasingly used as a conscious tool of business strategy, to protect markets, and establish lines of technological development for the future.

Most studies of litigation have been either of particular cases, of large samples (particularly of the disputes underlying them, as in the Wisconsin study[3]), or of aggregate cases which are then at least partially disaggregated (as in Galanter and Rogers).[4] In this chapter I look at a locality significant for the development of an industry, to see the changing nature and incidence of its litigation. I then set it against the discussion in Galanter and Rogers, and suggest that we should see litigation in the context of other moves in industry to restructure business governance mechanisms in favor of particular companies.

The Industry

The basic story is described by Krislov[5] and Gilder,[6] and revolves round silicon, and its functional development.[7] Though the integrated circuit was invented both at Texas Instruments, far away from Silicon Valley, and at Fairchild, a few miles from Stanford, and its practical development made possible by licenses from each, it was in Silicon Valley that it was most strongly developed; that was regarded as the mainstream. Although Motorola, in Phoenix, Arizona, was Fairchild's major competitor in the 1960s[8], it was in Silicon Valley, at Intel, that the next major functional advances were made, the development of computer memory in successful integrated circuit form[9] and the invention of the single-chip microprocessor, along with the EPROM.[10]

It is important to recognise that the companies which revolved round silicon and the integrated circuit did not start in a vacuum. One of the most important factors was the presence of the satellite and missile divisions of Lockheed a few miles away, which provided an important part of the market for their early products.[11] At Stanford University Terman had inaugurated an approach of linking the university and industry, both through the laboratories which trained PhDs in electrical engineering suitable for local employment, as well as engaging in fundamental research, and also by providing land at modest rents in the Stanford Industrial Park for the potential employers and exploiters of technology. There were already three successful local electronics companies, Watkins Johnson, Hewlett Packard and Varian, and it was individuals from Hewlett Packard who were responsible for the first effective personal computer. While specialists had already used Intel-designed chips to create personal computers which required the users to be programmers, it was Jobs and Wozniak who produced the Apple computer, which could be programmed to be used by all. The IBM PC, introduced in 1981, which is credited with legitimating the personal computer for business use, was designed in consultation with Intel engineers. In the 1980s there have been a substantial number of makers of advanced chip designs,[12] and these have given rise to many of the so-called high-end workstations, with graphics capabilities for the scientist and the engineer, which have been produced in the area (Sun, Silicon Graphics, Hewlett Packard), In addition there have been a number of successful software companies, notably Oracle (a few miles to the north), a very successful database company, and Adobe Systems, whose Postscript language and type fonts contributed substantially to the success of the Apple Macintosh. Not all computer companies in the area deal only in workstations and personal computers; Amdahl was one of the first manufacturers of mainframe computers "plug-compatible", with those from IBM, Hewlett Packard were very successful in minicomputers, and Tandem grew rapidly as producers of failure-proof computers which could handle thousands of transactions simultaneously. In addition, the Valley has a substantial presence in communications, an important neighbouring technology. There are also a number of biotechnology and specialist pharmaceutical companies in the area.

The area, however, is not where the computer industry itself began. Although IBM has long had a facility in San Jose, just to the south, the centers of mainframe computing have been elsewhere, New York State and Minnesota, for instance. When mainframes were challenged by the minicomputer, that was the work of DEC, from outside Boston. Nor are the fundamentals of personal computing all to be found in Silicon Valley. Although the first operating system for Intel chips was comparatively local (Digital Research, discussed later), when IBM introduced its PC it used a company in Seattle to design the operating system; this company later became Microsoft. Ashton Tate, whose dBase II was the first successful database program for the personal computer, was based in Los Angeles, while the first spreadsheet, which gave the Apple computer a business use, came from the East. Texas Instruments shared with Fairchild the invention of the integrated circuit, while Motorola has always been a successful competitor for Intel. Nevertheless, no other area rivals Silicon Valley in the number, concentration and significance of related businesses.

What happened to make Silicon Valley "take off", develop such radical and far-reaching innovations and generate so much employment? This has been the subject of continuous study, largely generated by those who have sought to recreate it in other areas and countries. Geographers have made a special study of the spatial location of industry, and what gives rise to this form of aggregation of enterprise. They have focussed on the relationships between the local companies. It is not enough, they say, to have a strong local university and supportive services, such as venture capital; it is the shared technical interests of the companies and a degree of interdependence which makes for such a successful aggregation. In the earlier years, the well-known spin-offs, along with a general mobility of employment, ensured a diffusion of technical advances. In addition, there were formal and informal (read "social") channels for communicating information and ideas; an anecdote[13] describes an engineer going in a presentation to the edge of what was secret in his company to elicit questions which might reveal what their rivals were working on. Further, there came to be specialists in particular fields, who could provide state-of-the-art services to a number of different companies with similar needs, without each having to be involved in the R & D costs.

Saxenian[14] has analyzed this process particularly for the 1980s, at a point when the semiconductor business was enjoying a particular resurgence. She describes the growth of arrangements in which companies pool their expertise and facilities; thus, one might bring expertise in chip-design, the other advanced fabrication facilities. Another example is that of computer companies, Apple and Sun, which acted as systems integrators, bringing together engineers from a number of companies each with specific skills in components such as disk drive controllers. These arrangements required a fair amount of trust and continued cooperation in ways which could not always be predicted at the beginning of the relationship, and thus could not easily be specified in contracts.[15] She quotes an executive from Apple as saying that it was trust that was needed, not "armies of attorneys". What is also important for the study of localization is the need for the cooperating parties to be close to each other; it was difficult to work with someone hundreds of miles away.[16]

Technological joint ventures, of course, pervade these as well as other high-tech industries. We have interviewed a number of lawyers involved in them. Although approaches may differ, we were shown a contract between a German and a fairly small English company which was an inch thick, involving the expenditure of substantial lawyer time. Those involved in them as in-house lawyers at the biggest companies see them as exceedingly complex and beyond the abilities of even large-firm lawyers in private practice.[17] Though much more work would be needed to demonstrate this, it does seem likely that local connection can create specific forms of relationship which will affect the legalization of relations; this may have some influence on patterns of litigation.

That the use of litigation is in some way determined by the relationships between potentially litigating parties has long been taken as self-evident.[18] It has been assumed that parties in "long-term continuing relations" would not litigate with each other. Krislov, elsewhere in this book, describes the early days of Silicon Valley as exhibiting a "subtle mixture of cooperation and competition", which might, on this basis, have been enough to inhibit litigation. But certainly as time went on, the range of relationships between companies might become greater; some might be arms' length suppliers or customers, some might be customers or suppliers cooperating on product development or manufacture, or otherwise linked by the need for continuity of supply, some might be competitors with a common interest in expanding the size and significance of the field, or who were cooperating in some other way, while others might be competitors who were geographically or otherwise outsiders, or even thieves of physical or intellectual property. All these situations might provide different opportunities and incentive structures for litigation, and should be borne in mind as a background for what follows.

Litigation and Its Categories

This paper concentrates on civil litigation, with some mention both of arbitration (and other forms of alternate dispute resolution) and of proceedings before the International Trade Commission ("ITC"), which have assumed considerable importance in relation to imports into the United States. To some extent this limitation is arbitrary. The rough general category might be something like "enlisting the help of authoritative third parties against other businesses", and the behavior it includes might be a continuum all the way up to successful legislative lobbying. Even a limitation to those third parties who act (or are supposed to act) under comparatively stable and recognisable standards might not be workable, if it excluded civil litigation which was pushing at the edges of currently applicable law. Nevertheless, civil litigation is the archetype of party initiative in the legal field, and so offers a sensible starting point.

Two forms of activity might be seen as close parallels. The first is the instigation of criminal investigation and prosecution, in cases in which for some reason those to be investigated are not merely seen as overstepping the bounds of competition. Since the prosecuting authorities may have attitudes and methods of their own, they are likely to bring a different approach to problems which, in this kind of industry, may be very unfamiliar to them.[19] The second is the use of complaints to government departments. An elegant recent example is a case in which a Swiss company complained to the International Trade Commission[20] over patent infringement by a Japanese company, while the Japanese company instigated a Department of Defense investigation of the Swiss company for export control violations.[21] And, relatedly, one should mention antitrust actions and FTC enforcement. It may be that some of the industry's attitudes towards licensing stemmed from the conditions about licensing patents imposed on AT&T in 1956, and although the antitrust battles between IBM and its competitors did not directly affect the microcomputer or the chip, some of the attitudes against size and monopoly may have affected the way the Valley did business. It is only recently that the FTC has been taking a serious interest, with investigations of Microsoft and Intel.[22]

There are good reasons, when one is considering the effects of the law on an industry, not to concentrate too much on the legal categories which are used, but to look at relationships, substantive grounds for complaint and outcomes. Nevertheless, this is an industry in which intellectual property has come to play, and intentionally so, an increasingly significant part, and a fair amount of effort is spent on orienting the company's activity towards its creation. Contract, of course, is a staple, but five forms of protection of intellectual property are significant; they are not only litigated over but lobbied for. They are trade marks, patents, copyright, the special mask protection given by the 1984 legislation described by Krislov, and trade secrets. Members of the industry in California have certainly recently lobbied over trade secrets (in the California legislature), over mask protection (in the Congress), and over copyright protection for software (in the European Community). Interviews both locally and in England, as well as articles in the press, suggest how much effort goes into identifying intellectual property and protecting it according to the most appropriate intellectual property category. In the case of some items, for instance, the most recent Intel microprocessors, all might apply.[23] Perhaps the other part of the law with the greatest impact was that related to the raising of capital; here again enormous efforts went into the initial capital structures which provided the incentives and rewards for the venture capitalists, the entrepreneurs and the engineers, and also into the initial public offerings, which to some extent provided the pay-off for the most successful enterprises. Aspects of the tax code are also significant, and electronics company trade associations took an active part in the successful lobbying in the late 1970s on reduced capital gains tax rates, which preceded a dramatic increase in the amount of available venture capital.

The background to some of the more important cases will be described later. Plainly, Silicon Valley companies, like any others, engage in the ordinary transactions in which, from time to time, customers do not pay, the goods are alleged to be defective, or not to do what the buyer says that the seller gave him to understand that they would do.[24] They have problems with employees they have dismissed,[25] with safety regulations and injuries at work,[26] and substantial environmental problems. Problems with unions and unionizing activity were next to non-existent. For the companies which were more successful, and then met setbacks after their initial public offerings, litigation over their public offering statements might safely be expected.[27]

Three main categories of problem were or became recurrent from soon after the invention of the integrated circuit. The first was that of departing employees. It soon became part of Valley culture that it was acceptable to leave one company to establish or join another, whether to develop another product, to have more interesting or more responsible work, to have the possibility of an equity stake in the new company, or simply for better pay or working conditions.[28] For reasons discussed later, actions against such employees, and sometimes their new companies, became a staple of Silicon Valley life.

Secondly, there were the problems often lumped together under the heading of intellectual property. This may, however, be to confuse the problems with the means for their solution. A determination to secure license fees for the use of an invention may be different from trying to establish a protected market segment, or from the run-of-the-mill effort to keep the company's trade identity clear by protecting trade marks.[29]

Thirdly, perhaps more recent than the others, there are the after-effects of failed cooperation. As has been said, this is an industry with a lot of cooperation, partly to achieve technological advances, but also to ensure the prevalence of standards. Thus, it was initially common practice, to ensure the success of a particular chip design, to ensure that there was a second source licensed to produce it, so that those considering the adoption of the chip in their equipment would not feel themselves vulnerable to shortages of supply or the vagaries of a non-competitive pricing policy.[30] This practice might involve the disclosure of not only design but also manufacturing details. In any cooperation, there comes a point where it is tempting for one party or the other to break ranks, and take for itself a greater share in the benefits of the cooperation; plainly in such a position it is the other party which can mount the most effective competition. As we shall see, some of the most bitter litigation seems to come from broken down cooperation.

Finally, by the middle 1970s at the latest the industry and competition had become international. Both straight copying and debated patent infringements might have to be pursued in courts even less suited to the speedy enforcement of rights than those in the U.S. One U.S. interview by the SVRP mentioned a case where patent infringement in Japan was only remedied by the intervention of the president of a friendly and influential Japanese company. The most effective means of dealing with the problem was seen as attacking imports to the U.S., either in the courts or eventually through the International Trade Commission. This did not, however, deal with the problem of sales outside the U.S., which has required pressure on a number of fronts to improve (from a U.S. point of view) local laws and procedures on the establishment, recognition and enforcement of intellectual property rights.

History

There is some temptation to regard the early period of Silicon Valley as some kind of litigation-free Golden Age, in which employees went from company to company without being sued, and patents were not applied for, not enforced or freely cross-licensed.

The accepted picture is described by Krislov elsewhere in this volume: this state of affairs lasted till the 1980s when everything changed. Companies became more assiduous in the identification and protection of their intellectual property,[31] and more aggressive about suing departing employees and competitors.

In this spirit, Roger Borovoy, former patent counsel for Fairchild, has recently written of a time in which Fairchild and Texas Instruments could sit down and settle a patent licence in a few months.[32] But he was described by Malone[33] as spending years litigating with Texas Instruments over the patent rights to the invention of the integrated circuit (a case which went to the Court of Appeals) and chasing down royalties for Fairchild. In the first year or so of Fairchild's existence employees went off to form another company (Rheem Electronics), apparently taking with them a "cook-book" of Fairchild's manufacturing recipes for transistor-based components. Fairchild recovered $70,000 in the settlement, although one of the other side said that the judge was indignant when he learned that the Fairchild management had themselves left Shockley Laboratories in a group.[34] Similarly, a few years later, when yet other employees (the seventh Fairchild spin-off) left Fairchild to set up a new company, the owners in the East insisted that they be sued; on this occasion no money passed, but it is said that the departing employees promised not to use a process they had no intention of using anyway.

The episode which is seen as typifying the Golden Age comes towards the end of the 1960s, when employees were leaving Fairchild in large numbers to join Sporck at National Semiconductor.[35] No actions were brought, although Malone suggests that National cheated by promising not to hire certain employees, who then left, joined other companies for a few months, and were then hired. What seemed to matter to Noyce, then in charge of Fairchild, (and perhaps to Bay, the general manager) was whether employees had actually taken proprietary information, rather than whether they could achieve some competitive advantage by litigating.[36] Hoefler, writing only a couple of years from the event, was more sceptical; although one reason was Sporck's strong friendship with the Fairchild top line and the many real contributions he had made to that company, another reason might have been that a number of Fairchild's insiders made substantial capital gains in National's stock, buying it at very depressed prices before the Sporck move was made public.

Without a thorough search of the case records, one cannot say with certainty that this situation was as typical as it has since been taken to be. Though written sources about Silicon Valley do not have much, if anything, to say about litigation in the 1970s until towards the end, an attorney who arrived in Palo Alto in the early 1970s to do litigation work said that much of the litigation was of the "split-off, start-up kind of thing" in what was then becoming known as Silicon Valley.[37] In the computer industry generally antitrust litigation against IBM seems to have been frequent. In the middle 1970s AT&T was making claims on a manufacturing patent against Intel and other companies, who were refusing to pay, and had too few patents to cross-license.[38] The case proceeded to discovery before being settled at a moderate fixed fee. Here the company suing was, from the Valley point of view, an outsider.

It is also unclear whether as little attention was paid to the establishment of intellectual property rights in the late 1960s and in the 1970s as is now said. There are, it is true, famous examples of the failure to patent basic inventions. There was no apparent attempt to create any intellectual property protection for the Graphical User Interface first created at Xerox PARC, nor for the basic use of the mouse as a method of interaction with the screen and for the input of commands. In the field of biotechnology a basic technique (monoclonal antibodies) was not patented. Intel's first microprocessor was not patented as such; only a particular aspect of it.[39]

I know of no assessment of patent activity in the industry in the 1970s, or the extent to which, as is now common, there were systematic reviews in companies to ensure the creation of patents where possible. A patent attorney who started practice at the end of the decade said that there were only 4 patent attorneys in the area at the time, and that clients were quite relaxed even when sued for patent infringement, thinking it was worthwhile to go on and market the allegedly infringing products. In other fields we know that Intel, who by 1975 were facing intense international competition, were in 1978 suing (unsuccessfully) to seek to require the Copyright Office to register the copyright on one of their chips. In 1979 they took part in the first effort to persuade Congress to give semiconductors *sui generis* protection, an effort which failed because the industry was divided as to the extent of the protection to be given. In practice, however, they were licensing their chips, though whether or not on favorable terms I do not know.[40]

With some reservations because the 1970s have been so little documented, I would accept that there was some change from the early 1980s, though less than the conventional picture suggests. A Palo Alto lawyer interviewed by the SVRP agreed that companies pursue departing employees more frequently,[41] and a judge who had tried such cases thought that attitudes had definitely become much harder, and that "almost any employee leaving to form a new company can expect, unless he has prepared himself very well with his former employer, to be on the receiving end of a lawsuit."[42] Like child abuse, it goes through generations; one case represented the third generation of spin-off to be sued. Not all such lawsuits will be vigorously pursued, at least where the new employer is an existing company; the CEO of Cypress Semiconductors claimed to have been sued 23 times without any case having come to court.[43] Krislov discusses the increase in patent litigation elsewhere in this volume. The number of patents is growing at an enormous rate, fuelled by tactics of patent bracketing and clustering, while there are estimated to be 10-20,000 applications for software patents that have been filed.[44] More than one source describes the need for new start-up companies to acquire patent portfolios of their own as soon as possible, as part of their business plan, so as to have something with which to bargain with those who will inevitably sue them. Recent SVRP interviews in which the issue has been specifically addressed, tend to confirm a sense of an increase in litigation, including patent litigation, in the early 1980s, along with an increase in the vigor with which it has been pursued.

In addition, the aims of intellectual property changed for some companies; they were not just trying to keep other people off their backs, but consciously seeking a return on their R & D activities; some, too, were seeking to establish a monopoly in a particular area; their litigation, that is, was aimed at stopping their competitors completely from engaging in particular courses of action. The strongest examples are Apple in relation to its operating system and Intel in relation to their most recent generations of chips.[45] On the "look and feel" side (the appearance of the screen and the lay-out of the commands necessary to operate the program) we know that Lotus has so far stopped competitors entirely.[46] The biotechnology field also seems to be one in which patent litigation is not merely about license fees.

The other growth area in litigation has been that of shareholders' suits over the decline in the value of a company's stock after its Initial

Public Offering, which has already been mentioned, and which has been shown to be the product of insurance (or other cash fund) and an enterprising plaintiffs' bar.[47] Nearly half the litigation department of one of the major Palo Alto firms is dealing with such cases for high-technology defendants.

Illustrative Cases

An earlier section outlined the most frequent and significant kinds of case, and mentioned the special situation where companies had been in some kind of previous relationship, as is the case with the departing employee. The case of *Hitachi* v *Motorola* is illustrative; Hitachi were engaged in research which would produce faster versions of the Motorola 68000 (which powered the original Macintosh).[48] In their cross-litigation over the Motorola 68030 chip the judge eventually banged their heads together by granting each an injunction against the other for patent infringement.[49] Here I describe two sets of cases in greater detail, to illuminate some of the connections which litigation can have to technological change. One is the litigation brought by Apple to maintain its exclusive position in relation to the Macintosh user interface, and the other is the litigation brought by Intel, mainly against AMD. Both, as has been said, sought to maintain a monopoly position; Apple could do so because of its enormous success with the Apple II, and Intel because of its position as the initial designer of the microprocessors for all IBM-compatible machines.

The legal background to this litigation is substantial uncertainty about the relevant law. Even when it had become clear that some aspects of software attracted copyright protection, specific applications of the law remained undecided, whether the availability of patent protection for hardware meant that there could not be copyright protection for the contents of ROMS, or for the microcode in the CPU, and what line should be drawn in the context of software between unprotected idea and protected expression. The limits of software patents, first recognized by the Supreme Court at the beginning of the decade, have not yet been seriously litigated. Thus, Apple's earliest litigation was against Franklin for copying its operating system, which was in ROM in the Apple II, and it was not until 1983, after Apple had lost at first instance that a Federal appeals court settled that it was protected by copyright.[50] When the Macintosh was introduced it was its user interface that was the key to its success, and Apple's efforts turned to that. One interesting point is that although Apple has so far not licensed either its operating system or its graphical interface,[51] it was in some kind of contractual relationship with both the companies it has sued over the latter.

Apple had the disadvantage (which many people thought disqualified them from claiming copyright) that Apple employees had admitted taking important ideas for the Apple interface from the Xerox Star (a commercially unsuccessful computer introduced in 1981) and from a visit to the Xerox research center in Palo Alto. However, the company seems to have acted with vigor and good judgement. Several graphical interfaces were coming onto the market at that time. Apple certainly did not sue IBM, whose product was in any case not very likely to be successful. In relation to Microsoft, the companies entered into an agreement in November 1985. Microsoft acknowledged that the visual display in version 1.0 of their product, Windows, was a "derivative work" and Apple agreed to grant to Microsoft "a nonexclusive, worldwide, royalty-free, perpetual, nontransferable license to use these derivative works in present and future software programs and to license them to and through third parties for use in their software programs."

Apple appears to have taken this course for three reasons; firstly, Microsoft was a prosperous company, in full co-operation with IBM, secondly, that version of Windows never looked to be a serious competitor with the Apple user interface, and if a successor was likely to fare better (as has been the case with Windows 3.0 and 3.1), the acknowledgment might be invaluable, and thirdly (as industry commentators suggest), Microsoft had hurried to bring out full-featured word-processor and spreadsheet programs for the Macintosh at a time when the Macintosh's ultimate success was still not certain.

Its other competitor was a very different proposition. Digital Research ("DR") had never recovered the central position it had in the earliest days of the personal computer, but it remained an innovative company,[52] and in 1985 had produced the GEM graphics interface, which could sit on top of the MS-DOS operating system which ran on IBM and IBM-compatible machines and also run on other innovative machines, such as the Atari ST, which was being rushed to market at the time as a possible competitor to the Macintosh. GEM's success could have had a radical effect, since it would made available a graphical interface on hardware which was not Apple's, and was much cheaper. Unfortunately, the actual appearance of the screen followed the new Macintosh screen quite closely, and in a case in 1985, apparently at a time when DR was short of cash[53] and needed to introduce a new product quickly, it was forced to withdraw its original design, as well as paying an undisclosed sum of money to Apple. DR agreed to produce new versions that differed substantially in both appearance and operation, and to remove comparisons with the Macintosh from their advertising. There had also apparently been non-disclosure agreements, so this may be another of the cases where cooperation had turned into hostility. The revised version of GEM never became of particular importance on IBM-compatible machines.

Apple further sought to defend themselves when Steve Jobs, who was behind the Macintosh, left to set up another company relying heavily on a graphical user interface, suing him to restrain him from using Apple secrets. The action was settled, and no further action seems to have been brought against his new company, NeXT, although its interface uses many of the features on which Apple relied on against Microsoft.

As the decade went on, the courts seemed to be moving in the direction of upholding, not the use of windows and icons, as such, but a more general concept of the "look and feel" of the user interface, the way the components were arranged on the screen, and the appearance of the menus of choices with which users were faced. Thus, if one manufacturer's software took an early lead, it might be the case that other software, with totally different underlying coding, could not build on the way of working or the facility which users had developed with the earlier software, even if the makers offered improved performance or features. Apple began their litigation against Microsoft and Hewlett-Packard in 1987 with a strategy (developed in-house) slanted towards this more general concept. Their position seemed to be strengthened when in the meantime Lotus Development, in successful litigation, maintained a hold on the standard set by the interface of their spreadsheet product.

However, whether or not concern for U.S. competitiveness has led to a strengthening of intellectual property generally, as Krislov argues elsewhere in this volume, at least in the field of software protection there has recently been a pull-back in the U.S. courts from its more extreme versions, possibly in recognition of the interest of users in competition in the substance of the operating system or application software which lies behind a more or less standard user interface. The Apple-Microsoft-Hewlett-Packard case seems to be an illustration of this tendency, as the court has, over the years, gradually whittled down the bases on which Apple might claim to something like virtual equivalence, at which point Apple, at the time of writing, seems to have given up, at least pending an appeal.

One lesson is that strategic litigation may have its assumptions challenged while it goes through the courts. When this case began, Microsoft and IBM were cooperating, and there seemed little reason to believe that the version of Windows under attack in the case was really the software of the future. Whether Apple were attempting to gain a monopoly in graphical user interfaces, whether they were just hoping for license revenues or whether, as has been suggested, it was an attempt to set back the cooperative efforts of Microsoft and IBM is not public knowledge. With the success of later versions of Windows[54], there has been some distancing of Microsoft (who had less interest in ensuring compatibility with IBM software which has not proved successful) and IBM (who may have been concerned that the Apple lawsuit was likely to succeed), and there is now a partnership between Apple and IBM in which the Apple user interface will be used on IBM equipment and new operating system software will be jointly developed. The litigation, if successful, might then have had value in diminishing Microsoft's ability to compete with the new alliance.

We see, then, that litigation has a time-scale unsuitable for an industry with rapid product turn-over, sudden and frequent realignments and shifting and uncertain law. Intel, however, has some continuities in the series of microprocessors which are its central products, and has sought since the middle 1980s to keep itself from entangling alliances. But in earlier days it did have cooperation agreements with other microprocessor manufacturers, and much of its litigation has been with two of these former partners (NEC and AMD), in each case outlasting several versions of the original technology involved. It is also just getting going on patent litigation, where it will not have to prove copying.[55]

Though Intel attempted, as already mentioned, to achieve protection for its chip layouts by lobbying for the passage of mask-protection legislation its actual case against NEC proceeded under copyright, again with some uncertainty as to whether the microcode in its 8086 and 8088 chips was protected. It was held to be protected in principle, although it lost its protection for technical reasons of marking.[56] The chips in question were long outdated by the time of the ultimate decision, though the principle may have had some use.

The AMD case seems an object-lesson in the need for care in drafting joint ventures or technology-sharing agreements. Arbitration and subsequent proceedings have been going on for some six years, and the amount of time spent in the arbitration, and in the courts arguing about the arbitrator's jurisdiction, illustrate well-known arguments against Alternative Dispute Resolution. Again, cooperation broke down. When Intel introduced the 80286 chip, which was used for the IBM AT, it needed second sources for it. One was Advanced Micro Devices, with whom it made a complicated agreement calling for a pooling of inventions, a points-based assessment of their value, and monetary compensation for any difference in the value of the innovations contributed to the pool. By the time Intel decided to keep the next generation of chips, the 80386, for itself and IBM, it had also (coincidentally?) decided that AMD was not pulling its weight, and sought to terminate the agreement, which still had several years to run. Fortunes have continued to change in the arbitration and the courts; but although the situation remains in some doubt, Intel has enjoyed considerable success in delaying AMD's access to the market for the 80486, till recently the most advanced IBM-compatible chip, and its profits have reached record heights,

In the meantime, several smaller companies designed alternatives for Intel's floating-point chips, and they, too, were met by litigation; here though Intel's efforts totally failed to keep the competing chips off the market, and the price of these chips crashed.

Intel has plainly been pursuing a concerted strategy of establishing rights which it can then, and does, enforce by litigation.[57] It can be said for Intel that it has used the very substantial profits from its near-monopoly position on R & D for the next generations of chips; on the other hand, its use of all five legal methods of protection for its designs and its dominant position in the field of IBM-compatible computers attracted the interest of the FTC; both AMD and one of the floating-point chip manufacturers have brought anti-trust actions against it. But it may be that the industry has no need to turn to government to counteract monopoly; the new IBM-Apple strategy, mentioned above, relies initially on Motorola chips, and there are distinct signs of shifts away from any particular chip, or indeed any particular operating system.[58]

Effects

One of the ideas behind the SVRP has been to investigate what, if any, effects the law, lawyers and litigation have had on this remarkable economic and technological development. Thinking of the Intel and Apple stories told above I am tempted to suggest that litigation has had some effect in prolonging a monopoly in a way which encourages innovation and fresh combinations in order to bypass it. An English interview[59] suggested that Xerox's stranglehold on copier patents, which it did not license, led to Japanese manufacturers' developing lower-cost plain-paper copiers which took over particular parts of the market, and certainly Intel has now made powerful competitors for itself. Conversely, at least one of the companies describing itself as not litigious is also quite ready to license its technology and encourages its use in the hope of becoming a standard. Such arguments seem quite contingent, and would need a lot of detailed examination.

Those who attach importance to rights as the basis of economic activity may see litigation as their guarantor; I myself prefer to be less certain about its function and effects, but recognize that this may then say very little. It is true that once one leaves generalities statements about particular effects seem rather uninteresting. The Palo Alto lawyer already quoted thought that some companies had been diverted by the threat of litigation from activities they could usefully (and also legitimately, though this is not relevant in this context) have pursued. A specific example of his point might have been the withdrawal of a venture capitalist from financing a company when named as a "co-conspirator" in a trade secrets case;[60] in any case litigation against a start-up is likely to affect the minds of creditors, suppliers and customers, and lead, for instance, to a new employee not being allowed to work in his own field for a period. Often one cannot know the effects of litigation, as is the case with the Fujitsu-IBM arbitration, or the Intel-Seeq litigation, because the parties have in effect sealed the record. Even when one knows the amount of a judgment it is difficult to assess its effect on the parties without a very detailed knowledge of their financial position.[61] And generally there are so many factors affecting the success of a company or a process that litigation cannot be isolated. The earliest case I have mentioned, *Fairchild v Rheem*, is an example. Rheem actually went out of business a couple of years after the settlement, but it seems just not to have got into the new technology.

Perhaps one can see the precautionary effects, the careful documentation of legitimate practices of reverse engineering ("clean room techniques"), and possibly also the careful review of behavior and language in the period leading up to an Initial Public Offering.[62] Software developers, who may now face patent disputes, are advised to keep careful records of their work in bound and witnessed notebooks, and a number of in-house counsel, both in the US and in England, are engaged in intellectual property auditing. It is right to say that participants can be more downright. An attorney defending a software company from an inventor not seen in the industry as having made any contribution to the technology said: "Forget the money that's lost in legal costs. That's just part of it. It's the diversion of engineering talent in evaluating these patents, and trying to fend them off that is the great hindrance."[63]

Explanations

Although I can give no figures, I accept that there has been a rise in the amount of litigation in the industries discussed here. How should we account for it? Krislov argues that the industry has matured, and that there has been a period of shake-out and consolidation. "Where there is not enough market share to go round—no sense of a rising tide—companies tend to fight market battles in the courtroom", he says.[64]

It is a theme of Gilder's book *Microcosm*, that the concept of "maturity" in the context of this industry is one used by people who want competition to proceed on well-understood lines rather than accepting that radical innovation is still possible,[65] and I will be arguing a related point. But those involved in these events who have been interviewed find the Krislov account acceptable; in fact, they too use metaphors from the relationship of mankind and nature. A judge compared the scene to a fishing-hole someone discovers; first, he fishes himself, then he tells his friends, then they tell their friends, and suddenly there are not enough fish to go round. A lawyer speaking about departing employees said that there were enough trees for everyone in the forest; no need to worry if someone went off and started his own farm. The same man used the metaphor of kids in a candy-store to describe the early days of the industry. Similarly, though not in the context of litigation, Malone[66] describes the sense of limitless demand in the late 1970s after the invention of the personal computer. Nevertheless, even in these flush times companies failed, although the reaction of those in them might have been to go off and join or form a better one.

I would suggest that although the maturing market argument may have some force it is somewhat undifferentiated, and does not do justice to a number of points.

Firstly, we can look at the motivations for particular cases and see that they only partly fit within the maturing market explanation, which needs to be supplemented at least by some consideration of changing attitudes. Secondly, analysis using a concept operative in the industry at the time suggests that resort to the court-room may be only one means of achieving the desired end. Finally, I consider the application of a well-known discussion by Galanter and Rogers,[67] and argue that the data discussed here require a slight extension of their account, but that it then describes the situation fairly well.

There would seem to be some scope for looking at the motivations for specific cases, although the discussion above shows how difficult it may be to find out what they are. I have mentioned Reuter's reference to the need to look at specific fields to see the effects of liability, and to the fact that in the semiconductor industry frequent lay-offs and an educated workforce increased the amount of litigation.[68] More specifically still, a Silicon Valley lawyer familiar with trade secret litigation spoke of motivations he had frequently come across for suing departing employees. One was merely a sense of breach of loyalty, of being let down, which in its outcome could verge on spite, a desire to damage the new competitor without regard to the costs and benefits to the plaintiff. Sometimes action against the departing employee might be recommended to make him a scapegoat for the failings in the department he had left. This lawyer felt that the proportion of cases for which there was a good reason might have risen, firstly because lawyers had come to have a moderating effect in pointing out the disadvantages of litigation, particularly of grudge litigation, but also because the industry had become more specialized, people had a narrower area of expertise, and so, if they left to set up a new company it was a real possibility that that company would be competing with the old one. Though his emphasis was on motivation, this is a structural argument, to some extent supporting Krislov's case.

These are the reasons for specific cases. But it looks as if companies such as Texas Instruments, Apple and Intel, for varying reasons, developed a strategy of which litigation was a part. In the case of Texas Instruments, this was not so much to maintain market share as to bring in revenue, to exploit intellectual property rights in themselves, rather than to use them to protect its own products from competition.[69] In the case of Intel it was to buttress innovation. In an English pharmaceutical company it turned out that the company lawyer had designed and implemented a systematic campaign of litigation to protect the company's trade marks and to keep out parallel imports; he proudly showed me the original drawing of a cartoon about it which had appeared in a trade journal.

More generally, the view that it is the maturing market which brings companies to the court-room does not account for variations over time or between companies, particularly variations in attitudes. If it were the only factor one would expect there to be a neutral attitude towards litigation, one which was concerned not with rights and wrongs, but with costs and benefits. Yet we have seen that in the Fairchild-NSC situation the reason given for not suing was a legal or moral one. There are also companies which articulate a position against litigation; those which did so in some 1987 interviews conducted by the SVRP tended to be amongst the biggest and most successful. Some said that the company was litigation averse. One described his company as not trigger-happy; it preferred to settle things,[70] and this was confirmed by the general counsel of their English subsidiary. Another said that they regarded litigation as a waste, and the in-house lawyers would go in and see whether there was not merit in the other side's case, even if they were not entitled to as much as they thought; they associated litigation with leaving things to outside counsel to deal with. A contrasting view (from the lawyer to the English subsidiary of a US company) was that businessmen underestimated the costs in time and effort of litigation; he would do anything to keep them out of it. One said that the people who litigated were the ones "being killed in this business," because there was a problem right in their strategic path. Apart from people in that situation, one could, and should, choose not to litigate.

In between these positions there can be variations as to what people see as costs. Thus, when engineers from Digital (DEC) left to form Data General, Olsen, the founder of DEC, did not sue in spite of his conviction that they had taken with them designs done in Digital paid time; he later said that he was glad they did not sue, because the destructive emotions would have torn them apart: they made computers instead.[71] Perhaps the item whose valuation is most uncertain is the impact of litigation on long-term continuing relations. It has been a truism of law and society studies that litigation does not take place in the context of such relations, and an in-house counsel in England thought that it would be impossible. The view that it is culturally impossible has been expressed very strongly by the President of Cypress,[72] who was being sued and taken to the ITC, along with others, by Texas Instruments over a claim of patent infringement. They were customers of each other in other areas, and Cypress claimed to have helped TI in its relations with government. Plainly either TI did not think it impossible, or thought that it was a cost outweighed by the benefits, or that it was a cost which would go away, in that other companies would come to see suing and being sued not as hostile acts but as ordinary concomitants of business.[73]

Although, then, there may be something to the situational argument put forward by Krislov, I think that both the concept of different ways of protecting market segments put forward by Davidow and these perceptual ideas may be useful modifications to it.

Davidow[74] argues that companies seek to achieve a market segment for their product sufficient in size for stability and profitability but protected in some way from competitors. He scarcely mentions property rights and does not mention litigation, but plainly these would be barriers against competition of the kind he thinks that companies try to achieve. But he sees the principal barriers as created by innovation and product differentiation. In particular he contrasts devices and products, and describes how Intel's device (its microprocessor), when he became Marketing Director, was not actually as good as Motorola's, but they concentrated on integrating it into a system, and providing sales and customer support through skilled engineers. The total product became the sum of processor, system tools and support, better and more useful to customers than anything Motorola could provide; once adopted it was hard for customers to give it up. Devices, though, are usually what intellectual property rights defend, and we can see that the rights are likely to become significant when for some reason the device becomes easily replaceable in the product. Thus, for mass-market shrinkwrap software companies enforcement of the copyright protection of their software (their device, as it were) is vital, whereas for a corporate database company, I was told, it is unimportant, since the user needs the whole product, including support, tailoring and maintenance.[75]

Conclusion

To the extent that there is an increase in business-against-business litigation to be seen in Silicon Valley it parallels the developments charted by Galanter and Rogers[76] in their examination of the reality of the "litigation explosion;" they argue that the explosion, at least in the federal courts, is in the business sector and are now trying to work out the different business areas in which this growth is concentrated.

They have suggested that this increase in business-against-business litigation is the result of a breakdown in other governance mechanisms. They emphasise that litigation is "only one form of business 'governance' necessary to secure orderly commercial dealings", and by "governance" they mean "the rules and sanctions regulating inter-organizational dealings."[77] The litigation decision is seen, not as a decision whether to litigate or not, using the criteria outlined by Priest and Klein,[78] but as "*a choice between alternative governance mechanisms*"[79] (their emphasis), so that the result of a calculation of the costs and benefits of litigation is weighed against the costs and benefits of pursuing alternative routes. They rely on Macaulay's classical study of non-contractual relations in business for this approach, and from him they also take a concern with long-term-continuing-relations (LTCR) between businesses, which "simultaneously helped to secure the availability of such informal mechanisms of governance and encouraged their use,"[80] since damage to LTCR from litigation might outweigh the benefits otherwise to be expected from it.

An increase in litigation, they argue, might arise from an increase in the number of transactions, or of the kind of transactions which go sour, or, on the other hand, there may be a change in the relative efficacy of legal and informal governance mechanisms. They instance, as economic factors which might give rise to increased litigation, "competition, product specialization, turnover of parties to deals, the number of parties to and complexity of deals, spatial and cultural dispersal of parties, instability in prices, high-stakes transactions, the rate of economic change."[81]

These are likely to increase the numbers of disputes and erode the structures which permit less contentious dispute handling. The authors say that many of these factors "can be summarized as increases in (and immediate firm response to) competition, uncertainty and instability (CUI)." They expect that as CUI rises further (or its costs become apparent) new sorts of governance mechanisms (other than litigation) will be established to handle an unstable environment.[82]

The area on which Galanter and Rogers have focussed their main attention is business-against-business contract litigation, but their reasoning goes wider. In a footnote important for this paper,[83] they describe some of the ways that firms can "govern" business relations; particularly relevant seems this heading: ". . . by forcing issues of legal interpretation and implementation, or in other ways influencing the exercise of authority over commercial dealings." Just as Macaulay added a second tier of decisions, in which litigation calculations are set against calculations of the possible outcomes of other courses of action, so this footnote adds a third tier, in which the "framework of established systems of governance relations" within which disputing decisions are made (p. 40) is not "established", but problematic.[84] Resources can be devoted to making the environment more predictable, particularly in this context the legal environment, thus favoring a litigation solution over others.

Making the environment more predictable, however, is not, at least in the short term, a neutral activity. One of the reasons that dealings may not be "orderly" is that the governance framework may not be sufficient to give a player in the market a return which either subjectively he regards himself as entitled to or which objectively can give him sufficient return to justify investment in the relevant field. Much of the story of law in Silicon Valley might be understood in terms, not of ensuring the performance of contracts, but of defining "reasonable limits" and methods for the protection of investments. What limits were "reasonable" has been the subject of substantial debate and use of litigation, partly because of the mixture of co-operation and competition to which Krislov refers; user interfaces and reverse engineering both raise this problem in the context of establishing a legal framework. Similarly, the systematic use of non-disclosure agreements and patenting programs are methods of investment protection, the latter dependent, as Krislov shows, on a changed attitude towards patent protection which itself takes its rise from a desire to reduce uncertainty in the interests of US innovators. Characteristically, it is not the party with whom the innovator has LTCR who wishes to take advantage of his innovation (opportunistic behavior presumably bringing the relationship to an end), but a third party, so that establishing proprietary rights is likely to be a preface to protecting them by litigation or the threat of litigation, whether to derive income by licensing the innovation or so as to establish a monopoly.[85] Once again, what is innovation may be subjective; thus the establishment of legally enforceable proprietary rights may achieve a definition of innovation which could not have prevailed in any informal mechanism.[86]

The insight contained in their footnote 88, then, is that "established systems of governance relations" may favor or be seen to favor particular market participants; increased litigation may be explained not just by an externally caused change in the relative costs/benefit calculation for litigation and other mechanisms but by deliberate attempts to increase the costs/benefit ratio for litigation. This may accompany changes in attitude about what those costs are, or about whether litigation is only justified if there is wrong-doing. This is not to argue that the desire for orderly dealings is not one of the motivations behind a rights-and litigation-based strategy, but merely to draw out the suggestion implicit in the footnote in the Galanter and Rogers article already cited that there may, in a given situation, be more than one way of achieving order.

Notes

1. This paper is part of the Stanford Law School's Silicon Valley Research Project (the "SVRP"). Previous work is described in Friedman L, Gordon R *et al.*, "Law, Lawyers, and Legal Practice in Silicon Valley", 64 *Indiana L.J.* 555 (1989). I thank Lawrence Friedman and Robert Gordon, who began the Project, for their help generally, Lawrence Friedman and William Simon for their comments on an earlier version of this chapter, Stanford Law School for its hospitality during the research described and its writing up, and the staffs of the Stanford Law School Library and the Silicon Valley Information Center at the San Jose Public Library for their help in getting me information I did not know was available.

2. M. Galanter and J. Rogers, "A Transformation of American Business Disputing? Some Preliminary Observations," DPRP 10-3, Institute for Legal Studies, University of Wisconsin (1991).

3. D. Trubek, J. Grossman *et al.*, *Civil Litigation Research Project Final Report*, SPR-2, Institute of Legal Studies, University of Wisconsin (2nd ed. 1987).

4. *Supra*, note 2. Continuing efforts to generate data which would be closer to particular sectors and firms, and firms' decisions to litigate are described in M.

Galanter, S. Macaulay *et al.*, *The Transformation of American Business Disputing: A Sketch of the Wisconsin Project*, Working paper DPRP 10-6, Institute of Legal Studies, University of Wisconsin (1991).

5. See chapter 3 of this volume.

6. Gilder, George F. *Microcosm : the quantum revolution in economics and technology*, Simon and Schuster, New York, 1989. I have also found very helpful Michael S. Malone, *The big score: the billion-dollar story of Silicon Valley*, Doubleday, Garden City, N.Y.(1985). As a local journalist, Malone is particularly good on the geographical and social environment of the Valley industries, whereas Gilder aims at pursuing threads of decrease in size and increase in information content in the development of the industry, as well as arguing a case against what he sees as a protectionist attitude which will be inimical to its success. Other sources include court records, the press and interviews with lawyers in the area. I have relied heavily on Hoefler's articles in *Electronics News*, January 1971, while Hoefler's later gossip-sheet, *Microelectronics News*, is a mine of information about industry-related litigation. Malone's "The Great Patent Wars", *Upside*, January 1991, has also been an invaluable source. I also refer to "SVRP" interviews conducted at various times between 1986 and 1992; references to English lawyers without citation are to interviews I conducted under grant R000233849 from the Economic and Social Research Council.

7. One of the most difficult part of telling the story by and for non-technologists is the interweaving of the technological advances in technological design and manufacturing processes with functional advances, such as memory, the microprocessor and their combination into working systems. The former made the latter possible, but visions of the functional possibilities to a large extent drove the technological advances. The non-technical can understand the functional advances much more easily, so that the story is told in terms of advance to the personal computer. For that really to take off, as Krislov points out, moderately-priced small disk drives were also essential. I suspect also that not enough weight is given to the more arcane areas of communications, which have also flourished in the area.

8. Hogan is quoted in Malone, *The Big Score*, p. 109, as saying that though he regarded Fairchild as the industry leader in technology, and though they had invented the silicon planar transistor, Motorola probably had 60% of the world-wide market for them. Both TI and Motorola overtook Fairchild in sales and profits some time after 1965: *id*, p. 108.

9. Whatever we now take for granted, ferrite core memory systems were used and improved until the second half of the 1970's: Gilder, *Microcosm*, pp. 90-95. Intel also developed the Read Only Memory which made it possible to store without power the basic programs which start up the computer.

10. The Eraseable Programmable Read-Only Memory, which gave engineers flexibility in the injection of permanently available information into systems.

11. Other important companies with local facilities before Fairchild were Sylvania, General Electric, and Kaiser. According to the *Palo Alto Weekly*, September 25, 1991, 17 electronics firms began in Palo Alto in the years 1956 and 1957.

12. This last development is described in Gilder, *Microcosm;* for him these designs are the logical and highest embodiment of the Silicon revolution.

13. Everett M. Rogers & Judith K. Larsen, *Silicon Valley fever: growth of high-technology culture* 31, Basic Books, New York (1984).

14. Annalee Saxenian, "The Cheshire Cat's Grin: Innovation and Regional Development in England," *Technology Review,* Feb/Mar 1988, v. 91, pp. 66-75; "Regional Networks and the Resurgence of Silicon Valley," *California Management Review,* Fall 1990, v. 33, pp.89-112; "The Origins and Dynamics of Production Networks in Silicon Valley," *Research Policy,* Oct 1991, v. 20, pp. 423-437.

15. Davidow, a former marketing manager at Intel, points out that similar relationships arise between large suppliers and large customers; they become interdependent. "The industry term in vogue to describe the phenomenon is 'co-destiny'. In a relationship of co-destiny, the buyer and seller deal in an environment of trust and understanding.... Above all, the relationship is long-term." W.H. Davidow, *Marketing High Technology: An Indiser's View* (New York: Free Press, 1986), 65-66.

16. A similar point was made in a recent discussion of the alleged failure of Japanese manufacturers of chip-making equipment to supply their latest models to U.S. chip manufacturers. It was conceded that such equipment had to be developed in cooperation with customers who were nearby: "Japanese criticized by chip-makers," *New York Times,* 7 May 1991.

17. From an English interview.

18. Since the publication of S. Macaulay, "Non-Contractual Relations in Business: A Preliminary Study," 28 *American Sociological Review* 55 (1963).

19. Accounts of the prosecution of computer "hackers" have a slightly surreal feel to them. For an example, see J.P. Barlow "The law comes to cyberspace," *Byte,* October 1992, 332. A games manufacturer was raided by the Secret Service on the basis that one of its bulletin boards had stolen material on it. The material proved to be public, and the company won more than $50,000 damages as well as attorney's fees for the government's conduct during and after the raid: P. Hoffman, "Steve Jackson Games Case," *Microtimes,* May 3, 1993, 17

On the other hand, FBI investigations of industrial espionage and theft seem to have been successful. Malone, *The Big Score,* 243-4, suggests that while the local police, at least until 1980 or so, were mainly both uninterested and unqualified in relation to thefts of integrated circuits and other electronic components, the companies themselves (except for Intel) were anxious to keep the police out of their affairs.

20. Since about 1986 the ITC has become a principal forum for firms seeking to restrain the importation into the United States of goods alleged to infringe domestic patents. See "Intel files investigation against Twinhead over 'paging' patent enforcement," *Personal Computer World,* July 1993, p. 214, for an example in which Intel appears to be combatting Intel-compatible processors made by others which might not themselves infringe on Intel's rights by claiming a patent on their use with generally used operating system software and filing a request with the ITC rather than initiating litigation.

The ITC seems a reliable forum in which to protect US interests, as it sees them; see the case in which it found dumping of advanced Japanese computer screens at the suit of US manufacturers who are quite unable to meet their customers needs, at any price: A. Pollack, "Duties on Japanese screen for laptops cleared by U.S.," *New York Times*, 16 August 1991.

21. C. H. Farnsworth, "Patent Suit Becomes Trade Battle," *New York Times*, March 9, 1990.

22. Malone, *The Big Score* 381-2, suggests that it was the new attitude of the Reagan Administration towards antitrust that made it possible for IBM (which had had a long anti-trust struggle with the government) to enter the personal computer field in 1981. Since it appears that Novell has been behind complaints against Microsoft both in the United States and Europe, the analogy with litigation seems close. See *e.g.* L. Kehoe, "A case that doesn't compute," *Financial Times*, July 23, 1993 (Novell leading the crusade); L. Kehoe, "EC to probe antitrust allegations against Microsoft," *Financial Times*, September 6, 1993 (complaint filed by Novell).

23. Although Intel could not maintain trademark protection for the 80286 and 80386 chips by number, without more.

24. A search in the records of the Santa Clara courts for cases involving microelectronics companies up to 1968 uncovered cases for unpaid bills, allegedly defective parts and such non-industry-specific matters as the interruption of production caused by a workman's severing a gas main. There was a case on the residual value of computers, a reflection of the accelerated rate of technical change.

25. A Rand researcher found these especially significant for semiconductor companies, because they had a highly educated work force and a cyclical business, giving rise to lay-offs: Peter Reuter, *The Economic Consequences of Expanded Corporate Liability*, Institute for Civil Justice, Santa Monica (1988). An SVRP interview with a lawyer at a foreign-owned company found potential problems because when the time came for lay-offs it was less likely to let its own nationals go.

26. Malone, *The Big Score* 403 ff., describes the problems of drug-taking amongst lower-level employees engaged in repetitive work, which may have been of more legal consequence than those of higher-level employees.

27. See J. Cooper Alexander, "Do the merits matter? A study of settlements in securities classactions," 43 *Stanford L.R.* 497 (1991). This litigation is not special to high-tech companies, but they were particularly liable to the hyperbole and subsequent disenchantment which leads to the collapse in share prices which Alexander describes as triggering such litigation.

28. I repeat this with some caution; the employee turnover for large companies with good employment practices like Hewlett-Packard may have been quite low (in spite of Wozniak, who left to start Apple). A lawyer interviewed by the SVRP suggested that feelings of betrayal were often behind suits against departing employees; not everyone accepted the free movement.

29. Discussion with in-house lawyers, both in the U.S. and England, reveals considerable effort spent on this mundane task, even apart from the special efforts directed against counterfeiters.

30. Economic justifications for the practice are discussed in A. Shepherd, "Licensing to Enhance Remand for New Technologies," 18 *Rand Journal of Economics* 360 (1987); the argument is taken up in D North, *Institutions, Institutional Change and Economic Performance*, Cambridge, Cambridge University Press (1990), 65-66. It is now clear that it should be seen as one of the main alternative strategies, standardization as against monopolization.

31. In the *Intel v NEC* case, a judge said that Intel did not seem to be taking the protection of its intellectual property very seriously. While it may be true that it was not doing as much as the law required to ensure that all its chips were properly marked for copyright protection, one cannot accept this as a general judgement on the company's operations. See S.M. Marconda, "NEC Corp. v. Intel Corp.: a brief analysis," 5 *Santa Clara Computer and High-Technology L.J.* 559, 5 (1989).

32. *Upside*, January 1991.

33. *The Big Score*, 94.

34. According to Hoefler's 1971 articles, from which this account is taken. Since the account refers to the doctrine of "clean hands", presumably the judge had refused any temporary restraining order. A search in the court records of Santa Clara County for the period up to 1968 has not thrown up the record of this case, or any similar cases brought by Fairchild or by or against any of the earliest spin-offs from it.

35. According to Hoefler when National was set up in Connecticut in 1959 by employees who had left Sperry they were hit devastatingly in an ensuing lawsuit which would not have been taken seriously in California.

36. Malone, *The Big Score*, p. 109, describes what happened after Sporck and others left Fairchild for National. "To keep from getting sued, National agreed not to hire directly from Fairchild; but for those people they wanted, like Jerry Sanders, they cheated by getting the person hired somewhere else first and then bringing him into National several months later. Fairchild did not react. Noyce, whose future company Intel would be notorious for suing the bejesus out of spin-offs, will say only that he saw no reason for a law-suit: after all, Sporck 'took absolutely nothing in terms of proprietary information.'" Malone records (109) an interview with Marshall Cox from marketing: they had terrific guys in R & D, in marketing, legal counsel industrial relations, a lot of activities. They were weak in manufacturing because people had gone to National. "What Fairchild should have done when those guys left is what everybody does now when somebody leaves: sue their ass."

37. From an SVRP interview.

38. This seems an early case which shows the internal inconsistency of the view that patent licenses were seen only as a way of keeping other companies off one's back; someone had to be using them offensively.

39. Gilbert Hyatt received his patent for the microprocessor in 1990. For articles on the subject, together with interviews with those who had been working in the field at the time, see *Byte*, January 1991. The interviews strongly suggested that all Hyatt's ideas were current and well-known at the time, which is why Intel did not patent the 4004; on the other hand, it is unreasonable to

expect any straight answer from potential witnesses on this question until the validity of Hyatt's patent is settled by litigation. It seems that attention at Intel at the time was not focussed on Hoff's achievement, and its value was not appreciated at the time: Davidow, *Marketing High Technology* 137. Borovoy did not come to Intel as General Counsel until 1974.

40. Some of the licences have remained to haunt them, such as that to AMD described later. One early cross-licence, to a company later bought by SGS-Thomson, allows Cyrix to have its microprocessors, which compete with Intel's, fabricated by SGS-Thomson, and so be protected from a patent suit: "Nice one, Cyrix", *Economist*, November 13, 1993.

41. However, an SVRP interview in 1993 suggested that this kind of litigation was no longer seen as an effective competitive tool.

42. An analysis of three months issues of *Microelectronics News* in 1983 showed that this was by far the most frequent class of case recorded. However, since Hoefler seems to have got his information from disgruntled individuals, cases of this kind may have been over-represented.

43. M. Malone, "The Great Patent Wars." *Upside*, January 1991.

44. A speaker at the Bay Area Next Group in November 1991 described some of them as looking as if the applicants had gone systematically through basic textbooks on software, filing applications on everything they had found. Patents on some basic features could potentially be very far-reaching, for instance. a 1985 patent on the means of running several windows simultaneously in workstations being asserted by A.T. & T: J. Markoff, "Patent Action On Software By A.T.& T," *New York Times*, 26 February 1991. For very recent criticism of a patent on methods of searching in multimedia databases, see note 63, *infra*.

45. In the novel field of software patents, apparently Honeywell refused to license a data-compression program it had patented, and the infringer had to withdraw its own program completely.

46. At the time of writing (December 1993) Apple seems to have failed, at least at first instance, in its long battle against Microsoft and Hewlett-Packard over their graphical user interfaces. Since Apple and Microsoft also have interests in common (Microsoft is a major supplier of software for Apple's Macintosh computer), it is not known what Apple's strategic aim was or what it would have done about Microsoft's Windows system if it had succeeded in its litigation.

47. See Alexander, "Do the merits matter?" *supra* note 27.

48. Though the case did not involve Silicon Valley companies directly, it was of immediate relevance to computer companies relying on the Motorola chip in question.

49. L. Forkner, "Pact protects 030 shipments," 20 *Computer Design* 1.

50. Apple has also used or been afforded the protections of the criminal law to an unusual extent. The FBI has pursued vigorously the release by apparently disgruntled Apple employees of the code for parts of the Macintosh operating system. In 1990 (see *Microtimes*, October 29, 1990) there was a successful prosecution of someone counterfeiting the Macintosh ROMs.

51. In announcing an agreement signed on October 2 1991, Apple stated that

its visual interface would be running on IBM hardware, and it is now likely to license its software to other manufacturers: J. Weber, "Apple plans to license new Macintosh software," *L.A. Times*, 5 July 1993.

52. Digital Research had made a major contribution to the extension of personal computing by the design of CP/M, which ran on the earliest Intel chip to be generally used in personal computers, the 8080, and on the more sophisticated Z80 from Zilog. In spite of some interesting later products, it was essentially marginalized by IBM's adoption of an operating system from Microsoft. It has maintained an innovative but minor presence, mainly at the operating system level, and was eventually acquired by a company specialising in Local Area Networks.

53. "Visual Copyrights," *Byte* April 1986. A pro-Apple attorney suggested in the same issue, however, that DR had easily sufficient resources to fight the action had they thought it justified. DR officials were quoted as saying that they needed a program then, not two years later.

54. Which have sold tens of millions of copies.

55. Its fortunes have been mixed, since some of the competing chips are fabricated by companies with which it has cross-licensing agreements see note 40, *supra*. See footnote 20 for an example of an unusual claim in an advantageous forum.

56. The parties summarise their cases usefully in "NEC v. Intel: a discussion of the case by both parties," 3 *Santa Clara Computer and High-Technology L.J.* 1 (1987).

57. For an illustrative passage, see S. K. Yoder, "Changing Game", *Wall Street Journal*, 8 April 1991. He quotes Intel's general counsel as saying that Intel was entitled to a monopoly in certain areas through patents and copyrights, and continues: "But critics charge that Intel uses the courts to milk its rights for more than they're worth. Intel casts a pall over companies that clone its chips by launching barrages of suits and motions that drag out the litigation for years, they say. By the time a ruling is handed down, the market for the chip may have vanished. U.S. computer makers avoided NEC Corp.'s Intel-compatible chips, for instance, while the Japanese company was battling Intel in the courts over certain copyrights. The judge ruled NEC had the right to sell its chip, but by then the opportunity was gone."

58. Thus new versions of Microsoft's Windows will be available for any of a number of processors, while programs written for Windows may now be run on other operating systems: L. Kehoe, "Sun attacks Microsoft dominance in software," *Financial Times*, 7 May 1993; J. Schofield, "Sun/USL WABI translator opens Windows to run under standard Unix," *Personal Computer World*, July 1993, 216.

59. With a former Xerox employee. It is also suggested that the Dutch electric lamp industry developed because the stranglehold of Edison's patents in Britain encouraged development offshore. E.N. Todd, reviewing *The History of N.V. Philips' Gloelampenfabrieken*, Vol. 1: 63 *Business History Review* 230 (1989).

60. Pooley, *Trade Secrets* 178, Osborne/McGraw-Hill, Berkeley, 1982.

61. For instance, the amount made by companies in some successful patent

actions are known, and one can compare them to the companies' reported earnings. But it would take more financial analysis to see the effects on the companies' business, and still more to know whether the recoveries have enhanced their power to innovate.

62. The process of going public in a microprocessor company is described in M.S. Malone, *Going Public: MIPS Computer and the Entrepreneurial Dream,* New York: Harper Collins, 1991. The part played by the legal department is emphasized, but the concern seems to be more that the Securities and Exchange Commission will not allow the offering to go forward than the avoidance of subsequent litigation. Some outsiders may decline to become directors at all, of course, for fear of being sued.

63. Peter H. Lewis, "The New Patent that Is Infuriating the Multimedia Industry," *New York Times,* November 28 1993.

64. In chapter 3 of this volume.

65. Gilder, *Microcosm, supra,* note 6.

66. *The Big Score,* pp. 261-2, 379.

67. "Transformation?", *supra* note 2.

68. *Supra,* note .

69. The ultimate example is that of Refac, which buys up and prosecutes infringement claims; it has never had any business in the area. There are also the individuals who are seen as pursuing a deliberate policy of securing strategically placed patents which they have no intention of using themselves. See also T. Harbert, "Patent portfolios emerge as corporate money-makers," 16 *Electronic Business* 53.

70. "We are fortunate that we don't have much litigation now. We happen to be a somewhat litigation averse company. We are not trigger happy when it comes to suing people, and in general we'd like to settle something as opposed to sue someone or be sued." It had however gained quite a large verdict against a company it thought had improperly used its proprietary information.

71. G. Rifkin and G. Harrar, *The Ultimate Entrepreneur* (Chicago: Contemporary Books, 1988), 94 ff.

72. See Malone, *Upside,* January 1991

73. The Apple-Microsoft litigation might be seen as another example, since it was continued by Apple in spite of the leading role that Microsoft has continued to play as a leading supplier of Macintosh software.

74. The phrase is taken from Davidow, *Marketing High Technology, supra* note 15. See *e.g.* p. 15.

75. For a parallel argument see Malone, *Going Public* 165, on the protection of the MIPS processor by what surrounded it.

76. *Supra,* note 2.

77. *Id,* 35.

78. G.L. Priest and B. Klein, "The Selection of Disputes for Litigation," 13 *Journal of Legal Studies* 1 (1984)

80. Galanter and Rogers, *supra* note 2, 37.

81. *Id.* 39.

82. *Id* 41.

83. *Id.* 46. One source interviewed by the SVRP suggested that ADR had increased substantially in the late 1980's, and would spread even further, which may be an example of the point.

84. *Id.* 36 note 88.

85. *Id.* 40. Their note 92, on the same page, also recognizes that the second-tier mechanisms can be unstable.

86. In some circumstances, as Krislov says, it might have been a prelude to cross-licensing, and there is still a fair amount of this, for all the "Great Patent Wars" described in *Upside*, January 1991; it may even be on the upsurge.

87. It is highly unlikely that Gilbert Hyatt could achieve anything outside the patent system, in which remote third parties are brought in to determine the state of community knowledge. But, apart from honor, it is not clear that industry, unlike academia, has ever recognised the claims of innovation, however meritorious, to be rewarded in the absence of some legal enforcement mechanism.

PART FOUR

Property Rights in an Advanced Capitalist Economy

9

Lochner v. New York in Japan: Protecting Economic Liberties in a Country Governed by Bureaucrats

Shigenori Matsui

Introduction

Almost every American lawyer knows *Lochner v. New York*,[1] a 1905 decision which struck down a state maximum working hour legislation as an unreasonable infringement of liberty of contract. It was a decision symbolic of the era when the United States Supreme Court invalidated social and economic legislation in the name of the Constitution. Many thought that *Lochner* and company improperly interfered with the economic policy-making of the legislature and intruded into the domain of the political process. The Court later came to repudiate *Lochner* and to refrain from interfering with economic policy-making function. Since then, *Lochner* has been treated as a prime example of bad constitutional decision. Now economic liberties are given no serious constitutional protection by the Court in the United States.

In 1975, the Japanese Supreme Court handed down a decision in the Pharmaceuticals Act Case which subjected an economic regulation to strict scrutiny and invalidated it. Involved was the section of the Pharmaceuticals Act which required proper location as a precondition for granting a license to operate a new pharmacy or drug store, as well as the local ordinance adopted under that Act specifying the required distance from existing pharmacies or drug stores. We are justified in calling this decision the Japanese version of *Lochner v. New York*. For it subjected an economic regulation to strict scrutiny and substituted the judgment of the Court on the necessity and reasonableness of regulation for that of the Diet. Indeed, this decision had the potential for wiping out a huge number of statutory restrictions on economic liberties. Curiously, however, unlike *Lochner*, this decision has been applauded by the overwhelming majority of Japanese constitutional commentators. Also curiously, its potential for wiping out numerous regulatory statutes has never been realized. Many restrictions on economic liberties which might have been struck down under its reasoning still remain on the code book. Few dare to take them to the courts in the first place and no courts are willing to apply its reasoning to other economic regulations. Moreover, economic liberties are subject to countless extra-legal restrictions in addition to legal restrictions.

This paper attempts to explore these curious contrasts between American and Japanese experience. This paper consists of four parts. The first part briefly portrays how economic liberties are protected in the United States. It emphasizes the doctrinal framework within which the United States Supreme Court decides economic liberties cases. The chief purpose of this part lies in setting the background for comparative analysis, by illuminating the American perception of how the Government should and should not regulate economic liberties. The second part contrasts this American perception with the Japanese perception. Close attention is paid especially to the doctrine by which the Japanese Supreme Court decides economic liberties cases. The third part considers how economic liberties are actually protected in Japan. This part is of special importance since in Japan economic liberties are subject to numerous regulations despite the explicit constitutional guarantee. The discrepancy between law and reality is far greater in Japan than in the United States. The fourth and final part considers how this discrepancy is accepted in Japan. This section illuminates thereby the protection of economic liberties in a unique Japanese style. It then attempts to explore the significance of that Japanese style and its implications for the issue of the relationship between law and economic development, and further for the general issue of the relationship between law and society.

The Protection of Economic Liberties in the United States

The United States Constitution

The United States Constitution does not have any provision specifically protecting property rights or economic liberties. There were two provisions which indirectly protected property rights or economic liberties in the original Constitution: the contract clause[2] and the privileges and immunities clause.[3] The contract clause prohibits the state legislature from impairing the obligation of contracts. The clause was initially intended to prohibit debtor relief laws but its reach was expanded to protect public contract as well. Yet the protection to be accorded to economic liberties under this clause is quite limited.[4] The privileges and immunities clause on the other hand is essentially an equal protection provision. It protects a resident of other states from discrimination by guaranteeing the same privileges and immunities given to local residents. The protection to be accorded to economic liberties under this clause is again limited.[5]

The Bill of Rights added to the Constitution after the ratification also did not contain a provision guaranteeing property rights or economic liberties. Instead it merely contained a provision which indirectly protects property rights: the Fifth Amendment's taking clause.[6] The taking clause, however, only demands just compensation as a precondition for taking. It is thus not a substantive restraint on the power of the Government to regulate property rights or economic liberties. The Fifth Amendment contains one another provision indirectly protecting property rights or economic liberties: the due process clause which prohibits the deprivation of "life, liberty or property, without due process of law."[7] It is generally believed that this clause was primarily meant to assure fair procedure prior to deprivation of life, liberty or property.[8] It thus gives essentially a procedural protection to property rights or economic liberties.

Taken together, therefore, the United States Constitution seems to be assuming that the scope and dimension of property rights should be essentially defined by the state. The Constitution was meant to provide indirect protection to property rights thus defined by prohibiting retroactive impairment of contractual obligations, by requiring just compensation for taking of private property, and finally by requiring due process (fair procedure) prior to its deprivation. Similarly, instead of enumerating economic liberties, the Constitution contemplates that economic liberties should be given protection under the contract clause and the due process clause. The privileges and immunities clause of Article IV and the equal protection clause of the Fourteenth Amendment[9] would also afford equal protection to property rights and economic liberties. But beyond these, there is no explicit textual authority to afford substantive constitutional protection either to property rights or to broader economic liberties.

Yet when the states came to regulate business and economic activities in the late nineteenth century, lawyers representing business gradually came to invite the courts to afford substantive constitutional protection to such economic liberties. Precisely because the United States Constitution does not have any explicit textual authority for such economic liberties, they came to turn their eyes to the due process clause of the Fourteenth Amendment. They in effect invited the courts to afford substantive constitutional protection to such unenumerated economic liberties under the due process clause.

Lochner v. New York

As every American lawyer knows, during the period between the late nineteenth century and the early twentieth century the United States Supreme Court accepted this invitation and subjected various social and economic regulations to strict scrutiny. The Court construed the due process clause as substantively protecting "life, liberty and property" against arbitrary infringement even if the procedure is perfectly fair. The Court also construed the term of "liberty" broadly enough to encompass "not only the right of the citizen to be free from the mere physical restraint of his person, as by incarceration," but also "the right of the citizen to be free in the enjoyment of all his faculties; to be free to use them in all lawful ways; ... to pursue any livelihood or avocation; and for that purpose to enter into all contracts which may be proper, necessary, and essential to his carrying out to a successful conclusion the purposes above mentioned." [10] The Court then employed strict scrutiny for any restrictions on this liberty of contract and often found them unreasonable and hence invalid.

Lochner v. New York was a symbolic decision of this era. Involved was a state maximum working hour legislation for bakery workers. The Court first found liberty of contract among the "liberty" interests protected by the due process clause of the Fourteenth Amendment. It then asked whether the statute was a reasonable exercise of police power or an unreasonable and arbitrary deprivation of that liberty. The state asserted two state interests to justify the regulation: the protection of bakery workers and the protection of public health. Yet the Court dismissed the state interest in protecting bakery workers for it found no reason for the legislature to protect such workers. The Court did not deny the legitimacy of the state interest of protecting public health. Yet it doubted whether the maximum working hours legislation bore a reasonable relation to this goal. Consequently the Court found the statute unreasonable and held it invalid.

The Court applied similar strict scrutiny in other cases involving social legislation and held them invalid.[11] Yet the same attitude can also be found in cases involving purely economic regulations. Typical was *New State Ice Co. v. Liebmann,*[12] in which an Oklahoma statute declared the manufacture, sale, and distribution of ice a public business and prohibited the manufacture, sale, and distribution of ice without first having secured a license from the state commission. The New

State Ice Company engaged in the business of manufacturing, selling, and distributing ice under a license duly issued from the commission brought a suit against Liebmann to enjoin him from manufacturing, selling, and distributing ice without first having obtained such a license. The Court affirmed the district court's dismissal of the complaint. The Court did not accept the argument that the manufacture, sale, and distribution of ice had a special public nature to justify the licensing requirement. The business of manufacturing, selling, and distributing ice was, according to the Court, purely private and there was no reason to require a license from the state. The Court thus found the regulation unreasonable.

Liberty of contract was thus accorded heightened judicial protection during this period. Indeed, the Court may be said to have acted like a guardian of *laissez-faire* capitalism.

The Post–New Deal Era

Many thought that *Lochner* and company were wrongly decided and arbitrarily interfered with economic policy-making by the legislature. Ultimately the Court came to repudiate the *Lochner* philosophy in the late 1930s and to refrain from ever interfering with the economic and social policy-making of the legislature. It came instead to hold that economic and social legislation should be upheld so long as it has a rational basis and a rational relationship to some legitimate purpose. The Court then presumes the constitutionality of such legislation and thus concedes to the legislature a wide discretion in judging the necessity as well as the reasonableness of such legislation.[13]

Typical was *United States v. Carolene Products Co*,[14] which involved the constitutionality of the federal Filled Milk Act which prohibited the interstate shipment of filled milk. Filled milk, though not harmful in itself, was banned because it did not contain a vitamin allegedly essential for the public health and because its sale caused confusion and deception among the public. The constitutionality of such statute must be presumed, the Court declared, and there was a rational basis for enacting the statute. Although the necessity of prohibiting filled milk was questionable,[15] the Act was thus upheld.

In the 1950s and 1960s, the Court made even clearer that it had no intention of interfering with economic and social legislation. The Court has never denied that the "liberty" protected by the due process clause includes liberty of contract and that the due process clause affords substantive protection to such liberty. Yet the Court came to presume the constitutionality of a statute restricting liberty of contract. The

Court, while employing the rational basis test, then speculated on possible legitimate legislative purposes to sustain the statute and found it reasonably related to them. As a result, when the state employs the police power to regulate economic liberties, it is quite likely that the Court will sustain it.[16]

"There was a time," the Court recalls, "when the Due Process Clause was used by this Court to strike down laws which were thought unreasonable, that is, unwise or incompatible with some particular economic or social philosophy."[17] Yet "[t]he doctrine that prevailed in *Lochner*... that due process authorizes courts to hold laws unconstitutional when they believe the legislature has acted unwisely," the Court now tells us, "has long since been discarded. We have returned to the original constitutional proposition that courts do not substitute their social and economic beliefs for the judgment of legislative bodies, who are elected to pass laws."[18] The Court also says that "[w]e refuse to sit as a 'super-legislature to weigh the wisdom of legislation,' and we emphatically refuse to go back to the time when courts used the Due Process Clause 'to strike down state laws, regulatory of business and industrial conditions, because they may be unwise, improvident, or out of harmony with a particular school of thought.'"[19] "Whether the legislature takes for its textbook Adam Smith, Herbert Spencer, Lord Keynes, or some other," the Court added, "is no concern of ours."[20] As McCloskey puts it, "there could be little doubt as to the practical result: no claim of substantive economic rights would now be sustained by the Supreme Court. The judiciary had abdicated the field."[21]

The Court showed a similar hands-off attitude toward economic regulation under the equal protection clause in the 1950s and 1960s.[22] The Court upheld an overinclusive classification, holding that the legislature could rationally decide that such a classification was necessary. The Court also upheld an underinclusive classification holding that the legislature could deal with problems only one by one. Although the completely hands-off attitude seems to be gradually changing in the 1980s,[23] yet no outright reinvigoration of equal protection doctrine to afford more protection to property rights or economic liberties is still likely.[24]

This does not mean, however, that economic liberties are totally devoid of constitutional protection. The contract clause, the privileges and immunities clause, and the taking clause surely give indirect constitutional protection.[25] Moreover, state economic regulation which substantially interferes with interstate commerce, especially protectionist economic regulation, can be invalidated under the commerce clause. The commerce clause jurisprudence thus serves to afford some safeguards to economic liberties against state regulations.[26] Beyond these, however, the main constitutional protection for economic liberties lies rather in the procedural one supplied by the due process clause. Substantive protection to economic liberties, if any, are largely supplied by the state courts under the state constitutions and not by the federal courts.

One can thus conclude that, after all, protection for property rights and economic liberties must be sought in the political process. Indeed, how economic activities should be regulated has been a major political issue. The Congress has enacted various regulatory statutes and entrusted their enforcement to administrative agencies. These administrative agencies, mostly established outside the Executive departments, are independent commissions which are supposed to enforce statutes outside politics. The number of regulatory statutes has gradually grown, especially since the New Deal. We also saw the dramatic rise of social regulation like environmental protection and consumer protection in the 1970s.[27] But these regulatory statutes, while restricting economic liberties, set the outer limits of regulatory power. If the agency exceeds those limits and abuses its power, the courts can invalidate the agency action. Individual regulatory statutes also serve to afford legal protection against governmental abuse of power.

Moreover, the Administrative Procedure Act (APA)[28] provides procedural protection to economic liberties. Significantly for our purpose, the APA established fairly formal procedure for economic regulation and the courts have been fairly active in enforcing these procedural requirements. The relationship between bureaucrats and business is highly "legalized" and it has become rather quite "formal." The courts have given a liberal construction to the standing requirement of the APA, thus enlarging the room for judicial intervention.[29] The courts have also accepted the preenforcement suit, thus providing effective relief for the public.[30] Although critics claim that the Court has recently been cutting back these protections, it is undeniable that economic liberties are afforded considerable judicial protection under the APA.[31]

Commentators

The retreat from *Lochner* has been generally accepted favorably among commentators. This does not mean, however, that broad and far-reaching social and economic regulations have been immune from criticism in the United States. In fact, much has been written about the abuses of licensing power.[32] Moreover, there are voices criticizing excessive social regulation as crippling the economy.[33] Yet the criticisms appear to be directed to the wisdom of such regulation and not to its constitutionality.

There are some commentators, however, who express dissatisfaction with the total abandonment of any judicial scrutiny in economic liberties cases. Some commentators, for example, find the primary vice of *Lochner* in its use of strict scrutiny of legislative ends and argue for the use of slightly heightened means scrutiny in economic liberties cases.[34] Some commentators criticize the Court for its insufficient protection of the material welfare of the public. They are not interested in revitalizing economic substantive due process doctrine to invalidate social legislation. Instead, they would like to subject, for example, economic legislation which tends to have a discriminatory impact upon the poor to more rigorous review under the equal protection clause.[35]

There is a growing tendency, however, to revitalize *Lochner* in its own context. Indeed, "there is a movement afoot (among scholars, not as yet among judges) to make the majority opinion in *Lochner* the centerpiece of a new activist jurisprudence."[36] Epstein,[37] for instance, has espoused a view which would severely restrict the range of legitimate regulation and taking of private property. Siegan has also espoused a view which would accord more judicial protection to economic liberties.[38] Moreover, he has specifically argued for the rehabilitation of *Lochner*.[39] This view is not limited to these two.[40] Some other commentators have come to find a vice of class legislation in economic regulation, and to support the economic substantive due process doctrine as a safeguard for the process of open competition.[41] As one commentator has put it, property rights may be indeed "now like the ugly duckling before it became a swan."[42] Yet the overwhelming majority of commentators seem to be still unconvinced that the Court should be actively involved in reviewing economic regulations.[43]

The Constitutional Guarantee of Economic Liberties in Japan

The Japanese Constitution and Economic Liberties

Constitutional Guarantee. Unlike the United States Constitution, the Japanese Constitution of 1946 has specific provisions which directly guarantee property rights and economic liberties. Article 22, Section 1 thus provides that

> [e]very person shall have freedom... to choose his occupation to the extent that it does not interfere with the public welfare.

Article 29 also provides that:

> [t]he right to own or to hold property is inviolable.
> Property rights shall be defined by law, in conformity with the public welfare.
> Private property may be taken for public use upon just compensation therefore.

Most commentators construe Article 29, Section 1, as guaranteeing the right to own or to hold property of each individual.[44] Moreover, most commentators view Section 1 as guaranteeing private property as an institution.[45] It would be unconstitutional, according to this view, to abolish the private property system and to move from capitalism to socialism.

The Japanese people did not have a clear notion of property rights before the Meiji Restoration. They did not have any economic liberties like the freedom to choose an occupation. The Meiji Government, in its modernization effort, introduced the modern notion of property rights for the first time.[46] Nevertheless, pre-modern feudal customs persisted. Land was owned by a limited number of landlords. Most of the farmers did not have their own farmlands and worked as peasants paying rent to their landlords. Business was dominated by a limited number of Zaibatsu, the famous family-like business associations.

The Allied Powers believed that these pre-modern elements of the Japanese economy were among the main reasons for the rise of extreme militarism. The General Headquarters of the Allied Powers (GHQ) thus strived to eliminate these feudal elements from the Japanese economy. They in effect attempted to democratize the economy.[47] The Farmland Reform took the farmlands from landlords and distributed them to farmers. The GHQ also dismantled the Zaibatsu. They also encouraged a union movement to democratize the economy. The Japanese Constitution purported to protect property rights and freedom to choose an occupation against this background.

The Constitution mentions only freedom to choose an occupation but does not mention freedom to do business. Yet most commentators agree that the freedom to choose an occupation guaranteed by Article 22 includes the freedom to engage in a chosen occupation, i.e. freedom to do business.[48] As will be stated below, the Supreme Court has accepted this interpretation.[49] Economic liberties are thus all entitled to constitutional protection under Article 22.

Public Welfare Limits and Standard of Review. The explicit guarantee of economic liberties entails, however, also explicit limitations. Article 22, unlike other bill of rights provisions, has a qualifying clause of "to the extent that it does not interfere with the public welfare." Article 29, Section 2 also made it clear that property rights should be defined by law "in conformity with the public welfare."[50] These limitations reflect, it is generally believed, the lessons of the past. Under *laissez-faire* capitalism the economic order itself was destroyed by unrestrained competition. Thus it became necessary for the government to intervene in the economy to secure basic order. Moreover, workers were exploited by companies because of their relatively weak bargaining power. The Japanese Constitution thus specifically provides for the welfare right as a constitutional right.[51]The Government is thereby constitutionally obliged to provide assistance to the needy. The Constitution also guarantees the right to work[52] and three basic rights of workers: the right to unite, the right of collective bargaining, and the right of collective action like strikes.[53] The Constitution is thus committed to the welfare state. Liberty of contract must be subject to special constitutional restrictions to accomplish this commitment.

As a result, Japanese commentators have come to believe that economic liberties must be subject to two different kinds of restriction. The first is a restriction in order to prevent infringement of the rights and interests of others. In other words, property rights and economic liberties can be restricted to protect the health and safety of the public. This kind of restriction must be allowed with respect to all freedoms. The second is a restriction necessary to achieve the welfare state. In other words, property rights and economic liberties can be restricted for the promotion of the welfare state. This kind of restriction is unique to property rights and economic liberties. To put it differently, there are two kinds of public welfare interest which justify the restriction of property rights and economic liberties: the protection of public health and safety and the promotion of the welfare state.[54] There can be thus no question as to the legitimacy of social legislation in Japan.

Many commentators argue for a bifurcated standard of review for these two different types of economic regulation. They accept the doctrine of a constitutional double standard. The restriction on property rights and economic liberties, they thus argue, should, unlike personal freedoms, be subject to a lenient standard of review. Yet the Court should employ the most lenient standard of review for social regulation purporting to promote the welfare state and should employ a slightly more searching standard of review, the rational basis test with bite or the intermediate standard of review, for economic regulation purporting to protect public health and safety.[55] [56]

The First Public Bath Act Case and the Marketplace Case

Early Cases. Despite Article 22 and Article 29, the Court, in its early days, had not given any serious judicial protection to economic liberties.[57] The Court, for instance, easily upheld the constitutionality of the Antiques Dealer Act which set up a licensing system for antiques dealers.[58] Even though Article 22 of the Constitution guarantees freedom to choose an occupation as a right of citizen, the Court said, it does not guarantee unrestricted freedom. It instead admits the permissibility of restrictions so long as the public welfare dictates. The licensing system established by the Antiques Dealer Act and its punishment of those engaged in the business without a license, the Court continued, do not run afoul of the Constitution when they are necessary to preserve the public welfare. It then concluded without hesitation that the Act was constitutional because it was necessary to give protection to victims of theft or burglary and to facilitate the prevention or detection of these crimes. Yet the Court here did not inquire whether the licensing system was excessive for accomplishing these legislative purposes.

The same attitude could be found in other cases in the early 1950s to early 1960s. In all of them the Court quite summarily upheld the constitutionality of restrictions on economic liberties.[59] It is noteworthy that the Court did not defer to the judgments of the legislature as to the necessity of restrictions, but made the finding of necessity itself. But the Court did not look to the legislative facts. It simply recited the text of the statute involved or accepted the Government's arguments without any critical assessment to support its judgment.

The First Public Bath Act Case. This attitude of the Court toward the regulation of economic liberties was typically shown in the First Public Bath Act Case.[60] Japanese houses used to have no private bath. Instead people went to the public bath. The public bath constituted thus an integral part of Japanese life. As a result, the Public Bath Act requires a license from the Governor to operate a public bath and regulates the sanitary condition of the facility. But its section 2, subsection 2 also authorizes the Governor to refuse a license if he or she believes that the location of the public bath is improper. The authority to set specific standards is relegated to local ordinance. The ordinance of the Fukuoka Prefecture involved in this case required that a new public bath should keep a distance of 250m in urban areas and a distance of 300m in rural areas from any existing licensed public baths. The defendant operated a public bath without a license and was fined. The defendant attacked his conviction as an infringement of his right to choose an occupation guaranteed by Article 22 of the Constitution and appealed up to the Supreme Court.

Yet the Supreme Court rejected the appeal. It held:

> The public bath is a business of a highly public nature essential to many people. If everyone can freely operate a public bath and no measure is taken to assure proper location by preventing the location imbalance and the excessive increase of public baths, there might be a danger of causing inconvenience to many residents when they use public bath in their daily lives. Moreover, there is a danger of inviting economic trouble for the public bath business because of unnecessary competition resulting from its excessive increase. Undesirable consequences such as the deterioration of safety conditions might then ensue. In light of the special nature of the public bath, it is desirable to prevent these dangers as far as possible in order to protect the safety and health of the general public. The improper location of the public bath and resulting location imbalance and unnecessary increase are therefore against the public welfare. It is thus not repugnant to Article 22 of the Constitution for the Diet to authorize the Governor to refuse a license because of these dangers.[61]

The Court thus justified the regulation involved on the public safety ground.

Implications of the First Public Bath Act Case. It may certainly not be possible to deny the importance of securing the safety of the public bath facility since most Japanese houses did not have a private bath at that time. Yet it was quite doubtful whether the proper distance requirement would accomplish its main legislative purpose of preventing deterioration of safety conditions. It was also quite doubtful whether safety conditions could not be secured by less restrictive measures such as administrative regulations or regular inspections. The Court did not even bother to answer these doubts.

Indeed, in light of its legislative history, the purpose of the proper location requirement seems to lie elsewhere. The Public Bath Act was enacted in 1948. The original Act authorized the Governor to refuse a license only when the place or structure of public bath is improper from a sanitary standpoint. The administrators interpreted this provision, however, as authorizing the Governor to refuse a license also when the new public bath did not keep a proper distance from the existing public baths. Yet the adequacy of this interpretation had been questioned and the Government was thus not eager to add this proper distance requirement to the Act. The bill was then introduced to the Diet by Diet members under the pressure of the public bath organization. The proper location standard was thus inserted into the Act. In light of this legislative history, it was fair to say that this proper location requirement was a protectionist entry restriction in order to protect existing public baths.[62] The failure of the Court to address this point and its willingness to uphold its constitutionality by simply accepting the arguments advanced to justify this requirement vividly show the reluctance of the Court to interfere with economic regulations.

Naturally, the First Public Bath Act Case holding was severely criticized by commentators. The absence of scrutiny of legislative facts and the failure to take into account the real motive led commentators to question the plausibility of the Court's holding.[63]

In response to these criticisms, the Court came to spend some more time before upholding the regulation.[64] The Court even showed some willingness to give meaningful protection to economic liberties.[65] Yet that willingness was quite aberrational. In other cases, the Court continued to take an extremely permissive attitude toward economic regulations.[66]

The Marketplace Case. This permissive attitude of the Court reached its apex in the Marketplace Case.[67] The Special Measure Act Concerning Accommodation of Retail Business requires a license from the Governor to operate certain marketplaces in specified cities. Most marketplaces to be regulated are located in Osaka Prefecture and its vicinity. The purpose of the Act is "adequately to secure business opportunities for retail stores and to eliminate factors hindering the proper order of retail business, thus contributing to the healthy development of the national economy." The Governor must grant a license unless the application falls into one of the listed exceptions. One such exception is "when, as a result of the opening of the new marketplace, the competition between the retail stores in that marketplace and retail stores in other marketplaces or the competition between the retail stores in that marketplace and the retail stores in the vicinity becomes excessive and when there is a danger that the management of small or medium size retail stores is thereby destabilized." The authority to set a more specific standard is left to local ordinance. The relevant ordinance of the Osaka Prefecture required that new marketplace should keep a distance of at least 700m (some half mile) from existing marketplaces. The defendants, the corporation which built the marketplace without a license and its manager, were prosecuted and appealed up to the Supreme Court.

The Court, while acknowledging that Article 22 protects freedom to engage in a chosen business as well, announced the following general limits to its protection:

> Legal regulation of economic activities of individuals is permissible, needless to say, when various vices resulting from the free economic activities of individuals become hard to ignore in light of the maintenance of public safety and order. Such regulation, preventive in nature, is permissible, when the regulation is a necessary and reasonable means to eliminate or ameliorate such vices. Besides such regulation, however, the Constitution, considered together with other provisions, contemplates as a whole the balanced development of social economy under the ideal of the welfare state. It thus evidently demands adequate protective measures for the economically disadvantaged by guaranteeing in that spirit the so-called welfare right to every citizen and further by guaranteeing the right of citizen to work as a part of its guarantee. Taking these into consideration in totality, the Constitution presupposes implementation of an affirmative social and economic policy as a duty of the Government. As far as individual economic freedom is concerned in contrast to individual personal freedom, it is within the contemplation of the Constitution and is thus permissible for the Government to take certain reasonable regulatory measures as a means to implement such social and economic policy . . .[68]

In short, the Court distinguished preventive public safety regulation and affirmative social policy regulation. It then allowed both types of regulation as to economic liberties in contrast to personal liberties as to which only preventive public safety regulation is permissible.

The Court then declared that the most lenient standard of review should be applied in reviewing the necessity and reasonableness of such affirmative social policy regulation.

> The decisions as to whether it is necessary in the social economic field to take legal regulatory measures, what kind and manner of regulatory measure if necessary is adequate, or which subjects such regulatory measures should cover are to be left to the discretion of the legislature as a matter of legislative policy judgment. For these decisions demand correct data and information as to the social and economic reality of the subject. They also demand the consideration of the impact of such legal regulatory measure to be adopted upon the actual social economy, with its costs and benefits, and further of the balance with broader economic policy as a whole, thus necessitating adequate evaluation and judgment upon the interrelated factors. The function of such evaluation and judgment belongs precisely to the job of the legislature. It is the legislature that is a governmental branch fit for such function. Accordingly, the aforementioned decisions as to the legal regulatory measures on individual economic activities should be left to the policy-based, technical discretion of the legislature. It is thus proper to conclude that the courts should ordinarily respect such discretionary judgment of the legislature. The courts should invalidate the adopted legal regulatory measure and negate its legal effect

> only when the legislative discretion exceeds the bounds and its unreasonableness is evident and gross.[69]

Turning to the facts before the Court, the Court found the Act as adopted to be part of the policy to protect small and medium size retail stores. Based upon the felt necessity to assure business opportunity for small and medium size retail stores with scant economic power and to eliminate the danger of disturbing the peaceful order of such retail industry, the Act aimed at protecting small and medium size retail stores from the danger of extinction due to excessive competition resulting from the improper increase of marketplaces. It was not thus intended to vest a monopoly of distribution in the hands of small and medium size retail stores. Moreover, the Act regulates only certain marketplaces. It was thus impossible to say, the Court concluded, that the regulation involved does not serve a prima facie reasonable purpose of protecting small and medium size retail stores from the standpoint of promoting balanced development of the social economy and that its unreasonableness is evident and gross.

The distance requirement for marketplaces enacted to protect small and medium size retail stores was thus upheld by the Court.

The Pharmaceuticals Act Case

The Supreme Court Decision. The Court took, however, a radically different attitude in the Pharmaceuticals Act Case.[70] The Pharmaceuticals Act sets up a licensing system for pharmacies and drug stores. It vests the licensing power in the Governor and authorizes the Governor to refuse a license if the new pharmacy or drug store is not in a proper location. The authority to set a more specific standard is relegated to each local ordinance. The plaintiff in this case was a corporation operating supermarkets chiefly in Fukuyama Prefecture. The plaintiff filed an application to open a drug store. The Governor of the Fukuyama Prefecture refused a license because the location of the store did not meet the standard specified by the ordinance. The ordinance involved required the new store to keep a distance of roughly 100m from existing stores, in the absence of exceptional circumstances. The plaintiff then filed a suit seeking judicial revocation of the refusal decision and argued that the Pharmaceuticals Act and its accompanying ordinance unconstitutionally violated Article 22 of the Constitution. Although the district court accepted the plaintiff's argument and revoked the refusal decision, the High Court reversed. It upheld the constitutionality of the proper location requirement as well as the distance requirement and rejected all the plaintiff's arguments. The plaintiff then appealed to the Supreme Court. On appeal, the Supreme Court reversed the High Court decision and invalidated the Pharmaceuticals Act.

The Court, in affording constitutional protection to freedom to engage in business activity, emphasized the significance of freedom to choose an occupation at the outset.

> The occupation, has, in addition to its character of supporting one's living through its continuous activity, a character of undertaking a social function, in a society of division of labor, by contributing to the maintenance and development of society through one's activity. It has thus an essential relationship with the personal value of an individual as a forum to realize one's personality... In light of this character and significance of one's occupation, not only the choice of occupation, i.e., the decision to start, continue and to quit the occupation should be free but also the undertaking of that chosen occupation, i.e., the scope and manner of that occupational activity should be free in principle. Accordingly, [Article 22] is to be construed to include the guarantee not only of freedom to choose an occupation but also of freedom to engage in occupational activity.[71]

Freedom to engage in business activity, however, must yield to broader regulation because of its social and economic character and even the Court had to concede that limit. The Court here made a distinction between an affirmative social and economic policy purpose of promoting the smooth development of the national economy, providing benefits for the public or protecting the economically disadvantaged, and a preventive purpose of guarding the safety of social life or maintaining order. It then announced the following standard of review.

> Whether a particular regulatory measure is permissible as a public welfare restriction in the meaning of Article 22, Section 1 cannot be stated in categorical terms. It should be carefully decided by way of balancing, taking into consideration the purpose, necessity, and scope of regulation, the nature of the occupation regulated, and the scope and extent of the regulation. Such consideration and balancing primarily should be left to the province of legislature. If the regulatory purpose is found to conform with the public welfare, the courts should, therefore, pay deference to the policy judgement of the legislature as to the choice of a particular regulatory measure as well as to its necessity and reasonableness so long as the judgment remains within the bounds of reasonable discretion.[72]

The licensing system, however, operates to restrict the freedom to choose the occupation itself in contrast to other regulation on the scope and extent of business activity. The Court thus held:

> In order for the licensing system to be upheld, it must be shown to be a necessary and reasonable means serving an important public interest. Moreover, when the licensing system is a preventive public safety measure to prevent vices to the public resulting from unrestricted business activity in contrast to when it is an affirmative measure for the sake of social or economic policy, it must also be shown that the purpose cannot be adequately achieved by less restrictive means of regulating the scope and manner of business activity compared to the licensing system.[73]

According to the Court, not only the licensing system itself but also each precondition for a license must satisfy these criteria.

Turning to the licensing system established by the Pharmaceuticals Act, the Court found the licensing system for pharmacies and drug stores a necessary and reasonable measure to protect the health and safety of the public from defective drugs. The Court then turned its eyes to the proper location requirement of the Act. At the time that requirement was added to the Act, two reasons for its addition were mentioned. One is to prevent the supply of defective drugs which might be caused by the unstable business condition of some of the pharmacies or drug stores as a result of excessive competition. The other is to facilitate the dispersion of new pharmacies or drug stores in areas where there are no or few pharmacies or drug stores. The Court found the former purpose to be primary and the latter secondary. The Court thus concluded that the proper location requirement together with the distance requirement was a preventive public safety measure intended to protect the health and safety of the public. The Court thereby distinguished this case from the Marketplace Case which was concerned with social or economic policy regulation.

The Court then conceded that the purpose of the regulation was legitimate. It also conceded that unrestricted establishment of pharmacies and drug stores might invite a location imbalance and excessive competition. Some stores might be forced into economic trouble as a result of the competition. Yet the Court questioned whether the distance requirement was necessary to prevent the supply of defective drugs. For the manufacture and distribution of drugs are tightly regulated and supervised by the Government. Moreover, the Court found no solid evidence to show that the supply of defective drugs would result from excessive competition. The Court thus concluded that the proper location requirement together with the distance requirement could not be upheld as a necessary and reasonable measure to protect the safety and health of the public.

The Court also found that the proper location requirement did not actually serve the second purpose, i.e., the facilitation of dispersion of pharmacies and drug stores. For the Court doubted its effectiveness and it also found the distance requirement way out of balance as a means to that purpose. The Court thus unanimously invalidated the proper location requirement of the Pharmaceuticals Act.

Implications of the Decision. This decision was a surprise to many. For the same proper location requirement together with the distance requirement was upheld in the First Public Bath Act Case.

In retrospect, the proper location requirement was added to the Pharmaceuticals Act in 1963 in response to an increase of fierce price competition in the late 1950s. Some of the supermarkets sold pharmaceuticals regardless of profit in order to attract customers. At the time the Pharmaceuticals Act was enacted in 1960 as a total revision of the old Pharmaceuticals Act, pharmacies and drug stores strongly demanded that the proper location requirement should be added. Yet there were doubts as to the constitutionality of such an entry restriction and no such requirement was incorporated. The Welfare Ministry instructed, however, each Prefecture to set internal rules to guide the proper location standard. The proper location requirement was thus introduced first by administrative guidance. In 1963, however, a bill was introduced to add that requirement to the Act by Diet members led by Councillor Kazuo Takano, who was a president of the Pharmacist Association. Councillor Takano, when questioned about the constitutionality of this requirement, stressed the fact that pharmaceuticals have a highly public nature, important to the public health. He then developed the same logic employed in the Public Bath Act together with the First Public Bath Act Case.[74] Apparently, in spite of the severe criticisms from many commentators, the First Public Bath Act Case provided a precedent for encouraging the introduction of similar entry restrictions in other statutes.

It is thus not surprising that most commentators are generally supportive of the holding.[75] Indeed, the reasons for such support are not hard to understand. For it is virtually the only Court decision which has applied strict scrutiny to invalidate a statutory restriction on any fundamental human right in Japan.[76] Moreover, the distance requirement appears to be utterly unreasonable. Indeed, the constitutionality of the distance requirement had been questioned by many and the justifications marshalled to support it seem murky at best. The conclusion reached by the Court looks quite natural.

Yet the decision left one wondering why the Court was justified in substituting its judgment on the necessity and reasonableness of regulation for the judgment of the legislature. The Court used to uphold regulations simply accepting the arguments advanced by the Government. Now, suddenly, the Court completely dismissed them. It is doubtful whether the Court convincingly explained its sudden departure from its precedents. Moreover, the theoretical framework adopted by the Court was filled with ambiguities and doctrinal difficulties. The distinction between preventive public safety regulation and affirmative social policy regulation may look fine at first sight. Yet the theoretical justification for this dichotomy is not so strong as it first appears. It is unclear why the former should be subject to more searching review than the latter. Moreover, application of strict scrutiny to public safety regulation would severely restrict the Diet's power to enact such regulation. Furthermore, when we apply this dichotomy in actual cases, one faces difficulty in categorizing each regulation in its terms. In this case, the Court characterized the regulation in the Pharmaceuticals Act as preventive public safety regulation. The Court found the interest of dispersing pharmacies and drug stores secondary. The purpose of protecting existing pharmacies against competition was shrugged off. The Court thereby ignored the legislative history which indicates that the real motive of introducing the distance requirement was apparently anti-competitive. The Court also failed to explain why strict scrutiny should be applied when a regulation serves both the preventive public safety purpose and the affirmative social policy purpose.

The Pharmaceuticals Act Case could be thus equated with *Lochner v. New York*. More precisely it is much closer to *New State Ice Co. v. Liebmann*. For the Pharmaceuticals Act Case employed strict scrutiny and struck down purely economic legislation. As such it provides a strong precedent for employing similar strict scrutiny to other economic regulations. It thus cast doubt on the constitutionality of numerous other economic regulations.

Aftermath

The Forest Act Case. Yet nothing like an avalanche of invalidation of economic regulations occurred.

The Court did in fact apply similar strict scrutiny in the Forest Act Case[77] to invalidate another economic statute. The plaintiff and the defendant in this case were brothers and both were given a half share of the forest involved by their father. The plaintiff sued the defendant seeking damages resulting from the sale of trees by the defendant without the plaintiff's consent and a division of the forest. The district court upheld the plaintiff's damage claim. Yet it rejected the division claim because section 186 of the Forest Act prohibits such a claim unless the claimant's share is more than half the forest. This provision was an exception to section 256, subsection 1 of the Civil

Code, which allows a division claim in such a case. The district court was not persuaded by the plaintiff's argument that the Forest Act was unconstitutional in violation of Article 29 of the Constitution. The High Court affirmed, and the plaintiff appealed to the Supreme Court.

The Court conceded that property rights must yield to preventive public safety regulation as well as to affirmative social policy regulation. It also conceded that whether a particular regulation is permissible should be decided by way of balancing, taking into consideration the purpose, necessity, and scope of regulation, the kind and nature of the property regulated, and the extent of regulation. It further conceded that the court should give deference to the judgment of the legislature. So far the Court seems to be following the framework established by the Pharmaceuticals Act Case. Nevertheless, the Court here suddenly formulated different criteria for reviewing an economic regulation. According to the new criteria,

> the courts should hold the regulation repugnant to Article 29, Section 2 and negate its validity only in the following circumstances: when legislative judgment exceeds the bounds of reasonable discretion, namely when the regulatory purpose of the legislation, serving no social goal or purpose, evidently does not conform with the public welfare, or when the regulatory means, even if the purpose does conform with the public welfare, evidently lacks necessity or reasonableness as a means to accomplish that purpose.[78]

Applying these new criteria, the Court found the purpose of section 186 of the Forest Act in the stabilization of forest management by preventing balkanization of the forest and the promotion of the national economy by preserving forest and promoting its productivity. Such a regulatory purpose, the Court found, cannot be said not to conform with the public welfare. Yet the Court doubted whether the restriction on division claims did contribute to the stabilization of forest management. For the restriction on division claim does not secure that co-owners of a forest manage their forest responsibly and it may bring about simple deadlock if co-owners disagree badly over the management. The Court thus concluded that the means lacked reasonable relation to its purpose.

Moreover, the Court found the restriction on division claims by the Forest Act exceeded what was necessary since balkanization of the forest could be caused even by a single owner of the forest or by a division claim by a co-owner with a share of more than half of the forest. The Act also unnecessarily prohibits the division claim indefinitely without regard to the period necessary for growing trees.

Furthermore, it is not impossible to grant a division without causing balkanization by, for instance, selling the forest altogether and dividing the money.

The Court thus concluded that the restriction on division claims lacked both reasonableness and necessity and that the legislative judgment exceeded the bounds of reasonable discretion. It thus held the section 186 of the Forest Act to be repugnant to Article 29 of the Constitution and void.[79]

Like the Pharmaceuticals Act Case, the Forest Act Case was a surprise but for a different reason. For almost no one had heard of the Forest Act prior to the Supreme Court decision. Moreover, since the constitutional attack was rejected in both lower courts, no commentator expected that the Supreme Court would suddenly reverse these decisions and strike down a statute. Many wondered what led the Court to strike down the restriction on division claims in the Forest Act. Probably the restriction involved was just an outdated imprudent one. Yet it was at least debatable whether the restriction was reasonable or not. In such a case, the Court might be better off to presume its constitutionality and defer to the judgment of the Diet. It was indeed unclear why the Court was inclined to invalidate that restriction. In the end, this judgment was announced in the 40th anniversary year of the Japanese Constitution, and may be nothing more than just a 40th anniversary present: just a reminder to the public that the Court is here to say something. Indeed, this decision had no significant political impact. The invalidated provision of the Forest Act was easily repealed by the Diet.

But from the theoretical perspective, this decision was significant precisely because of the refusal or inability of the Court to categorize the restriction on property rights involved within the preventive public safety regulation and affirmative social policy regulation dichotomy. In this case, the Court did not make clear which category the regulation fell in. If it fell in the preventive public safety regulation, the Court could be seen as following the Pharmaceuticals Act Case. But it is hard to characterize the Forest Act as a preventive public safety regulation. If it was an affirmative social policy regulation, however, then the Forest Act Case means that the Court applied strict scrutiny also in a case involving an affirmative social policy regulation.

The Forest Act Case thus cast doubt on the validity of the theoretical dichotomy of the Pharmaceuticals Act Case. Now it has become completely unclear when the Court employs strict scrutiny in reviewing economic regulations. Suddenly the potential of wiping out much economic legislation is let loose.

The Second and Third Public Bath Act Cases. Yet that potential was soon allayed by two subsequent cases on the Public Bath Act. The Pharmaceuticals Act Case cast doubt on the validity of the First Public Bath Act Case. For it struck down essentially the same type of distance requirement, rejecting the same arguments advanced in support of the distance requirement for public baths. Some thus predicted that the distance requirement in the Public Bath Act might be invalidated.[80] The Court nevertheless made it clear in these two cases that it had no intent of reversing its previous holding.

In the Second Public Bath Act Case,[81] the defendant was prosecuted for a violation of the Public Bath Act and attacked its constitutionality. Yet the second petty bench of the Court reaffirmed the First Public Bath Act Case and added:

> It was true at the time of enactment of this Act and is still true today that the public bath is an essential institution in the daily life of residents. It is necessary to maintain and preserve the public bath in order to serve the needs of residents dependent upon it. It is even more so today because the public bath business is facing economic trouble. To prevent public baths from closure or change of business because of the economic trouble and to take various legislative measures to secure its healthy and stable management do contribute to the maintenance of health and welfare of the citizen and thus conform with the public welfare. The aforementioned proper location regulation together with the distance requirement has sufficient necessity and reasonableness as a means to that end. The courts should hold such affirmative social or economic policy regulation invalid only when the chosen means exceeds the bounds of discretion and its unreasonableness is evident (see [the Marketplace Case]). It needs not so many words before concluding that this proper location regulation and the distance requirement do not meet that test.[82]

In the Third Public Bath Act Case,[83] the plaintiff, the same person who was prosecuted in the Second Public Bath Act Case, attacked the rejection of his application to open a new public bath. The third petty bench of the Court here again reaffirmed its First Public Bath Act Case. The Court did not here use the words "affirmative social policy regulation." But apparently the Court found one legislative purpose of the Act to be the protection of the public bath business. The Court could thus easily conclude that the proper location requirement was a necessary and reasonable means to achieve that purpose.

Times have changed. In the 1950s when the number of public baths increased, it was a fear of excessive competition that justified the distance requirement. But now most of the Japanese houses have a private bath in their houses and the number of public baths is rapidly declining. Indeed, the industry is facing the possibility of extinction.

The Diet in 1981 passed a Special Measures Act to Secure Public Bath to provide aid to the public bath business. Thus it is now a fear for extinction that justifies the distance requirement. Yet the fact remains that at the time of the enactment, the proper location requirement of the Public Bath Act was justified as a public safety measure. It was not a protective measure for the public bath industry. The Court holding thus raised the question as to why the Court could substitute the social policy justification for the initial public safety justification. Moreover, even if the provision can be seen as a social policy restriction, it is still doubtful whether the means chosen has a rational relation to that goal. For the distance requirement does not seem to serve the public bath industry because now there is no fear of an unrestrained increase in new public baths and resulting excessive competition. The Court's stance in the Second and Third Public Bath Act Cases is quite contrasting with that adopted in the Pharmaceuticals Act Case and the Forest Act Case.

The Liquor Store License Case. The Court has continued to take this highly deferential attitude in the Liquor Store License Case.[84] The Liquor Tax Act requires a license to sell liquors but no license can be granted unless the applicant can show a sufficient financial foundation. This provision was meant to secure a stable tax revenue by assuring that licensed liquor stores could maintain stable management. The lower courts had upheld the requirement but had some difficulty in characterizing the purpose of this Act in terms of the dichotomy established by the Supreme Court.

The Court also upheld the requirement but here again it refused to employ the dichotomy. Stressing that this case involved a tax provision which necessitates highly technical and policy-based judgments, the Court held that the legislative discretion should not be disturbed unless the judgment exceeds the bounds and is grossly unreasonable. The Court easily concluded that the license as well as the stable financial foundation requirement were necessary to assure a stable and certain tax revenue and were not grossly unreasonable.[85] It thereby ignored the fact that the Revenue Service has administered this licensing system in the interests of existing (mostly small) liquor stores by preventing supermarkets or discount stores from entering the market.

Protection of Economic Liberties — Its Reality

Legal Regulation

One surely would have a wrong impression, if one comes to believe by way of the constitutional guarantee of property rights and economic liberties or through the Pharmaceuticals Act Case and the Forest Act Case that economic liberties are well protected (or better protected) in Japan. One must look to the reality before concluding how well property rights and economic liberties are protected. For the reality is that they are heavily regulated in Japan.

Indeed, it is a well known fact that most of the major financial institutions and major industries are tightly regulated.[86] But regulation is not limited to such major industries. In fact, one is hard pressed to imagine any occupation which can be engaged in without governmental license (besides of course working for companies as a salaried worker). There are more than ten thousand licensing provisions and the administrative agencies can exercise broad regulatory powers based on their licensing powers. The discretions vested in the agencies are quite broad. This is not surprising since most bills are drafted by bureaucrats and introduced into the Diet by the Cabinet. There are virtually no constitutional limits to delegation of legislative power. Moreover, the administrative agencies interpret these regulatory statutes as authorizing discretion even more broadly.[87]

Nevertheless, despite the Pharmaceuticals Act Case, the courts are very reluctant to overturn these regulations. The Pharmaceuticals Act Case seems to be carefully contained. The courts do not have any intention of applying the strict scrutiny there employed to other regulations. They have simply continued to apply deferential minimum scrutiny when regulations have been attacked and have upheld them.[88] The courts are also quite reluctant to overturn social and economic regulations when they are challenged as infringing the equality right guaranteed by Article 14 of the Constitution.[89] [90]

No one would be surprised to learn this fact because property rights and economic liberties are not given serious judicial protection even in the United States. For that matter, it may be rather remarkable that property rights and economic liberties are given at least partially serious protection by the courts. Moreover, it is more remarkable that public safety regulation is subject to more searching review than social policy regulation. For public safety regulation tends to receive the greatest deference in the United States.

It is also noteworthy that as a result protectionist regulation receives almost no judicial scrutiny and almost always passes constitutional muster. There are many protectionist entry restrictions in Japan, serving to guard the industry against newcomers.[91] Those regulations, however, are quite likely to be sustained in Japan. This is well illustrated by the Public Bath Act Cases, the Marketplace Case and the Liquor Store License Case.

This absence of scrutiny of anti-competitive regulation is curious since the initial justification for the less stringent standard of review toward affirmative social policy regulation was the commitment to the welfare state. It was necessary to give the possible broadest discretion to the legislature, it was argued, to regulate economic liberties in order to secure a harmonized economic order and to protect the workers and the poor. Surely it would be permissible to prohibit unfair trade restrictions or unfair trade practices. It would be also permissible to introduce a progressive income tax or to collect funds to maintain the social security system. Yet nothing seems to justify anti-competitive entry restrictions simply to protect one industry even when that industry is facing economic difficulty. Nevertheless, the courts and commentators alike seem to believe that the legislature enjoys the same wide discretion when its purpose is to protect such an industry.

This seems to imply that the Japanese conception of the welfare state is quite unique: it includes the protection of small and medium size stores or companies against competition as a goal. As stated below, this ideology of the welfare state has justified entry restrictions to protect small and medium size stores or companies instead of giving aid or subsidies to them.

Extra-Legal Regulation—Administrative Guidance

Moreover, it must be noted that, in addition to pervasive legal regulation, economic liberties are also subject to even more pervasive extra-legal regulation. Indeed there is a voluminous amount of extra-legal regulation called administrative guidance which in effect restricts economic liberties in Japan. The close intersection of legal regulation and extra-legal regulation such as administrative guidance can be said to be the most distinctive characteristic of Japanese economic regulation.[92]

Much has been already written, even in the English-language literature, about the unique role administrative guidance plays in Japanese administration.[93] Administrative guidance is a name generally attached to instructions or directions the administrative agency uses to guide and direct the conduct of the public. Some guidance is written but much is transmitted orally. Much of it is issued on the basis of the general jurisdictional authority of the agency and has no explicit statutory authorization. The agency can thus employ this administrative guidance to direct the public to perform an act not specifically required by law.

The guidance has no legal binding force. The parties concerned are free to accept or ignore it. Yet it has great *de facto* binding force. For it is not easy for the parties concerned to ignore it, especially when the agency has a licensing or regulatory power.

The merit of using such administrative guidance is great flexibility. The administrative guidance is issued without explicit statutory authority. The agency can thus quickly respond to new needs and can easily change its guidance. Moreover, administrative guidance makes it possible to maintain the image of cooperation between bureaucrats and private business. This image is especially significant in Japan. That is a reason why bureaucrats are inclined to invoke administrative guidance even when they have formal regulatory powers. The agency can avoid the impression by using administrative guidance that it regulates the business through the force of law.

There are without doubt limits to what administrative guidance can do. Moreover, since it has no legal binding force, the agency cannot directly use any legal sanction even when the public has refused to accept it.

Furthermore, there are serious demerits to the use of administrative guidance. The most significant is the lack of formality and transparency. It is often difficult to know what kind of regulation is enforced through administrative guidance. Furthermore, the use of such guidance makes it impossible for the courts to control the administrative agency by law. The agency can easily circumvent the mandate of law by using administrative guidance.[94]

The Reality Illustrated—The Large Scale Retail Store Act

The most vivid example of such mixed use of legal rule and administrative guidance can be seen in the regulation of large scale retail stores under the Large Scale Retail Store Act (LSRS Act).

The LSRS Act (formally an Act Concerning the Accommodation of Retail Business Activities in the Large Scale Retail Store) was enacted to "accommodate" retail business in the large scale retail store with the local small business community. This Act symbolizes the unique style Japanese bureaucrats employ when they regulate business.[95]

The LSRS Act was enacted in 1973 as a successor to the Department Store Act which required a license to operate a department store. In the 1960s, a different type of large scale retail store, generally called a supermarket, arose with increased commercialism and advances in technology. Supermarkets, unlike traditional department stores, took advantage of the loopholes in the Department Store Act and expanded their business unregulated by that Act. Department stores and small retail stores called strongly for regulation of supermarkets. But the

Ministry of International Trade and Industry (MITI), aspiring to modernize the retail industry, planned to relax the Department Store Act in the interests of consumers. Small retail stores, together with many politicians, both opposition party members and some ruling Liberal Democratic Party (LDP) members with economic ties with small retail stores, strongly criticized the plan and pressured the MITI. The LSRS Act was enacted as a compromise.

The LSRS Act thus adopted a registration system instead of a licensing system but instituted a system of advance review for the registration. Upon receiving a registration from a large scale retail store and its building owner, the International Trade and Industry Minister is authorized within 4 months to make recommendations, if necessary, concerning the opening date or the floor space. Before making such recommendations, the Minister must hear the advice of the Council for the Large Scale Retail Store (Council). The Council is then required to hear the opinion of the local chamber of commerce and other local consumer and retail store groups before giving its advice.

The legal framework for handling application for registration appears simple and fine. Yet the actual operation of this Act was, from the beginning, far different from what might be suggested by the text of the Act. The chamber of commerce is advised to consult with the Conference for Accommodating with Local Business (Conference) before giving its advice. The Conference consists of some 10 to 20 members chosen from business persons, consumers and other citizens, and the critical authority to accommodate the interests of the large scale retail store with local small retail stores is delegated to it. The Conference gradually came to be involved soon after the filing of registration from the building owner, even before the filing of registration from the retail store. The Conference, thus administered, is often called the Pre-Council. Since its opinion is virtually honored by the chamber of commerce, the Pre-Council becomes the actual forum for compromise.

Local small retail stores have a very strong influence on the Pre-Council. Consumer representatives and other citizens are often deprived of any actual voice. As a result, an applicant has tremendous difficulty in obtaining consent from this Pre-Council. All of this has made the applicant prepare well in advance of registration by the building owner. The MITI itself has advised the applicant to conduct an advance explanation, thus practically forcing the applicant to obtain consent from local small retail stores beforehand. The actual battleground has shifted again. It is now before the initial operation of the Act that the applicant must face local small retail stores. The forum for this negotiation is often called the Pre-Pre-Council. The applicant has to obtain consent from this Pre-Pre-Council even before filing an application.

Some cities even went beyond this and declared that they would not accept any more applications. Even though such declarations do not have any legal binding force, they practically functioned to preclude further application in those cities. The MITI, though admitting that these declarations do not have any legal force, partially responded to them by designating cities where applicants were advised to refrain from filing an application.

This whole regulatory scheme made it tremendously difficult to build a large scale retail store. In some cities the opening of a large scale retail store was made virtually impossible. Even when the applicant successfully obtained consent from the community, the applicant had to spend several years before finally becoming able to open the store, and significantly reduce the floor space or cut the business hours to obtain consent from opposing small retail stores. There are many reports of arbitrary recommendations by the Conference. Recommendations differ radically according to the place and applicant. Some applicants who are notorious for destabilizing the retail market or who are outsiders receive very hostile recommendations. Many even point out that the applicant who wants to build the store smoothly must spend huge amount of money to persuade local small retail stores.

The LSRS Act has been attacked as a symbol of how closed the Japanese market is.[96] For our present purpose, however, it is especially important that all of these regulations are not parts of the statutory regulatory scheme. They are in practice mandated by administrative rules and guidance.

The Reality Restated

The story of the LSRS Act vividly illustrates how economic liberties are regulated by law as well as outside the law in Japan. Yet the LSRS Act is not an exception. Rather, the existence of pervasive legal regulation and the wide use of administrative guidance is a standard practice in Japan.[97]

All of this does not mean, however, that the Government has been eager to regulate economic activities in every respect. Antitrust regulation in Japan has been notoriously pro-industry. The Japanese Anti-Monopoly Law is often criticized as toothless.[98] The Fair Trade Commission (FTC) has not enforced the law with vigor. It is well known that the MITI has allowed the industry to evade the Act by letting the industry association curtail production or set prices to survive the crisis and the FTC has often acknowledged such practices.[99] Moreover, there is no products liability law to protect consumers in Japan.[100] The legal system for consumer protection is visibly deficient. The Government has not been active in protecting informational privacy against data processing companies or credit companies either. Also the Government has not been eager to regulate corporate activities in order to protect the environment.[101] Moreover, there is no civil rights legislation in Japan. This means that private discrimination is largely unregulated.[102] Accordingly, the picture is, as it must be, a mixed one. Economic liberties are heavily regulated in many aspects but left unregulated in many other aspects.

It is hard to conclude which country has more regulation of economic liberties: the United States or Japan. It is also hard to tell whether regulation of economic liberties is excessive or not. For there seem to be no objective criteria to show what regulation is necessary. Yet it is true that many people claim that there are too much economic regulation in Japan.[103] Japanese society is without doubt a tightly regulated society.

Protection of Economic Liberties, Japanese Style

The Limits of Judicial Protection

To what extent then does the constitutional guarantee of economic liberties afford actual protection? How can we make sense of the Pharmaceuticals Act Case? Did the Court holding provide any relief for companies or consumers? The Court holding certainly implies that the court can intervene and invalidate unreasonable economic regulation. But the decision is unlikely to exert much influence upon economic regulation.

First of all, it is quite rare to find challenges against such regulation in the court. When one owner of a chain-store filed a suit attacking the constitutionality of the LSRS Act in March, 1990, for example, it was the first constitutional suit ever filed against this regulatory statute.[104] The plaintiff spent 9 years in vain trying to obtain consent from the local business community even before filing an application in one of the suburban cities of Tokyo which had declared a policy of not accepting any more applications. He finally gave up the plan of building a store and instead filed a suit seeking damages. But other supermarkets are reluctant to join the constitutional fight.[105] The fact that the LSRS Act has been administered without constitutional challenge for decades and the fact that the first constitutional challenge was greeted unfavorably by other supermarkets certainly manifest the unwillingness of those regulated to launch a constitutional fight before the court.

Moreover, it is highly unclear when the Court would employ strict scrutiny and invalidate economic regulation. For the whole distinction between public safety regulation and social policy regulation is highly ambiguous. There are no objective criteria for deciding which category the regulatory statute falls into. It is in fact all too naive to believe that economic regulation necessarily falls into either category. As a result, the Pharmaceuticals Act Case cannot provide a powerful precedent for attacking a regulatory statute.

Thirdly, the dichotomy allows the Government to defend much protectionist regulation as social policy regulation, which can easily pass constitutional muster. The Government can even defend the statute initially enacted as a public safety measure as social policy legislation. Despite the Pharmaceuticals Act Case and the Forest Act Case, the Marketplace Case is then likely to provide a precedent to sustain such protectionist regulation. It is the ideology of the welfare state in the Japanese version that legitimizes such legislation.

The Constitution is thus unlikely to afford any actual protection to economic liberties in Japan.

Where Does the Japanese Public Find Protection?

Where can one then find protection for economic liberties? In order to answer this question, we must examine the characteristics of economic regulation in Japan.

There are certain basic differences in the nature of economic regulation in Japan and the United States. In the United States the federal Government has only limited authority to regulate the economy whereas in Japan most economic regulation is administered by the central government. In the United States it is primarily the independent administrative commissions that are entrusted with economic regulation whereas in Japan it is entrusted to departments of the Executive. As a result, it is far easier to set industrial policy within the executive department in Japan, although each department has its own independent interest and authority. Moreover, the existence of a corps of able bureaucrats in the Japanese executive departments certainly makes a notable difference. Japanese bureaucrats have more prestige than American bureaucrats. Japan has been indeed famous for the strong authority of its bureaucrats. It is indeed a country governed by bureaucrats.

Besides these differences, however, we may be allowed to point out some of the characteristics of economic regulation in Japan. One notable characteristic concerns the scope of governmental regulation that is deemed justified. Whereas in the United States governmental regulation tends to be deemed justified only where there is market failure or malfunction, it tends to be deemed justified in Japan even in their absence. Or to put it differently, the scope of market failure or malfunction that is deemed to justify regulation is perceived more broadly in Japan.[106] Indeed, the role of the Government as a promoter and protector of the economy has been long accepted in Japan.

As a result, free competition is often regarded as threatening to the harmony of society. It is true that many Japanese companies are engaged in fierce competition and that this is apparently one of the major reasons for rapid economic growth. It cannot be denied, however, that such competition is allowed only within the boundaries set by bureaucrats. Indeed competition is always controlled and coordinated by bureaucrats in Japan. Such control and coordination become especially prominent when the industry faces economic troubles. But there are also many anti-competitive protectionist entry restrictions to prevent a fragile industry from falling into economic trouble. Moreover, even in healthy industries, small and medium size companies and stores are often protected against competition by various regulations. All such regulations are justified in the name of the necessity of maintaining the orderly development of the economy.

The key term which often appears even in the Court opinion is "excessive competition." "Excessive competition," it is argued, produces various undesirable consequences like excessive price slashing, a rush of bankruptcies and industrial disorder and must be hence curtailed. This reasoning is found in the Public Bath Act, the Pharmaceuticals Act, the LSRS Act, and many other regulatory statutes.[107] Cartels or unfair trade practices are certainly forms of excessive competition which must be curtailed to preserve the market mechanism. Yet often what is regarded as a usual trade practice in the United States is regarded as a form of excessive competition and is hence restricted in Japan. Although there may be special reasons for guarding against excessive competition in Japan,[108] it is more likely that the term "excessive competition" is used as a pretext for protectionist regulation.[109]

The second notable characteristic is the orientation of regulation. Many regulations are designed to protect producers and distributors.[110] Some of them are overtly protectionist. Some of them are regulatory on their face but are in fact administered for the benefit of producers and distributors. In the end, both function to protect producers and distributors. As a result consumers' interests are relatively ignored. The LSRS Act is in point here. One of the principal thoughts behind regulation under the LSRS Act is the ideology of "prospering-together." Large scale retail stores, it is believed, should not prosper at the cost of sacrificing neighboring small and medium size retail stores. This ideology surely burdens the large scale retail store. Once it opens successfully, however, this ideology makes it possible for it to enjoy a virtual monopoly over the market preventing the entry of another large scale retail store. The net result is the neglect of consumers' interests, to the benefit of all retail stores.[111] This characteristic can be observed with respect to many other regulations.

The third characteristic is concerned with the manner in which regulation is designed. Business is certainly widely regulated in Japan. But this does not mean that Government actually tightly regulates every aspect of business activities. Rather, administrative regulations are designed to assure maximum discretion to bureaucrats. Bureaucrats, taking advantage of this wide discretion, can form economic policy and enforce it. The law is intentionally designed to prevent those regulated from challenging their exercise of discretion before the court. The Administrative Case Litigation Act, as explained below, intentionally sets up an elaborate scheme for not disturbing the discretion of bureaucrats. This broad discretion, isolated from judicial control, is the most prominent characteristic of economic regulation, Japanese style.[112]

Japan may indeed be characterized as the "soft state" in contrast to the "strong state."[113] Even though the Government has broad regulatory powers over the private economy, it has not exercised these powers vigorously in reality. Even when the Government feels the necessity of regulation, it tends to explore informal alternatives to formal legal regulation such as administrative guidance. A symbiotic relationship between bureaucrats, politicians and business corporations, or at least the appearance of it, has made this soft state possible. As is pointed out by many, bureaucrats, LDP politicians and business corporations have had very strong ties in Japan. The business corporations accepted ex-bureaucrats as their executives after retirement. This practice, called the "descent from heaven," ensures that business corporations can keep good relations with bureaucrats. Bureaucrats know that the welfare of the regulated industry is directly linked to their regulatory power. They also know that a good relationship with business corporations is essential to secure their descent from heaven. LDP politicians heavily relied upon business corporations for their support. A huge amount of political contributions from business corporations was essential for LDP politicians. Business corporations have had to count on bureaucrats for help and rely upon LDP politicians to prosper. Often ex-bureaucrats served as power mediators as LDP politicians in the Diet. This triangle between bureaucrats, LDP politicians, and business corporations has contributed to the flexibility of economic regulation.[114]

This does not mean, however, that bureaucrats or politicians could dictate the economic policy as they wished. One of the prevailing myths about Japan is that the Government or bureaucrats can set industrial policy and let every private corporation follow its goal. This is simply not true.[115] Moreover, even bureaucrats could not set policy by themselves. The relationship between bureaucrats and politicians was more subtle. In the end, it is more appropriate to view the relationship between bureaucrats, politicians, and business corporations as an interactive one.[116] It is true that bureaucrats have broad discretion immune from judicial control. Yet bureaucrats cannot disregard politicians and business corporations in deciding policy. Politicians exert influence upon bureaucrats in both the legislative and the administrative process. Bureaucrats also need cooperation from business corporations in order to accomplish governmental objectives. It is more appropriate to say, therefore, that bureaucrats have simply had relatively strong voices in this interactive relationship between bureaucrats, LDP politicians and business corporations.[117]

It is fair to say, therefore, that the actual protection for economic liberties has been in this interactive relationship between bureaucrats, politicians and business corporations. This is indeed the fourth and most significant characteristic of economic regulation in Japan. It is true even in the United States that the main protection for property rights and economic liberties lies in the political process. Yet in Japan the protection for property rights and economic liberties has depended to a far greater extent on informal interactions in the political process despite the constitutional guarantee. Moreover, the relatively strong authority of bureaucrats in this interaction, as above stated, constitutes its most distinguishing characteristic.

Indeed, when market failure or malfunction occurs, people have sought redress in this relationship between bureaucrats, politicians, and business corporations. The chief protection usually lies in the broad discretion of bureaucrats immune from judicial control. Bureaucrats, if convinced that intervention is necessary, may seek new legislation or can intervene benevolently by using informal administrative guidance. Yet the discretion of bureaucrats is partially restricted by the roles played by politicians and business corporations. Politicians can enact regulatory legislation but more often they have pressured bureaucrats to intervene at the request of industry, expecting in return political contributions or support at election time. Business corporations seek help from bureaucrats as well as from politicians.

The protection has been practical and subtle. It is highly non-legalized and informal. For better or worse, it has been this protection that is critical in Japan.[118]

Reasons Why People Do Not Seek Judicial Protection

All of this makes one wonder, however, why people do not seek help from the courts. As the story of the LSRS Act illustrates, citizens are not willing to challenge regulation before the courts. One is naturally tempted to ask why people are simply so content with the vast regulatory powers of bureaucrats.

One of the reasons is definitely the difficulty of winning the lawsuit. As stated above, it is utterly unclear when the courts will employ the reasoning of the Pharmaceuticals Act Case, and the courts are rather reluctant to apply it. It is thus natural that the public is discouraged from filing a suit. However, that is not the only reason why people do not seek help from the courts. There are other reasons. Among them the following four seem to be important. The first is the reluctance of the Japanese to go to courts and the small number of lawyers in Japan. The second is the difficulty of administrative litigation. The third is the pervasive use of administrative guidance and the difficulty of attacking it. The fourth and final is the role of ideology.

Few Lawyers and the Reluctance to Sue. There has been much talk about the small number of lawyers in Japan and the reluctance of the Japanese to sue. These features used to be regarded as a reflection of a traditional cultural attitude.[119] Japanese people tend to emphasize group harmony and prefer consensual decision-making to open discussion and formal confrontation. That has been said to be the reason why the Japanese hesitate to resort to courts for solving social problems. Yet recently many commentators have come to doubt this cultural explanation and instead look to institutional reasons for the reluctance of the Japanese to sue. According to this revisionist thesis, Japanese are not necessarily inherently reluctant to sue. The small number of lawyers and small amount of litigation are thus explained as a result of the deliberate design of bureaucrats to divert disputes away from the courts.[120]

It is true that the number of lawyers is few compared to the United States. It is also certainly true that the amount of litigation is small compared to the United States. Moreover, it would be true that the Japanese public are reluctant to go to courts to solve a problem. Yet it cannot be denied that the reluctance of the people to sue is also a result of a deliberate effort by bureaucrats to divert disputes away from the courts. The number of lawyers is intentionally limited and the civil procedure is intentionally designed so as to prevent the public from using litigation as a means to social reform.[121]

The revisionist thesis is justified, therefore, to that extent. Nevertheless, it still fails to answer how bureaucrats can manage to divert so many disputes away from the courts.[122] There still seems to be room for inquiry how the Japanese understanding of law or attitudes toward the court has made such diversion from litigation possible.[123]

It seems undeniable that many Japanese people still subscribe to traditional beliefs and tend to avoid courts for solving disputes. We should not disregard these beliefs even if bureaucrats have capitalized on them to divert litigation. Moreover, they still constrain those who do not personally subscribe to them. For, as explained below, such traditional beliefs still serve to control the conduct of the public as ideologies.

The Difficulty of Administrative Litigation. In Japan a lawsuit attacking administrative action must satisfy the requirements and follow the procedure set up by the Administrative Case Litigation Act. During the Meiji era, administrative cases were heard by the Administrative Court; judicial courts did not have jurisdiction. The Administrative Court was an administrative organ and the function of judging administrative cases was considered as administrative. The Japanese Constitution abolished the Administrative Court and vested the function of judging administrative cases in the judicial courts. Yet bureaucrats as well as administrative law professors thought that special procedures should be required for administrative cases because they involve the exercise of administrative power. The Administrative Case Litigation Act was thus enacted.

As a result, the requirements and procedure are deliberately structured by the Act to assure the maximum discretion and deference to the administrative agency.[124] The principal form of action allowed is a suit for judicial revocation of administrative order (section 8). The suit must be filed therefore only after the agency action. In other words, no pre-enforcement suit like an injunction can be filed.[125] There is a very short statute of limitations (section 14). The suit can be only filed against an "administrative order" (section 3, subsection 1). No suit can be filed, it is believed, against rulemaking, informal activity or planning by the agency.[126] The Act stipulates that only a person who has a "legally protected interest" can file a suit (section 9). This standing requirement has been interpreted by the Court as only conferring standing when a particular statute specifically protects the legal interest of an individual citizen.[127] As a result, citizens have had extreme difficulty in arguing their standing to challenge administrative actions.[128] Even if the citizen files a suit, that does not stop the administrative agency from enforcing the challenged order (section 25, subsection 1). Only in quite exceptional circumstances is the court authorized to order the agency to stop and wait for final judicial determination (section 25, subsection 2). Yet even in these rare circumstances, the Prime Minister can override the judicial order (section 27). No temporary relief can be granted to the citizen-plaintiff since the Act specifically prohibits the court from issuing it (section 44). As a result, the administrative agency can simply enforce its order while defending it before the court. Finally, the Act still has one more safeguard for the administrative agency. For the Act specifically authorizes the court not to invalidate an administrative order even when it is found illegal if the court believes that invalidation would not serve the public interest (section 31).

It is thus no exaggeration to say that the whole structure of administrative litigation is designed to prevent the public from filing a suit against administrative action. These barriers would prevent legal challenges from any parties. But the most significant disadvantage will fall upon the ordinary public and consumers since they are most likely to find no relief in the political process and administrative agencies. These barriers make sure that they cannot find relief also in the courts.

The courts seem to have no intention of giving a liberal construction to these provisions to provide more help to the general public. On the contrary, the courts have given them a very restrictive construction. By so doing, the courts have sided with bureaucrats against challenges from the public.

The absence of any Administrative Procedure Act has aggravated the general public's plight. There is no comprehensive procedure for the administrative agency to follow. Formal hearings are rarely required. The administrative process is rather designed to preclude citizen participation. Almost everything is left to the discretion of bureaucrats. The absence of a Freedom of Information Act further aggravates the already miserable plight of the general public. For the public are not allowed to seek disclosure of governmental documents. They have no means of even knowing how bureaucrats manage administration. Moreover litigation takes many years in Japan. If the Government is determined to appeal up to the Supreme Court, it may take indeed more than ten years. Finally, the plaintiff must bear all the litigation costs and attorney fees even when he or she wins the suit. There are no attorney fee provisions to force the Government to pay the attorney fees when it loses a suit. It is thus not surprising to find that the public are not inclined to resort to litigation in order to attack administrative actions in the first place.

The Difficulty of Attacking Administrative Guidance. Furthermore, the particular technique widely used by bureaucrats to regulate economic liberties makes it even more difficult for citizens to challenge regulation. For it is even more difficult to challenge administrative guidance before the court.

First of all, administrative guidance has no legal binding force. Legally speaking, it can be accepted or ignored. Citizens are thus regarded as voluntarily complying with administrative guidance when they accept it. The courts thus tend to refuse judicial review when it is challenged.[129] Moreover, even in exceptional cases where the courts agree to hear attacks on administrative guidance, the courts are not willing to annul it.[130] Thus, citizens are discouraged from filing a suit attacking administrative guidance.

Moreover, disobeying administrative guidance or challenging it before the court tends to entail serious adverse consequences. Surely one must anticipate strong condemnation and all kinds of counterattacks (even retaliation) from bureaucrats. Sudden on-site safety inspection and strict enforcement of health and safety regulations are just some examples. Moreover, one will not be able to count on the favor of bureaucrats in the future. The costs of ignoring the guidance can indeed be extraordinary. It is a risky decision to disregard administrative guidance. It is no wonder if people are inclined to refrain from doing so.

As a consequence, pervasive extra-legal restrictions on economic liberties are likely to be left unchallenged.

Ideologies. Yet the difficulty of administrative litigation in general and the difficulty of attacking administrative guidance in particular cannot by themselves fully explain the unwillingness of Japanese citizens to challenge broad regulations on economic liberties. We must not ignore the role ideologies play in this context.

As suggested above, there still remains a belief among many Japanese that Japanese society is a homogeneous society, which emphasizes harmony and prefers consensual decision-making to public discussion and voting. Citizens are thus supposed not to disturb the harmony of the group by raising an opposing voice or filing a lawsuit.

Some surely accept such a belief and act according to it, although it is questionable whether the overwhelming majority do accept such a belief. It is less significant, however, for our purpose, whether Japanese society is indeed such a society or whether the overwhelming majority of the public have succumbed to such a belief. What matters more is, as Ramseyer points out, the fact that many people still tend to view themselves and their society in this way.[131] Even when one finds such a belief ridiculous, he or she is still likely to act according to it. For he or she knows that there are many other people who do accept the belief and expect him or her to act according to it.

We may be allowed to call this kind of mind-set ideology. It is a view on society or on the relationship between the individual and society widely shared by the public. Ideology tells the public how to think and how to act. It also tells the public what kind of society is desirable and what kind of relationship between the individual and society is desirable.[132] It is such an ideology that tells the public to act according to a traditional belief even when they personally do not share it.

Apparently, the ideology of a harmonious society and consensual decision-making mentioned above serves to legitimize bureaucratic discretion and its informal decision-making process.[133] It also serves to legitimize the symbiotic relationship between bureaucrats, politicians and business corporations, and induces the public to accept governance by bureaucrats and the reality of pervasive bureaucratic interference as natural and legitimate. At the same time, it discourages the public from challenging economic regulation before the courts.

Moreover, the Japanese public had been taught not to challenge authority. Challenges to authority were deemed to deserve death in the past. Especially during the Meiji era, the Emperor was declared to be sacred and inviolable (Meiji Constitution, Article 3). Unquestioning acceptance of the governmental order has been regarded as a virtue. "It's no use kicking against the pricks" is an often repeated maxim even in daily life. Challenging the Government is thus still regarded as something grossly improper. As a result, the plaintiff in constitutional or administrative cases must often anticipate intimidation and harassment from the rest of the public. The ideology of obedience together with the fear of intimidation and harassment thus dissuade the public from filing suit.

Another ideology which keeps the public from legal challenge is a view, which many Japanese share, of bureaucrats and administrative agencies. It is an ideology of bureaucrats as coordinators of the economy. Japan started its modern industrialization after the Meiji Restoration. Since there was no modern industry at that time, the Japanese Government had to play a major role in promoting industry and in protecting domestic industry against foreign competitors. Ever since then, the Japanese public tends to share a view that the Government, administrative agencies and bureaucrats, should promote and protect industry. This view did not change drastically even after World War II. Much has been written about the role the MITI has played in this post-war history.[134] It was made possible by the public perception toward bureaucrats and administrative agencies. *Laissez-faire* capitalism has never been a part of Japanese ideology. It is thus no wonder again if the public are inclined to accept governmental intervention.

It is not only these social ideologies, however, that lie behind the reluctance of the public to attack economic regulation. It is also legal ideologies that we have inherited from our past that has made the existence of broad regulation of economic liberties possible.

The first is the ideology of "executive power" as residual power. The Japanese Constitution vested "executive power" in the Cabinet (Article 65). Interestingly for our present purpose, this "executive power" has been defined broadly to encompass all governmental powers with the exception of "legislative" and "judicial" powers.[135] "Executive power" is a residual power and thus encompasses very broad authorities. In other words, "executive power" in Japan includes not only "executive power" but also "administrative power" as the term is employed in the United States. It is very close to the concept of "police power."

Moreover, the "executive power" has been conceived as involving the exercise of public authority and has been afforded superior status over the general public. The view has been taken, therefore, that the exercise of "executive power" should not be disturbed by the individual citizen. When administrative law commentators talk about the separation of powers principle in Japan, it is a separation of powers among legislative, judicial and "executive" powers in this sense that has been supposed to be mandated by the Constitution. The separation of powers principle has been thus interpreted to preclude legislative and judicial interference with the "executive power."

Apparently, this ideology of "executive power" as a residual power and the ideology of the superiority of executive power are inherited from our past when the Emperor was sovereign and had all governmental powers. Although under the Meiji Constitution the Emperor received assistance from the legislature in the exercise of his legislative power and although judicial power was exercised by the judicial courts in his name, the Emperor had certain prerogatives and could exercise administrative power with the assistance of individual Ministers. The definition of "executive power" as a residual power and the superiority of executive power surely fit the Meiji Constitution. Yet the Japanese Constitution adopted a totally different governmental structure. It stripped all governmental powers from the Emperor and vested "executive power" in the Cabinet while vesting legislative power in the Diet and judicial power in the judiciary. The Japanese Constitution therefore seems to be adopting the American conception of "executive power."[136] Nevertheless, the difference was never fully appreciated. As a result, the traditional conception has outlived the constitutional change.

This ideology of "executive power" as a residual power and the ideology of the superiority of executive power has made it possible to preclude public challenge of economic regulation. The ideology of "executive power" as a residual power has made people believe that it was the responsibility of the administrative agency to solve social problems when no other governmental organs are helpful. Indeed, when there is a problem, the Japanese public tend to go to an administrative agency for help. It has also certainly helped to create the view that an administrative agency could use extra-legal regulation such as administrative guidance even without explicit statutory authorization.[137] On the other hand, the ideology of the superiority of executive power has provided a rationale for setting up a special litigation procedure for administrative cases which functions to preclude judicial interference with administrative agencies.[138] It is certainly the same ideology that has precluded the courts from issuing injunctive relief or even temporary restraining orders.[139]

These legal ideologies without doubt have functioned to preclude legal challenge of economic regulation in Japan.

Why Are the Courts Playing Such a Minimal Role?

It may not be so astonishing, therefore, if we learn that the Japanese public are reluctant to challenge broad and far-reaching economic regulations. Yet it must be still inquired why the courts are not willing to make it easier for the public to challenge restrictions on economic liberties.

It is of course conceivable that Japanese judges share various ideologies with their fellows. They may thus be cherishing the harmony of society and preferring the Japanese way of dispute resolution through consensual negotiation between bureaucrats, LDP politicians and business corporations. They may be viewing litigation as something disruptive and improper. It is hard to prove any of these speculations. But it is evident that judges are strongly influenced by the ideology of "executive power" as a residual power and the ideology of superiority of executive power. The judges are thus reluctant to disturb the exercise of executive power by accepting lawsuits.

Moreover, there is a strong positivist impulse among Japanese judges. Raised and trained under the strong influence of civil law tradition, the Japanese judges still share a highly positivist conception of law. They are not willing to give a liberal construction to statutes in favor of the public. Even when they interpret the Administrative Cases Litigation Act, the judges are reluctant to go beyond the statutory provision. Such an attitude is apparent in the inclination of judges to dismiss injunctive suits against administrative agencies.

Even when the citizen decides to file a suit and all the barriers are cleared, the courts, as stated above, are quite deferential toward the Government and administrative agencies. They are eager to uphold economic regulation if its constitutionality is challenged. Here the ideology of judicial restraint and the ideology of the welfare state play significant roles. The ideology of judicial restraint has constantly characterized the judicial philosophy of the Japanese courts. The courts have been extremely reluctant to overturn legislative judgments in any cases involving individual rights.[140] Moreover, as stated above, the ideology of the welfare state legitimizes protectionist regulation, and counsels the courts to refrain from invalidating regulation in the name of social policy.

The reluctance of the courts can be also observed when administrative action is challenged as arbitrary or illegal. The courts are inclined to sustain the exercise of administrative powers by emphasizing the broad discretion given to them by the statutes. Even when administrative guidance without explicit statutory authorization is challenged, the courts tend to sustain it.[141]

This tendency is well illustrated by statistics. According to the Secretariat General Office of the Supreme Court, Administrative Branch, 1,198 new administrative cases were filed before the courts in 1990. Of the 1,305 cases handled, a decision was reached in 941 cases (72.1%), 338 cases (25.9%) were dropped, and 17 cases (1.3%) were settled. Of the 941 cases in which a decision was reached, 899 cases (68.9% of all cases handled) were decided by judgment and 42 cases (3.2%) were decided by order. Of the cases decided by judgment, only 141 cases (partially or totally) upheld the plaintiff's claim, 554 cases were dismissed after reaching the merits, and 204 cases were dismissed without reaching the merits. The winning ratio of the plaintiff is 10.8% of all cases handled. It is merely 15.7% even in all cases decided by judgment and at most 20.3% in all cases in which the merits were reached. This means only one of ten plaintiffs wins at first instance.[142] If we further consider the fact that many of those judgments upholding the plaintiff's claim are reversed on appeal, the actual winning ratio of the plaintiff is less than 10%.[143]

One is naturally tempted to ask why the courts are so deferential. Why are the courts playing such a minimal role in Japan? Certainly the regulatory statutes are intentionally designed to vest broad discretion in regulators. The courts are thus practically precluded from holding regulations invalid. Moreover, the Administrative Case Litigation Act is designed to preclude the courts from invalidating the administrative action. The courts are simply ill-equipped to constrain the regulators in the first place.

Yet the reluctance of the courts to scrutinize administrative action, let alone invalidate it, cannot be fully explained by these alone. Legal ideology also plays a significant role again here. The ideology of "executive power" as residual power and the ideology of superiority of executive power make judges even more restrained in invalidating administrative action. Moreover, the civil law tradition counsels judges to refrain from interfering with administrative action without explicit statutory authorization. The positivist impulse here has the same effect.

But the role of ideologies, even though significant, should not suffice to explain the reluctance of the courts to scrutinize and invalidate administrative action. For politics has played a far more critical role here.

First of all, the Chief Judge of the Supreme Court is appointed by the Emperor upon nomination by the Cabinet and other judges are appointed by the Cabinet. Since the conservative parties occupied the Government almost ever since the end of the war (the LDP occupied the Government from 1955 to 1993), almost all judges have been appointed by the conservative Cabinet. Because the appointment is highly discretionary, it is natural that the Supreme Court consists of those judges who shared a conservative ideology with the Cabinet.[144] It is natural that they have shown a reluctance to overturn the acts of administrative agencies.

Secondly, the Court has been eager to direct lower court judges to follow the lead of the Court. The Secretariat General Office of the Supreme Court has often invited in judges dealing with a particular subject and has held non-public conferences where judges discuss what kind of result should be obtained. Even though the Court has claimed that it is just a study conference, there is evidence to show that the Secretariat General Office has used it as an occasion to direct lower court judges to follow the Court decisions or to hand down a conservative decision.[145]

Thirdly, the Court has been very active in promoting personnel exchange between the judiciary and the prosecutor's office. An increasing number of judges have resigned and worked for the Government as prosecutors. They have then been reappointed and heard administrative cases. Even though the Court has defended this practice as a way for judges to widen their knowledge, one cannot be blamed for doubting whether such a judge can sit and hear administrative cases fairly.[146]

Finally, there have been mechanisms to make sure that judges hand down conservative decisions. Those judges who are likely to give a decision unfavorable to the Government are likely to be precluded from appointment in the first place. Indeed some of the applicants who have successfully completed the legal training necessary to become judges have been denied appointment. It is generally believed that their appointment was denied for political reasons.[147] Those judges who have given a decision unfavorable to the Government may be denied reappointment when their ten year tenure expires.[148] Or they may be treated unfavorably within the judiciary. Indeed there are some data to show that judges who ignore the Court's decision and hand down a decision unfavorable to the Government are slow to be promoted.[149]

All of this certainly functions to make sure that judges do not invalidate statutes and administrative action.[150] It is thus no wonder that the courts are playing such a minimal role in scrutinizing economic regulation in Japan.

Economic Development and the Role of Law

Much has been written about the role of the Government's economic policy in post-war Japan.[151] Much has been written also about many other factors which have contributed to this economic growth.[152] Yet little has been written specifically on the role the law has played in this economic development. Does the constitutional guarantee of property rights and economic liberties have something to do with the rapid economic growth in Japan? How about the pervasive regulation of economic liberties? Have they facilitated the economic growth or somehow constricted it?

One may be justified in saying that at least some regulations did contribute to economic growth by vesting broad discretion in bureaucrats. Especially in the early days foreign exchange regulation made it possible for the MITI to control imports and exports. Yet the causal relationship between regulation and economic growth seems to be somewhat indirect. Perhaps the absence of regulation or the failure to enforce regulations has more impact on economic growth than the existence of regulation. The toothless anti-monopoly law, for instance, may have enabled industry to co-operate under the coordination of the MITI.[153] The absence of any products liability law and the poor consumer protection must be a relief for manufacturers. Yet some regulations apparently hindered economic growth. Some protectionist regulations, like the LSRS Act, surely hindered the modernization of the retail industry.

It is thus hard to figure out how and to what extent a particular law or regulation (or absence of it) or the whole structure of regulation did contribute to the economic growth of Japan. Moreover, regulation is just one method of economic policy enforcement. The Government can employ non-regulatory measures to facilitate or to deter particular conduct, such as subsidy or tax-incentives. These non-regulatory measures may even have much more impact than regulatory measures upon the economy.[154] It is indeed a well known fact that the Japanese Government facilitated the development of semiconductor and electronic industry by subsidizing further research and development.[155] Although the broad discretion vested in bureaucrats may have contributed to economic growth, the impact of economic regulations on economic growth seems to be undemonstrable.

Then how about the constitutional guarantees of property rights and economic liberties? We have already seen that the fact that the Japanese Constitution, unlike the United States Constitution, has explicit provisions guaranteeing property rights and economic liberties is largely irrelevant in this context. The constitutional guarantee has not prevented bureaucrats from enacting voluminous economic regulations and has not led the courts to protect property rights or economic liberties vigorously.

Nevertheless, the constitutional guarantee of property rights and economic liberties seem to have at least some crucial functions for economic regulation and possibly for economic growth in Japan.

First of all, the Japanese Constitution first enabled the public to have a modern notion of property rights and economic liberties. By removing pre-modern feudal elements from the economy, the Constitution thereby contributed to the establishment of a modern market mechanism. It is probable that this change made it possible to lay the foundation for economic growth.

Second, the explicit limits on property rights and economic liberties in the Constitution made it easier for bureaucrats to introduce economic regulations. The Diet and bureaucrats could easily invoke the existence of explicit limits as a justification for the broad discretion vested in bureaucrats. The same explicit limits also serve to justify protectionist regulation in the name of the welfare state.

Third, the Pharmaceuticals Act Case and other Supreme Court decisions perform a significant legitimizing function in this context. By upholding the broad legislative discretion in regulating economic liberties, the Court has essentially legitimized the existence of pervasive economic regulations. While leaving room for invalidating some (perhaps politically insignificant) economic regulations, the Court lends support to the authority of bureaucrats by sending messages that their authority is constitutional and legitimate. As a result, the Diet and bureaucrats can introduce and implement any economic regulation almost free from fear of invalidation by the Court.

Fourth and finally, on the other hand, the Diet and bureaucrats can invoke the constitutional guarantee of economic liberties to rationalize the refusal or failure of regulation. Since business activities are entitled to constitutional protection, they can thus respond to a call for regulation, the Government has to respect that constitutional guarantee and should not unnecessarily restrict such activities. Moreover, they can also invoke the constitutional guarantee as a rationalization for using extra-legal informal governmental actions such as administrative guidance. The constitutional guarantee of property rights and economic liberties is a convenient excuse for bureaucrats to refuse to regulate.

The constitutional guarantee of property rights and economic liberties as well as Supreme Court decisions on this guarantee have thus allowed the broadest discretion to bureaucrats and thereby enabled them to set industrial policy. They have served to legitimize that policy by upholding the discretion so allowed. If that industrial policy somehow did contribute to the economic growth of Japan, then the constitutional guarantee as well as the Supreme Court decisions may be said to have contributed, even though indirectly, to that growth.

Law and Society Reexamined

A brief look at the Japanese experience seems to suggest the important role ideologies play in controlling public conduct and legitimizing bureaucratic governance.

Many Japanese people still tend to view Japanese society as a homogeneous society which emphasizes harmony and prefers consensual decision-making to open discussion and confrontation. One is thus supposed not to disturb the harmony of society by raising an opposing voice or by filing a lawsuit. These beliefs certainly constrain public conduct. Indeed, many Japanese, especially in rural districts, simply accept these beliefs and act according to them. Yet the importance of such beliefs is not confined to those who subscribe to them. Even when one is not necessarily subject to such beliefs, he or she must consider the fact that many others do expect him or her to stick to such beliefs before deciding to reject them in public. Such beliefs thus function as ideologies and constrain public conduct even when the public know that they are simply myths. The function of ideologies is quite subtle. Ideologies tell the public that the traditional beliefs about Japanese society are natural and legitimate. They then tell the public to act according to them.

In fact various ideologies—of harmonious society, of consensual decision-making, of obedience, and of bureaucrats as coordinators of the economy—serve to persuade the public to accept governmental regulations. They dissuade the public from filing lawsuits attacking these regulations. Moreover, the ideologies of "executive power" as a residual power and of the superiority of executive power have made it possible to set up the special procedure for administrative cases designed to preclude the courts from interfering with bureaucrats. The same ideologies and the strong positivist impulse of Japanese judges have allowed them to refuse to interfere with administrative actions. Apparently such ideologies have more influence on the people and the judges than the text of the Constitution.

It is true that bureaucrats have capitalized on the influence of such shared ideologies to enact pervasive economic regulations which vest broad discretionary powers in them. They have also capitalized on the existence of such ideologies to prevent the public from filing a suit against their power and also to prevent the courts from interfering with them. As a result, bureaucrats are allowed to exercise their powers almost without fear of invalidation by the courts. Although their powers have been partially constricted by the roles played by politicians and business corporations, these ideologies have made bureaucrats leave the issue largely to the symbiotic relationship between bureaucrats, politicians and business corporations. The governance of bureaucrats is made possible only with the help of these ideologies.

Conclusion

Even though Japan is now struggling to escape from serious recession caused by the explosion of the so-called "bubble economy," it cannot be denied that it has managed to achieve an unprecedentedly rapid economic recovery from the devastation after World War II. This recovery was accomplished under the Japanese Constitution which guarantees property rights and economic liberties.

This paper has examined how the constitutional guarantee of property rights and economic liberties is judicially enforced and how property rights and economic liberties are regulated in Japan. We have seen that *Lochner v. New York* is alive in Japan. But we have also seen that it has not served to invalidate various economic regulations. Despite the constitutional guarantee, economic liberties are pervasively regulated and are subject to even more pervasive extra-legal regulation such as administrative guidance. It is rather the most prominent characteristic of Japanese economic regulation that a quite broad discretion immune from judicial control is vested in the hands of bureaucrats. The actual protection of economic liberties does not lie in the judiciary but in the interactive relationship between bureaucrats, politicians, and business corporations.

It is not clear whether and to what extent the constitutional guarantee of property rights and economic liberties or the existence of pervasive regulations have any bearing upon economic growth. Bureaucrats have without doubt taken advantage of the broad discretion given to them by law and formed economic policy in response to changing circumstances. Probably this has contributed to the great success of the Japanese economy. One may be then justified in concluding that the constitutional guarantee of property rights and economic liberties and its explicit limitations have played a significant role in lending support to the legitimacy of these broad discretionary regulatory powers.

But we are now at the crossroads. Plagued by prolonged recession, there are growing voices for reconsidering the Japanese economic system from its foundation. What have been considered as strengths of the Japanese economy like the ethic of hard work or the permanent employment system are now criticized as hindering the restructuring of the Japanese economy. There are growing voices criticizing the vast number of licensing and regulatory statutes, especially protectionist ones. Japan is now facing the challenge of moving to being a society which emphasizes the quality of life rather than a society which emphasizes economic development.

Moreover, in the summer of 1993, there was a dramatic political change. The LDP lost power and became a minority in the Diet for the first time in its almost forty years of history. Instead a coalition of several previous opposition parties and new parties has formed the new government. This political change has undermined the symbiotic relationship between bureaucrats, politicians, and business corporations. As a result, bureaucrats, politicians, and business corporations are forced to formulate a new relationship. Since political reform is the most urgent issue of the day, strict limits will be placed on political contributions from business corporations. Election reform would change the party system together with the close relationship between politicians and business corporations. Since the new government places much emphasis on a consumers' perspective, it is striving hard to deregulate the economy for the benefit of consumers. Any such move is destined to face strong opposition from bureaucrats who want to maintain their regulatory powers. Since the new government does not have enough experience to control the bureaucrats, many speculate that bureaucratic influence will be greater than before. Yet deregulation cannot be achieved without reducing the regulatory powers of bureaucrats. The Diet has already passed the Administrative Procedure Act, which requires certain procedures for permit refusal and sets limits on the use of administrative guidance. It is still to be seen how far this political change will entail a change in the political and legal protection of economic liberties in Japan.

Notes

1. 198 U.S. 45 (1905).

2. "No State shall . . . pass any . . . Law impairing the Obligation of Contracts . . . " U.S. Constitution Article I, Section 10, Clause 1.

3. "The Citizens of each State shall be entitled to all Privileges and Immunities of Citizens in the several States." U.S. Constitution Article IV, Section 2, Clause 1.

4. The contract clause protects only contractual obligations. Moreover, it protects contractual obligations only against retroactive impairment. Finally, it does not constrain the conduct of the Federal Government.

5. First of all, the privileges and immunities clause does not restrict the power of the state to regulate economic liberties so long as the state regulates local residents and out-of-state visitors equally. It also does not limit the Federal Government. Moreover, privileges and immunities do not include every common or garden variety of economic interest. It is only certain rights and interests that can qualify as "Privileges and Immunities of Citizens in the several States." See, e.g., *Baldwin v. Fish and Game Commission of Montana*, 436 U.S. 371 (1978).

6. "[N]or shall private property be taken for public use, without just compensation." U.S. Constitution Amendment V.

7. "No person shall... be deprived of life, liberty, or property, without due process of law." U.S. Constitution Amendment V.

8. See, e.g., John Ely, *Democracy and Distrust: A Theory of Judicial Review* 15 (Cambridge, Mass.: Harvard University Press 1980). There are commentators, however, who insist that the due process clause was originally also meant to protect liberty and property against arbitrary infringement. See *infra* notes 37-40.

9. "No State shall make or enforce any law which shall abridge the privileges or immunities of citizens of the United States; nor shall any State deprive any person of life, liberty, or property, without due process of law; nor deny to any person within its jurisdiction the equal protection of the laws." U.S. Constitution Amendment XIV, Section 1. Corporations were held to be "persons" within the

meaning of the due process clause. *Santa Clara County v. Southern Pacific Railroad*, 118 U.S. 394 (1886).

10. *Allgeyer v. Louisiana*, 165 U.S. 578, 589 (1897).

11. *Adair v. United States*, 208 U.S. 161 (1908); *Muller v. Oregon*, 208 U.S. 412 (1908); *Coppage v. Kansas*, 236 U.S. 1 (1915); *Adkins v. Children's Hospital*, 261 U.S. 525 (1923).

12. 285 U.S. 262 (1932).

13. *Nebbia v. New York*, 291 U.S. 502 (1934); *West Coast Hotel Co. v. Parrish*, 300 U.S. 379 (1937).

14. 304 U.S. 144 (1938).

15. See Jeoffrey Miller, "The True Story of Carolene Products," 1987 *Sup. Ct. Rev.* 397.

16. *Williamson v. Lee Optical Co.*, 348 U.S. 483 (1955); *Ferguson v. Scrupa*, 372 U.S. 726 (1963).

17. *Ferguson v. Scrupa*, 372 U.S. 726, 729 (1963).

18. *Id.* at 730.

19. *Id.* at 731-32.

20. *Id.* at 732.

21. Robert McCloskey, "Economic Due Process and the Supreme Court: An Exhumation and Reburial," 1962 *Sup. Ct. Rev.* 34, 38. In refusing to overturn economic legislation, the Court may be seen as accepting the view of New Dealers that regulation is necessary for the preservation and best development of liberty. Bernard Schwartz, *The New Right and the Constitution: Turning Back the Legal Clock* 80 (Boston: Northeastern University Press 1990). See also Martin Shapiro, "The Constitution and Economic Rights," in M. Harmon (ed.), *Essays on the Constitution of the United States* 74 (Port Washington, N.Y.: Kennikat Press 1978).

22. *Williamson v. Lee Optical Co.*, 348 U.S. 483 (1955).

23. *City of Cleburne v. Cleburne Living Center*, 473 U.S. 432 (1985).

24. *New Orleans v. Dukes*, 427 U.S. 297 (1976); *Nordlinger v. Hahn*, 112 S. Ct. 2326 (1992).

25. There are some signs to show that the Court is beginning to afford slightly more protection to property rights under these clauses. See, e.g., *United States Trust Co. v. New Jersey*, 431 U.S. 1 (1977); *Allied Structural Steel Co. v. Spannaus*, 438 U.S. 234 (1978).

26. See, e.g., *Philadelphia v. New Jersey*, 437 U.S. 617 (1978).

27. For government regulation of economic liberties in general, see Louis Schwartz, John Flynn, & Harry First, *Free Enterprise and Economic Organization: Government Regulation* (Mineola, N.Y.: Foundation Press 6th ed. 1985); James Wilson (ed.), *The Politics of Regulation* (New York: Basic Books 1980).

28. 5 U.S.C. 551-559.

29. *Association of Data Processing Service Organizations, Inc. v. Camp*, 397 U.S. 150 (1970).

30. *Abbott Laboratories v. Gardner*, 387 U.S. 136 (1967).

31. See generally Alan Morrison, "Close Reins on the Bureaucracy: Overseeing the Administrative Agencies," in Herman Schwartz (ed.), *The Burger Years* 191 (New York: Viking 1987).

32. Walter Gellhorn, "The Abuse of Occupational Licensing," 44 *U. Chi. L. Rev.* 6 (1976).

33. See, e.g., Susan Tolchin & Martin Tolchin, *Dismantling America: The Rush to Deregulate* (Boston: Houghton Mufflin Company 1983).

34. Gerald Gunther, *Constitutional Law* 449 (Mineola, N.Y.: Foundation Press 12th ed. 1991); Gerald Gunther, "Supreme Court, 1971 Term — Foreword: In Search of Evolving Doctrine on a Changing Court: A Model for a Newer Equal Protection," 86 *Harv. L. Rev.* 1 (1972).

35. See, e.g., Lawrence Tribe, *American Constitutional Law* 778-79 (Mineola, N.Y.: Foundation Press 2nd ed. 1988).

36. Richard Posner, *The Federal Courts: Crisis and Reform* 209 n.25 (Cambridge, Mass.: Harvard University Press 1985).

37. Richard Epstein, *Taking: Private Property and the Power of Eminent Domain* (Cambridge, Mass.: Harvard University Press 1985).

38. Bernard Siegan, *Economic Liberties and the Constitution* (Chicago: University of Chicago Press 1981).

39. Bernard Siegan, "Rehabilitating Lochner," 22 *San Diego L. Rev.* 453 (1985).

40. See, e.g., Stephan Macedo, *The New Right v. The Constitution* (Washington, D.C.: Cato Institute 1987).

41. Christopher Wonnell, "Economic Due Process and the Preservation of Competition," 11 *Hast. Con. L. Q.* 91 (1983). See also Frank Strong, *Substantive Due Process of Law: A Dichotomy of Sense and Nonsense* (Durham, N.C.: Carolina Academic Press 1986).

42. Herman Schwartz, "Property Rights and the Constitution: Will the Ugly Duckling Become a Swan?," 37 *Am. U. L. Rev.* 9, 9 (1987).

43. Schwartz, *supra* note 21, at 73; Michael Phillips, "Another Look at Economic Substantive Due Process," 1987 *Wis. L. Rev.* 265.

44. Masami Itoh, *Kenpou* (Constitutional Law) 360-61 (Tokyo: Koubundo 2nd ed. 1990); Koji Satoh, *Kenpou* (Constitutional Law) 495 (Tokyo: Seirin Shoin 2nd ed. 1990); Nobuyoshi Ashibe, *Kenpou* (Constitutional Law) 172-73 (Tokyo: Iwanami Shoten 1993). See generally Mutsuo Nakamura, "Freedom of Economic Activities and the Right to Property," 53 *Law & Contemporary Problems* 1 (Spring 1990).

45. Itoh, *supra* note 44, at 360; Satoh, *supra* note 44, at 495; Ashibe, *supra* note 44, at 172-73.

46. Kenzo Takayanagi, "A Century of Innovation: The Development of Japanese Law, 1868-1961," in A. von Mehren (ed.), *Law in Japan: The Legal Order in a Changing Society* 5 (Cambridge, Mass.: Harvard University Press 1963).

47. Ryousuke Ishii, *A History of Political Institutions in Japan* 128-29 (Tokyo: University of Tokyo Press 1980).

48. Itoh, *supra* note 44, at 352-53; Satoh, *supra* note 44, at 488; Ashibe, *supra* note 44, at 165.

49. See *infra* note 71 and accompanying text. Corporations are believed to enjoy fundamental human rights guaranteed by the Constitution to the extent a

particular right is apt for corporations: judgment of June 24, 1970, Supreme Court, grand bench, Minshu vol. 24, no. 6, at 625.

50. Most commentators do not take the difference in structure between Article 22 and Article 29 seriously. Even though Article 29, unlike Article 22, stipulates that property rights "shall be defined by law in conformity with the public welfare," they construe Article 29 as authorizing restrictions on property rights for the public welfare. This construction places property rights ahead of statutory definition. In short, according to the prevailing view, property rights exist prior to their statutory definition and can be limited by law to the extent that the limitation is necessary to maintain the public welfare.

51. "All people shall have the right to maintain the minimum standards of wholesome and cultured living.

In all spheres of life, the State shall use its endeavors for the promotion and extension of social welfare and security, and of public health.": Japanese Constitution Article 25.

52. "All people shall have the right and the obligation to work.

Standards for wages, hours, rest and other working conditions shall be fixed by law.

Children shall not be exploited.": Japanese Constitution Article 27.

53. "The right of workers to organize and to bargain and act collectively is guaranteed.": Japanese Constitution Article 28.

54. Itoh, *supra* note 44, at 220-21; Satoh, *supra* note 44, at 489; Ashibe, *supra* note 44, at 166.

55. Itoh, *supra* note 44, at 354; Satoh, *supra* note 44, at 489-90; Ashibe, *supra* note 44, at 167.

56. There are some commentators who limit the protection of property rights under Article 29 according to the nature of property. The seminal view was first espoused by Takahara who proposed that "small property" (property essential for living including housing and minimal land) should be distinguished from "large property" (property not essential for living): Kenzi Takahara, "Shakaikokka ni okeru Zaisanken (Property Rights in the Social State)," in *Zaisanken to Sonsitsuhoshou* (Property Rights and Compensation) 2 (Tokyo: Yuhikaku 1978). Others came to join this view proposing that "property essential for personal development" or "property essential for living" should be distinguished from "capitalist property." See, e.g., Noriho Urabe, "Zaisanken Seigen no Houri (Theory of Restrictions on Property Rights)," *Kouhoukenkyuu* vol. 51, at 90 (1989); Toshiyuki Munesue, "Zaisanken no Seiyaku Konkyoron Saikou (Reconsideration of Theories of Restrictions on Property Rights)," *Kouhoukenkyuu* vol. 51, at 120 (1989). See also Nobushige Ukai, "Hou no Shihai no Gensoku to Gendaigyousei no Kadai (Principle of Rule of Law and the Tasks of Modern Administration)," *Kouhoukenkyuu* vol. 39, at 1 (1977).

57. Probably the first judicial encounter with the claim of invasion of economic liberties was the judgment of June 21, 1950, Supreme Court, grand bench, Keishu vol. 4, no. 6, at 1049. Involved was the Job Security Act which established a public placement office and banned commercial placement businesses. The defendant, convicted under this Act, appealed to the Court

claiming that it was unreasonable to ban commercial placement businesses altogether. Yet the Court found that commercial placement businesses had often exploited workers by offering jobs without regard to their ability or working conditions. The Court thus upheld the Act as justified in order to stabilize the labor market by eliminating these vices, which were contrary to the public welfare.

58. Judgment of March 18, 1953, Supreme Court, grand bench, Keishu vol. 7, no. 3, at 577.

59. The Court, for instance, upheld the constitutionality of the Narcotics Control Act's total ban on the distribution and even possession of narcotics as a means to maintain the public health: judgment of December 26, 1956, Supreme Court, grand bench, Keishu vol. 10, no. 12, at 1746. Similarly the Court upheld the constitutionality of the Dental Technique Act's ban on dental technicians taking an imprint for an artificial tooth or attaching an artificial tooth for public health reasons: judgment of July 8, 1959, Supreme Court, grand bench, Keishu vol. 13, no. 7, at 1132. The Court also upheld the constitutionality of the Unfair Competition Prevention Act's ban on acts conducted with an intent of unfair competition regardless of the size of the business because of the danger of inviting chaos in the industry and destabilizing the economy: judgment of April 6, 1960, Supreme Court, grand bench, Keishu vol. 14, no. 5, at 525.

60. Judgment of January 26, 1955, Supreme Court, grand bench, Keishu vol. 9, no. 1, at 89.

61. Id. at 93.

62. Nobuyoshi Ashibe, "Shokugyou no Jiyuu no Kisei (Restrictions on Freedom to Choose an Occupation)—part 2," *Hougaku Seminar* (September 1979) at 54, 59-60. Indeed, the Court in a different context admitted this fact. In its judgment of January 19, 1962, Supreme Court, 2nd petty bench, Minshu vol. 16, no. 1, at 57, the Court held that the existing public bath owner has standing (a statutory protected legal interest) to challenge the grant of a license to a competitor.

63. Ashibe, *supra* note 62, at 59 (criticizing the decision for its insufficient examination of legislative facts); Toshihiko Nonaka, "Eigyou no Jiyuu to Kyoriseigen (Economic Liberties and the Distance Requirement)," *Hougaku Kyoushitsu* vol. 131, at 34, 35 (1991)(criticizing the decision as quite conclusory with no demonstration of grounds).

64. See judgment of December 20, 1961, Supreme Court, grand bench, Keishu vol. 15, no. 11, at 1864 (upholding the Loan Business Control Act's registration requirement for loan business); judgment of October 24, 1962, Supreme Court, grand bench, Minshu vol. 16, no. 10, at 2143 (upholding the constitutionality of the amendments to the Real Estate Dealers Act which required the presence of a responsible person who has passed the examination at each office and demanded that every dealer make a security deposit).

65. Judgment of January 27, 1960, Supreme Court, grand bench, Keishu vol. 14, no. 1, at 33. The Massage Act prohibited anyone not duly licensed under the Act from conducting any quasi-medical treatment as an occupation. The defendant, without such a license, treated a patient with special equipment and was

convicted. On appeal, the defendant claimed that his equipment inflicted no harm to his patient and that it was thus unconstitutional to prohibit such an unharmful act. The Court agreed that the Act prohibited only harmful acts and remanded the case to the lower court to decide whether the defendant's act was harmful or not. Cf. order of May 7, 1964, Supreme Court, 1st petty bench, Keishu vol. 18, no. 4, at 144. Yet this decision was rather aberrational and the Court itself took quite a contrasting attitude in its judgment of February 15, 1961, Supreme Court, grand bench, Keishu vol. 15, no. 2, at 347. This case concerned another section of the Massage Act which allowed the commercial advertisement of a massage business only on specified subjects and prohibited the advertisement of ability or method of treatment. The defendant distributed handbills describing the effect of his treatment and was prosecuted. There was no false or misleading information in his handbill. Included was truthful information as to the possible effect of his lawfully licensed business. The Court nevertheless upheld the conviction. The Court agreed with the Government that there was a danger that unrestricted advertisement might lead to the spreading of misleading information to attract customers and thereby deprive the public of an opportunity to receive timely adequate medical treatment. It was thus constitutional, the Court concluded, to prohibit such an advertisement even though it was perfectly truthful and was concerned with a lawful activity. If the Court had applied this reasoning in the 1960 case, it could have easily upheld the ban on unharmful activity in order to prevent harmful activity or to secure the opportunity to receive timely adequate medical treatment. The Court in fact adopted this reasoning in its judgment of July 14, 1965, Supreme Court, grand bench, Keishu vol. 19, no. 5, at 554. Involved was the constitutionality of the old Pharmaceuticals Act's registration requirement for a pharmacy with its criminal ban on drug sale by unregistered persons. The defendant sold approved drugs without a certificate of registration and was prosecuted. The defendant then attacked his conviction because drugs he sold were apparently effective and unharmful. Yet the Court upheld the conviction. The registration requirement is necessary, the Court held, because the public health and safety might be endangered when effective and unharmful drugs deteriorate while being improperly stored or when instructions necessary for use are not given by the qualified person. The ban on unharmful business transaction was thus upheld. The Court here did not even mention its 1960 holding in the Massage Act case.

66. For instance, the Court upheld the Road Transportation Act which prohibits drivers of personal automobiles from receiving payment for carrying passengers: judgment of December 4, 1963, Supreme Court, grand bench, Keishu vol. 17, no. 12, at 2434. The Act requires a license from the Transportation Minister to engage in the taxi business. The defendant carried passengers and accepted payment and was charged with a violation of the Act. On appeal, the defendant claimed that his act itself did not cause any social harm and the ban was nothing but a protectionist entry restriction to protect existing taxi companies. Yet the Court summarily rejected the appeal. It simply recited the text of the Act and found that to allow drivers of personal automobiles to receive payment for carrying passengers amounts to permitting an unlicensed taxi

business, thus undermining the license requirement. It was constitutional, the Court thus held, to prohibit such activity in order to secure the licensing system.

67. Judgment of November 22, 1972, Supreme Court, grand bench, Keishu vol. 26, no. 9, at 586.

68. Id. at 591.

69. Id. at 591-92.

70. Judgment of April 30, 1975, Supreme Court, grand bench, Minshu vol. 29, no. 4, at 572.

71. Id. at 575.

72. Id. at 576.

73. Id. at 577.

74. Nobuyoshi Ashibe, "Shokugyou no Jiyuu no Kisei —part 3," *Hougaku Seminar* (October, 1979), at 28, 29-30.

75. Nobuyoshi Ashibe, "Shokugyou no Jiyuu no Kisei —part 4," *Hougaku Seminar* (November, 1979), at 58, 61.

76. See generally Shigenori Matsui, "A Comment upon the Role of the Judiciary in Japan," 35 *Osaka U. L. Rev.* 17 (1988).

77. Judgment of April 22, 1987, Supreme Court, grand bench, Minshu vol. 41, no. 3, at 408.

78. Id. at 411.

79. The opinions of the Supreme Court Judges were split in this case. Judge Ohuchi filed a concurring opinion, with Judge Takashima joining, in which he held section 186 of the Forest Act invalid only so far as it banned a division claim by a co-owner who has a half share in the forest. Judge Kagawa filed the only dissent. He found that the legislative purpose conformed to the public welfare and also found the restriction on division claims not evidently unnecessary or unreasonable.

80. Nobuyoshi Ashibe, "Shokugyou no Jiyuu no Kisei —part 5," *Hougaku Seminar* (December, 1979), at 32, 36.

81. Judgment of January 20, 1989, Supreme Court, 2nd petty bench, Keishu vol. 43, no. 1, at 1.

82. Id. at 3.

83. Judgment of March 7, 1989, Supreme Court, 3rd petty bench, Hanreijihou vol. 1308, at 111.

84. Judgment of December 15, 1992, Supreme Court, 3rd petty bench, Minshu vol. 46, no. 9, at 2829.

85. Judge Sakagami filed a dissent in which he found the license requirement unreasonable.

86. See generally Masu Uekusa, *Koutekikisei no Keizaigaku* (Economics of Public Regulation) 28 (Tokyo: Chikuma Shobou 1991).

87. One typical example is taxi regulation by the Transportation Ministry. The taxi business is subject to licensing, and the fare schedule must be approved by the Ministry. The Ministry has given licenses to a limited number of taxi companies in each city and taken a very restrictive attitude towards giving licenses to independent unaffiliated drivers. As a result, in many cities a limited number of taxi companies holds a virtual monopoly over the market. Moreover,

the Transportation Ministry is adopting the single-fare-schedule-for-each-area policy even though no such policy is specifically authorized by the statute. The Transportation Ministry has thus urged all taxi companies in each area to submit the same fare rise application. The Ministry justifies this policy as a means of preventing passenger confusion resulting from different fare schedules. Yet, as a result, even profitable taxi companies are practically compelled to file an application for a fare rise together with not-so-profitable ones. When one taxi company applied for a fare cut, the Ministry rejected the application: see judgment of January 31, 1985, Osaka District Court, Hanreijihou vol. 1143, at 46 (holding the refusal illegal). See also judgment of March 2, 1993, Osaka District Court, Hanreijihou vol. 1454, at 61. These regulations have been criticized as unnecessarily protectionist: Keizaikikakuchou Sougoukeikakukyoku (General Planning Bureau of the Economic Planning Agency), *Kiseikanwa no Keizairiron* (Economic Theory of Deregulation) 124-30 (Tokyo: Publication Bureau, Ministry of Finance 1989).

88. See judgment of April 26, 1985, Nagoya District Court, Gyoushu vol. 36, no. 4, at 552, aff'd, judgment of July 29, 1986, Nagoya High Court, Gyoushu vol. 37, nos. 7-8, at 1000 (upholding the Tobacco Act which gives exclusive right to produce and sell tobacco to the Japan Tobacco Company and prohibits anyone from selling tobacco except those duly franchised by that Company); judgment of January 26, 1990, Osaka District Court, Gyoushu vol. 41, no. 1, at 90 (upholding the Salt Act which gives the exclusive right to produce and sell salt to the Japan Tobacco Company and prohibits anyone from selling salt except those duly franchised by that Company); judgment of March 26, 1990, Tokyo District Court, Hanreijihou vol. 1344, at 115 (upholding the controversial Sales Tax Act).

89. See, e.g., judgment of March 27, 1985, Supreme Court, grand bench, Minshu vol. 39, no. 2, at 247 (upholding an income tax deduction system allegedly discriminatory against salaried workers).

90. It should be noted that the Court was quite deferential to the Diet also when the welfare legislation was attacked as insufficient to meet the welfare right guarantee of Article 25: judgment of May 24, 1967, Supreme Court, grand bench, Minshu vol. 21, no. 5, at 1043. See also judgment of July 7, 1982, Supreme Court, grand bench, Minshu vol. 36, no. 7, at 1235. See generally Akira Osuka, "Welfare Rights," 53 *Law & Contemporary Problems* 13 (Spring 1990). The Court also took an utterly deferential posture when the deprivation of rights of public workers was challenged: judgment of April 25, 1973, Supreme Court, grand bench, Keishu vol.27, no. 4, at 547.

91. Uekusa, *supra* note 86, at 25, 279.

92. See "Gyouseishidou ni kansuru Chousakenkyuu Houkoku (A Study Report on Administrative Guidance) (1)-(3)," *Gyousei Kanrikenkyuu* vol. 15, at 36, vol. 18, at 38, vol. 20, at 37 (1981-82). To be sure, such administrative guidance can be found in any country. In this sense, administrative guidance is not unique to Japan. What is unique to Japan is the degree such guidance is used.

93. Michael Young, "Judicial Review of Administrative Guidance: Governmentally Encouraged Consensual Dispute Resolution in Japan," 84 *Colum. L. Rev.* 923 (1984); Michael Young, "Administrative Guidance in the

Courts: A Case Study in Doctrinal Adaptation," 17 *Law in Japan* 120 (1984); Kozo Yamamura, "Success that Soured: Administrative Guidance and Cartels in Japan," in Kozo Yamamura (ed.), *Policy and Trade Issues of the Japanese Economy: American and Japanese Perspectives* 77 (Seattle: University of Washington Press 1982) (hereinafter cited as *Policy and Trade Issues*); John Haley, "Administrative Guidance versus Formal Regulation: Resolving the Paradox of Industrial Policy," in Gary Saxonhouse & Kozo Yamamura (eds.), *Law and Trade Issues of the Japanese Economy: American and Japanese Perspectives* 107 (Tokyo: University of Tokyo Press 1986) (hereinafter cited as *Law and Trade Issues*).

94. The recent stock scandal manifestly shows the limits as well as the lack of transparency of economic regulation through administrative guidance. See Nihonkeizai Shinbunsha, *Utage no Akuma* (Devils Hiding behind Fiesta) (Tokyo: Nihonkeizai Shinbunsha 1991).

95. Uekusa, *supra* note 86, at 279-86; Keizaikikakuchou Sougou-keikakukyoku, *supra* note 87, at 170-87. See also Nihonkeizai Shinbunsha, *Daitenhou ga Kieru Hi* (The Day When the Large Scale Retail Store Act Vanishes) (Tokyo: Nihonkeizai Shinbunsha 1990); Kazumitsu Sakata, "Daitenhou to Ohgataten Mondai (The Large Scale Retail Store Act and the Large Scale Store Problems)," *Reference* vol. 485, at 48 (1991); Atsushi Kusano, *Daitenhou — Keizaikisei no Kouzou* (Large Scale Retail Store Act — The Structure of Economic Regulation) (Tokyo: Nihonkeizai Shinbunsha 1992); Frank Upham, "Privatizing Regulation: The Implementation of the Large-Scale Retail Stores Law," in Gary Allinson & Yasunori Sone (eds.), *Political Dynamics in Contemporary Japan* 264 (Ithaca: Cornell University Press, 1993) (hereinafter cited as Dynamics).

96. Uekusa points out that a statutory entry restriction to protect small retail stores of the kind in the LSRS Act is quite unique: Uekusa, *supra* note 86, at 281. The LSRS Act is also unique in that the regulatory power is not exercised by the MITI but is in practice relegated to the local business community. This means that the regulatory authority is relegated to the group of competitors hoping to prevent the opening of a large scale retail store (282). Moreover, it should be noted that the LSRS Act also encourages a cartel between the large scale retail store and the local business community with the sacrifice of consumers' interests (284-86). Finally the LSRS Act has prevented the modernization of the retail industry by protecting inefficient small retail stores (285). See also Upham, *supra* note 95, at 288–292.

Under criticism from the United States Government, the Japanese Government finally agreed to amend the regulatory scheme under the LSRS Act. The MITI changed its guidance to speed up the process. Ultimately, in May 1991 the Diet passed an amendment to the LSRS Act and the MITI altered its regulations. From now on, the review process starts with the filing of an application by the owner and it is to be left to the Council to make recommendations. Since this amendment several Japanese as well as American large scale retail stores have successfully opened new stores. It is still to be seen how the LSRS Act will be actually administered after the 1991 amendment. See Upham, *supra*, 287.

97. To take another example, it is necessary for the developer to meet the standards set by the Construction Standards Act or the City Development Act in

order to construct a building. When the developer files a development application, the local government reviews the application. If the local government finds that the plan satisfies the standards set forth by the Acts, it has to grant a permit within the designated period. There is no way, legally speaking, for the local government to refuse a permit when the application meets the standards. Many local governments have adopted, however, additional development guidelines and employed administrative guidance. They set higher standards and direct the developer to obtain consent from local residents. They often require the developer to build public facilities and to make contributions to the local governments. Such administrative guidance, needless to say, does not have any legal binding force. It is up to the willingness of those concerned to accept the guidance. Yet in many cases, developers are practically forced to follow it. See *infra* note 141.

98. For an overview of the Japanese anti-monopoly law, see Mitsuo Matsushita, *Introduction to Japanese Antimonopoly Law* (Tokyo: Yuhikaku 1990).

99. Judgment of February 24, 1984, Supreme Court, 2nd petty bench, Keishu vol. 38, no. 4, at 1287 (the Oil Cartel Case). See also Frank Upham, *Law and Social Change in Postwar Japan* 176-82, 184-88 (Cambridge, Mass.: Harvard University Press 1987).

100. Koichi Hamada, Hidetoh Ishida & Masahiro Murakami, "The Evolution and Economic Consequences of Product Liability Rules in Japan," in *Law and Trade Issues, supra* note 93, at 83.

101. Environmental pollution and the governmental response to it are well illustrated in Upham, *supra* note 99, at 28-77. Indeed, in a series of cases involving environmental pollution or damage to life and health because of the side-effects of drugs, the Government has been sued for its failure to exercise adequate regulatory measures. See judgment of August 3, 1978, Tokyo District Court, Hanreijihou vol. 899, at 48 (the Sumon Case); judgment of March 30, 1987, Kumamoto District Court, Hanreijihou vol. 1235, at 3 (the Minamata Disease Case); judgment of February 7, 1992, Tokyo District Court, Hanreijihou Special Supplement (April 25, 1992); judgment of July 1, 1993, Kumamoto District Court, Hanreijihou vol. 1455, at 3 (holding the Government liable for its failure to prevent the spread of Minamata Disease).

102. The Labor Standard Act prohibits certain discriminatory practices in employment. Yet the Act is filled with loopholes and no general civil rights legislation exists outside the labor relationship area. The Court could and indeed occasionally did invalidate the discriminatory legal act of a private individual when it ran afoul of "public order and good morality": judgment of March 24, 1981, Supreme Court, 3rd petty bench, Minshu vol. 35, no. 2, at 300. Yet judicial protection against private discrimination is too limited without civil rights legislation.

103. The necessity of deregulation and administrative reform has been an urgent political issue for some time. Rinji Gyouseikaikaku Suishin Shingikai (The Ad Hoc Advisory Panel on Administrative Reform), *Kisei Kanwa* (Deregulation) (1988); Keizaikikakuchou Sougoukeikakukyoku, *supra* note 87.

104. There was a prior suit against the LSRS Act, filed by opposing small

stores and seeking revocation of recommendations by the International Trade and Industry Minister. The court denied standing and dismissed the suit: judgment of March 16, 1982, Tokyo District Court, Gyoushu vol. 33. no. 3, at 441, aff'd, judgment of June 24, 1985, Tokyo High Court, Hanreijihou vol. 1156, at 37.

105. The plaintiff ultimately dropped the suit because, according to the explanation of the plaintiff, the aim of litigation was, practically speaking, achieved by the 1991 amendment to the LSRS Act: *Nihonkeizai Shinbun*, March 9, 1992.

106. Daniel Okimoto, *Between MITI and the Market: Japanese Industrial Policy for High Technology* 10-12 (Stanford: Stanford University Press 1989).

107. Id. at 38-39.

108. Id. at 39-48.

109. Uekusa, *supra* note 86, at 59-61.

110. Okimoto, *supra* note 106, at 34-36

111. Nihonkeizai Shinbunsha, *supra* note 95, at 175-79 (Masanori Tamura). See also "Kiseigyousei no Gourika ni kansuru Chousakenkyuu (A Study Report on Rationalizing Administrative Regulation)," *Gyouseikanri Kenkyuu* vol. 28, at 38, vol. 33, at 48 (1984-86) (criticizing the regulation from the consumer perspective).

112. Upham, *supra* note 99, at 169-70. Haley argues that Japanese bureaucrats have almost limitless authority but relatively limited power. John Haley, *Authority without Power: Law and the Japanese Paradox* 142-43 (New York: Oxford University Press 1991). Haley correctly points out the fact that Japanese bureaucrats exercise broad authority beyond those powers specifically authorized by statutes. Yet he seems to be underestimating the existence of more than ten thousand statutory licensing provisions. Administrative guidance works effectively only with those discretionary powers given to them by statutes.

113. Masaru Mabuchi, "Deregulation and Legalization of Financial Policy," in *Dynamics*, *supra* note 95, at 130. See also Okimoto, *supra* note 106, at 2-3 (Japan can be considered among the world's smallest states, minimalist, in fact).

114. Upham, *supra* note 99, at 167-68.

115. Okimoto, *supra* note 106, at 24.

116. There has been much debate as to whether bureaucrats or LDP politicians had more influence upon economic policies. The conventional view is that bureaucrats had determinative power over economic policies. Yet a more recent view stresses the increasing role LDP politicians have played in formulating economic policy. Michio Muramatsu & Ellis Krauss, "Bureaucrats and Politicians in Policymaking: The Case of Japan," *American Political Science Rev.* vol. 78, no. 1, at 126 (1984); Michio Muramatsu & Ellis Krauss, "The Conservative Policy Line and the Development of Patterned Pluralism," in Kozo Yamamura & Yasukichi Yasuba (eds.), *The Political Economy of Japan* vol. 1, at 516 (Stanford: Stanford University Press 1987)(hereinafter cited as Muramatsu, Patterned Pluralism); Gerald Curtis, *The Japanese Way of Politics* 106-09 (New York: Columbia University Press 1988). See also Ellis Krauss, "Politics and the

Policymaking Process," in Takeshi Ishida & Ellis Krauss (eds.), *Democracy in Japan* 39, 50-54 (Pittsburgh: University of Pittsburgh Press 1989); Eisuke Sakakibara, "The Japanese Politico-Economic System and the Public Sector," in Samuel Kernell (ed.), *Parallel Politics: Economic Policymaking in Japan and the United States* 50 (Washington, D.C.: Brookings Institution 1991)(hereinafter cited as *Parallel Politics*); Haley, *supra* note 112, at 157-59; Takashi Inoguchi & Tomoaki Iwai, *Zokugiin no Kenkyuu* (A Study on Zoku Diet Members) (Tokyo: Nihonkeizai Shinbunsha 1987). Some even argue that bureaucrats in reality administered in the shadow of the LDP. Mark Ramseyer & Frances Rosenbluth, *Japan's Political Marketplace* 12-14, 99-141 (Cambridge, Mass.: Harvard University Press 1993). It is beyond the scope of this paper to delve into this issue. But it seems to be an overstatement to say bureaucrats simply served the LDP, because of their rather autonomous position vis-à-vis LDP politicians. Moreover, the power relationship between bureaucrats and LDP politicians varied according to time and field. Jirou Yamaguchi, *Ohkura Kanryou Shihai no Shuuen* (End of Dominance by the Ministry of Finance Bureaucrats) 10-11 (Tokyo: Iwanami Shoten 1987). It is thus more adequate to view the relationship between bureaucrats and LDP politicians as an interactive one. See Tomoaki Iwai, *Rippoukatei* (Legislative Process) 146-79 (Tokyo: University of Tokyo Press 1988).

117. Karel von Wolferen, *The Enigma of Japanese Power* (London: MacMillan 1989) finds only what he calls "the system" directing Japan. He is surely right in pointing out that no single party, bureaucrats, politicians, or business corporations, does have determinative power in Japan. Nevertheless it is a gross overstatement to suggest that something autonomous which can be called "the system" is directing Japan. An increasing number of political scientists rather view Japanese political system a kind of pluralism. Indeed, Muramatsu characterizes Japanese political system "patterned pluralism." Muramatsu, "Patterned Pluralism," *supra* note 116.

118. It could be even argued that judges constitute just one ingredient of this coalition of bureaucrats, politicians and business corporations. After all, judges are judicial bureaucrats in Japan. See *infra* notes 144-50.

119. Takeyoshi Kawashima, "Dispute Resolution in Contemporary Japan," in A. von Mehren (ed.), *Law in Japan* (Cambridge, Mass.: Harvard University Press 1963).

120. John Haley, "The Myth of the Reluctant Litigant," 4 *Journal of Japanese Studies* 359 (1978); Marc Galanter, "Reading the Landscape of Disputes," 31 *UCLA L. Rev.* 4 (1983); Mark Ramseyer, "The Costs of the Consensual Myth: Antitrust Enforcement and Institutional Barriers to Litigation in Japan," 94 *Yale L. J.* 604 (1985)(hereinafter cited as "Myth"); Mark Ramseyer, "Reluctant Litigant Revisited: Rationality and Disputes in Japan," 14 *Journal of Japanese Studies* 111 (1988).

121. Haley, who formerly argued that the number of lawyers in Japan was intentionally restricted by the Government, has recanted his argument, claiming that such motive has not yet been proven. He now argues that opposition by the bar and the unwillingness of the Government to increase the number of lawyers

at its own expense (Japanese lawyers are trained at government expense) are more persuasive reasons for its failure to increase the number of lawyers. Haley, *supra* note 112, at 110-11. Moreover, he argues that the small number of lawsuits in Japan can be explained by several factors that have little to do with aversion to formal adjudication; certainty of result, the existence of registration system, the existence of mediation, and the prevalence of interdependency relationships (115-16). Yet it cannot be denied that the small numbers of lawyers and lawsuits reflect the effort of bureaucrats to limit litigation to a manageable level.

122. Takao Tanase, "The Management of Disputes: Automobile Accident Compensation in Japan," 24 *Law & Society Rev.* 651, 655 (1990).

123. See Setsuo Miyazawa, "Taking Kawashima Seriously: A Review of Japanese Research on Japanese Legal Consciousness and Disputing Behavior," 21 *Law & Society Rev.* 219 (1987).

124. See generally Shoukitsu Tanakadate, "A Summary of the Limitations on Administrative Adjudication under the Japanese Constitution," 18 *Law in Japan* 108 (1986).

125. It is generally believed that the Administrative Case Litigation Act does not totally preclude a suit for an injunction. Yet the lack of explicit statutory authorization together with the view of a very influential scholar that a judicial injunction against an administrative agency would violate the constitutional separation of powers have made the use of an injunction suit virtually impossible: Jirou Tanaka, *Shihouken no Genkai* (Limits of Judicial Power) 40 (Tokyo: Koubundo 1976). See generally Isao Chiba, "Mumei Koukokusoshou (Unlisted Revocation Suit)," in Toshimasa Sugimura (ed.), *Gyousei Kyuusaihou* vol. I at 277 (Tokyo: Yuhikaku 1990).

126. Judgment of February 23, 1966, Supreme Court, grand bench, Minshu vol. 20, no. 2, at 271 (planning); judgment of December 24, 1968, Supreme Court, 3rd petty bench, Minshu vol. 22, no. 13, at 3147 (administrative guidance). See also Upham, *supra* note 99, at 170-71; Robert Dziubla, "The Impotent Sword of Japanese Justice: The Doctrine of Shobunsei as a Barrier to Administrative Litigation," 18 *Corn. International L. J.* 37 (1985).

127. Judgment of March 14, 1978, Supreme Court, 3rd petty bench, Minshu vol. 32, no. 2, at 211; judgment of September 9, 1982, Supreme Court, 1st petty bench, Minshu vol. 36, no. 9, at 1679; judgment of February 17, 1989, Supreme Court, 2nd petty bench, Minshu vol. 43, no. 2, at 56.

128. Judgment of March 14, 1978, Supreme Court, 3rd petty bench, Minshu vol. 32, no. 2, at 211. See also Upham, *supra* note 99, at 172-73. It must be also added that no class action is allowed in Japan.

129. Judgment of December 24, 1968, Supreme Court, 3rd petty bench, Minshu vol. 22, no. 13, at 3147; judgment of June 24, 1985, Tokyo High Court, Hanreijihou vol. 1156, at 37.

130. See *infra* note 141.

131. Ramseyer, "Myth," *supra* note 120, at 637-38.

132. Although I disagree with the Critical Legal Studies Movement on some issues, I agree with it in so far as it emphasizes the role such ideologies play in law; see, e.g., Mark Kelman, *A Guide to Critical Legal Studies* (Cambridge, Mass.:

Harvard University Press 1987); Robert Gordon, "Critical Legal Histories," 36 *Stan. L. Rev.* 57 (1984).

133. Ramseyer, "Myth," *supra* note 120, at 639-40.

134. Chalmers Johnson, *MITI and the Japanese Miracle: The Growth of Industrial Policy, 1925-1975* (Stanford: Stanford University Press 1982). However, the authority of the MITI has been rapidly declining and the MITI itself is now attempting to regain it. See Shakaikankyou no Henka to Gyousei Sutail no Hen-you ni kansuru Kenkyuukai (Conference on Changing Environment and Changing Administrative Style), *Gyouseikanri Kenkyuu* vol. 54, at 49 (1991)(Toshiya Kitayama).

135. This view is widely shared among Japanese constitutional law as well as administrative law scholars. See, e.g., Itoh, *supra* note 44, at 503.

136. In fact, in the early decades of the postwar period, various independent administrative agencies were created. Yet they were gradually abolished or reorganized into the departments of the Executive.

137. Tanaka, *supra* note 125, at 260.

138. Tanaka, *supra* note 125, at 25; Naohiko Harada, "Gyouseisoshouhou Sousetsu (Basic Theories of Administrative Litigation)," in Ichirou Okawa, Hiroshi Shiono, & Itsuo Sonobe (eds.), *Gendai Gyouseihou Taikei* vol. 4, at 103 (Tokyo: Yuhikaku 1983).

139. Tadashi Murai, "Yobouteki Soshou (Injunctive Suit)," in Ichirou Okawa, Hiroshi Shiono, & Itsuo Sonobe (eds.), *Gendai Gyouseihou Taikei* vol. 5, at 23 (Tokyo: Yuhikaku 1984).

140. Matsui, *supra* note 76.

141. For instance, the courts tend to sustain administrative guidance under local development guidelines even though there is no statutory authorization for it: judgment of April 28, 1988, Yokohama District Court, Hanreijihou vol. 1302, at 129. The courts also tend to sustain agreements between the city and developer to make a contribution in order to receive municipal approval: judgment of May 23, 1989, Tokyo High Court, Hanreijihou vol. 1343, at 26; judgment of October 31, 1989, Tokyo High Court, Hanreijihou vol. 1333, at 91. Only in exceptional circumstances has the Court conceded that there are limits to such administrative guidance. The agency is not allowed, for instance, to force the party concerned to follow the guidance if the party has expressed a sincere intent not to accept the guidance and that intent is justified: judgment of July 16, 1985, Supreme Court, 3rd petty bench, Minshu vol. 39, no. 5, at 989; judgment of February 18, 1993, Supreme Court, 1st petty bench, Minshu vol. 47, no. 2, at 574. The mayor of the city also cannot violate the mandate of the statute and refuse to supply water even when the developer has declined to comply with administrative guidance: order of November 7, 1989, Supreme Court, 2nd petty bench, Hanreijihou vol. 1328, at 16. See also Upham, *supra* note 99, at 174-75.

142. Saikousaibansho Jimusoukyoku Gyouseikyoku (The General Secretariat of the Supreme Court, Administrative Division), "Heisei 2 Nendo Gyouseijiken no Gaikyou (Overview of 1990 Administrative Cases)," *Housou Jihou* vol. 43, no. 8, at 101.

143. The actual winning ratio of the Government including partial victory is

reported to reach as high as 97 or 98%. Asahi Shinbunsha, *Kokou no Oukoku: Saibansho* (Isolated Kingdom—The Judiciary) 72 (Tokyo: Asahi Shinbunsha 1991).

144. Jirou Nomura, *Saikou Saibansho* (The Supreme Court) 57 (Tokyo: Kodansha 1987). See also Ramseyer & Rosenbluth, *supra* note 116, at 152-53; Setsuo Miyazawa, "Administrative Control of Japanese Judges," chapter 10 of this book.

145. Asahi Shinbunsha, *supra* note 143, at 120; Mainichi Shinbunsha, *Kenshou: Saikou Saibansho* (The Supreme Court Reconsidered) 221-32 (Tokyo: Mainichi Shinbunsha 1991).

146. Asahi Shinbunsha, *supra* note 143, at 133-40; Mainichi Shinbunsha, *supra* note 144, at 196-206.

147. From 1966 to 1990, 51 applicants were denied appointment. No reason has been ever given. Asahi Shinbunsha, *supra* note 143, at 106. It is now generally believed that one has to be conservative or at least moderate to be considered as a candidate for appointment. Nomura, *supra* note 144, at 100.

148. Judge Yasuaki Miyamoto of the Kumamoto District Court was denied reappointment by the Supreme Court when his ten year tenure expired in 1971. No reason was cited but many suspected that this decision was based upon his affiliation with the liberal lawyers group.

149. Asahi Shinbunsha, *supra* note 143, at 129-30; Mainichi Shinbunsha, *supra* note 144, at 249-54. See also Ramseyer & Rosenbluth, *supra* note 116, at 152-56; Setsuo Miyazawa, "Administrative Control of Japanese Judges," chapter 10 of this book.

150. Upham points out that when the destabilizing power of litigation begins to surface, that power is usually undercut by the deliberate efforts of bureaucrats. Bureaucrats led the Diet to enact regulatory statutes to vest broad discretionary regulatory power in themselves and precluded the courts from actualizing that destabilizing power. Upham, *supra* note 99, at 56-66, 219-20. Upham seems to be overstating the destabilizing capacity of litigation, for litigation has serious limits as a means of social reform. In any event, litigation cannot have any destabilizing power in the first place since there are mechanisms for preventing judges from giving it such power. On the other hand, it is inadequate to regard, as Ramseyer and Rosenbluth do, Japanese judges as having been effectively controlled by the LDP and in reality its agents. Ramseyer and Rosenbluth, *supra* note 116, at 178-79, 185. Political pressure from the LDP was without doubt a major factor. But the decision to restrain judges from invalidating statutes was also a professional response by judges to outside pressure. Moreover, the ideology of judicial restraint and the positivist impulse of Japanese judges helped to legitimize this decision.

151. The success story of the MITI has been somewhat overstated. Moreover, the MITI's power over the market has changed dramatically in its 50 years of history after the war. The MITI did have wide authority in the early post-war period, especially under statutes such as the Foreign Exchange Law. Yet its authority is rapidly declining due to liberalization of the market. It is interesting in this context to find that in financial regulation more administrative guidance

has been incorporated into statutes despite deregulation. Mabuchi, *supra* note 113, argues that this shows the Finance Ministry's attempt to offset its loss of authority by seeking more statutory authorizations from the Diet.

152. Okimoto points out that the success of industrial policy in Japan is based upon "its unique combination of effective political institutions and a resilient private sector characterized by the commingling of market and organizational elements": Daniel Okimoto, "Regime Characteristics of Japanese Industrial Policy," in Hugh Patrick (ed.), *Japan's High Technology Industries: Lessons and Limitations of Industrial Policy* 35, 40 (Seattle: University of Washington Press 1986) (hereinafter cited as *High Technology Industries*). The factors he refers to include a long tradition of competent bureaucratic administration represented by the MITI with its high quality civil servants, its organization, its large corps of ex-bureaucrats in key private sector positions, and its unique broad scope of jurisdiction, the unbroken dominance of the pro-business LDP over the Diet, the comparative weakness of national labor unions, and the unique convergence of state and industrial interest (40-45). See also Okimoto, *supra* note 106, at 178-228, 232. The structure of Japanese manufacturing industry may have also contributed to this economic growth: David Friedman, *The Misunderstood Miracle: Industrial Development and Political Change in Japan* (Ithaca: Cornell University Press 1988).

153. Iyori Hiroshi, "Antitrust and Industrial Policy in Japan: Competition and Cooperation," in *Law and Trade Issues, supra* note 93, at 56; Kozo Yamamura, "Joint Research and Antitrust: Japanese vs. American Strategies," in *High Technology Industries, supra* note 153, at 171.

154. Haruo Shimada, "Structural Policies in Japan," in *Parallel Politics, supra* note 116, at 281.

155. Shimada, *supra* note 154, at 295-96. But see Okimoto, *supra* note 106, at 55-86 (the success story of governmental targeting is overstated). For an overview and assessment of industrial policy for high technology industry, see Hugh Patrick, "Japanese High Technology Industrial Policy in Comparative Context," in *High Technology Industries, supra* note 152, at 3; Ken-ichi Imai, "Japan's Industrial Policy for High Technology Industry, in *High Technology Industries, supra*, at 147. See also George Eads & Richard Nelson, "Japanese High Technology Policy: What Lessons for the United States?," in *High Technology Industries, supra*, at 243.

10

Administrative Control of Japanese Judges

Setsuo Miyazawa

Introduction

Japan has been known for her low civil litigation rate.[1] Various explanations have been proposed. The most recent of these focuses on the higher predictability of court decisions and the higher probability of out-of-court settlement as its result.[2] There are different ways to produce highly predictable court decisions. One of them is to abolish jury trials. Ramseyer and Nakazato emphasize this point.[3] Their premise is that professional judges are more predictable than lay people. Then, is it possible to further increase the predictability of the outcome of a court when only professional judges decide the case? This is the subject of this paper.

While the civil litigation rate is generally low in Japan, there is one area in which the rate is particularly low. Specifically, it is litigation that challenges the legality or constitutionality of governmental actions (*gyosei sosho* in Japanese). Only 1,119 such suits were filed in 1989. This figure is considered to be extremely low compared to other developed countries. One observer argues that the per-capita rate of such administrative litigation in former West Germany, for instance, was more than seven hundred times that of Japan.[4] The main reason for this fact is easy to hypothesize. It has been uniformly difficult for plaintiffs to win in such cases and this fact deters litigation against governmental actions. Then, how does the Japanese judicial system maintain such uniformity among professional judges who are supposed to make independent decisions according to their own conscience, bound only by the constitution and statutes.[5] This paper deals with this question.

I assume that at least in most liberal capitalist countries, appellate courts unify interpretations of law by reviewing lower-court decisions in individual cases. Lower-court judges cite supreme-court precedents and other appellate-court decisions on the basis of their own judgments. That is why socio-legal scholars have analyzed case-citation patterns in their studies on mutual influences among courts. Even the supreme court must wait until the case reaches it before having a chance to express its own interpretations of the relevant law.

The Japanese Supreme Court needs not to be so passive in its relationship with lower-court judges. It can convene a conference of judges who are presiding over the cases in which the central government has been involved as a defendant, and can express its opinions about proper interpretation of the relevant law before those cases actually reach it. Such opinions are usually favorable to the government. This and other administrative mechanisms make it possible for the Supreme Court to control or influence lower-court judges and ensure that lower-court judges do not cause problems to the government, business, and friendly foreign governments. This paper will provide an outline of such mechanisms and discuss their cultural and political backgrounds.

Status of Japanese Judges

Japan has approximately two thousand judges who are qualified lawyers to staff fifty district courts, fifty family courts, eight high courts, and their branches. In addition, there are approximately eight hundred summary court judges most of whom are not qualified lawyers. They hear petitions for warrants and decide cases in which the value of a plaintiff's claim is worth less than nine hundred thousand yen or which carry only a possible fine. This paper will focus on the first group of regular judges.

The occupational status of most judges in Japan is similar to that of employees of the executive branch of the government. They are virtually life-time employees of a national governmental bureaucracy called the judiciary.

Some five hundred people from among approximately twenty thousand applicants pass the bar examination in Japan each year. On the average, those who pass the bar examination have spent six years since finishing undergraduate legal education and their average age is around twenty eight. Then they spend two years at the Judicial Research and Training Institute for practical training in all three branches of the legal profession, namely, the judiciary, prosecution, and private bar. After finishing this two-year training, sixty to one hundred trainees are recruited by the Supreme Court as assistant judges. The Supreme Court presents the Cabinet a list of trainees it wishes to hire and the Cabinet appoints them.

They are promoted to full judgeships after working for ten years and can be reappointed every ten years thereafter, until the mandatory retirement age of sixty-five. While the law permits the Supreme Court to appoint full judges from among private attorneys, prosecutors, and law professors, such appointments have been rare. Judges are appointed not to work at a specific court, but to work in the national court system.

During each ten year term, they are transferred from one court to another three times on the average. The expectation is that they spend approximately three years each at a small, a medium, and a large court. Judges are promoted in the process of such transfers. Except for branch courts which have only one or two judges, every court is divided into sections, each of which consists of a chief judge and two or three associate judges. A judge starts his career as an associate judge at a district or a family court, moves up to a high court as an associate judge, returns to a district or a family court as a chief judge, and then goes back to a high court as a chief judge. Salary also rises according to their seniority. By the time they reach the age of mandatory retirement, approximately half of the same entering cohort has left the judiciary and become private attorneys. Many of the remaining judges can expect to become the head of a district or family court at least once before their retirement.

However, differences in the speed of promotion and the rate of salary increase among judges particularly after the second renewal of appointment, after serving for twenty years. By that time, a small number of judges have been promoted to the rank of chief judge at a large court earlier than most of their cohort mates. Differences in salaries are not made public, but anyone can determine them because seating of judges at official meetings is arranged according to the applied pay scale. Many judges realize that they are ranked lower by the Supreme Court than their elite cohort mates and that there will not be much chance of promotion for them. This is a major consideration in their decision to leave the judiciary. This power to decide transfer and promotion of lower-court judges, therefore, gives considerable leverage to the Supreme Court. I will later cite some cases in which this power appears to have been used quite consciously to encourage certain judges to leave the judiciary.

A small number of judges who have been promoted faster than most of their cohort mates can expect to head more than one district or family court before reaching the age of sixty. Heads of high courts are selected from among this group. Usually, one or two judges of the same cohort can reach the rank of high court head. I will later describe what types of judges usually can get this fast-track promotion.

The Supreme Court consists of fifteen justices. The constitution does not require them to be qualified lawyers. Associate justices are appointed by the Cabinet and the chief justice is appointed by the emperor upon nomination by the Cabinet. Usually, the chief justice recommends a specific candidate to the prime minister. There is no open hearing for the selection, nor is there any legislative confirmation. It is now an established custom to appoint five or six justices from among career judges who have moved up in their judicial careers to the rank of high court head, particularly in Tokyo or Osaka, before sixty-three or -four years of age. It is also an established pattern to appoint the chief justice from among them. (Other justices usually include five private attorneys, a prosecutor, a diplomat, a head of the Cabinet Legislative Bureau, and a law professor.) On the average, only one judge from two entering cohorts can become a Supreme Court justice. The mandatory retirement age for Supreme Court justices is seventy.

The system of ten-year terms was introduced by the post-war constitution as a guarantee of judicial independence. It in fact gives the Supreme Court important leverage to control lower-court judges. It is true that denial of reappointment is rare. That happened only once in 1971. This judge was an active member of an organization of lawyers called *Seihokyo* or the Young Lawyers Association (YLA) that included private attorneys and law professors as well as judges. The suspected reason for the denial of reappointment was this membership. In saying "It was not the only reason," the Supreme Court officially admitted it. The Supreme Court also actively asked judges in this organization to leave. The message was clear and there was no need to deny another reappointment. The YLA was divided into two sections: one for practicing attorneys and academic lawyers and the other for judges. The YLA's section of judges continued to lose members and no new members were joining. The section was dissolved in 1984. I will later describe how its members have been discriminated against by the Supreme Court.

The law provides that no judge shall be transferred against his own will. However, resistance to the Supreme Court's intention to transfer a judge will certainly damage his future career and thus most judges follow orders given by the Supreme Court. In this sense, lower-court judges are like employees of executive branch agencies. Moreover, the theoretical possibility of denial of reappointment makes their status much weaker than the latter.

General Secretariat of the Supreme Court

I have so far implied that the entire Supreme Court is involved in the administrative control of lower-court judges. Many of you must have thought that all of the fifteen justices are involved in it. That is not the case. Among justices, only the chief justice is involved in it. Daily operation of the administrative control of lower-court judges is carried out by the General Secretariat (GS) of the Supreme Court under the secretary general. The law simply provides that its function is to handle *shomu* or the general affairs of the judiciary. It sounds like a mere support function, but it is actually the most powerful part of the Japanese judiciary.

Under the secretary general and the deputy secretary general, the GS has seven bureaus of general affairs, personnel affairs, accounting, civil cases, criminal cases, administrative cases, and family cases. The bureau of personnel affairs handles recruitment, promotion, and transfer of judges, while the bureaus of civil, criminal, administrative, and family cases provide "reference services" upon request from judges in the field and convene judicial conferences in their respective areas. Since cases involving administrative agencies are special types of civil cases, the bureaus of civil and administrative cases are combined. Approximately forty five judges work full-time. The secretary general, the deputy secretary general, and the bureau chiefs are all judges.

While they are technically lower-court judges, judges working in the GS have supervisory power over those actually handling real cases in the field. The problem is that a small number of the same judges are repeatedly assigned to the GS and promoted faster than other judges. These judges do not decide real cases as often as other judges, but they still have a better chance to become a Supreme Court justice. In fact, all four of the most recent chief justices were formerly this type of judge.

I would like to give some examples of the career patterns of these elite judges.[6] Between 1983 and 1990, four judges (Katsumi, Kusaba, Onishi, Kawasaki, and Sakurai) became deputy secretary general or secretary general. All of them were old-timers of the GS. For instance, Katsumi spent only eight years outside the GS in his thirty years of his service prior to becoming deputy secretary general. Kusaba spent eighteen years of his thirty-five, Onishi spent fifteen years of his thirty-one, Kawasaki spent ten and a half of his thirty, and Sakurai spent eleven years of his thirty-one.

Except for Sakurai who is still deputy secretary general, all of them who had finished their terms as deputy secretary general became head of a district court near Tokyo and later returned to the GS as secretary general. After that, Katsumi became the head of Nagoya High Court and Kusaba and Onishi successively became the head of the Tokyo High Court. Kusaba went on to become Supreme Court justice and soon was promoted to chief justice. One outside observer predicted in early 1991 that, considering the well-established promotion pattern, Onishi would also become Supreme Court justice in the near future.[7] That happened in May of 1991.

Many of these and other judges working in the GS started their careers as assistant judges right in the GS and have repeatedly been assigned to it. By the time they have reached the position of bureau chief, they have worked together for a large part of their careers. As we have just seen, they successively occupy the same or similar positions and are virtually appointing each other to GS positions and other favored locations outside the GS. In this way, GS positions are retained by a small group of self-appointed elite judges who spend a large part of their career in administrative control of other judges.

The GS presents its own justifications for strengthening its authority, for assigning same judges to positions in the GS and courts in or near Tokyo, and for assigning judges to specific courts and gradually giving different ranks to judges of the same cohort. First, the judiciary is the politically weakest branch of the government, so that it needs a full-time staff to defend its own independence and integrity. Second, GS positions need special administrative ability and political sensitivity in dealing with other governmental agencies, political parties, and other outside forces. Third, GS positions are so exhausting that its staff judges deserve preferential treatment in assignment to local courts. Fourth, there are inevitable differences in the ability in efficient disposition of cases and propriety in legal reasoning, so that only those who can properly handle complex cases even under higher case loads should be assigned to major courts and receive faster promotion.

However, the GS does not present any plausible reason to believe that those judges who have spent a large part of their careers in administration are also better jurists in deciding real cases and should be represented in the Supreme Court with an overwhelming percentage share among those who have been appointed from among career judges. I also suspect that the specific content of decisions and outside activities of judges, rather than the efficiency of case disposition or the ability in legal reasoning, are major considerations in deciding judicial assignment. I will later present some evidence to support this suspicion.

Personnel Exchange Between the Judiciary and the Justice Ministry

In addition to assignment to GS positions, there is another way to give judges a chance to perform administrative functions. That is to loan judges to the Justice Ministry for a limited term as a solicitor to defend the government in civil cases or to staff its bureau of civil legislation. This arrangement was introduced because prosecutors generally prefer to deal only with criminal cases as the highest position in the Justice Ministry is the prosecutor general. Now the heads of the Justice Ministry bureaus of solicitors and civil legislation and a majority of solicitors working at the Justice Ministry headquarters and local solicitor's offices are loaned judges.

These loaned judges are likely to get preferential treatment after returning to the judiciary, particularly after working in the Justice Ministry headquarters. Among the Supreme Court justices at the end of 1990, for instance, six were former lower-court judges, and two of them actually spent most of their career in the Justice Ministry.[8] One of them, Justice Kagawa, was an exceptional case. He joined the Justice Ministry after working for only one month as an assistant judge and stayed in the Ministry for the next twenty nine years, eventually becoming the head of the civil legislation bureau. He then returned to the judiciary, working only three and a half years as a chief judge at the Tokyo High Court and as the head of the Urawa District Court near Tokyo before becoming the head of the Sapporo and Nagoya High Courts and, then, Supreme Court justice.

In return, the Justice Ministry loans prosecutors to the judiciary as judges. In 1989, approximately twenty judges and prosecutors were exchanged.[9] Particularly noteworthy is the preferential assignment of those loaned prosecutors to major courts. From 1975 to 1989, 264 prosecutors moved to the judiciary and 67% were assigned to Tokyo and 14% were assigned to Osaka.

The GS justifies this practice of sending judges to the Justice Ministry to defend the government, as a measure to give judges a chance to know the outside world, something that is particularly needed under the present system of recruiting most judges directly from the Judicial Research and Training Institute. In addition to the Justice Ministry, the GS in fact sends a small, yet increasing number of judges to other governmental agencies, law firms, and major business corporations. However, considering other measures to ensure that uniform legal interpretations are adopted by judges who are handling cases that involve governmental agencies and businesses, I suspect that this system of loaning judges as solicitors is also a measure to promote governmental perspectives among judges.

Indeed, this policy of loaning judges to the Justice Ministry to defend the government has been criticized because of the possibility that those judges return to the judiciary with pro-government attitudes and decide cases accordingly. This problem becomes more serious when it is combined with the practice of establishing sections specializing in administrative cases involving governmental defendants. The two sections of administrative cases at the Tokyo District Court are the most important because the central government is most likely to be sued there. In the period between 1982 and 1989, seven judges served there as chief judges. Two of them worked in both the GS and the Justice Ministry, four worked in the GS, and one worked in the Justice Ministry. Similar patterns appear for associate judges. It appears that the most trusted judges are assigned to these critical positions.

The GS also appears to assign a judge with a background as Justice Ministry solicitor in order to get a desired result in a particular case at a local court. The GS can get information about important cases at local courts because judges are required to report to the GS at major junctures in the process of litigation in administrative and labor cases. (Judges are also required to file case-clearance records.) I would like to cite an example where the GS appears to have most effectively used this information.

In 1979, the banks of the Nagara river in Gifu prefecture was broken under heavy rain and the towns of Anpachi and Sunomata were flooded.[10] Residents of the two towns filed separate civil suits in Gifu District Court against the government seeking damage awards as the Nagara river was classified as a major river under the management of the national government. The two cases were heard at different times by the same section of the Gifu court, but the court reached opposing conclusions. While the court decided for the Anpachi plaintiffs in 1982, it decided against the Sunomata plaintiffs in 1984. The associate judges of the two decisions were the same, but the chief judge was different. Chief Judge Akimoto in the Anpachi decision was replaced by Chief Judge Watanabe in 1982, the same year as the Anpachi decision. Watanabe's background is the point. He worked for five years between 1975 and 1980 as a solicitor at the Justice Ministry headquarters, finally at the rank of none other than the head of the administrative litigation. He was at the Tokyo High Court when ordered to move to the Gifu District Court. For a judge who had remained in the jurisdiction of the Tokyo High Court until that time, transfer to a district court under the jurisdiction of the Nagoya High Court was an unusual move. He later returned to the Tokyo District Court in 1986, apparently having satisfied the expectations of the GS, and moved on to work at the Yokohama District Court, right next to Tokyo. In contrast, Judge Akimoto was first transferred to the Nagano District Court, and then to the Numazu branch of the Shizuoka District Court. I will later describe that assignment to a branch court often implies negative evaluation by the GS.

This case suggests both the influence of prior experience in defending the government on later judicial decisions and the relationship between judicial decisions and later treatment of judges. Japanese judges appear to need tremendous courage to decide a case in the way that is likely to displease the GS. This applies especially well to decisions that challenge Supreme Court precedents. Here is one such example.

It is prohibited for political candidates to visit households during election campaigns. This prohibition was considered to be a countermeasure against increasingly more active political campaigns by leftist parties right after the war, particularly those of communists. There was a series of lower-court decisions in the 1950s and 1960s that held this prohibition unconstitutional in violation of the freedom of expression, but the Supreme Court held it constitutional in 1969. However, in 1979, Judge Hirayu of the Yanagawa branch of the Fukuoka District Court in western Japan, an obscure court with only himself, handed down a contrary decision.[11] He had already spent a year there by that time, but was then kept there for another five years, and was later transferred to the Ina branch of the Nagano District Court in central Japan, another minor court with only himself. He stayed there for four more years. The distance of the transfer itself is exceptional, but ten continuous years at one-judge courts should be seen nothing other than a punishment. It is ironic, then, that with leftist parties having been weakened, that when the then ruling conservative party was planning an overhaul of the electoral system one of the proposed reforms was exactly the partial legalization of household visits.

Judicial Conferences

The GS convenes conferences of judges to discuss important issues in the administration of the court system and in interpretations of law. I will focus on the latter issue, as I suspect it is a way for the GS to promote certain lines of legal interpretations without waiting for such cases to reach the Supreme Court.

The critical importance of these conferences was made clear to those outside the court system in 1987 when an attorney representing plaintiffs in a river flood case, which was filed against the government, accidentally found an internal document marked as "requiring special care."[12] This was a thick document entitled "Materials on Handling Civil Damage Suits Against the Government Caused by Flood" and was circulated by the GS to both district and high courts in March, 1985. It contained a record of a conference of district and high court judges held at the Supreme Court in December, 1983. The topic of the discussion was the responsibility of the government in cases where floods have been caused by negligence in management of rivers. Its timing was telling. The conference was held only a month before the Supreme Court decision that severely limited the governmental responsibility in such cases. It appears that the GS tried to inform the lower-court judges of the probable content of the imminent Supreme Court decision and to encourage the attending judges to decide their cases accordingly.

The character of such judicial conferences has changed much since they started in the 1950s.[13] They started as forums for free discussion and judges were invited from among all of the courts. Each court sent a judge based on their own selection. Records of conferences were published and available to outsiders. Courts presenting specific opinions were identified.

They changed around 1970. Lower courts are now instructed to send a judge who is actually handling a case involving the specific issue selected for a given conference. Records are no longer available to outsiders. Participating courts are not identified even in documents for internal circulation. The GS bureau in charge of a given topic invariably presents its opinions at the end of the conference and this presentation takes the greatest amount of time. These opinions are ostensibly presented as information for lower courts that lack library, time, and staff to conduct careful analysis of these complex issues, and the lower courts are free to follow their advice. In reality, however, the GS takes these opinions seriously, and the concerned bureau presents them as their own official opinions after careful examinations among its staff, which include the bureau chief himself. Attending lower-court judges know the weight of such opinions and convey them to their colleagues after they return. Lower-court judges know what will happen to their career if they defy GS policies and many attending judges now consider these conferences as chances to ask the GS to tell them about its policies.

A good example of such control over lower-court judges is the two conferences held in Tokyo in 1976 and 1982. The issue at both conferences was the standing of third parties to sue in administrative cases.[14] The Act of Administrative Litigation provides that only those who have "legal interests" to do so may file a suit to nullify the governmental action. This procedure was often used in cases of environmental litigation that challenged the prefectural governor's judgement in granting permission for the reclamation to build power plants and other potentially polluting facilities. A series of cases since 1968 had granted rights to sue to local residents who did not have fishing and other interests clearly recognized by statutes. The conclusions of the conferences in 1976 and 1982 clearly denied standing to such residents and all decisions on this issue since 1976 took the same position. In one case, for instance, the district court did grant standing in 1976, but it was reversed by the high court in 1982 and the high court decision was upheld by the Supreme Court in 1985.

Some might wonder why lower-court judges assigned to the GS bureaus were able to make correct predictions of future Supreme Court decisions. The Japanese system of Supreme Court clerks is the key. Supreme Court clerks were apparently modeled after the system in use at the U.S. Supreme Court. Unlike the U.S. system, however, clerks are not young lawyers who have just finished law schools. Japanese clerks are experienced judges who have often worked in the GS or who have taught in the Judicial Research and Training Institute. Moreover, also unlike the U.S. system, clerks do not work for individual justices, but for the entire court. The office of clerks now has approximately thirty judges. They are divided into three groups under the direction of chief clerk who manages the entire office and the three senior clerks who each manages one of the respective groups. The fifteen justices are divided into three petty courts each consisting of five justices. When a case is filed, it is heard by one of these petty courts. One of the justices is assigned to the case to draft a decision, but research in relevant precedents, theories, and other materials is carried out by a clerk who is also assigned to the case. This clerk presents materials and alternative conclusions to the assigned judge and, hence, to the entire court. One former clerk in fact told me that one of their major functions was educating justices. The assigned clerk even publishes explanations of the decision and his explanations are often taken as authoritative interpretations.

I do not claim that GS judges and Supreme Court clerks routinely discuss cases pending in the Supreme Court. However, since the GS selects judges to work as clerks, only the most trusted judges are likely to be sent to the office of clerks. As the Supreme Court clerks and the judges at the GS share the same perspective, the Supreme Court's decisions might be at least predictable to the GS.

Returning to the impact of judicial conferences on lower-court judges, official justification of this influence is the lack of ability of most lower-court judges to decide complex cases. A second justification is the benefit of a court system that works like a hierarchical governmental agency. Judge Sonobe, one of the best known judges in Japan who moved from a university law faculty to the judiciary and worked as a Supreme Court clerk as a leading specialist in administrative litigation, once said that it was natural for lower-court judges to accept GS policies, for GS judges are the ones who are the most capable and whose opinions are the most persuasive.[15] He also said that given the way in which the court system now works, it is futile for outside administrative law scholars to try to influence local judges through their books, articles, or briefs.[16] Any legal question of importance is decided by GS judges, Supreme Court clerks, and other elite judges and handed down to local judges. However, this practice undermines the principle of judicial independence as it applies to the relationship among judges. It also undermines the significance of having a system to settle differences in interpretations through appeals of individual cases. A footnote here is that Judge Sonobe left the judiciary, briefly returned to teaching, and was later made Supreme Court justice as the replacement for a retiring justice who was formerly a Tokyo University law professor. Since he was appointed with the qualification of having been a former law professor, no other academic lawyer will have a chance to become justice before his retirement.

Membership in Outside Organizations

The official justification for the judicial conferences I have just described is that they are occasions for judges to freely discuss matters in which they are interested. However, the reality is that they are carefully orchestrated by the GS as a mechanism to promote its own policies among judges. When judges seek forums where they can truly engage in free discussions about topics of their own selection, the GS punishes them. The GS can discriminate against such judges in terms of transfer, promotion, and salary.

The best known cases of discrimination were members of the judicial section of the YLA. This organization was established in 1954 by approximately 280 young lawyers including some ten judges.[17] Its main purpose was the promotion of ideals expressed in the present constitution. The YLA recruited new members from trainees at the Judicial Research and Training Institute. Eventually, a pattern emerged in which approximately one third of the new assistant judges joined the YLA every year. The total number of judges in the YLA reached 140 in 1963 and the judges' section of the YLA started to publish its own periodical dealing with current legal issues from a liberal perspective.

Around 1968, a conservative political magazine published a list of judges who were allegedly members of the YLA and called them "reds." There was also a series of liberal decisions, including some handed down by the Supreme Court, particularly in the area of labor law. Conservative politicians started to pay greater attention to the judiciary and, in 1969, the justice minister said "The judiciary has been out of our control, but there are biased decisions, and we should do something about the judicial system."

Also in 1969, Judge Fukushima of the Sapporo District Court who was presiding over a case involving the constitutionality of the self defense forces, exposed the fact that the head of the court had asked him to honor the government's position. Initially, the head of the court was reprimanded and called back to Tokyo. Eventually, however, conservative politicians put both of them through the impeachment procedures in the Diet. The decision was handed down in 1970. There was no impeachment of the head of the court, while the impeachment of Judge Fukushima was suspended. In other words, Fukushima's exposure was taken to be a more serious crime than the fact that the head of the court had intervened in the decision of another judge's case. Another factor for the harsher treatment of Fukushima was undoubtedly his membership in the YLA.

In 1970, the secretary general of the GS stated that "since membership in political organizations could invite public suspicion of political influences in decisions, judges should not join such organizations," and Chief Justice Ishida stated "Extreme nationalists, militarists, and anarchists, and clear communists are morally undesirable as judges." While Ishida named various ideologies, the message was clear. The YLA was considered as a communist organization and its membership was made a most serious offense for judges. The GS asked member judges to leave the YLA. All of the assistant judges in the GS who belonged to the YLA sent a withdrawal notice to the YLA by certified mail and other judges followed them. The membership of the YLA's judicial section dwindled and, as I have already described, the section was dissolved in 1984.

Since that time, judges who have not clearly discarded their membership have received discriminatory treatment. I would like to give three examples.[18] All of them share Judge Hirayu's problem, namely, controversial decisions which were contrary to the Supreme Court's position on the issue of prohibition of house visits for political campaigns.

The first example is Judge Haruhiko Abe, a graduate of Tokyo University and formerly a leading theoretician in the judicial section of the YLA. Like Hirayu, he held the prohibition of house visits for political campaigning unconstitutional in 1968. In 1972, he was also a member of the court that held that the heavier penalty proscribed by the penal law for homicide of a parent was unconstitutional. While the Supreme Court took the same position in 1973 for the latter issue, Judge Abe has been assigned only to family (five years) or branch courts (twelve consecutive years) ever since. In spite of his experience of more than thirty years, he has never been given a position of chief judge.

The second example is Judge Hanada. Also a graduate of Tokyo University, he was sent to the United States for study when he was an assistant judge. However, he took a similar position to that of Hirayu and Abe in a house visits case in 1969 and was also a leading theoretician of the YLA. He publicly defended the YLA and has also been assigned only to family (five years) or branch courts (twelve years). He resigned in 1987 when ordered to move to another branch court to replace a much younger judge.

The third example is Judge Kunio Ogawa. His career was unusual from the very beginning. He was first assigned to a summary court for seven years and later assigned mostly to branch courts (fifteen years, including twelve consecutive years). He held the house visits prohibition unconstitutional in 1979.

These judges are most untrustworthy from the perspective of the GS. Discrimination against most members of surviving YLA members is more subtle. There is a survey of transfer patterns of judges who joined the judiciary between 1966 and 1970.[19] This survey analyzed for each cohort how many judges have been twice transferred to a branch court or failed to get transfer to a major court in three consecutive transfers. Depending on the cohort, percentage of such judges varied from thirty six to sixty percent for members and from twelve to nineteen percent for non-members. The YLA members clearly face a higher risk of getting such unfavorable assignment.

Another group that has been discriminated against by the GS is members of *Saibankan Konwakai* or the Friendly Meeting of Judges (FMJ). This group was formed in the middle of the conservative attack on YLA members and, unlike the YLA, participation is limited to judges. The FMJ still holds annual meetings and publishes the papers presented in a leading law journal. Academic quality of such papers is quite high. Unlike the YLA, the FMJ does not have fixed members, except some leaders who plan meetings and send out announcements. Discriminatory treatment focuses on such leaders in the same manner as that applied to YLA members.

In these cases, impacts of organizational membership and legal interpretations are difficult to distinguish as the two factors tend to coexist. It seems, however, that organizational membership has been used by the GS as the primary index to classify judges and individual decisions have worked as an aggravating factor.

Culture and Politics

How has this system of administrative control developed? One may try both cultural and political explanations.

A cultural explanation might focus on the legacy of the prewar structure of the Japanese judiciary and the conception of the judiciary as a governmental agency without much difference from agencies of the executive branch. Before the war, the judiciary was part of the Justice Ministry and judges and prosecutors freely changed their jobs. In spite of the American occupation that separated the judiciary from the Justice Ministry, the centralized court structure was maintained, and prewar judges remained in the judiciary and kept the prewar organizational culture with them. While the legal education under the post-World-War-II constitution brought in more independent-minded, liberal judges into the judiciary and gave them a chance to liberalize legal interpretations in many areas, the political climate around 1970 allowed those conservative judges to regain control over the entire structure.

However, this cultural explanation itself assumes the impact of political factors that allowed the legacy of prewar organizational culture to resurface in the judiciary. I have already described the political factor which I believe was the most important, namely, the conservative attack on liberal judges around 1970. Tightening of administrative control of judges since that time can at least partially be understood as a measure to avoid a potentially more damaging intervention by conservative politicians. I should note, however, that there was also an element within the judiciary that shared the perspective of conservative politicians and actively responded to their expectations. The case in point is Justice Ishida who headed the Supreme Court from 1969 to 1973, exactly when the judiciary was under the strongest pressure from conservative politicians.[20]

In 1966, the Supreme Court handed down an epoch-making decision in a case involving the labor union of mail workers. While the constitution guaranteed the right of workers to form a union and take collective action, statutes prohibited strikes by employees of governmental agencies and public corporations and provided criminal punishments for strikes. In this decision in 1966, the Supreme Court held that unless they caused grave adverse effects to the public, no criminal punishment should be applied to strikes even carried out by employees of public corporations. The theoretical leader behind this decision was Justice Jiro Tanaka, a former Tokyo University law professor and the founding father of modern administrative law scholarship in Japan. In the same year, the Supreme Court handed down a similar decision in a case involving teachers, namely, employees of local governments. In this way, the constitutional protection of worker's rights was extended to employees of both public corporations and governmental agencies.

These and other liberal decisions alerted conservative politicians, particularly Tokutaro Kimura. Kimura was the last justice minister right after the war prior to the separation of the judiciary and the prosecution. He took these decisions to mean a national crisis and was particularly worried about one scenario, namely, the promotion of Justice Tanaka to chief justice. The prime minister at that time was Sato, who later received a Nobel peace prize. The incumbent chief justice was to retire in 1969 and Sato, a Tokyo University graduate, was considering the promotion of Tanaka. Realizing this possibility, Kimura met Sato in December, 1968, told his ideas, and recommended another person as chief justice. Kimura's choice was Justice Ishida. Kimura had known Ishida for nearly thirty years because Ishida was the head of the personnel department of the Justice Ministry under Kimura and they together fought against the occupation authority to preserve the status quo of the judiciary and the Justice Ministry. Sato took Kimura's advice and Ishida became chief justice in January, 1969.

Since Tanaka and other liberal justices still remained, Ishida had to wait a few more years to overturn liberal decisions. He did so by replacing retiring liberal justices with conservative ones, including a former ambassador to the United States and a former head of the Cabinet Legislative Bureau that reviews bills proposed by the government. The Foreign Ministry and the Cabinet Legislative Bureau have kept at least one justiceship ever since. The turning point came in April, 1973. The Supreme Court decided three cases involving strikes by employees of the governmental agencies and public corporations and overturned its 1966 decisions with a eight-to-seven majority. Tanaka had been disappointed and demoralized and left the Supreme Court in March, 1973, one month before the conservative victory, leaving three years before retirement age. Ishida retired with satisfaction in May, 1973, one month after his victory. Conservative justices continued to increase and, in a similar case decided in 1976, the decision was unanimous. By the way, Ishida's loyalty to Kimura did not end by his retirement from the chief justiceship. In March, 1974, Kimura retired from the presidency of the Japanese Association of Japanese Swordsmanship and Ishida succeeded him.

After Ishida, excluding two brief terms served by a former private attorney and a former prosecutor, the chief justiceship has been held by people like Ishida who accumulated their career in administrative control of other judges. Such administrators have justified the present system in terms of the need of political neutrality of the judiciary. Their conception of neutrality simply means the sharing of the perspective of the dominant political group in the legislative and administrative branches of the government. They have appointed like-minded judges to the GS and other key positions to control other judges and such elite judges have promoted each other to higher positions including the chief justiceship of the Supreme Court.

They have not only promoted conservative interpretations of law, particularly of the constitution. They have also kept the judiciary very small in spite of tremendous economic growth of Japanese society which undoubtedly has increased potential sources of legal disputes. The per capita number of judges, including summary court judges, has constantly decreased since 1950.[21] The number of judges for one million people was twenty eight in 1950, twenty five in 1970, and twenty two in 1989. Conscious reduction of organizational size and authority by its own members is totally against an accepted wisdom of organizational sociology. Organizational sociologists particularly expect that governmental agencies always try to expand their size and authority. However, the reduction of the size and authority of the Japanese judiciary can be understood as a rational behavior from the perspective of elite judges. An expanded judiciary will make it more difficult for them to control other judges and increase chances for the public to challenge the government. Elite judges seem to find their satisfaction in their role as a rear guard of the status quo of the government.

Unlike the United States, Japan has no popular election nor legislative confirmation of judges. Unlike Germany, we do not decide judicial appointment with consideration of political identifications. Our judiciary may then appear to be more independent from political influences. However, this also means a lack of democratic control, and this alienation from democratic process allows internal elites to promote a single political perspective and deprive independence of a vast majority of judges.

I suspect that there are different ways to change the Japanese judiciary in order to give more freedom to judges and, thus, greater chances for the public to win in administrative litigation. One way may be to abolish the system of recruiting the vast majority of judges directly after they have finished their two-year practical training at the Judicial Research and Training Institute and thus drastically reduce the chances for the Supreme Court General Secretariat to influence the views of these younger judges. The Japanese Federation of Bar Associations has proposed this reform and asked the judiciary to recruit judges from among experienced practicing attorneys.

Another possibility may be to appoint judges to specific courts until their retirement and abolish the present practice to relocate them every few years. Judges could then decide more freely without the need to worry much about possible adverse effects on their future career.

Still another, more radical possibility may be to politicize the judiciary in such a way that judicial appointments, at least those at the Supreme Court, are publicly reviewed and different political perspectives are guaranteed to have representation in the judiciary. A thoroughgoing cross-national socio-legal study on Japan and West Germany suggests the need for such a restructuring of the Japanese judiciary.[21]

Notes

1. This chapter is reprinted (with minor changes in style and wording) from 25 *Kobe University Law Review* 45 (1991). Andrew L. Beaton, a research student in the Graduate School of Law of Kobe University, kindly edited it for the original publication.

All articles cited in this chapter (except for Ramseyer and Nakato, *infra* note 2, are written in Japanese. Article titles are translated into English, while journal and book titles are not for the convenience of those who might have access to them. The articles marked with * were originally presented at the panel I organized for the 1990 annual meeting of the Japanese Association of the Sociology of Law on May 12, 1990. The three panelists kindly spent their expensive time as private attorneys to prepare these papers. Those who wish to verify the career patterns of Japanese judges described in this paper might consult the following directory of all judges appointed since 1947: Nihon Minshu Horitsuka Kyokai Siho Seido Iinkai (ed.), *Zen-saibankan Keireki Soran: Kaitei Shinpan*, Tokyo: Kojinsha, 1990.

2. J. Mark Ramseyer and Minoru Nakazato, "The Rational Litigant: Settlement Amounts and Verdict Rates in Japan" 18 *Journal of Legal Studies* 263 (1989).

3. *Id.*

4. Shigeo Kisa, *Ningen no Songen to Shihoken* (Human Dignity and the Judiciary), Tokyo: Nihon Hyoronsha, 1990, 316..

5. Article 76 (3), Japanese Constitution.

6. Kuniaki Shioya, "Treatment of Judges Revisited," *Horitsu Jiho*, Vol.63, No.1, 1991.*

7. *Id.*

8. *Id.*

9. Shigeo Kisa, "Professionalism and Independence of Judges (1)," *Hokudai Hogaku Ronshu*, Vol.40, Nos.5-6 (1990).

10. Yoshitomo Ode, "Present Status and Problems of the Participants in the Judicial System," *Ho no Kagaku*, No.15 (1987).

11. Eiji Tsukahara "Judicial Careers and Judicial Decisions," *Horitsu Jiho*, Vol.62, No.5. (1990).*

12. Tadashi, Matsumoto, "Judicial Conferences and Supreme Court Clerks," in *Hogaku Semina* special issue, *Konnichi no Saiko Saibansho*, Tokyo: Nihon Hyoronsha (1988).

13. Kisa, *supra* note 9.

14. Jiro Yukawa, "Judicial Conferences in Administrative Cases," *Horitsu Jiho*, Vol.62, No.5.(1990).*

15. Itsuo Sonobe, "Structure and Roles of the Supreme Court," 67 *Hogaku Kyoshitsu* (1986), p. 42.

16. Itsuo Sonobe, *Gendai Gyosei to Gyosei Sosho* (Contemporary Administration and Administrative Litigation), Tokyo: Kobundo, 1987, p. 302.

17. Seinen Horitsuka Kyokai *Seihokyo*. Tokyo: Nihon Hyoronsha (1990).

18. Tsukahara, *supra* note 11.

19. Tokuo Sakaguchi, "The Reality of Unfair Practices in Discriminatory Transfer, Promotion, and Salary," *Ho to Minshushugi*, No.229 (1988).

20. Yuji Yamamoto and Keiko Okada, "A Coup in the Supreme Court," *Hogaku Semina*, No.378 (1986).

21. Kisa, *supra* note 9.

22. Kisa, *supra* note 3.

PART FIVE

Education for the New Lawyer

11

Challenges to Legal Education in Korea

Sang-Hyun Song

Introduction

Since the 1970s, chronic problems in legal education have frequently been discussed in legal academic circles and various proposals for reforms have been made.[1] Korean law professors have described Korean legal education and made reform proposals[2] and foreign scholars have also examined the diagnoses of malaise in our legal education.[3]

The legal and educational institutions of each nation have been molded by its own distinctive history and culture. Korea is no exception. In the present age of ever increasing interdependence worldwide, however, an international and comparative approach to legal education is apt for Korea, which is now undergoing the processes of democratization and internationalization.

Although the law and legal system presently in operation in Korea are by and large legacies of Japan's colonial rule of Korea from 1910 to 1945 or imitation from the West imposed by the Japanese more than a century ago, some of the legal institutions were created and molded by the dictatorial governments of former Presidents Park and Chun over the past thirty years partly to help them strengthen their own power base. Since changes in legal education have been proposed with respect to the broader issues of educational objectives and policies, graduate programs for law, the national judicial service examination, and judicial training systems, this note will deal briefly with some of those issues.

Legal Education at Law College

Approximately speaking, about 5,300 high schools across the country produce approximately 800,000 graduates annually and more than half of them want to go to college. If anyone excels in their class in high school, teachers as well as parents and friends pressurize the student to apply for Seoul National University (SNU) and its law faculty, regardless of their wishes, aptitude, and talents. It is no exaggeration to say, therefore, that the law faculty of SNU takes the 270 or so highest scorers in the nationally administered college entrance examination, which is rather like the Scholastic Aptitude Test in the U.S. Although those chosen few are undoubtedly the cream of the crop, examination-focused credentialism and careerism, to which almost all the freshmen of law faculties are long used, tend to set in virtually upon admittance to the law department of a top university, for the future avenue of those who survived such a tough competition seems to be well guaranteed at that point. Students are required to complete 150 credits over four years in law college, which is ten credits more than required by other departments. The curriculum for law colleges commences with one year of general education. From the beginning of the second year, studies focus largely on legal topics and the list of required law courses becomes quite crowded. Too many subjects are listed as compulsory and there is little room for the students to take any electives. Several attempts to change the law college curricula so as to free students to take more electives have failed largely due to the self-interest of individual law faculty members. Almost all of the students begin serious preparations for the judicial service examination from the second year, if not in the first year. There are very few who choose a non-judicial career by refusing to prepare for the examination. The hot wind of examination preparation thus envelopes the entire law school as well as the students. Two consequences can be observed: firstly, worrisome paralysis of the legal education and related academic activities; second, unbalanced nourishment of the students' legal knowledge. As one way to remedy this abnormality in legal education, the SNU law faculty has proposed that the LL.B. program be expanded from four to five years so that a five-year LL.B. course could give an additional year for extra law courses as well as more electives in the non-law areas.

Although such proposals were by and large influenced by the American legal education system and have long been endorsed by the Law Professors Association, they have met with skeptical responses on a number of counts. Firstly, pointing out that the four-year LL.B. course is already followed by the two-year course of the Judicial Research and Training Institute (JRTI) for those who have passed the national examination, most legal professionals have argued that the extension by a year is unnecessary. Second, most of the National Assemblymen belonging to the Educational Committee have voiced their concern that the additional costs of another year of legal education without any corresponding benefit such as exemption from the first part of the national examination would be seen as a severe additional economic burden for less affluent aspirants to the legal profession, whose parents have already endured considerable sacrifices. Third, some educators' argument in opposition to the proposal has been to the effect that even if the social and private costs of an additional year of legal studies can be justified, a longer course of study is unlikely to achieve very much without concurrent qualitative changes in the curriculum, in the graduate program, and in the examination system.

Whereas law schools in the United States devote themselves mainly to the training of practitioners, the situation at Korean law colleges is entirely the opposite. Although the institutional context is quite different in that Korean law students are undergraduates, unlike American law students, the whole course, regardless of subject, places its main focus on teaching theories and meticulous exegeses of legal dogma so that students emerge with limited know-how of practical use in their subsequent careers. The apprenticeship training provided in Korea's JRTI is thus considered by some legal professionals as a needed supplement to the theoretical bias of law college education.

Traditionally, the main purpose of the Korean LL.B. programs has been controversial. Some have said that it was more of a general education. Others have argued that it should be for professional purposes, aiming at cultivating future judges and prosecutors, and identifying bureaucrats for the higher civil services, for whom there are also the Higher Civil Service and the Diplomatic Service Examinations. Under present circumstances many law faculties are of opinion that as long as the major role played by the legal profession remains dogmatic interpretation of black-letter law, career building for government service might be more meaningful, for technocrats could carry out more active and important missions in the policy-formulating process of the country. Recognizing the importance of technocrats' role in national development in developing countries like Korea, faculty members urge law students to take either of these two examinations. Yet, very few law students choose to take them, and almost all of them tend to plan a judicial career.

Therefore, the objectives of law teaching have to be reassessed in a broader context, and it is essential at least that law colleges are prevented from becoming a mere preparatory school for the examinations.

National Judicial Service Examination

For the National Judicial Service Examination, a group of about sixteen thousand applicants annually takes a multiple choice test, the first part of the examination, that covers eight subjects such as constitutional law, civil law, criminal law, history, some social science disciplines like basic economics and a foreign language, etc. This part being to weed out most of the unqualified applicants, usually around 800 to 900 are selected in this process. Those who have passed the first part go on to take the second and third parts. If, however, they fail at this stage, they are allowed to take the second and third parts once more only, in the following year.

The field is thus drastically narrowed to around 1,500 students who sit for the second part of the examination, an essay test covering seven required legal topics, that is, constitutional law, administrative law, Commercial Code, Civil Code, civil procedure, criminal law, and criminal procedure as well as "national ethics." Finally, the successful examinees, numbering around three hundred annually, undergo an interview process, the third part of the examination, which is now largely perfunctory. Once your name is announced amongst the three hundred successful examinees after the second part of the examination, you may now remain assured of final success, because the government no longer uses the third part as an opportunity to flunk the applicants who have shown an anti-government propensity.

Although there is no prerequisite of holding a university degree, or law degree, to take the examination, almost all successful examinees are, in actuality, graduates of the law faculties of leading universities located in Seoul. Slightly less than a half of those three hundred are from SNU alone.

West[4] observes that "the prestige attached to licensure as jurist in Korea may permit the regulative function of screening out unqualified aspirants to the bar to be subordinated to a constitutive function of reproducing an exclusive segment of the political elite on the basis of mastery of a highly esoteric corpus of legal dogma. This process of elite recruitment is actually meritocratic, exhibiting a degree of continuity with the Confucian cultural ideals once embodied in Chosun dynasty civil service examinations."

The examination system has long been unreasonable, irrelevant, anachronistic, sometimes politically tainted, and thus ill-adapted to the institutionalization of a modern legal profession. Law colleges attract the brightest few annually, but only too small a number of them pass the examinations. Since to pass them is the quickest and surest way to satisfy everyone's desire for upward mobility in our highly stratified society, almost every ambitious young man and woman tries and repeats the attempt for many years, despite the difficulties and frustration that they have to endure. The vast majority of applicants make it a perennial or even a life time job to repeat the examination, and reluctantly seek a job in the business or other sectors only after several tries. The bench, the bar and the prosecution do not, in fact, need this brightest chosen few as long as all that the whole judiciary does is merely to indulge in dogmatic interpretation of the black-letter law, as they do now. Therefore, it is a blatant example of a waste and misallocation of human resources nationally.

Professional Training

Until 1962 the basic format of the judicial training was just a one year individual apprenticeship program; those who passed the National Judicial Service Examination were assigned to experienced judges, prosecutors and practitioners for one year in total on a rotation basis.

From 1962 to 1970, Korean judicial training was carried on in a new format, in the Graduate School of Law of SNU. It was a result of the tenacious efforts on the part of a few American-educated law faculty members of the SNU to launch such a law college-managed judicial training program. However, in 1970, President Park Chung-Hee decided to copy the Japanese training model by establishing the JRTI under the supervision of the Korean Supreme Court. Whether or not such a change was considered a move to centralize ideological control over the legal profession, it also had considerable support from the legal profession and the students. It was at this time that the new reform of the examination and training programs were so designed as to sever any link with the legal education, as mentioned above. This reform thus made it possible for anyone to take the examination, and the law faculties have since been excluded from the operation of the judicial training program.

It was only in the 1960s that several graduates of the Graduate School of Law were first sent to the U.S. for advanced legal studies on Fulbright grants. A small number of them were the first generation of Korean jurists who undertook academic study of foreign legal systems other than those of Japan and Germany. They came to have fundamental doubts as to whether law should be taught as a part of general education or as a specialized professional training. Furthermore, the kind of education in law they received in the U.S., designed mainly to teach lawyerly problem-solving skills necessary for private practice, differed drastically from the narrow focus on conceptual jurisprudence necessary for a judge or prosecutor. Those Korean legal professionals were really perplexed at American colleagues being ardent defenders of private interests. Nowadays many of these Western-educated Korean lawyers are engaged in transnational commercial practice for their clients, specializing in foreign investment, technology transfer, off-shore financing, securities regulation, international trade, intellectual property, and international commercial arbitration, etc.

The course of professional training at the JRTI and elsewhere has become formalistic and dogmatized to such an extent that no occasion arises to reflect on professional ideals of public service and their implications for lawyers. The statistics of legal aid for the poor amply indicate this. There were merely 9,796 free counselling cases and only 14 pro bono litigation cases handled by 1,529 members of the Seoul Bar Association in 1991, and this is a negligible number even if taking account of the government-funded legal aid agency and others which render such services. This illustrates the results of a system in which, as West describes it,[5] "the learning of law may come to resemble the mastery of a technique of symbolic manipulation detached from social reality and devoid of sensitivity to the human needs driving the conflicts that the legal order regulates."

The Legal Profession in Korea

The structural changes in the Korean legal profession can be approached from several points of view, all of which have a bearing on legal education and training and the judicial service examination.

First, it has been a perennial debate whether to increase the number who pass the judicial service examination to more than the present 300 a year. The bench, the bar and the Justice Ministry are strongly opposed to the idea and argue rather in favor of decreasing the number, because they do not want to see their scarcity value diluted. On the other hand, law faculty members always propose increasing it, in the hope of enhancing the possibility of a few more of their own students joining the elite rank, because they believe that the reputation of their law school depends on how many of their students pass the examination. Second, the national examinations including the judicial service examination are administered by the Ministry of Government Administration. This fact implies that practising attorneys, judges and public prosecutors are just an extension of the administrative bureaucracy, although there is a debate whether the judicial service examination ought to be managed by the Supreme Court. Third, traditionally the practical training for those who pass the examination has been narrowly focused on litigation. Counselling, business planning and contract negotiation, etc., which occupy a large portion of the professional activities of lawyers in the United States, are as yet underdeveloped as specialties among Korean attorneys. On the one hand, however, lawyers are gradually realizing that this is a new area of practice, and on the other their clients come to feel it necessary to rely on lawyers for this kind of non-litigation work. While litigation services are monopolized by licensed lawyers, shortage of lawyers compels many less affluent clients to seek legal assistance from quasi-lawyers such as judicial scriveners, tax accountants and land appraisers. Corporate employees doing law-related work often consult closely with working-level bureaucrats in the government who themselves may have been law majors in college. The legal departments of corporations have yet to be properly organized and utilized.

There is an immense shortage of sophisticated international legal expertise in Korea. The transactional history of many Korean corporations amply indicates enormous costs incurred due to the inadequacy and shortage of legal professionals as well as the inexperience and unpreparedness of corporations in planning international business activities, typical examples in great numbers being the legal problems that challenged Korean contractors in the Middle East construction markets in the 1970s.

In such an urbanized country as Korea there are still only less than fifty law firms with more than five lawyers, most of which were formed to secure authority for notarization from the Ministry of Justice, as required by the Lawyers' Act, rather than for the more effective practice of international law. It was only in the beginning of the 1970s that a few of the American-educated Korean lawyers launched a big experiment to institutionalize American style law firms in the legally sterile soil of Korea. By and large they have been growing rapidly and successfully. Yet it still remains to be seen whether most of them will survive the legal services market in Korea, soon to be opened internationally.

The vast majority of legal professionals lack an adequate understanding of how rules actually operate in complex social and transnational environments. For many decades they felt little necessity to broaden their understanding of the world outside the courts and the state bureaucratic apparatus. Forming a kind of a fraternity among judges, public prosecutors and practitioners, they operate in a closed network in which hierarchies are fixed according largely to past records, such as the seniorities in their law school graduation and in the examination, and their previous or present office holding in the public service, etc. Expectations are changing in Korea, however, and changing expectations mean new professional roles and new demands on legal education.

International and Comparative Legal Studies

The export-oriented development strategy adopted by successive Korean governments since the 1960s has entailed an increasing need for expertise in the law of transnational, commercial and financial relations. Unavailability of the more sophisticated legal services in Korea at this period made reliance on foreign lawyers unavoidable.

The main job that a small number of lawyers practising international law were asked to do in the 1970s was to review all sorts of documents prepared by foreign lawyers and referred to them to check whether any of the provisions in the documents was repugnant to Korean law, and also to translate legal documents between Korean and English. It was a learning process for Korean lawyers, and no Korean lawyers could then draft any legal document of an international nature, due to the language barrier and the perception that drafting was no part of lawyering. Soon some of the large law offices began to hire American lawyers whose job was drafting various agreements or mere English proofreading, depending upon how the talents of foreign lawyers were utilized. Transfer of such legal know-how and international expertise to Korean lawyers was largely made possible by their foreign clients retaining them.

In the 1980s, the local supply of such sophisticated expertise was ameliorated somewhat, but less through improvement in Korean legal education and training than through a growth in the number of Korean lawyers sent abroad for advanced legal studies and practical training with leading law firms overseas.

The Uruguay Round negotiations, entry to the United Nations, the rapprochement of the two Koreas and many other bilateral negotiations such as our relations with the U.S., EC, Russia, and China present new legal issues and opportunities of critical importance. Unfortunately Korean corporations seldom consult Korean lawyers in advance, for instance, when they enter such a new market as China, Russia, Vietnam and Southeast Asia. The Korean Government as well as business have yet to fully realize the importance of law and lawyers and to utilize experienced lawyers who are now well equipped with international expertise.

The study of foreign and international law, in particular, should be accorded a high priority in legal education. In fact, however, these areas of legal studies have been underdeveloped and under-funded in the universities, and attracted little attention from government policy-makers.

The initial impediment arises from the language barrier. Compulsory study of the English language for at least six years at middle and high schools is not coupled with any extensive exposure to the Anglo-American legal system for most legal professionals. While there is strong demand on the part of law students and lawyers for pursuing international and comparative legal studies, law colleges are not well equipped with the human and material resources necessary to make it possible. Furthermore, law is perceived by policy makers to be playing a remedial function in Korean political and economic affairs, and international law is perceived as public international law in the traditional narrow sense of the word that has no relevance to the typical career in the legal profession. Lawyers are hardly ever asked to participate in any policy formulating process and it is usually economists who dominate. Low-ranking government bureaucrats who are not even law majors are routinely asked to draft a legal framework or a bill.

From the 1960s, judges, prosecutors and professors were sent both to common law and civil law countries. Advanced studies in common law jurisdictions have grown more popular in the 1980s, perhaps due to a recognition that the important trade and financial relations between Korea and the United States make it imperative to cultivate relevant legal expertise. As Korea's economic relations diversify, expertise in European Community law and in other legal systems is also necessary.

As of April 1993 there were 2,634 practising lawyers in Korea with a population per lawyer ratio of 18000:1. The number of individuals who can proudly identify themselves as judges, prosecutors and attorneys is very small—only 2,634 lawyers, 1,156 judges,and 930 prosecutors in a nation of 43,000,000. Furthermore, 1,678 lawyers out of 2,634 practise law in Seoul, and fewer than two hundred licensed Korean attorneys are regularly engaged in working on legal matters with a transnational dimension.

Conclusion

The present system of legal education and training leads career decisions to be framed in terms of a choice among three roles—judge, prosecutor and litigation attorney. The legal adviser's crucial roles as business planner and negotiator, international mediator, interpreter of foreign legal requirements and so forth are not fully recognized in the general perception or even in the curriculum of law college, even in the JRTI.

With the advent of a new era that marks the inauguration of the first legitimate civilian government in 1993, a number of important goals were projected: improved legal protection of human rights, normalized labor relations, eradication of corruption and crime, restoration of local autonomy, freedom of the press, university autonomy, the restructuring of electoral procedures to enhance their fairness and justice, and establishment of Korea's position in the international society as a responsible member.

Achievement of these objectives depends largely on commitment to democratic and international values within the legal profession. Tasks for constructive legal education, including comparative and international legal studies, are urgent and indispensable. In the past, there seems to have been little understanding that law has a major role to play in changing society, for the role of judges, prosecutors and lawyers was simply to see to it that the laws on the books were effectively enforced.

Whether this attitude will change, and whether the Korean people will come to view the judicial system as a positive and responsive part of the institutional picture largely depends on the younger legal professionals who will soon assume more responsible roles in our society.

Notes

1. This short note is based on the author's own experience of passing the national judicial service examination and the higher civil service examination, brief practice within and without Korea, and law-teaching experience for more than twenty years. Views expressed in this note are the author's own.

2. E.g., D.K. Choi, *Legal Education in Korea: Problems and Reform Efforts*, International Conference on Legal Education held on October 30-31, 1987 at Seoul National University; Kiljun Park, "Problems Concerning the Reform of Legal Education in Korea," 6 *Korean Journal of Comparative Law* 56-91 (1978).

3. See Jay Murphy, "Legal Education and the Development of Law in Traditional Cultures: Learning from the Korean Experience," 27 *Journal of Legal Education* 234-249 (1975); James West, *Education of the Legal Profession in Korea*, International Legal Studies, Korea University, 1991.

4. West, *supra* note 3, 25.

5. West, *supra* note 3, 27.

12

Legal Education in Japan

Yasuhei Taniguchi

Organization of Japanese Legal Education: An Outline

In the late 19th century Japan adopted a European style system of legal education.[1] Legal education within the university has since been primarily at the undergraduate level, but, except for certain periods, undergraduate legal education itself has not entitled graduates to pursue a professional legal career as a "full jurist", either as a member of the practicing bar, as a judge or as a prosecutor.[2] To become a full jurist, one must take a rigorous state examination. Administrative agencies, in central as well as local government, and private industries are eager to employ law graduates without the full jurist qualification. Therefore, only a small portion of law graduates become "full jurists" while others go into other fields which are not strictly legal. This basic pattern of Japanese legal education has remained unchanged for more than a century, although many important reforms took place after the Second World War.

Before the war, university education was a highly limited opportunity available only to a small portion of the population. After the war the so-called democratization wave also washed over the whole educational system. Along with primary and secondary education,[3] higher education underwent great changes, namely:

1. Compulsory liberal arts education was introduced into the university curriculum, and the period of university education was extended from 3 to 4 years. Under the pre-war system a university student took courses only within his or her chosen field. Students now entered a university normally at age 18 and the first 2 years were devoted to liberal arts subjects, namely 3 social science subjects, 3 humanities subjects and 3 natural science subjects, in addition to one or two foreign languages and physical

education. This means that the period of specialized study became one year shorter than in the pre-war system. As a result, many universities have adopted a system allowing second year, and sometimes even first year students, to take some of the specialized subjects.

2. The number of universities was greatly increased, initially by raising the former technical colleges to the status of university. Later, many universities, mostly private ones, were and still continue to be established to meet the demands of applicants.[4] The number of universities with a separate law faculty increased from fewer than 15 in the pre-war era[5] to the present 87. In addition there are various combination departments, e.g., faculties of law and economics, which have their own law faculty and curriculum.[6] They number roughly 10. As a result Japan now turns out almost 45,000 university graduates every year who have done specialized legal study. This is more than twice as many as in 1972.[7]
3. Graduate legal education was also reformed, and American-style graduate programs were established, with a two year master's program followed by 3 years of doctoral work. These graduate courses, especially those for a doctorate, are intended primarily, but not necessarily, to be a training for an academic career. There are presently 65 graduate programs in law (including political science).[8] Under the pre-war system, the training of future legal academics mostly consisted of academic assistantship in the European style. Academic assistantship has today become mostly a position for those who have done graduate study, although some law faculties still hire a limited number of good graduating undergraduate students as academic assistants.

Another significant change in legal education at the graduate level was a reform in the training of future members of the legal professions. After passing the annual National Legal Examination, university graduates enter the Legal Training and Research Institute (hereinafter called LTRI), which is attached to and managed by the Supreme Court. A uniform two year training is given in class rooms, courts, a public prosecutor's office and a practicing attorney's office. During this period the students receive a respectable salary from the Government. Another examination at the end of the two years qualifies the students for the legal profession as full jurist or *Hoso*. They then become eligible to apply to the Supreme Court or the Ministry of Justice for employment as assistant judge or public prosecutor, or to the local bar association for admission to practice. A few pursue an academic career by joining a university law faculty.[9] This unified training for all legal professions is particularly significant since before the war judges and public prosecutors received a distinctive training, generally superior to that given to private attorneys, although there has been a unified national legal examination since 1923.[10]

The National Legal Examination and the subsequent LTRI training, as the exclusive way of entering the legal profession, have a certain impact on legal education in the universities. The number of students passing the examination and therefore eligible to apply to the LTRI for admission has been very limited. It started with 250 and gradually increased to 500 where it stayed for a long time until it was finally increased to 600 in 1992; in 1994 it will be 700, as explained later in more detail. Since there are approximately 45,000 graduates annually and many graduates take the examination several times, the chance of success is little more than a miniscule 2 percent. Consequently, even in the better universities at best 15 percent of graduates succeed in the examination even after many attempts, and the rest must seek jobs outside the legal profession. Central and local governments are favored employers but there also the students must face the difficult National Civil Service Examination or a similar examination given by each local government, prefecture or city. As a result, most law graduates in the country go into private industries of various sorts. Large financial firms and manufacturers are favored but not available to everyone, of course.

Some of those employed by a company may work in the legal department and deal with the kind of legal affairs handled by qualified lawyers in other countries, but in Japan these people are not called lawyers because they have not qualified as full jurist or *Hoso* by receiving the LTRI training. They are sometimes called quasi-lawyers. These people often become, however, through their in-house training, real experts in the field in which they work. For large companies, it has become customary to send a selected number of such employees abroad for full time legal study, mostly in the United States for a graduate degree in law. Many of them return after having passed the New York bar examination.

Some graduates may also become a legal scrivener (*Shiho-Shoshi*), patent agent (*Benrishi*) or tax agent (*Zeirishi*). All of these professionals are also called quasi-lawyers and do what a lawyer would do in some other countries.[11] Thus, Japanese legal education at the undergraduate level produces overwhelmingly non-lawyers, more exactly non-"full jurists". Full jurists are produced by the LTRI which is at a graduate level but not a part of any university. Universities have their own graduate schools and academic assistantships for training legal academics. Thus, the world of practice and legal academia are quite separated and independent from each other.[12]

Problems and Recent Reform Movements

Undergraduate Level

Basic Dilemma. The source of a basic dilemma for Japanese legal education at the undergraduate level has been and will continue to be the fact that very few of its graduates will enter the legal profession. What should legal education be like when most graduates do not become lawyers? Legal education in the technical sense, namely professional training, does not seem to fit here. The LTRI is the place for that. Should undergraduate legal education play the role of preliminary or introductory education to the LTRI? This is unrealistic because only a very small minority of students can get there. The idea may be valid for a limited number of elitist universities where a majority of students seriously want to enter the legal profession although only a small part of them can really do so because of the barrier of the National Legal Examination. A danger here is that the universities might become mere prep-schools for the examination. In most universities, a great majority of students probably have never thought of becoming any kind of legal person. Thus, some law faculties have described their objective as a kind of liberal arts education with an emphasis on law. The definition may vary from school to school, and, even if a meaningful goal is found, to decide how to achieve it may prove to be even more difficult. One obvious question is whether curriculum and/or teaching methods should be modified as the objective is differently defined. It may be most realistic to assume that as long as the "law" faculty is allowed to exist, any drastic change is highly unlikely and that the dilemma of a system of legal education which does not train lawyers will remain a source of problems and ambivalence.

Curriculum and Related Problems. Each law faculty determines its own curriculum although generally the traditional European pattern is followed. No substantial central control, gevernmental or otherwise, is exercised. The Ministry of Education fixes the number of credits required for graduation and the size of the budget for the national universities. But within this framework there is considerable freedom for each faculty to build up its own curriculum. There is no such thing as an association of law faculties controlling the curriculum. Thus, one faculty, e.g., Kyoto University, has virtually no required courses, while another, e.g., the University of Tokyo, divides the students into three groups, namely public law, private law and political science, and assigns certain required courses to each; one makes the full year course the rule, but another provides for half-year courses; one gives more credit hours to a particular course than others; in one the class hour runs for 110 minutes while in others 90 minutes and so on. With this situation in view, it is difficult to talk generally about the curriculum, but there seem to be some common problems facing all of us.

Liberal Arts v. Law. One of the big curriculum problems for post-war universities has been the relation between the pre-existing specialized curriculum and the newly introduced liberal arts curriculum. The original aim of the post-war reforms was to allocate the first 2 years to liberal arts and the following 2 years to specialized education, but the desire of the law faculties to maintain pre-war standards, which were based on 3 years of legal education, has led to the inclusion of some specialized courses in the second year. Students have welcomed the move; they are bored by some of the liberal arts courses which seem to them mere repetition of their high school education. Thus, a variety of mixes of liberal arts and specialized subjects has been tried by various schools. It is hoped that a flexible curriculum will bring about a better combination of liberal arts and legal studies and better motivation on the part of students.[13] The idea has been put in practice in many universities today.[14]

Laissez-faire v. Compulsion. The choice between a *laissez-faire* policy and a compulsory policy is a basic decision. The former relies heavily on the student's motivation to study, and represents a philosophy which dominated the pre-war universities. This policy probably worked better when higher education was a real elite privilege than it does today. Thus, policies are divided among law faculties. As mentioned before, some law faculties have made certain courses compulsory and assigned them to particular years, so that students can learn more systematically and efficiently, as the particular faculty sees it. But others leave most decisions to the student. The student movement in the late 1960s and early 1970s brought more freedom in terms of course selection and extra-curricular activities of an academic nature. Nobody denies the educational value of the *laissez-faire* policy when accompanied by adequate guidance and facilities, but establishment of a proper balance between these two philosophies is perhaps an eternal issue in all education; it will surely continue to plague Japanese legal educators.

Curriculum. The courses offered vary from place to place, but there is a traditional minimum adopted by all law faculties, that is, the courses related to six basic laws, namely constitutional law, civil law, commercial law, civil procedure, criminal procedure, and penal law. Each of these basic subjects is divided into several courses. For example, in Kyoto University the civil law breaks down into I (general part), II (property), III (obligations including contract and tort) and IV (family and succession). This traditional division of courses has been criticized as not suitable for making legal study interesting and stimulating for the young students in our undergraduate legal education. The common law division of basic law courses into contract, tort, property, etc. has been considered as a possible alternative. In the international fields, the standard curriculum includes one or more courses in public and private international law. At Kyoto University, International Law I and II, Conflict of Laws, and International Organization are available as full courses and European Community Law, French Law, German Law, English Law, American Law and Chinese Law are annually or biannually offered as half courses. In this internationalized world, we need improvements not only in the number of offerings in this direction but also in the way they are offered and taught. Any reform is largely dependent on the initiative of an individual teacher or a group of them in a particular faculty; so far no drastic and systematic reform seems to have taken place anywhere.

The need for new kinds of courses is strongly felt. Non-traditional courses like anti-trust law, intellectual property, securities law, tax law, sociology of law, international transactions, for example, have been added to the regular curriculum of many law faculties. Even traditional courses need more class hours than before. In Kyoto, for instance, tort law was included in Civil Law III which also included contract and quasi-contract (restitution). But tort law has become such a large subject that we now offer it as a separate subject. Similar things have happened in many areas of law. On the other hand we still keep such "basic" subjects as Roman Law in which very few students are really interested. Courses offered in most Japanese law faculties are certainly not very responsive to the needs of a society with highly sophisticated and internationalized economic systems. Some years ago, the association of corporate legal departments published a statement of their dissatisfaction with the kind of training their new employees had received in their universities. It criticized law faculty education as dispensing only abstract theories of little practical use in corporate legal work. Their complaint is understandable. But in view of the nature and a dilemma of the current undergraduate legal education it seems unreasonable to demand too much of it. For example, most law faculties offer courses in which students are trained in reading foreign legal texts. But the professor usually chooses the foreign text for its general interest. Advanced business oriented courses, such as banking law, international finance, international taxation, commercial arbitration etc., which are taught in many American law schools, are normally unavailable in the Japanese curriculum. Even rather basic tax law, anti-trust law and securities law, subjects which are currently offered at Kyoto University, are not necessarily popular with students. At present, more advanced subjects are left to in-house training by the companies and government agencies which hire our graduates. We must be satisfied with dispensing a basic general training in law. In this respect, the *senshu* graduate program introduced recently may have some potential, as will be suggested later.

Demand for more class hours has resulted in a proposal to extend undergraduate legal education from the present 4 years to 5 years. This proposal, advanced more than twenty years ago by the University of Tokyo law faculty, received much attention, but a uniform enforcement of such a reform throughout Japan was impossible because of the different sizes and resources of each law faculty. There was insurmountable opposition to converting only a limited number of schools to a five year school which would become elite schools distinguished from the others. This was not acceptable in the very egalitarian atmosphere of the post-war Japanese academic community.[15] Quite recently, however, the proposal has been realized at least in part by creating a new graduate program which is not intended for an academic career, as explained later.

Teaching Methods. The choice of teaching method has been treated as a matter for the personal decision of the individual teacher. The traditional idea of academic freedom is considered as including the freedom to decide how to teach one's own students. The traditional teaching method has been a lecture delivered by the professor to a mass of students who are supposed to take notes. Students are not necessarily expected to prepare for the class. Although they are not prohibited from raising questions, they usually do not. This passivity on the part of students has long been unquestioned. But after the war, many legal scholars had an opportunity to observe and experience American methods of law teaching. Now a few professors try to teach by the socratic method, using a cases and materials kind of book they have edited. But this is not yet a wide-spread practice. Many professors admit the usefulness of the method but are reluctant to change their style. There are many reasons for this. Those who have tried it have been disappointed because the students did not respond properly and the method was more time-consuming than anticipated. In a large class of several hundred students, not an uncommon size, the method does not work. However, a dialectical teaching method has been almost always adopted in seminars. Because of student demand, in most universities the weight of seminars in the legal curriculum has increased. The educational value of seminars cannot be overemphasized because in most schools they are the only place where the students can have personal contact with the professors.

Examination. In most schools, only a final examination is given at the end of each course, which may run a whole or half year. The type of examination varies by professor. But the tradition has been to ask for the definition of legal concepts, testing merely the students' memory rather than their analytical capability. Recently, however, more problem-oriented questions are becoming common. The examination consists of a simplified fact situation and a couple of specific questions. But the presentation of facts is rarely more than a few lines, and the time allowed is normally less than two hours.

Student Demands. Nowadays we cannot totally ignore student demands for participation in the framing of the curriculum, whether they are officially recognized or not. Student criticism has always been directed against the so-called "mass-production" education, namely, large lecture classes. They have demanded smaller classes, more seminars, and a better student-professor ratio, which in national universities is about 10-15 to 1, but in most private schools 30 to 1 or even worse. They demand, quite understandably, better library facilities, which in most places are far from satisfactory. Unlike in the US, Japanese students have not demanded any affirmative action to admit more females or minorities like Koreans. They seem to take the traditional method of admission for granted, that is, on the basis of an entrance examination only. They have never demanded more female faculty members either. Many student demands are difficult to satisfy simply because of budget, space, etc. But sometimes they raise a question touching the very basic dilemma of Japanese legal education mentioned earlier. For example, those who are taking the National Legal Examination demand courses and seminars squarely oriented to it; this sometimes goes counter to a professor's wish to approach a legal subject from broader historical, economic and sociological perspectives

Graduate Level

As explained above, an overwhelming majority of law graduates find employment with private companies. A much smaller number of them go into government service. A very limited number continue legal study or training at the graduate level. Of those who are fortunate enough to pass the National Legal Examination, most go to the LTRI for professional training. An even smaller number go to a graduate school aspiring to an academic career.

National Legal Examination and Professional Training

The problems concerning professional education in the LTRI are somewhat unusual because the students there are a kind of government employee and the teachers are all selected judges, public prosecutors and attorneys.[16] The Institute, nonetheless, certainly does function as an educational institution constituting an important part of the Japanese scheme of legal education, and its problems should be reviewed here.

Probably the most salient characteristic is the extremely selective admission policy. For a long time, only 500 students a year from all over Japan were admitted to the Institute after a rigorous National Legal Examination. The examination takes place only once a year and is divided into three parts; a multiple choice examination in three basic legal subjects (Constitutional Law, Civil Law and Penal Law) in May, an essay examination in several subjects (in July), and finally an oral examination in October. At every stage, the number of candidates shrinks. The pass rate has been a little more than two percent, never exceeding three percent. Those who fail can take it again, repeatedly. Therefore, there has been an average of six attempts before a success and the average age of those who pass has been around 28.[17] A rather modest reform was finally put in force from 1991. That year the number of successful candidates was increased to 600. In 1992, the number of subjects in the essay examination was decreased by one to 6, eliminating the non-legal subject.[18] In 1993 the number will be increased to 700. In 1995, the effect of the reform will be reviewed and if the number of successful younger applicants does not significantly increase, more drastic action will be taken by giving them priority treatment. This was the result of a compromise finally reached between the Ministry of Justice and the judiciary on the one side, both of whom wanted to introduce limitation by age or by the number of attempts (three or five times), and the bar association on the other which resisted any kind of reform.

The LTRI training lasts for two years. During the first and last four months, all the students attend classes at the Institute in Tokyo. Students from outside Tokyo can live in the Institute's dormitory. The students spend the remaining 16 months in one of some 20 cities while they receive training for eight months in the court, for four months in the prosecutor's office and four months in an attorney's office. Throughout these two years the students receive a salary roughly equivalent to that of new university graduates.

The second examination (which is not difficult) at the end of the two years qualifies the students as "full jurist" and enables them to apply for employment as a judge (assistant judge) or a prosecutor or for admission to a local bar association. It used to be that out of 500 some 70-90 became judges, 40-60 prosecutors and the rest practicing lawyers (more than 350). Since so few are added every year, Japan probably has the smallest number in the world, for its population and economic status, of fully qualified lawyers, even including judges and prosecutors. In the early years of the Institute in the 1940s and early 1950s, younger and promising students invariably chose to become either a judge or a prosecutor. From the 60s the situation started to change. Good students now tend to go into practice, and it has been very difficult to recruit them as judges and prosecutors. There has not yet been any coherent response to this growing problem. The recent reform of the Legal Examination was a tiny step in this direction. A proposal was made more than twenty years ago by the then Minister of Justice to separate out the candidates who wanted to become judges or prosecutors. It was severely criticized as reactionary and as destroying the whole spirit of the post-war legal education reforms. Since then no such proposal has been heard.

In the forty-five years since its foundation, the LTRI has undergone a substantial functional change. It was created to train primarily prospective judges and only ancillarily prosecutors and lawyers. The curriculum was thus heavily oriented toward the techniques of drafting judgments. This emphasis was justified for the first few years because the mainstream students demanded it. All this time later, the curriculum remains essentially the same while the mainstream flows to private practice. The justification is that the art of judgment writing is useful and necessary for practitioners too. But it is a good question whether the weight and the way it is taught are justifiable. In any event, some reform of the LTRI itself seems inevitable. Exactly what type of reform is necessary and possible is not clear. A very drastic reform will be to make the LTRI like an American law school.[19] Any significant reform at the LTRI would certainly have a great impact on legal education in universities.

Graduate Schools of Law

Graduate legal education within universities has been a source of many problems since its inception after the war. When the graduate schools were established, they were made totally dependent on the pre-existing faculties and facilities. A major post-war change was that a doctoral degree required successful completion of at least 5 years of graduate work. But this requirement was later abolished and the degree is now open to anyone who has submitted a suitable thesis and satisfied certain other requirements. Unlike in many countries, a doctoral degree is not a passport to an academic career. It is obtained mostly by already well established academics late in their career, say in their 40s or later. This practice tends to keep the academic standard required for the degree so high that young scholars do not dare to submit a degree thesis for examination.

Most graduate students obtain a Master's degree in two years and proceed to become a doctoral candidate unless they decide to go somewhere else, like public service, private employment, or the LTRI by passing the Legal Examination while in graduate school. It is extremely rare for a doctoral candidate to complete a doctoral thesis within three years. Sometimes they leave within three years to be employed as an academic assistant, a lecturer or even as an a tenured assistant professor in a university. If they have completed all the requirements except the thesis in the minimum three years, they can write a thesis within about three years. But very few people do. A doctoral degree, foreign or domestic, is not necessary for academic employment or promotion.

As suggested earlier, another avenue for an academic career is the academic assistantship. One can be hired as an academic assistant after finishing graduate study or in the middle of it, for example, after obtaining a Master's degree. But in a limited number of elitist law faculties, a recent graduate from the undergraduate program can be invited to become an academic assistant, which in fact is not very much an "assisting" position but rather an independent full-time paid research post. This practice, prevalent in the University of Tokyo and to a more limited extent in Kyoto University, has generated some conflict with the graduate students who have to pay tuition and rank behind the assistants. But the practice is maintained by the necessity of recruiting promising young scholars to the academic world, which must compete against the judiciary, prosecutors, the bar, the bureaucracy and a variety of occupations in the private sector.[20] The term of these assistantships is normally three years and on successful completion of a dissertation the holder will be able to find a position as tenured assistant professor with a major law faculty including the one where he or she has been an assistant. Our adherence to the assistantship would become unnecessary if we adopted the American practice of hiring faculty from the bar. But this is very unlikely to happen generally, although in recent years a small number of law faculty members have been recruited from the judiciary, the bar and corporate legal departments.[21]

Recent Reform: "Senshu" Course

Recent years have been marked by the creation of the *senshu* program within the graduate program. *Senshu* literally means "only learning," that is, not academic study.[22] A need has long been felt for an advanced and continuing education for those who have been working in society after graduation from a university. Some universities have opened their undergraduate program to returning students even on a part-time basis. To accept them in the graduate program was felt difficult because they are not oriented to an academic career. The Ministry of Education encouraged universities to create a new graduate program for that purpose by promising an increase in budgets. The University of Tokyo law faculty was the first to start such a course, in 1991. Kyoto University law faculty followed in the next year. Other state universities are also contemplating it. Private universities have started similar programs.

The class in the *senshu* program is about 40 at Kyoto. The students are varied. Government ministries, local governments and large corporations have given study leave to selected young employees for enrollment in the program. Some come to the university only part-time. The University of Tokyo program is designed to allow well qualified students to obtain a Master of Law degree in one year. Kyoto requires two years. Admission to the program is not as restrictive as for the traditional graduate program, so that about half those admitted were recent university graduates. They are supposed to find a job outside the academic world. Whether there is a sufficient job market for them remains to be seen. But my limited experience for one year with this new kind of graduate students has given me a refreshing impression. Many of them were older, experienced and more mature than the ordinary graduate students coming directly from the undergraduate program. Whether companies and government agencies will keep sending their employees to our program depends on the quality of the education we can provide and also economic conditions, especially for companies. As to the quality of education, the faculty is not entirely sure if it, with most of its members having little practical background and interest, can fulfill the task of giving a meaningful education. It is hoped, however, that the *senshu* program will mark the first step toward a transformation of the whole legal education system in Japan. Probably, this is an answer to the ill-fated proposal to expand the undergraduate program to 5 years and also to the aforementioned criticism by the association of corporate legal departments. But it is still premature to predict the future of the *senshu* program. The subjects taught, as well as the way they are taught, are all up to the individual professor. Some conduct the class as a seminar, while others just lecture. Some demand a great deal of student preparation, while others do not. I taught a course entitled "International Trade Dispute Resolution," and noticed considerable differences among the students in terms of ability and motivation. As the word *senshu* means, I think, a more intensive "teaching" and "learning" should be emphasized. This will mean more compulsion on students, in the American style.

Job Situation

For graduate students in the traditional "academic" program, finding an academic position is not always easy. Unemployment after completing a five year graduate program is not uncommon. This problem (the so-called "over-doctored" problem) is not limited to law, and is even more serious in other fields (typically, basic physics). The retirement of an older professor or the creation of a new position or a new university are the only remedies as long as students are seeking an academic position. Graduate students are, though only occasionally, employed by a private company or a government department after having completed the two year program for a Master of Law degree. This is different from other departments: in the engineering faculty a majority of undergraduates go to graduate school to take a Master's degree, and then go to private companies, which require better trained students to catch up with technological innovation. This is not the case with legal education. Employers of law graduates want to train their new employees themselves. That means that we, the universities, are not providing our students with a practically useful training. Hopefully, the new *senshu* program will change the situation. But it remains to be seen if its graduates can cultivate a new job market.

International Legal Education in Japan

Japanese law has attracted much attention, practically as well as academically.[23] Japanese law is extensively taught in many leading law schools in the United States, and also in Australia, Canada and, though to a lesser degree, in Europe. Because of historical affinities, students from neighboring countries such as Korea, China, Taiwan and Hong Kong have come to Japanese universities to study law. In recent years, however, the geographic area has been expanded to cover the whole world. They are mostly at the graduate level but a smaller number of them are enrolled in an undergraduate program. The graduate level students may be officially enrolled in a graduate law program or stay as simple visiting scholars. Some are on a scholarship from Japanese or foreign sources. But many students, particularly from Asia and North America, are supported by their family or supporting themselves.[24] It is the government's announced policy to increase the total number of foreign students to 100,000 by the year 2000. There will be a considerable number of law students then.

Apart from foreign students, there are Japanese students admitted from a foreign educational system. Most of them were taken abroad by their parents for an extended period of time. Since the normal entrance examination does not fit them and is too demanding, a special admission procedure is adopted in many law faculties. Kyoto University law faculty was the first law faculty to introduce this system. They are not foreign students and their number is quite limited (at Kyoto law faculty only 20 of the class of 420) but some problems are common to both kinds of students.

Admissions policy and procedure as well as study conditions for foreign students vary from school to school a great deal. But some basic problems can be pointed out.

Language

In order to study a foreign legal system, one must be sufficiently good at the language in which it operates. After all the law is nothing but the language. I have noticed that incoming foreign students have sometimes not been well prepared in Japanese. This makes real study impossible. The recipients of a government scholarship (*Monbusho* scholarship) are entitled to receive extensive language training in an institution for that purpose. But privately financed students have to manage for themselves. Privately run language schools are very expensive and not affordable for most students. Most universities provide some kind of language course which is usually limited, qualitatively and quantitatively.

Degree

As mentioned above, a doctoral degree in law, LL.D., is not given to anyone unless highly qualified. Students from many developing countries need a doctoral degree in order to obtain an academic or other position in their home country. Even if a degree is available, one must spend many more years than required in the United States and major European countries. Law faculties in Japan are considered as not being friendly to foreign students and tend to be avoided if there is a better opportunity in another country. The government has been trying to encourage law and other difficult faculties (such as literature) to relax their standards. But so far the situation has not changed at all dramatically.

Others

There are a host of problems surrounding foreign students such as housing, administrative support staff (foreign students service), immigration formalities, study space, local contacts, etc. But these are not specific to foreign "law" students.

Generally speaking in conclusion, the "internationalization" of Japanese university campuses is superficial. Unlike American universities, for example, no Japanese university is authorized to issue a paper which officially qualifies its holder to apply for a visa. It must instead be issued by the Ministry of Justice's Immigration Bureau on a request from a university which has admitted the foreign student. This process takes time. And then a visa takes a long time to issue to citizens of certain countries. Some sort of "academic exchange agreement" has been signed on numerous occasions by numerous university presidents. But very little activity has resulted, whether for financial reasons or otherwise. The organizational scheme of most Japanese universities does not seem to fit novel undertakings. Any project of a university as a whole must be approved by every faculty; they have strong autonomy and often differ in policy and mentality from each other. Moreover, as is often said about private industries, the "internationalist" tends not to prevail.

Conclusion and Prospects

Legal education is not an isolated subject, but closely related on the one hand to the nation's educational system and on the other to its legal traditions. Some problems are shared by all education and some are unique to legal education. The latter are more "legal" than educational and can best be understood against the background of the general legal system.

There was no such thing as legal education in pre-modern Japan, except perhaps a kind of internal apprenticeship training within the feudal courts, because there was no established legal profession. Furthermore, it is questionable whether legal education in the true sense of the word has ever existed even in modern Japan outside of the LTRI, if by "legal education" we mean the training of the legal profession. Japanese legal education in a formal sense began when the new Meiji government invited foreign teachers after 1868 to train the upper echelons of the new central bureaucracy. The government was also in a hurry to build up a European-style judiciary in order to abolish a series of so-called unequal treaties which granted extraterritorial privileges to foreign residents. Modern judges and prosecutors were badly needed. But a demand for practicing lawyers was not pressing. The practice of law, which had been officially prohibited under the Tokugawa feudal regime, became legal and gradually emerged as a by-product of the "legal" education of the bureaucrats, including judges and prosecutors. Under such circumstances, the practicing bar could enjoy only limited social prestige and importance until quite recently.[25] As stated earlier, there was no concept of a legal profession embracing both the legal bureaucracy (judges and prosecutors) and the private bar. When private industries developed, their managerial staff came to be also recruited from the graduates of law schools not because of the usefulness of legal knowledge but because of the prestige of a law degree. Thus, a diploma in law became a passport to the social elite in a society which remained essentially pre-modern. Legal knowledge was a new import from the West and probably of almost no immediate use in the daily business of government or industry. Even the courts, which now had to solve disputes in accordance with the Western concept of law, played an extremely limited role in such a society.[26]

This history explains many aspects of the present condition of our legal education. If the problems are so closely related to society and social values, our dilemma will not be easily solved. But it is also true that values are rapidly changing. There is every sign of a growing role for law and the legal profession. Increasing international contact has given an added impetus in that direction. This will necessarily bring about a change in the system of legal education. The recent development of the "*senshu*" program can be considered as one such change. Society is demanding better trained legal technocrats for the private as well as public sectors. In such a society, a mass non-professional legal education may have a great significance when properly organized. The same trend has given rise to a need to reform the system of professional legal education. The recent increase in the size of the LTRI is a sign in this direction.

Japan is sometimes characterized as an unlegalistic society. But can a society with a mass of ordinary people with a background of legal education be properly called unlegal? Japan seems to have a unique experiment, producing a mass of law graduates while limiting the number of full jurists. Japan is still in the process of seeking the mode and ideology for its legal education.

Notes

1. It has been more than two decades since I wrote about Japanese legal education: Y. Taniguchi, "Problems of Under-Graduate and Graduate Legal Education in Japan," in S.K. Agrawala (ed.), *Legal Education in India* pp.112-124 (Bombay, India, Tripathi 1973); the present paper can be seen as a second edition. Although there have been some important developments since the original, what I wrote there is still basically valid today. Therefore, I repeat most of what is in the old edition and merely add these new developments. This is for the convenience of readers, because the above mentioned book, being intended for readers in India, is not widely available.

2. Japan has a career judiciary and career prosecutors. There is no broad concept of "lawyer" or legal profession in the Anglo-American sense. In this paper the legal profession includes judges, prosecutors and private attorneys, who have to be "full jurists," but not law professors; theirs is a purely academic career, available even to those who are not a full jurist.

3. Pre-war system: 6 years of compulsory primary school, 5 years of middle school and then 3 years of technical school or 3 years of high school usually followed by 3 years of university. After the war, this was changed to: 6 years of compulsory primary school followed by 3 years of compulsory middle school, 3 years of high school and 4 years of university or 2 years of junior college. In short this was the American pattern at the time.

4. As of 1991, the number of students enrolled in higher education was 2,709,532 (four year universities 2,205,435 and two year junior colleges 504,097). In 1989 36.7 percent (35.8% male and 36.8% female) of high school graduates were enrolled in higher education. Most male students went to a four year university, but a majority of females entered a two year junior college. Since the 60s, Japan has ranked third behind the United States and the former Soviet Union in this respect. The number of universities (in 1992) and junior colleges (in 1992) is shown below in comparison with the numbers in 1972 (in parentheses) when the original version of this paper was written:

	Universities	Junior Colleges	Total
State	98 (76)	41(25)	139(101)
Municipal	41 (32)	54(44)	95(76)
Private	384(291)	497(426)	881(717)
Total	523(399)	592(495)	1,115(894)

5. Among 9 state universities only 2 had separate law faculties, namely Tokyo Imperial University and Kyoto Imperial University. Private universities outnumbered the state ones but the latter enjoyed greater importance and prestige. This condition generally holds true even today, although several eminent private universities now outperform in every respect many state universities of lesser rank.

6. Following probably the French tradition, Japanese law faculties, even those separate and independent, usually include political science faculty. They also allow students to take economics subjects for credit. Thus, a "law" student may

study only political science and/or economics and still graduate with a "law" degree if permitted by the pertinent school regulation. The proportion of such students cannot be ascertained but must be less than 10 percent.

7. 1992 statistics show the following numbers of law faculties and law students (1972 numbers in parenthesis for comparison):

		Statutory Number of Students per Year	
	Number of Institutions	Day Program	Night Program
Separate Law Faculty			
State	15	4,206	225
	(9)	(2,090)	(60)
Municipal	3	550	153
	(2)	(250)	(90)
Private	69	32,710	3,730
	(41)	(12,990)	(3,050)
Law in Composite Faculty			
State	7	1,175	70
	(11)	(1,100)	110)
Private	3	510	60
	(2)	(520)	(320)
Total	97	39,051*	4,240*
	(65)	(16,960)	(3,630)

* It is generally admitted that the private universities take more students than the publicly announced statutory number. Therefore, the total number of law students annually admitted to day programs is around 45,000. Once admitted, most students graduate with a law degree.

8. The number of graduate programs in law in 1992 is as follows (1972 figures in parenthesis):

	Number of Programs
State	19 (12)
Municipal	2 (2)
Private	44 (28)

Although there are figures for the maximum number of admissions in each program they are misleading, since the number of actual admissions is usually much smaller. For example, at the Kyoto University graduate school of law, we admit only some 20 students annually although the maximum is set around 70. Our policy is to admit only students who deserve graduate studies directed towards an academic career. This does not apply, however, to the newly created "*senshu*" graduate program described later.

9. In most law faculties, less than 10% of faculty members have this

background, although there are more who have passed the National Legal Examination. The Lawyers' Law of 1949 provides, however, that law professors of more than five years of teaching experience can apply for admission to the bar (Sec. 5). Similar provisions exist for employment as a judge (Judiciary Law of 1947, Secs.41,42,44).

10. For further details on the LTRI, see Hakaru Abe, "Education of the Legal Profession in Japan," in A. T. Von Mehren (ed.), *Law in Japan* p.153 (Cambridge, Mass., Harvard University Press, 1963); The Legal Training and Research Institute (*Shiho-Kenshusho*), *Shiho-Kenshusho* (The Legal Training and Research Institute of Japan), Tokyo, 1989). See also text to notes ff., *infra*.

11. For a discussion of their numbers and an assessment of their significance, see Kahei Rokumoto, "The Issues of Lawyer Population in Japan," in K. Rokumoto (ed.) *The Social Role of the Legal Profession*, Proceedings of the International Colloquium of the International Association of Legal Science, September 1991, pp. 201-206: Tokyo, International Center for Comparative Law and Politics. University of Tokyo (1993).

12. For detailed accounts of legal education in Japanese universities, see Takashi Uchida, "Legal Education in Japan", 12 *Cornell Law Forum* 7 (1985) describing Hokkaido University Law Faculty; Mark Thompson, "Taking Law at Chou" (*sic*), 10 *Canadian Lawyer* 21 (1986), describing Chuo University Law Faculty; Edward I. Chen, "The National Law examination of Japan," 39 *J. of Legal Education* 7 (1989), describing the law faculties of the University of Tokyo, Chuo University and Waseda University, and Richard S. Miller, "Apples vs. Persimmons: The Legal Profession in Japan and the United States," 39 *J. of Legal Education* 27 (1989).

13. It is well recognized that many freshmen students are disappointed by their liberal arts courses. The initial disappointment and boredom are likely to continue for the full 4 years. The introduction of novel specialized subjects would give a fresh stimulus to incoming students. Students also would find it stimulating to work on basic humanities and social and natural sciences after having studied legal subjects.

14. In many state universities, it used to be common to have a separate liberal arts faculty which specialized in the preliminary liberal arts education for the students who would later graduate from one of the specialized faculties, like law. The relationship between these liberal arts faculties and the specialized faculties has been unsatisfactory in many respects. The present tendency is to upgrade this kind of liberal arts faculty to an independent faculty which not only produces its own graduates but even provides a graduate level education. Such a reform has recently been carried out in Kyoto University where this author teaches. Reform of the liberal arts curriculum has become necessary to fit in with this organizational change. In many private universities, each faculty includes teachers of liberal arts subjects. So, for example, a law faculty has professors not only of sociology and economics but also of mathematics and German. This system has its own problems, of course.

15. Faculties of medicine have been granted the exceptional privilege of six years of undergraduate education. The special character of medical education as

a professional education justified this. But no equivalent idea is likely to apply to law because of the "lay" character of Japanese undergraduate legal education.

16. See Jiro Matsuda, "The Japanese Legal Training and Research Institute," 7 *American Journal of Comparative Law* 366 (1958); "The Legal Training and Research Institute, *supra* n. 10.

17. For details of the National Legal Examination, see Chen, *supra* n. 12.

18. The subjects of the essay examination up to 1990 were Constitutional Law, Civil Law, Commercial Law, Penal Law, either Civil Procedure or Criminal Procedure, and one other legal subject, chosen from Civil Procedure or Criminal Procedure (if not already chosen), Administrative Law, Bankruptcy Law, Labor Law, Public International Law, Private International Law,and Criminology; there was also one non-legal subject, chosen from Political Science, Economics, Public Finance, Accounting, Psychology, Economic Policy and Social Policy. Until the 1960s, both Civil and Criminal Procedures were required and there was no non-legal subject. This change in the 1960s proved a fruitless attempt to make the examination more accessible to younger applicants.

19. I have advocated such a reform: Y. Taniguchi, *Shiho Kenshu sho niokeru hoso kyoiku*, translated as "Legal Education at the Legal Training and Research Institute: An Introduction," in D.F. Henderson & J.O. Haley, *Law & the Legal Process in Japan* at 439 (Seattle,University of Washington Press, 1978 Edition).

20. Uchida, *supra*, n. 12.

21. Recently, the chief officer of Toshiba's legal department joined the Kyushu University law faculty as professor of international trade law. There have been several cases like that. An attraction is that five years of teaching with a law faculty with a five year graduate program can qualify one for the practice of law. See n. 9, *supra*.

The largest problem in recruiting academics from the bar is a substantial reduction in income.

22. The word *Senshu* is officially used to denote a class of schools called *Senshu Gakko* (learning school) which specialize in training in practical skills, like computer technique, accounting, cooking, etc., where high school graduates can go instead of going to a university.

23. The value of Japanese law as an object of study was pointed out in Charles Stevens, "Modern Japanese Law as an Instrument of Comparison," 19 *American J. of Comparative Law* 665 (1971).

24. Official statistics show that 90% of social science students are privately financed (law students are included under "social science," but there are no separate figures for them): Ministry of Education, Science and Culture (*Monbusho*), *Japanese Government Policies in Education, Science and Culture*, p.237 (*Monbusho*, Tokyo 1990).

25. As to the historical development of the Japanese bar, see Richard W. Rabinowitz, "The Historical Development of the Japanese Bar," 70 *Harvard L. Rev.* 61 (1956); Michael Young, "Foreign Lawyers in Japan: A Case Study in Transnational Dispute Resolution and Marginal Reform," 21 *Law in Japan, An Annual* 84, especially at 95 ff. (1988).

26. On the role of courts and litigation, compare conflicting views represented

by Takeyoshi Kawashima, "Dispute Resolution in Contemporary Japan," in Von Mehren ed., *Law in Japan* 41 (1963); Takeyoshi Kawashima, "The Notion of Law, Right and Social Order in Japan," in C,A. Moore (ed.), *The Status of Individual in East and West* 429 (Honolulu, University of Hawaii Press, 1968); John O. Haley, "The Myth of the Reluctant Litigant," 4 *Journal of Japanese Studies* 359 (1978); and J. Mark Ramseyer, "Reluctant Litigant Revisited: Rationality and Disputes in Japan," 14 *Journal of Japanese Studies* 111 (1988).

13

Implications of International Legal Integration for Law Teaching

John H. Barton

The Pacific Basin high technology legal community described in this book is but one example of the type of integration taking place throughout the legal system.[1] Business is now conducted on a global level. International environmental law can no longer be separated from domestic environmental law. Even family relations are more and more reflecting a variety of cultural traditions and imposing a new globalism of their own.

This evolution is extremely important for the future of legal education. Just as it was once necessary to move from teaching the law of a single U.S. state to teaching a national law, it is now essential to teach a global law. This paper explores ways to bring such globalism into legal education. The paper concentrates on two examples: the contract area and the administrative law area.

The paper recognizes that it will be impossible to teach a student all the specific legal issues that will later be confronted in practice. Hence, the task is to teach the student to "think like a global lawyer." The paper emphasizes a "pervasive method" in which global factors are considered in the context of more traditional legal subjects—for it is in the contexts of those subjects that graduates will face international issues. But the pervasive method must also recognize that teachers in all courses are stretched for time; they will not incorporate international material unless that material appears valuable for the points they want to make.

Contracts and Negotiations

The contract and negotiation area is an obvious candidate for considering international issues. There are many ways in which national differences among parties can affect a transaction. Moreover, contracts are usually taught in a law student's first semester; it is wise for a student to begin legal education with a sense of the need for cross-cultural understanding.

Typical International Contract Situations

Much existing international contract law is oriented toward sales transactions. This is the case, for example, with the United Nations Convention on Contracts for the International Sale of Goods,[2] which could be used for an introductory contract course in much the way the Uniform Commercial Code is currently used.

More complex relationships are also emerging. Corporate acquisition transactions, for example, now pose extremely difficult issues as different compensation and employee benefit regimes or non-discrimination principles apply to different parts of an integrated international corporate entity. Strategic alliances—a key integrating mechanism in the Pacific Basin high-technology legal community—combine contract questions, corporate questions, and intellectual property questions. It is unlikely that any of these questions could be faced adequately in a first-semester course, but it is essential that the student be prepared to understand the role of contract negotiation and structuring in dealing with such transactions.

Examples of Possible International Misunderstanding

Probably the most important point in the contract sector is to prepare the student for the variety of possible forms of misunderstanding that can occur in an international transaction.

The obvious examples arise from difference in the relevant law. Thus, the United Nations Sales Convention includes a battle of the forms resolution quite different from that typical of U.S. law.[3] Civil law concepts of good faith are stronger than those in the United States and reach into the contract formation process.[4] Examples of misunderstanding arising from differing vocabulary are nearly as obvious. The classic case of *Frigaliment Importing Co. v. B.N.S. International Sales Corp.*, 190 F. Supp. 116 (S.D.N.Y. 1960) shows the result when two parties may have entered into a transaction with quite different understandings of the quality implications of the term "chicken."

What may be more important are differences in negotiating style. Many are familiar with the stories of negotiations in Japan in which the key concessions are not made until an airplane is about to be missed. Comparably, what are the implications of negotiations between traditions in which a lawyer is regularly included in the negotiations and traditions in which it is regarded as inappropriate to include a lawyer? And what about the role—important in many cultures—of agreements in principle as distinguished from fully-detailed agreements?

Even more important are differences in the concept of an agreement. At the extreme, how does one negotiate or contract in a society, such as many Asian societies, in which resort to the courts is inappropriate—or in current Russia in which the courts are not operating? At less extreme levels, it is important to consider the implications of parallel negotiations between the businesspeople, the lawyers, and the engineers. How does one wisely advise a client as to choosing between detailed planning early on in a negotiation or leaving that planning for the execution of the agreement?

Possible Teaching Materials and Approaches

There are very few good materials available here. In showing differences among national laws, the best is perhaps the United Nations International Sales Convention, whose battle of the forms provisions can give rise to an unanticipated duty to arbitrate. This was the topic, although not the grounds of decision, of the first U.S. case interpreting the Convention, *Filanto, S.p.A. v. Chilewich Intern. Corp.*, 779 F. Supp. 1229 (S.D.N.Y. 1992). And a teacher interested in developing the UCC's concept of good faith may wish to consider civil law analogues.

With respect to negotiating style, one should certainly consider the variety of "Doing Business in X" articles.[5] Moreover, there is at least one case that demonstrates the problems of fitting a "Chinese way" of doing business, i.e. heavy reliance on good faith, into a Western contract framework: *Wang v. Hsu* (N.D. Ca.) 1991 U.S. Dist. Lexis 4398. The case involves sharp enough distinctions between culturally-based contracting strategies that it may be difficult to teach in today's culturally sensitive classrooms!

For the student, the issue may in large part be one of maintaining sensitivity to potential inter-cultural issues in the contract context—and some of these can be found in domestic analogues. Thus, indefiniteness in U.S. contract law can provide a place in which to consider the reasons why issues are settled at different times in different communities and negotiations and give the students a chance to focus on these issues from a negotiating strategy perspective as well as a contract doctrine perspective. Similarly, the questions of enforceability and resort to litigation can be discussed in the context of prohibitive U.S. litigation costs or through a distinction between single-shot relationships and repeat transactions. At least part of the necessary intercultural sensitivity can be prepared for by supplementing a traditional contract doctrine course with thoughtful consideration of the different factors involved in a variety of domestic transactions.

Administrative Law

One of the most important implications of the internationalization of law is that a single transaction must deal with a variety of national regulatory systems. It follows at once that a student should have a sense of the kinds of differences that arise among administrative law systems—and yet comparative administrative law (let alone international administrative law for those few situations of genuinely international regulation) is an underdeveloped area.

The Variety of Patterns of Administrative Law

The variety of patterns of administrative regulation can be suggested by simply noting a few examples. The United States has a detailed system of regulatory review based on the Administrative Procedure Act, Act of June 11, 1946, 60 Stat. 237, codified at 5 U.S.C. §§ 551-559, and an extensive, but generally procedure-based, review by the regular courts. The traditional civil law nations, in contrast, have a special administrative court system, subject to very technical rules, with ultimate appeal to a court such as the French Conseil d'État, that appears (at least to the outsider) to be as much a part of the nation's political system as a part of its legal system.[6] In Latin America, *amparo* plays the role that we might give to judicial review.[7] In many Asian nations, one senses that the administrative law system constitutes a formal legal structure that conceals rather than reveals the underlying decision-making process. The administrative system seems like an onion-skin system; each layer of formalism conceals a deeper layer of new formalism. This is complemented, in Japan, by a process of administrative guidance that appears to bypass the formal administrative process.[8] And, looking at the Russian example again, one sees the absence of administrative law. (Based on my experiences with Russian legal educators, the society has recognized that it needs both new private law and new constitutional safeguards for the individual, but has not yet realized that effective and predictable regulation will require a legal buffer between the bureaucracy and the emerging private sector.)

These descriptions, that reflect a lawyer's bias toward the role of the courts, ignore the deeper and more important realities of different types of administrative procedures. Here a taxonomy seems more possible. First, to what extent are the agencies independent from the groups they regulate? The extremes here might be the highly independent system of the United Kingdom and the close client-agency relationships of Japan. Second, to what extent are the agency's processes observable and available to the regulated sector or the public as a whole? Here, the contrast might be between the open U.S. system and the relatively closed U.K. system—or, perhaps as well, between the relatively open hearing processes of a U.S. agency such as the Nuclear Regulatory Commission and the relatively secret procedures of certain Immigration and Naturalization Service decisions. Third, is there any supervision or coordination of different agencies? In the United States, one looks at the roles of the Office of Management and the Budget in enforcing a regulatory agenda or the Office of Science and Technology Policy in coordinating the agencies that regulate biotechnology.[9] At the other extreme, in Japan, one sees each agency regulating in parallel for its own client sector. And there are many alternatives, shaped, for example, by traditions within a cabinet or traditions of interagency committees. Fourth, how does the agency implement its doctrine? The clear extremes are formal published regulations and informal unpublished administrative guidelines. Only after understanding a bureaucratic structure at this level can one usefully consider the role of outside (i.e. judicial) review.

Forces for Harmonization

In the face of this menagerie of alternatives, there are also strong forces for coordination and harmonization. One group of these forces comes from the fact that agencies are more and more facing the same problems and must thus work in parallel ways. The scientific issues involved in consumer or environmental regulation are much the same from nation to nation—and the scientific culture is international, thus creating a global force toward harmonization. Moreover, regulatory sectors are themselves seeking to harmonize their activities in order to simplify life for the private sector—and for themselves. Two outstanding examples can be suggested. The Federal Aviation Agency has attempted to coordinate its aircraft certification procedures with those of foreign counterparts.[10] And the Food and Drug Administration is involved in so many harmonization efforts that it has appointed a task force to consider the associated management problems.[11]

Potentially more important, international trade concerns have been forcing harmonization. The Services Code of the Uruguay Round is probably the strongest statement of an international norm for administrative law.[12] Although it is still in draft form, international trade experts generally believe that the Services Code will be accepted in its current form if the Uruguay Round is successfully concluded. The Code includes a number of provisions that amount to international restatement of the Administrative Procedure Act including, for example "transparency," which is similar to publication, and in some sectors a requirement for review procedures administered in a "reasonable, objective and impartial manner."[13]

Implications for the Lawyer

In this situation, probably the most important question for the practicing lawyer—and one that should at least be posed to students—is to develop a sense of when it is essential to hire local counsel. This is, of course, a function of the extent to which the details of the local law are relevant to the transaction; it is also a function of the character of the society and the role of local lawyers. Sometimes for example, local firms are in fact, and appropriately, oriented toward international clients and provide a package of language skills and understanding of the bureaucracy that is very useful for the foreign client, but unnecessary for the local client.

A second set of implications goes to the interpretation of the national laws and regulations. It is impossible to translate a legal document from one language to another and to have it retain the precise meaning it had in the original language. Moreover, the effective meaning of a regulation depends on the enforcement and interpretation procedures applicable to that regulation. A lawyer must be sensitive to these differences.

Third, a lawyer must be able to consider ways to structure a transaction defensively in order to avoid problems that may result from poorly-understood, politically malleable, corrupt, or non-existing administrative law. One thinks in terms of ensuring that as few assets as possible are placed in risky locations or of obtaining various forms of investment insurance. Similarly, one may ensure that there are local partners. And the possibility of political leaders shaping administrative decisions poses enormous questions of legal ethics, even when it does not reach the level of corruption.

Finally, a lawyer must understand the domestic and international political factors affecting foreign administrative law. When is it appropriate to go up the bureaucratic ladder to a foreign political leader with a complaint? What about the possibility of bringing in the U.S. Trade Representative, as so many firms are now doing?

Implications for Education

There are probably two points that are particularly important for a student in this area. The first is to develop a sensitivity to the underlying differences in administrative systems. At least one good example is essential; conceivably it can be developed from U.S. administrative systems as well as from foreign systems, provided the possibility of variety in administrative pattern is presented and analyzed.

Second, it is essential for the student to be exposed, again with at least one well-developed example, to the different ways and levels at which an administrative dispute can be faced. Ideally, such an example would compare such alternatives as straightforward foreign proceedings, more political foreign approaches, and international diplomatic pressure. A number of examples of such disputes are available.[14]

Conclusion

The direction suggested here will definitely require the development of new teaching materials. Few current materials attempt to develop the relevant forms of sensitivity. These new materials will require new vocabularies—for our vocabularies for describing negotiation or regulation approaches are relatively weak.

At the same time, the new materials can often be developed in the domestic context as well as the international one. Many of the same cultural issues can be seen domestically, whether culture is taken in the ethnic sense or in the weaker sense of a particular bureaucratic culture. But to present these issues will require stronger emphasis on the human and the transactional aspects of law and further movement away from the doctrinal approach to law. With the right emphasis, there is a good chance that we will prepare our students well for the Twenty-First Century.

Notes

1. This paper builds on a presentation given to the American Association of Law Schools on January 6, 1993. The work was carried out under grants to Stanford Law School from the Hitachi Foundation and from the Borchard Foundation. The author wishes to thank both donors.

2. Final Act of the United Nations Conference on Contracts for the

International Sale of Goods, April 10, 1980, U.N. Doc. A/Conf. 97/18, with Annex, United Nations Convention on Contracts for the International Sale of Goods, reprinted in 19 I.L.M. 668 (1980), *codified at* 15 U.S.C. Appendix (West Supp. 1991). See generally J. Honnold, *Uniform Law for International Sales Under the 1980 United Nations Convention* (Deventer: Kluwer, 1982); J.P. Griffin & M. Calabrese, "The New Rules for International Contracts," *ABA Journal*, March 1, 1988 at 62; A. Rosett, "Critical Reflections on the United Nations Convention on Contracts for the International Sale of Goods," 45 *Ohio St. L. J.* 265 (1984); P. Winship, "A Bibliography of Commentaries on the United Nations International Sales Convention," 21 *Int'l. Lawyer* 558 (1987), updated in 22 *Int'l. Lawyer* 605 (1988) and 24 *Int'l. Lawyer* 307 (1990).

3. Compare Article 19 of the International Sale of Goods Convention with Article 2-207 of the Uniform Commercial Code.

4. L. Aynes and P. Malaurie, *Cours de Droit Civil; Les Obligations* § 379 (2d Ed.) (Paris: Cujas, 1990).

5. E.g. P. Lansing & M. Wechselblatt, "Doing Business in Japan: The Importance of the Unwritten Law," 17 *Int'l. Lawyer* 647 (1983); D.A. Sneider, "The Baoshan Debacle: A Study of Sino-Japanese Contract Dispute Settlement," 18 *N.Y.U.J. of Int'l Law and Politics* 541 (1986).

6. G. Dupuis and M.-J. Guearodon, *Droit Administratif* (2nd Ed. Paris: Colin, 1989).

7. H.F. Zamudio, "A Brief Introduction to the Mexican Writ of Amparo," 9 *Calif. W. Int'l. L. J.* 306 (1979); *id.*, "The Writ of Amparo in Latin America," 13 *Lawyer of the Americas* 361 (1981).

8. M.K. Young, "Administrative Guidance in the Courts: A Case Study in Doctrinal Adaptation," 17 *Law in Japan* 120 (1984).

9. Coordinated Framework for the Regulation of Biotechnology (the "Matrix"), 49 *Fed. Reg.* 50856 (December 31, 1984), detailed more fully in Coordinated Framework for Regulation of Biotechnology, 51 *Fed. Reg.* 23302 (June 26, 1986).

10. See *Regulatory Cooperation with Counterpart Agencies Abroad: The FAA's Aircraft Certification Experience*, Administrative Conference of the United States, 1991 Recommendations and Reports. And see Recommendation 91-1: "Federal Agency Cooperation with Foreign Government Regulators," 1 CFR § 305.91-1.

11. Report of the FDA Task Force on Interntional Harmonization, December 1992, NTIS Doc. PB93-128155.

12. General Agreement on Trade in Services, MTN.TNC/W/FA, 20 December 1991 (The "Dunkel Draft").

13. Another important emerging theme is the application of international human rights law to administrative areas, turning the international procedural (and potentially private property) principles into another analogue of the Administrative Procedure Act. See, e.g. *Éditions Periscope*, 234 ECHR 56 (26 March 1992); *König v. Germany*, 27 ECHR 1, at 30 ff. (28 June 1978).

14. E.g., F. Upham, *Law and Social Change in Postwar Japan* (Cambridge, Mass.: Harvard U.P., 1987); P.B. Edelman, "Japanese Product Standards as Non-tariff Trade Barriers: When Regulatory Policy Becomes a Trade Issue," 24 *Stan. J. of Int'l. Law* 389 (1988).

About the Book

Most would agree that business and trade are now carried out in an international environment, but it is much less widely recognized that the practice of the law of business and technology is also becoming internationalized. Indeed, in many ways we seem to be rapidly moving toward a world legal order that may parallel the world economic order.

In this volume, distinguished Asian, U.S., and European scholars explore the role of law and the legal profession in the development of high-tech industries and in trade among the nations of the Pacific community. Focusing on the U.S., Japan, and South Korea, contributors do groundbreaking work on the international and governmental context of such issues as property rights, contracts, litigation, legal practice, and legal education. This is an essential book for scholars of international political economy and trade.

About the Contributors

Kyong Whan Ahn is a Professor of Law at Seoul National University. He has law degrees from Seoul National University, the University of Pennsylvania, and Santa Clara University, and is a member of the bars of the District of Columbia and California.

John H. Barton is a Professor of Law at Stanford Law School and also director of the Law and Technology Program. He is a specialist in international business transactions, international human rights and environmental problems, and has been specially interested in the impact of technology on law and the problems of technology transfer among nations.

Erhard Blankenburg is a Professor of the Sociology of Law at the Vrije Universiteit, Amserdam. He is author of many books and articles on the sociology of law, most recently *Mobilisierung für Recht,* containing studies of civil and criminal procedure, legal aid and labor courts. He has been conducting a major study of comparative legal cultures.

Lawrence M. Friedman is a Professor of Law at Stanford. He has written widely on law and society topics, including the relationship of law and the economy, and has also written a number of books on legal history, most recently *Crime and Punishment in American History.*

Susan Jordan is the Staff Attorney at the Environmental Law Foundation in Oakland, California. She has a law degree from Stanford, where she has taught environmental justice.

Dan R. Krislov is a third-year J.S.D. student at Stanford and a student in the Jurisprudence and Social Policy program at the University of California at Berkeley.

Philip S.C. Lewis was formerly a Senior Research Fellow of All Souls College, Oxford, and currently works with the Silicon Valley Research Project at the Stanford Law School. He is also engaged in a study of the work of lawyers in the high-technology field in England.

Shigenori Matsui is a Professor of Law at Osaka University. He has law degrees from Kyoto and Stanford and has written books in Japanese on media and constitutional law.

Setsuo Miyazawa is a Professor of Law at Kobe University. He has a Ph.D. in Sociology from Yale, and J.S.D. from Hokkaido, and has written several books and numerous articles, in Japanese and in English, on the sociology of law and criminology. His *Policing in Japan* (1992) received a Distinguished Book Award from the American Society of Criminology.

Sang-Hyun Song is a Professor of Law at the Seoul National University. He has law degrees and research training from Seoul, Tulane, Cambridge, Cornell and Hamburg, and has been a Visiting Professor at Harvard Law School. He is President of the Korea International Trade Law Association; and of the Korea Intellectual Property Research Society, and is a member of the Chief Justice's Committee for Judicial Reform. He has published many books and articles on civil procedure, computer software protection, maritime law and corporation law.

Yasuhei Taniguchi is a Professor of Law at Kyoto. He is a graduate of Kyoto and the Legal Training and Research Institute and has law degrees from the University of Berkeley and Cornell. He has taught at Harvard and other institutions outside Japan, and is the author of books, among others, on insolvency and civil procedure.

Seung Doo Yang is a Professor of Law at Yonsei University, where he took his doctorate, and has studied and visited at universities in the United States and England. He is a member of the Korean Supreme Court Committee on the Renovation of Judicial Administration, and author of books on administrative and industrial property law.

Index

For Product Safety Concerns and Information please contact our EU representative GPSR@taylorandfrancis.com Taylor & Francis Verlag GmbH, Kaufingerstraße 24, 80331 München, Germany

Batch number: 10726013

Printed by Printforce, the Netherlands